The Tourism Area Life Cycle, Vol. 1

ASPECTS OF TOURISM
Series Editors: Professor Chris Cooper, *University of Queensland, Australia*
Dr C. Michael Hall, *University of Otago, Dunedin, New Zealand*
Dr Dallen Timothy, *Arizona State University, Tempe, USA*

Aspects of Tourism is an innovative, multifaceted series which will comprise authoritative reference handbooks on global tourism regions, research volumes, texts and monographs. It is designed to provide readers with the latest thinking on tourism world-wide and in so doing will push back the frontiers of tourism knowledge. The series will also introduce a new generation of international tourism authors, writing on leading edge topics. The volumes will be readable and user-friendly, providing accessible sources for further research. The list will be underpinned by an annual authoritative tourism research volume. Books in the series will be commissioned that probe the relationship between tourism and cognate subject areas such as strategy, development, retailing, sport and environmental studies. The publisher and series editors welcome proposals from writers with projects on these topics.

Other Books in the Series
Sport Tourism: Interrelationships, Impact and Issues
    Brent Ritchie and Daryl Adair (eds)
Tourism, Mobility and Second Homes
    C. Michael Hall and Dieter Müller
Strategic Management for Tourism Communities: Bridging the Gaps
    Peter E. Murphy and Ann E. Murphy
Oceania: A Tourism Handbook
    Chris Cooper and C. Michael Hall (eds)
Tourism Marketing: A Collaborative Approach
    Alan Fyall and Brian Garrod
Music and Tourism: On the Road Again
    Chris Gibson and John Connell
Tourism Development: Issues for a Vulnerable Industry
    Julio Aramberri and Richard Butler (eds)
Nature-based Tourism in Peripheral Areas: Development or Disaster?
    C. Michael Hall and Stephen Boyd (eds)
Tourism, Recreation and Climate Change
    C. Michael Hall and James Higham (eds)
Shopping Tourism, Retailing and Leisure
    Dallen J. Timothy
Wildlife Tourism
    David Newsome, Ross Dowling and Susan Moore
Film-Induced Tourism
    Sue Beeton
Rural Tourism and Sustainable Business
    Derek Hall, Irene Kirkpatrick and Morag Mitchell (eds)
The Tourism Area Life Cycle, Vol. 2: Conceptual and Theoretical Issues
    Richard W. Butler (ed.)

For more details of these or any other of our publications, please contact:
Channel View Publications, Frankfurt Lodge, Clevedon Hall,
Victoria Road, Clevedon, BS21 7HH, England
http://www.channelviewpublications.com

ASPECTS OF TOURISM 28
Series Editors: Chris Cooper (*University of Queensland, Australia*),
C. Michael Hall (*University of Otago, New Zealand*)
and Dallen Timothy (*Arizona State University, USA*)

The Tourism Area Life Cycle, Vol. 1

Applications and Modifications

Edited by
Richard W. Butler

CHANNEL VIEW PUBLICATIONS
Clevedon • Buffalo • Toronto

Library of Congress Cataloging in Publication Data
The Tourism Area Life Cycle: Applications and Modifications
Edited by Richard W. Butler.
Aspects of Tourism: 28
Includes bibliographical references and index.
1. Tourism–Economic aspects. 2. Economic development. I. Butler, Richard. II. Series.
G155.A1T5898283 2005
338.4'791–dc22   2005015059

British Library Cataloguing in Publication Data
A catalogue entry for this book is available from the British Library.

ISBN 1-84541-026-2 (hbk)
ISBN 1-84541-025-4 (pbk)
ISBN 1-84541-027-0 (electronic)

Channel View Publications
An imprint of Multilingual Matters Ltd

UK: Frankfurt Lodge, Clevedon Hall, Victoria Road, Clevedon BS21 7HH.
USA: 2250 Military Road, Tonawanda, NY 14150, USA.
Canada: 5201 Dufferin Street, North York, Ontario, Canada M3H 5T8.

Typeset by Datapage Ltd.
Printed and bound in Great Britain by the Cromwell Press.

DEDICATION

To my wife, Margaret, and my children, Caroline, Richard and Antonia, who have lived with 'the cycle' and its demands and been there with support and encouragement over the last three decades, and:

IN MEMORIAM

To my father, Sgt. Pilot Richard Butler, RAF (VR), 106 Squadron, whom I never had the privilege of knowing, and the more than 55,000 men of Bomber Command, who like him, were killed in action in the Second World War.

'When you go home, tell them of us, and say:
For your tomorrows we gave our today'

Contents

Acknowledgements

There are many acknowledgements that have to be made for the publication of any book, but in the case of edited works there are inevitably more needed than for a single authored work. In the first place I must thank most sincerely the authors whose writings appear in this and the accompanying volume. They have done most of the academic work in terms of their contributions, and it is a truism to say the books would not have appeared without their efforts. Of all the people I approached, some old friends, some former students (and hopefully still friends), some recent acquaintances and some known only to me by their writings, only one did not reply, and only one was finally unable to contribute a chapter. Some responded early (5.00 am in one case), others performed more like myself, cutting it rather fine. Virtually all wrote exactly what was asked of them, sometimes at rather short notice, all took my comments and suggestions in good spirit and some have even yet to take me up on the offer of a beer. Perhaps above all, I wish to thank them for finding the TALC of interest and using it in the first place.

Second of course, there are those involved in the publication of the books. At the University of Surrey, my long-suffering secretary Margaret Williamson and at various times, Malcolm Thompson, for assistance with Word and word processing, and Paul Fuller and John Briggs for rescuing various items from faulty laptops and illegible files on more than one occasion. At Channel View Publications, first and foremost, Mike Grover, for his support, particularly as this project grew from one book of 80,000 words and 15 chapters to one book of about 20 chapters, and then to two books of nearly 40 chapters and over 200,000 words in total, and to his family team, whose efforts I appreciate greatly.

Third, there is the general support team. Conceptually in its creation the TALC owes a great deal to Jim Brougham, the nearest person to a Renaissance man I have ever come across in person. Many good arguments, parties, football matches and above all, incomparable folk singing (on his side) contributed greatly if tangentially at times, to the final product. He was one of many former students at the University of Western Ontario, including Brian Keogh, Peter Keller, James Strapp, Colin Harris, Dave Weaver, Winston Husbands, Dave Telfer, Stephen Boyd, Tom Hinch and Bryan Smale, all of whom helped develop, test and refine the model in various ways. There are also many more graduate and undergraduate students, unfortunately too many to list, at Western and at the University of Surrey who have used the model and also helped in its development. Peter Murphy (once English, then Canadian and now Australian) should be acknowledged (or blamed) particularly for TALC seeing the light of day in terms of publication, first by nagging me to produce a paper for the Canadian Association of Geographers' meeting in Vancouver, and then by persuading the Association to publish the first ever special edition of *The Canadian Geographer* (24 (1), 1980) (which he edited), one devoted to papers on tourism and recreation.

Since 1980 in particular, many colleagues have assisted greatly, either by using the model (including all those featured in these volumes), or by just being there to talk, and to share ideas and good times. Some legitimately might feel their research should be included (or may be relieved it is not!), Gareth Shaw and Allan Williams in the UK in particular, but I do have one representative from the south west at least included, who was influenced by their work. Klaus Meyer-Arendt, Paul Wilkinson, Ngaire Douglas and Gerda Priestly especially are also owed apologies for apparently being ignored, but only by noninclusion of papers I can assure them. There are also a vast number of other writers who have used the TALC, most, if not all, included in Lagiewski's bibliography, and an even larger number of students at universities around the world who have probably driven their supervisors mad by using the model. (Arriving at an Australian university on sabbatical in 1992 I was greeted at coffee by a staff member there, with the comment, 'So you're the bugger that wrote that, I've just had to mark 20 reports using it!') Finally there is the family support team, to whom these books are dedicated, who have been hoping to heaven 'it' is finished soon and doing their best to make sure it is. They have eventually won and I am very grateful, not only for their support and encouragement, but for the ideas, suggestions (mostly) and willingness to lose sandpits, rooms and furniture buried under TALC-related material for far too long.

More formally and finally, I should also like to thank the Canadian Association of Geographers, not only for publishing the article in *The Canadian Geographer* in the first place, but also for giving me permission to reproduce the original article (Chapter 1, this volume). I trust this book will relieve some pressure on their office at McGill University by reducing the number of requests for copies!

Contributors

Names and e-mail addresses of Contributors to TALC Books.

Book 1

Richard 'Rick' M. Lagiewski, Rochester Institute of Technology
Rick.Lagiewski@rit.edu

K. Michael Haywood, retired, at time of writing University of Guelph
Michael.Haywood@sympatico.ca

Gary Hovinen, retired at time of writing
ghovinen@yahoo.com

Jan O. Lundgren, McGill University
jan.lundgren@mcgill.ca

Jigang Bao, Sun Yat Sen University
eesbjg@zsu.edu.cn

Chaozi Zhang, Sun Yat Sen University
No e-mail, use Bao (above)

Stephen Boyd, currently University of Ulster (Coleraine Campus)
sw.boyd@ulster.ac.uk

Antonio Paolo Russo, Erasmus University
russo@few.eur.nl

Jane Malcolm-Davies, at time of writing University of Surrey
jane@jmdandco.com

David B. Weaver, University of South Carolina
dweaver@gwm.sc.edu

Charles S. Johnston, Auckland Institute of Technology
charles.johnston@aut.ac.nz

Jerry D. Johnson, Montana State University
jdj@montana.edu

David J. Snepenger, Montana State University
dsnep@montana.ed also dsnepenger@earthlink.com

Bonnie Martin
bmartin@mail.wcu.edu

Juanita Marois, University of Alberta
Juanita-marois@aol.com

Tom Hinch, University of Alberta
thinch@ualberta.ca

Sanda Corak, Institute of Tourism, University of Zagreb
sanda.corak@iztzg.hr

Charles Stansfield, retired from Rowan College, New Jersey
ruthig@rowan.edu

Bill Faulkner, deceased at time of writing, Griffith University

Carmen Tideswell, Auckland Institute of Technology
carmen.tideswell@aut.ac.nz

Brian Wheeller, at time of writing NHTV Breda, Netherlands
wheellerbrian@yahoo.com

Book 2

Tim Coles, University of Exeter
T.E.Coles@exeter.ac.uk

Andreas Papatheodorou, at time of writing University of Surrey, now
University of Aegean
academia@trioptron.org

C. Michael Hall, University of Otago
cmhall@business.otago.ac.nz

Rosslyn Russell, Royal Melbourne Institute of Technology
rosslyn.russell@rmit.edu.au

Sabine Weisenegger, University of Muenchen
weizenegger@bwl.uni-muenchen.de

Stephen Wanhill, at time of writing Bournemouth University, now
University of Limerick
Stephen@Wanhill.force9.co.uk

Sven Lundtorp, as Wanhill (above)

Neil Ravenscroft, University of Brighton
neil@ravenscroft.fsnet.co.uk

Ion Hadjihambi, KPMG Services (Pty) Ltd.
ion.hadjihambi@kpmg.co.za

Chris Cooper, University of Queensland
c.cooper@mailbox.uq.edu.au

Sheela Agarwal, University of Plymouth
S.Agarwal@plymouth.ac.uk

Mara Manente, CISET, University of Venice
mtourism@unive.it

Harald Pechlaner, Catholic University of Eichstatt-Ingoldstadt, Bavaria
Harald.Pechlaner@ku-eichstaett.de

Ted Berry, Lower Kuskokwin School District, Alaska
Tedberry_aus@yahoo.com

Introduction

C. MICHAEL HALL

It is an indication of the significance of a concept that it starts to attract not only articles but entire books as to its nature. And, as the reader will find in going through the various chapters in the two volumes of this book, the Tourism Area Life Cycle (TALC) is one of the most cited and contentious areas of tourism knowledge. Even as Butler (this volume), himself notes 'there was nothing devastatingly complicated or original in the data or facts on which the model is based'. The TALC has gone on to become one of the best known theories of destination growth and change within the field of tourism studies.

As the second volume highlights, there is a substantial body of contested theory and concepts that surround the TALC. Although 'Butler put into the realistic cyclical context a reality that everyone knew about, and clearly recognised, but had never formulated into an overall theory' (Lundgren, 1984: 22), the TALC is arguably one of the most significant contributions to studies of tourism development because of the way it provides a focal point for discussion of what leads to destination change, how destinations and their markets change and, even, what is a destination. Moreover, the two volumes together highlight the manner in which theory informs the development and generation of tourism knowledge, the importance of understanding the intellectual history of tourism ideas, and the disciplinary dimensions of tourism studies. These come from a number of different areas of knowledge, are applied at different scales, and often seek to tackle different dimensions of under-standing destination change. Nevertheless, they highlight the importance of the intellectual history of ideas in tourism, and of the intellectual heritage of the TALC in particular. Some of these issues are discussed at the outset of this volume in terms of the foundations of the TALC, however readers seeking to gain a wider appreciation and understanding of the TALC will need to read this section in conjunction with the discussions of the second volume. Nevertheless, it is readily apparent that the TALC remains one of the most oft-cited works in tourism studies even if many people have never read the original article and have instead only read interpretations of it in textbooks or journals.

This particular volume looks at the means by which the TALC has been applied in particular situations and settings. It commences with a reproduction of the original article from *The Canadian Geographer* and is followed by a chapter by Butler on the origins of the TALC. Being able to easily access the original article will be helpful to many students of tourism but the opportunity to read Butler discussing its background will be especially welcome. As noted in the introduction to the second volume, being able to encounter such a variety of insights into the TALC helps readers gain an appreciation not only of the significance of the TALC but also its intellectual history. In the case of Butler revisiting the origins of the TALC we see the significance of authors active in the 1960s and 1970s rarely cited in contemporary tourism studies, such as Roy Wolfe and Charles Stansfield, as well as even earlier authors from the 1930s and 1940s. Significantly, we also learn of the extent to which personal travel experiences, particularly in Scotland, may have influenced Butler's understanding of tourism destinations, as well as the role of his work with Jim Brougham, then a graduate student at the University of Western Ontario. These reflections highlight that in tourism research, as in other fields of knowledge, the generation of ideas rarely occurs in isolation and instead needs to be understood in relation to its personal and intellectual context.

The first section also includes a chapter by Lagiewski that provides an overview of some of the writings that have utilised the TALC and a chapter by Haywood that seeks to relate the TALC to understandings of destination change. The Haywood chapter in particular should be read in conjunction with the chapter by the same author in the second volume, which notes the extent to which concepts of life cycle and change have been poorly understood and appreciated by the tourism industry itself. As the introduction to Volume 2 notes, such a situation reflects the need for a broader understanding of the processes of the diffusion of tourism knowledge that the various contributions to the two volumes partly illustrate.

The second section of this volume deals with examples of the implementation of the TALC. Hovinen discusses the relationship between TALC and concepts of sustainability in Lancaster County, Pennsylvania. The reflections by Hovinen are particularly welcome as he was the first person to empirically apply the TALC to a specific location (Hovinen, 1981, 1982). Indeed, there are a number of chapters in this volume that illustrate the value of reflection on previous work and reconsiderations of its application. Similarly, Lundgren provides an empirical examination of TALC with respect to the eastern townships of Quebec, locations in which he has previously undertaken substantial research. The section is concluded with a case study of the role of TALC in tourism planning in China by Bao and Zhang.

The third section of the volume deals with the application of specific setting, that of cultural and natural heritage. The first chapter in the section is by Stephen Boyd, a former graduate student of Butler, who applies the TALC to Canadian national parks. Russo provides an appraisal of the TALC at a different scale by examining its relationship to heritage cities, while the final chapter of the section, by Malcolm-Davies, shifts the scale of analysis even further by dealing with its potential role at a site level.

One of the main points of debate that has emerged out of consideration of the TALC is its implications for the social and political dynamics that exist within a destination as it changes. Some of these issues are discussed in the fourth section of the volume, which discusses the TALC in relation to local involvement. Weaver and Johnston examine some of these concerns with respect to island destinations, examining the Caribbean and the Hawaiian islands respectively. Johnson and Snepenger discuss residents' perceptions of tourism development in a longitudinal investigation of Silver Valley, Idaho, with Marois and Hinch (another former graduate student of Butler) examining the links between TALC and sustainable tourism in Northern Thailand. The remaining chapter in the section, that of Martin on tourism and politics, discusses the significance of the political aspect of the growth that occurs as tourism progresses through the different stages of the life cycle. Martin provides a case study of Hilton Head, South Carolina to illustrate his general arguments regarding the politics of tourism growth.

The final section of the volume examines empirical studies of the rejuvenation stage of the TALC. Ideally, these should be read in conjunction with the chapters on conceptualising restructuring and rejuvenation in the second volume. Corak discusses the reinvention of a destination in terms of the Opatija Riviera in Croatia while Stansfield examines the rejuvenation of Atlantic City. Both locations have significance for the development of the TALC: Opatija in that it was the first continental destination visited by Butler; and Atlantic City, and the work of Stansfield (1972, 1978), because of the substantial insights it provided into the processes by which resorts rise and fall in popularity. Indeed, the length to which some of these ideas have now been circulating is reflected in Stansfield's chapter in which he refers to the recycling of the resort cycle. The final chapter in this section is by Faulkner and Tideswell and focuses on the rejuvenation of the Gold Coast, Australia.

The conclusion to this volume is an insightful and provocative chapter by Brian Wheeller who successfully managed to integrate issues of authenticity, sustainability and TALC with wildlife ecology, eco-lodges and Elvis Presley. Nevertheless, Wheeler's chapter has a serious message in that it seeks to bring together a number of significant concerns in contemporary tourism studies as well as question some of the assumptions made with respect to ethics, morals and tastes in tourism. The Wheeller chapter also provides a suitable springboard to some of the more theoretical and conceptual dimensions of TALC that are discussed in the other volume, particularly as it seeks to illustrate the manner in which empirical observation and experience and theory are interwoven.

This volume therefore provides a welcome overview of some of the ways in which the TALC has been applied and some of the implications of those applications for further theoretical and conceptual developments in understanding destination change. The second volume goes on to investigate some of these changes in further detail and the contested theoretical terrain that is the TALC. However, as noted above, it is important to realise that the contents of the two volumes are interwoven and ideally need to be read together in order to gain a wider appreciation of TALC, its intellectual history and its contribution to tourism studies, as well as understanding the processes of destination change.

References

Hovinen, G. (1981) A tourist cycle in Lancaster County, Pennsylvania. *Canadian Geographer* 15 (3), 283–286.

Hovinen, G. (1982) Visitor cycles: Outlook in tourism in Lancaster County. *Annals of Tourism Research* 9, 565–583.

Lundgren, J.O. (1984) Geographic concepts and the development of tourism research in Canada. *Geojournal* 9, 17–25.

Stansfield, C. (1972) The development of modern seaside resorts. *Parks and Recreation* 5 (10), 14–46.

Stansfield, C. (1978) Atlantic City and the resort cycle. Background to the legalization of gambling. *Annals of Tourism Research* 5 (2), 238–251.

Part 1

Foundations of the TALC

RICHARD W. BUTLER

This first section of the volume serves to introduce the TALC and review in general terms its origins and uses. It begins with a reproduction of the original article. While this may be felt redundant given the frequency with which it is still quoted, in fact it appears to be an elusive publication. As noted below (Butler, next chapter), the journal, despite its quality, is not commonly found in the holdings of a considerable number of institutions focusing on tourism, unless they also have departments of geography. This has meant over the years that a number of potential readers have, or appear to have had, considerable difficulty in obtaining access to a copy and have relied on summaries in other sources. It seemed appropriate, therefore, to republish the original article in its entirety to increase availability, as well as to enable readers of this volume to have a copy to hand should they wish to refer to it.

The chapter that follows traces the origins of the concept, including a fair amount of reflexive comment by the author, in order to provide a context for the model. It was felt necessary to point out the limited nature and scale of tourism research in the decades before 1980, as well as taking the opportunity to acknowledge the contribution to the theoretical and conceptual development of tourism of authors whose works are, unfortunately, relatively unknown to many of the present day's tourism students and scholars. As is the case of many models, the original focus and purpose was somewhat different to what finally emerged, and the spatial emphasis explicit in the original model had become implicit at best in the final version.

Lagiewski's chapter presents a review of several of the major initial applications of the TALC, and some of the authors whose work is reviewed have contributed chapters in this and the accompanying volume. Of particular value is the table listing applications of the model and the extensive bibliography resulting from it. While no bibliography is ever likely to be complete, this one would appear to have more references to the use of the TALC than any other single piece of work, and is in itself a valuable reference tool for other potential users of the model.

Finally in this first section of the book is the chapter by Haywood, who was one of the first to write a detailed full critique of the model once it had been published. His chapter in this volume focuses particularly on aspects of the model that need addressing in order to improve its potential value for application in areas such as destination development, policy and strategy formulation, and destination management. His comments are particularly valuable in identifying issues that still have to be resolved, some of them coming from the same points that he raised in his original review in 1986. In the section on Configuration and Transformation he discusses in detail issues such as the unit of analysis and unit of measurement most applicable for application of the TALC. He concludes by linking the TALC to sustainability, a theme dealt with in several chapters in this volume (Hovinen, Marois and Hinch, Russo, and Wheeller in particular).

After this the book proceeds with chapters applying the TALC in a variety of situations and locations, at different scales, and through different approaches. Hopefully this introductory section provides sufficient detail on the background and foundations of the TALC for the reader to be able to place these later chapters in an appropriate context.

Chapter 1

The Concept of a Tourist Area Cycle of Evolution: Implications for Management of Resources*

R.W. BUTLER
University of Western Ontario

There can be little doubt that tourist areas are dynamic, that they evolve and change over time. This evolution is brought about by a variety of factors including changes in the preferences and needs of visitors, the gradual deterioration and possible replacement of physical plant and facilities, and the change (or even disappearance) of the original natural and cultural attractions which were responsible for the initial popularity of the area. In some cases, while these attractions remain, they may be utilized for different purposes or come to be regarded as less significant in comparison with imported attractions.[1] The idea of a consistent process through which tourist areas evolve has been vividly described by Christaller:

> The typical course of development has the following pattern. Painters search out untouched and unusual places to paint. Step by step the place develops as a so-called artist colony. Soon a cluster of poets follows, kindred to the painters: then cinema people, gourmets, and the jeunesse dorée. The place becomes fashionable and the entrepreneur takes note. The fisherman's cottage, the shelter-huts become converted into boarding houses and hotels come on the scene. Meanwhile the painters have fled and sought out another periphery – periphery as related to space, and metaphorically, as 'forgotten' places and landscapes. Only the painters with a commercial inclination who like to do well in business remain; they capitalize on the good name of this former painter's corner and on the gullibility of tourists. More and more townsmen choose this place, now en vogue and advertised in the newspapers. Subsequently the gourmets, and all those who seek real recreation, stay away. At last the tourist agencies come with their package rate travelling parties; now, the indulged public avoids such places. At the same time, in other places the same cycle occurs again; more and more places come into fashion, change their type, turn into everybody's tourist haunt.[2]

While this description has most relevance to the European and, particularly, to the Mediterranean setting, others have expressed the same general idea. Stansfield, in discussing the development of Atlantic City, refers specifically to the resort cycle,[3] and Noronha has suggested that 'tourism develops in three stages: i) discovery, ii) local response and initiative, and iii) institutionalized 'institutionalization).'[4] It is also explicit in Christaller's concept that types of tourists change with the tourist areas. Research into the characteristics of visitors is widespread, but less has been done on their motivations and desires. One example is a typology conceived by Cohen, who characterizes tourists as 'institutionalized' or 'non-institutionalized,' and further as 'drifters', 'explorers,' 'individual mass tourists,' and 'organized mass tourists.'[5] Research by Plog into the psychology of travel, and the characterization of travellers as allocentrics, mid-centrics, and psychocentrics, substantiates Christaller's argument.[6] Plog suggests that tourist areas are attractive to different types of visitors as the areas evolve, beginning with small numbers of adventuresome allocentrics, followed by increasing numbers of mid-centrics as the area becomes accessible, better serviced, and well known, and giving way to declining numbers of psychocentrics as the area becomes older, more outdated, and less different to the areas of origin of visitors. While the actual numbers of visitors may not decline for a long time, the potential market will reduce in size as the area has to compete with others that are more recently developed. Plog sums up his argument thus: 'We can visualize a destination moving across a spectrum, however gradually or slowly, but far too often ineroxably toward the potential of its own demise. Destination areas carry with them the potential seeds of their own destruction, as they allow themselves to become more commercialized and lose their qualities which originally attracted tourists.'

While other writers, such as Cohen,[7] have warned against the problems of unilinear models of social change, there seems to be overwhelming evidence that the general pattern of tourist area evolution is consistent. The rates of growth and change may vary widely, but the final result will be the same in almost all cases.

A Hypothetical Cycle of Area Evolution

The pattern which is put forward here is based upon the product cycle concept, whereby sales of a product proceed slowly at first, experience a rapid rate of growth, stabilize, and subsequently decline; in other words, a basic asymptotic curve is followed. Visitors will come to an area in small numbers initially, restricted by lack of access, facilities, and local knowledge. As facilities are provided and awareness grows, visitor numbers will increase. With marketing, information dissemination, and further facility provision, the area's popularity will grow rapidly. Eventually, however, the rate of increase in visitor numbers will decline as levels of carrying capacity are reached. These may be identified in terms of environmental factors (e.g. land scarcity, water quality, air quality), of physical plant (e.g. transportation, accommodation, other services), or of social factors (e.g. crowding, resentment by the local population). As the attractiveness of the area declines relative to other areas, because of overuse and the impacts of visitors, the actual number of visitors may also eventually decline.

The stages through which it is suggested that tourist areas pass are illustrated in Figure 1.1. The *exploration stage* is characterized by small numbers of tourists, Plog's allocentrics and Cohen's explorers making individual travel arrangements and following irregular visitation patterns. From Christaller's model they can also be expected to be non-local visitors who have been attracted to the area by its unique or considerably different natural and cultural features. At this time there would be no specific facilities provided for visitors. The use of local facilities and

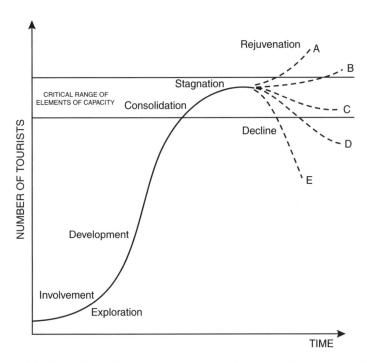

Figure 1.1 Hypothetical evolution of a tourist area. (For explanation of A–E see 'Implications.')

contact with local residents are therefore likely to be high, which may itself be a significant attraction to some visitors. The physical fabric and social milieu of the area would be unchanged by tourism, and the arrival and departure of tourists would be of relatively little significance to the economic and social life of the permanent residents. Examples of this stage can be seen in parts of the Canadian Arctic and Latin America, to which tourists are attracted by natural and cultural-historical features.

As numbers of visitors increase and assume some regularity, some local residents will enter the *involvement stage* and begin to provide facilities primarily or even exclusively for visitors. Contact between visitors and locals can be expected to remain high and, in fact, increase for those locals involved in catering for visitors. As this stage progresses, some advertising specifically to attract tourists can be anticipated, and a basic initial market area for visitors can be defined. A tourist season can be expected to emerge and adjustments will be made in the social pattern of at least those local residents involved in tourism. Some level of organization in tourist travel arrangements can be expected and the first pressures put upon governments and public agencies to provide or improve transport and other facilities for visitors. Some of the smaller, less developed Pacific and Caribbean islands exhibit this pattern, as do some less accessible areas of western Europe and North America.

The *development stage* reflects a well-defined tourist market area, shaped in part by heavy advertising in tourist-generating areas. As this stage progresses, local involvement and control of development will decline rapidly. Some locally provided facilities will have disappeared, being superseded by larger, more elaborate, and more up-to-date facilities provided by external organizations, particularly for visitor accommodation. Natural and cultural attractions will be developed and marketed specifically, and these original attractions will be supplemented by man-made imported facilities. Changes in the physical appearance of the area will be noticeable, and it can be expected that not all of them will be welcomed or approved by all of the local population. This stage can be seen in parts of Mexico, on the more developed Pacific islands, and on the north and west African coasts. Regional and national involvement in the planning and provision of facilities will almost certainly be necessary and, again, may not be completely in keeping with local preferences. The number of tourists at peak periods will probably equal or exceed the permanent local population. As this stage unfolds, imported labour will be utilized and auxiliary facilities for the tourist industry (such as laundries) will make their appearance. The type of tourist will also have changed, as a wider market is drawn upon, representing the mid-centrics of Plog's classification, or Cohen's institutionalized tourist.

As the *consolidation stage* is entered the rate of increase in numbers of visitors will decline, although total numbers will still increase, and total visitor numbers exceed the number of permanent residents. A major part of the area's economy will be tied to tourism. Marketing and advertising will be wide-reaching and efforts made to extend the visitor season and market area. Major franchises and chains in the tourist industry will be represented but few, if any, additions will be made. The large numbers of visitors and the facilities provided for them can be expected to arouse some opposition and discontent among permanent residents, paticularly those not involved in the tourist industry in any way, and to result in some deprivation and restrictions upon their activities. Such trends are evident in areas of the Caribbean and on the northern Mediterranean coast. The resort cities will have well-defined recreational business districts,[8] and, depending upon the length of time involved, old facilities may now be regarded as second rate and far from desirable.

As the area enters the *stagnation stage* the peak numbers of visitors will have been reached. Capacity levels for many variables will have been reached or exceeded, with attendant environmental, social, and economic problems. The area will have a well-established image but it will no longer be in fashion. There will be a heavy reliance on repeat visitation and on conventions and similar forms of traffic. Surplus bed capacity will be available and strenuous efforts will be needed to maintain the level of visitation. Natural and genuine cultural attractions will probably have been superseded by imported 'artificial' facilities. The resort image becomes divorced from its geographic environment.[9] New development will be peripheral to the original tourist area and the existing properties are likely to experience frequent changes in ownership. The Costa Brava resorts of Spain and many cottage resorts in Ontario manifest these characteristics. The type of visitor can also be expected to change towards the organized mass tourist identified by Cohen and the psychocentric described by Plog.

In the *decline stage* the area will not be able to compete with newer attractions and so will face a declining market, both spatially and numerically. It will no longer appeal to vacationers but will be used increasingly for weekend or day trips, if it is accessible to large numbers of people. Such trends can be clearly seen in older resort areas in Europe, such as the Firth of Clyde in western Scotland. Miami Beach would also appear to be entering this stage. Property turnover will be high and tourist facilities often replaced by non-tourist related structures, as the area moves out of tourism. This latter factor, of course, is cumulative. More tourist facilities disappear as the area becomes less attractive to tourists and the viability of other tourist facilities becomes more questionable. Local involvement in tourism is likely to increase at this stage, as employees and other residents are able to purchase facilities at significantly lower prices as the market declines. The conversion of many facilities to related activities is likely. Hotels may become condominiums, convalescent or retirement homes, or conventional apartments, since the attractions of many tourist areas make them equally attractive for permanent settlement, particularly for the elderly. Ultimately, the area may become a veritable tourist slum or lose its tourist function completely.

On the other hand *rejuvenation* may occur, although it is almost certain that this stage will never be reached without a complete change in the attractions on which tourism is based. Two ways of accomplishing this goal can be seen at present. One is the addition of a man-made attraction, as in the case of Atlantic City's gambling casinos. Obviously, though, if neighbouring and competing areas follow suit, the effectiveness of the measure will be reduced; a major part of Atlantic City's anticipated success is the element of uniqueness which it has obtained by the change.

An alternative approach to rejuvenation is to take advantage of previously untapped natural resources. Spa towns in Europe and the summer holiday village of Aviemore in Scotland have experienced rejuvenation by a reorientation to the winter sports market, thus allowing the areas to experience a year-round tourist industry. The development of new facilities becomes economically feasible, and simultaneously serves to revitalize the older summer holiday trade. As new forms of recreation appear, it is not impossible that other tourist areas will find previously unappreciated natural resources to develop.

In many cases, combined government and private efforts are necessary, and the new market may be not the allocentric section of the population (which would suggest a recommencement of the complete cycle), but rather a specific interest or activity group. Ultimately, however, it can be expected that even the attractions of the rejuvenated tourist area will lose their competitiveness. Only in the case of the truly unique area could one anticipate an almost timeless attractiveness, able to withstand the pressures of visitation. Even in such a case, human tastes and preferences would have to remain constant over time for visitors to be attracted. Niagara Falls is perhaps one example. Artificial attractions, such as the spectacularly successful Disneyland and Disneyworld, may also be able to compete effectively over long periods by adding to their attractions to keep in tune with contemporary preferences. Many established tourist areas in Britain, the United States, and elsewhere attract visitors who have spent their vacations in these areas consistently for several decades, and the preferences of these repeat visitors show little sign of changing. In the majority of cases, though, the initial selection of the area to be visited by these people was determined by cost and accessibility rather than specific preferences.

Implications

Although a consistent evolution of tourist areas can be conceptualized, it must be emphasized again that not all areas experience the stages of the cycle as clearly as others. The establishment of what has become known as the 'instant resort' is a case in point. The process whereby areas for development, such as Cancun in Mexico,[10] are selected by computer from a range of possibilities allowed by certain preselected parameters has meant that the exploration and involvement phases are probably of minimal significance, if they are present at all. Under these circumstances the development phase becomes the real commencement of the cycle. Even here, however, it can be argued that, at the national scale, Mexico is experiencing the cycle illustrated in Figure 1.1. Perhaps the later stages of the cycle are more significant, then, because of the implications which they hold for tourism in general and for the planning and arrangement of tourist areas in particular.

The assumption that tourist areas will always remain tourist areas and be attractive to tourists appears to be implicit in tourism planning. Public and private agencies alike, rarely, if ever, refer to the anticipated life span of a tourist area or its attractions. Rather, because tourism has shown an, as yet, unlimited potential for growth, despite economic recessions, it is taken for granted that numbers of visitors will continue to increase. The fallacy of this assumption can be seen in the experience of older tourist areas, such as those of southern Ontario, over the past two decades.

The process illustrated in Figure 1.1 has two axes representing numbers of visitors and time. An increase in either direction implies a general reduction in overall quality and attractiveness after capacity levels are reached. In the case of the first visitors, the area may become unattractive long before capacity levels are reached and they will have moved on to explore other undeveloped areas. It can be anticipated also that reaction to the visitors by the local population will undergo change throughout this period, a process suggested by Doxey in his 'irridex' (index of tourist irritation); the scale progresses from euphoria through apathy and irritation to antagonism.[11] More recent research has shown that resident reaction to tourists is not necessarily explained by increasing contact with visitors or increasing numbers of visitors alone. It is a more complex function, related to the characteristics of both visitors and visited, and the specific arrangements of the area involved.[12]

The direction of the curve after the period of stabilization illustrated in Figure 1.1 is open to several interpretations. Successful redevelopment, as for example in Atlantic City, could result in renewed growth and expansion as shown by curve A. Minor modification and adjustment to capacity levels, and continued protection of resources, could allow continued growth at a much reduced rate (curve B). A readjustment to meet all capacity levels would enable a more stable level of visitation to be maintained after an initial readjustment downwards (curve C) Continued overuse of resources, non-replacement of aging plant, and decreasing competitiveness with other areas would result in the marked decline (curve D). Finally, the intervention of war, disease, or other catastrophic events would result in an immediate decline in numbers of visitors (for example, Northern Ireland from 1969), from which it may be extremely difficult to return to high levels of visitation. If the decline continues for a long time, the area and its facilities may no longer be attractive to the majority of tourists after the problem is solved.

To date, the arguments put forward in this paper are general and are only now being substantiated in terms of quantifiable data. A major problem in testing the basic hypothesis and modelling the curve for specific areas is that of obtaining data on visitors to areas over long periods. These are rarely available, and it is particularly unlikely that they will date back to the onset of tourist visits. However, those data which are available for a few areas for periods in excess of thirty or forty years substantiate the general arguments put forward in this paper.

At the same time, the shape of the curve must be expected to vary for different areas, reflecting variations in such factors as rate of development, numbers of visitors, accessibility, government policies, and numbers of similar competing areas.

It has been clearly shown, for example, that each improvement in accessibility to a recreation area results in significantly increased visitation and an expansion of the market area.[13]

The development of health resorts in Britain, France, the north United States bears witness to this process.[14] If development of facilities and accessibility is delayed, for whatever reason (e.g. local opposition, lack of capital, lack of outside interest), the exploration period may be much longer than anticipated. In the case of new 'instant' resorts, where tourist facilities are established in an area in which there has been little or no previous settlement, the first two stages in Figure 1.1 may be of minimal significance or absent, a situation noted by Noronha as particularly applicable to some developing nations.[15] The classic, well-established tourist areas of the world (i.e. those which have been popular over several decades), frequently reveal evidence of having passed through all of the postulated stages.

The resort areas of the northern Mediterranean, Britain, the north-eastern seaboard of the United States, and parts of Florida have moved steadily through an evolutionary sequence. Other areas, such as Hawaii, the Caribbean and Pacific islands, and the resort areas of north Africa, are in earlier stages of the cycle, but the pattern of visitation strongly approximates the curve illustrated in Figure 1.1.

These observations also suggest that a change of attitude is required on the part of those who are responsible for planning, developing, and managing tourist areas. Tourist attractions are not infinite and timeless but should be viewed and treated as finite and possibly non-renewable resources. They could then be more carefully protected and preserved. *The development of the tourist area could be kept within predetermined capacity limits, and its potential competitiveness maintained over a longer period*. While the maximum number of people visiting an area at any one time under such arrangements may be less than most present policies of maximum short-term development, more visitors could be catered for in the long term. In a few localities already, limits to the growth of tourism have been adopted, chiefly because of severe environmental damage to attractions (e.g. the erosion of Stonehenge in England, or the damage to prehistoric cave paintings in Spain and France). Unless more knowledge is gained and a greater awareness developed of the processes which shape tourist areas, it has to be concluded, with Plog, that many 'of the most attractive and interesting areas in the world are doomed to become tourist relics.'[16]

Acknowledgements

I would like to acknowledge the valuable discussions and contribution of J.E. Brougham, International Centre for Research on Bilingualism, Laval University, to the ideas expressed in this paper.

Notes and References

* This article was first published in *The Canadian Geographer* 24(1), 5–12 (1980), and is reproduced by permission of the Canadian Association of Geographers.

1. R.I. Wolfe, 'Wasaga Beach-the divorce from the geographic environment,' *The Canadian Geographer*, 2 (1952), pp. 57–66.
2. W. Christaller, 'Some considerations of tourism location in Europe: the peripheral regions-underdeveloped countries-recreation areas,' *Regional Science Association Papers*, 12 (1963), p. 103.
3. C. Stansfield, 'Atlantic City and the resort cycle,' *Annals of Tourism Research*, 5 (1978), p. 238.
4. R. Noronha, *Review of the Sociological Literature on Tourism* (New York: World Bank, 1976).
5. E. Cohen, 'Towards a sociology of international tourism,' *Social Research*, 39 (1972), pp. 164–82.
6. S.C. Plog, 'Why destination areas rise and fall in popularity,' Unpublished paper presented to the Southern California Chapter, The Travel Research Association, 1972.
7. E. Cohen, 'Rethinking the sociology of tourism,' *Annals of Tourism Research*, 6 (1978), pp. 18–35.
8. C.A. Stansfield and J.E. Rickert, 'The recreational business district,' *Journal of Leisure Research*, 4 (1970), pp. 213–25.
9. Wolfe, op. cit.

10. F.P. Bosselman, *In the Wake of the Tourist* (Washington, DC: Conservation Foundation, 1978).

11. G. Doxey, 'Visitor-resident interaction in tourist destinations: inferences from empirical research in Barbados, West Indies and Niagara-on-the-Lake, Ontario,' Unpublished paper presented to the Symposium on the Planning and Development of the Tourist Industry in the ECC Region, Dubrovnik, Yugoslavia, 1975.

12. R.W. Butler and J.E. Brougham, *The Social and Cultural Impact of Tourism— A Case Study of Sleat, Isle of Skye* (Edinburgh: Scottish Tourist Board, 1977); J.E. Brougham, 'Resident Attitudes Towards the Impact of Tourism in Sleat,' unpublished PHD dissertation, University of Western Ontario, 1978; and P.E. Murphy, 'Perceptions and preferences of decision-making groups in tourist centres: a guide to planning strategy,' in *Tourism and the Next Decade: Issues and Problems* (Washington, DC: George Washington University, 1979).

13. C.A. Stansfield, 'The development of modern seaside resorts,' *Parks and Recreation,* 5: 10 (1972), pp. 14–46.

14. E.W. Gilbert, 'The growth of inland and seaside health resorts in England,' *Scottish Geographical Magazine,* 55 (1939), pp. 16–35; D.G. Pearce, 'Form and function in French resorts,' *Annals of Tourism Research,* 5 (1978), pp. 142–56; R.I. Wolfe, 'The summer resorts of Ontario in the nineteenth century,' *Ontario History,* 54 (1964), pp. 150–60; and Stansfield, 'Atlantic City.'

15. Noronha, op. cit., p. 24.

16. Plog, op. cit., p. 8.

Chapter 2
The Origins of the Tourism Area Life Cycle

RICHARD W. BUTLER

Introduction

The origins of the Tourism Area Life Cycle model have been discussed before in a number of academic papers, both by this author (Butler, 1990, 1998a, 2000) and others (see contributors to this and the accompanying volume). It is felt appropriate at this point to expand further upon those origins in order to place the model and its development in a clearer context. This is done partly to correct what may have been misperceptions of the real origins of the initial (1980) article (Hall, personal communication, 1996), and to elaborate upon comments made by this author in the earlier papers referred to above. As well, it is felt necessary to re-emphasise the importance of understanding from whence the academic literature on tourism, of which the TALC paper is a part, has evolved. All too often, in this writer's opinion, current students of tourism are led to believe, or come to the conclusion themselves, that tourism is a recent phenomenon, and that relatively little had been written on it before the 1990s. Such misperceptions have partly contributed to the still relatively low academic reputation which tourism has as an academic subject, and the all too familiar occurrence of scholars in more established subjects venturing into publication in tourism on the faulty assumption that it is a 'new' area waiting to be discovered and 'enriched' by their often somewhat limited contributions.

The TALC model as it initially appeared in its 1980 form had a distinct gestation period and was based on, and integrated within it, several strands of research and conceptual development. Although it may not appear overly so in its published form, it was inherently based in the geographic literature, reflecting the author's training and interests in geography. It is not by accident that several of the contributors in these two volumes (in particular Coles, Hall and Papatheodorou, all geographers themselves) draw attention to this linkage in their own chapters. The 'facts' on which the model is based are fairly obvious to any would-be observer of tourist resorts (as shown in the Postscript to this chapter), just as people were generally aware that apples appeared to always fall to the ground before one hit Newton on the head, resulting in the explanation of gravity. Before any reviewer draws the erroneous conclusion that the TALC is being compared to, or thought equal in significance to the theory of gravity, let me dispel any such arrogance of thought. The point that is being made is that there was nothing devastatingly complicated or original in the data or facts on which the model is based. Lundgren (1984: 22) summed up the situation very aptly when he commented 'Butler put into the realistic cyclical context a reality that everyone knew about, and clearly recognised, but had never formulated into an overall theory.' As noted below, at the time of its development, while it seemed to make good sense, the future wide application of the model was not anticipated. The chapter proceeds first by emphasising the reflexivity inevitably involved in the formulation of any model or concept.

Reflexivity and the TALC

Just as 'we are what we eat', our knowledge and understanding of the world around us is, to a large degree, based on what we observe first hand. My initial interest in tourist destination development came from personal experience with a number of British holiday resorts and destination areas from the 1950s onwards. Living in Birmingham, the major town in England that is furthest from the sea, meant that family holidays were not confined to the nearest resort linked to the home town by the railway, as was the normal pattern in that time period, because many resorts were equally distant and thus equally inaccessible. During my formative years holidays were spent in locations as varied as Rhyl (North Wales), Weston-Super-Mare and Skegness on the west and east coasts of England respectively, and Stonehaven, St Monans and the Isle of Arran in Scotland. A good sampling of classic railway-dominated resorts, mass tourist destinations and small fishing communities using tourism to support their traditional economic activity. Arran was an interesting and somewhat different example, because it could only be reached by boat, at that time by several of the fleet of steamers (some still paddle-wheelers then) that serviced the resorts of the Firth of Clyde. Some of my abiding favourite memories are of spending 10 days of a summer holiday on the Clyde steamers, setting out from Glasgow on the train to railheads such as Gourock and Wemyss Bay, to catch the steamers and visiting different resorts each day. By the time I began doctoral studies at Glasgow University in the mid 1960s, the fleet of steamers was rapidly diminishing and being replaced by roll-on roll-off car ferries, catering efficiently to a new breed of tourists but about as interesting to sail on as a modern day Ford car is to drive compared to a pre-war convertible Jaguar.

It became apparent that the resorts of the Clyde, as well as those elsewhere, were beginning to change significantly, in appearance, in accessibility, in tourists, in economic health and in attractivity. Like most Northern European resorts they were, for the first time, facing competition from Mediterranean resorts for the mass tourist market. Whereas in earlier years they had been shielded from such competition by continental conflict, relative inaccessibility, cost and what Plog (1973) might call 'pyschocentricity', from the 1960s onwards attitudes, accessibility and affluence had all changed dramatically. The old resorts were no longer as attractive to potential tourists, nor catering to the same market as effectively as in the past. Working alongside a colleague who was undertaking his own doctoral research on the Clyde resorts (see Pattison, 1968), these changes were frequently discussed. During the course of my doctoral research the same patterns became evident in other smaller resorts in the Scottish highlands and islands (Butler, 1973). In particular, the changes taking place in the Spey Valley, with the development of winter sports, meant that villages such as Aviemore and Grantown on Spey, previously quiet Victorian summer destinations, were now being developed or redeveloped to cater to a very different winter market. The physical, as well as social and economic changes were very obvious.

My first experience of continental Europe in 1966 included a visit to Opatija (see Corak, this volume), providing further visual evidence of changes taking place in well established resorts. A subsequent visit to Mallorca provided first-hand experience of why Mediterranean resorts were attracting a sizeable segment of the traditional British holiday market from British holiday resorts. Thus by the end of the 1960s I had witnessed very clearly the dramatic changes that were taking place in tourism in Britain and parts of continental Europe. At that time few people realised what might be the full extent of these changes and their implications, and extremely little had been written on the subject. In the 1960s and earlier the tourism literature was very limited, although publications such as those by Gilbert (1939, 1954), Ogilvie (1933), Pimlott (1947), House (1954) and Barratt (1958) had all discussed and analysed aspects of resort development, markets, morphology and dynamics. Their contributions today go almost unnoticed and uncredited, although they laid the foundations for much of the later work on resorts and tourist destinations. Barratt's model of resort morphology predates the work of Stansfield and Rickert (1978) on Recreational Business Districts, for example, but is rarely mentioned unless in the context of the citation in Mathieson and Wall (1982). The model Barratt produced is as valid in the 21st century as it was some five decades earlier when he first produced it. It is against this backdrop of personal experience and limited references that the resort cycle began to take shape.

Antecedent Literature and Concepts

In an earlier review of the TALC (Butler, 2000), two major bases for the model were identified, the Product Life Cycle and models of wildlife populations. While these were major influences, other specific writings predate these concepts in terms of influence on TALC establishment, in addition to those noted above. The first of these were articles relating to the flows of tourists and their patterns of movement, both at the micro (destination) and the macro (global) scales. This author's interest in modelling these flows and accounting for their patterns owes a very great deal to discussions with and contributions from Jim Brougham, then a research student at the University of Western Ontario. A paper produced jointly (Brougham & Butler, 1972) is, in reality, the first version of the TALC. Entitled 'The Applicability of the Asymptotic Curve to the Forecasting of Tourism Development', it was presented at the annual meeting of the Travel Research Association, held in Quebec City in 1972. To say that it did not set the audience on fire would be somewhat of an understatement, and despite a continuing interest in the ideas contained in the paper, neither author felt the topic practical to pursue much further at that time, mainly because of the perceived nonavailability of the data that would have been required.

That paper does deserve some attention, however, in the context of the origins of the TALC, as it introduced many of the key points of the 1980 model and appears to have been the first time 'the resort cycle' appears in print. (This is contrary to what I had stated in a paper and subsequent chapter (Butler, 1998a, 2000), where I mistakenly credited the origin of the phrase to Charles Stansfield in his 1978 article on Atlantic City.) The 1972 paper argued that much more attention should be paid to flows of tourists, building on the work of Williams and Zelinsky (1970) and Yokeno (1968). We stated that 'from the point of view of prediction of flows of tourists, and consequent growth of tourist destination areas, the need is greatest to explain the choice of specific locations and the process of movement from one location to another over time' (Brougham & Butler, 1972: 1). The second section of the paper was headed 'The Resort Cycle', and it utilised data from the resorts in the Firth of Clyde from 1949 to 1966 to illustrate (not tremendously convincingly it must be admitted) an asymptotic curve. It also made reference to the fact that an article in the Nice Matin (1971) suggested other areas were at 'this state in their cycle' and made reference to Christaller's (1963) article and the pattern of resort development described therein. We concluded that section by suggesting 'that a point will be reached, however, at which the rate of increase of visitors begins to decline, and may even, as in the case above, become a decline in numbers. Such a trend may be due to a number of factors, such as increasing pollution, increasing land values limiting expansion of facilities, congestion of facilities, and the availability of alternative areas' (Brougham & Butler, 1972: 6).

Most of the rest of that paper was taken up by attempting to model a hypothetical pattern of development of a tourist destination. It was suggested that the process 'may be satisfactorily approximated by the solution of the logistic equation:

$$\frac{Dv}{Dt} = kV(M - V)$$

where V is the number of visitors, T is time, M is the maximum number of visitors and K is an empirically derived parameter representative of the telling rate, or the spread of knowledge of the resort from tourists to potential tourists' (Brougham & Butler, 1972: 6).

The solution was proposed as:

$$V = MV \\ \frac{O}{V + (M - V) - Mkt}$$

where V is the number of tourists at time t. The resulting curve is shown in Figure 2.1.

It should be emphasised that the main focus in the 1972 paper was the prediction of where tourist development and flows would be in the future, not the resort cycle per se. Undoubtedly reflecting the authors' geographical roots, we referred to the 'shifting rule' of Garrison, as cited in Bunge (1966: 27).

> Where capacity increases require physical expansion, where the expansion cannot be in the vertical dimension and where the new space is made more 'expensive' by the presence of the phenomena itself, a shift is likely during times of capacity strain and the shift will probably occur to a new location as near to the old location as the area of induced expense will allow.

It was argued in our paper that when relocation to a new development took place in the same general location or region as the original tourist development, the pattern of development would be as illustrated in Figure 2.2.

The paper concluded with a brief discussion on the way that such a curve might be used for predicting the future patterns of tourism development (see Marente & Sheclader, and Berry, other volume, for examples of how the TALC can be used in a predictive manner). It suggested sufficient empirical regularities might illustrate patterns, assuming tourists would opt for nearby alternative developments,

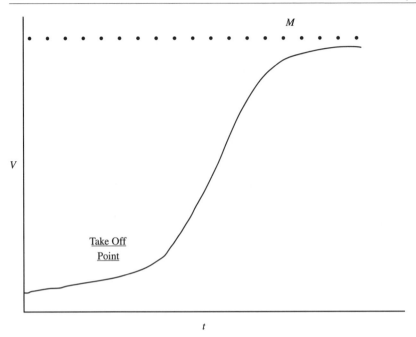

Figure 2.1 A theoretical asymptotic curve

although this was recognised as being a dubious assumption. An alternative approach suggested involved manipulating potential surface maps of migrant populations of specific regions, an idea not pursued in the context of tourism flows. A tentative pattern of tourist development matching the 'shifting rule' was suggested in the Mediterranean, beginning on the French Riviera, spreading to the Italian Riviera, then to Spain, the Adriatic coast and to North Africa. At this point, perhaps puzzlingly with the advantage of hindsight, Malta and Cyprus were overlooked, and Turkey not anticipated.

Contemporary Literature

(In this section contemporary is used in the context of the development of the TALC, not the present day.) Reference has already been made to Christaller (1963) and his seminal work, although it is interesting to note that the key comments in that article on the development process of tourists resorts are not the main focus of the article, but like that by Brougham and Butler (1972) were on explaining the flows and patterns of tourists. Christaller's contribution was significant, not least because, coming as it did from someone who was generally regarded as one the

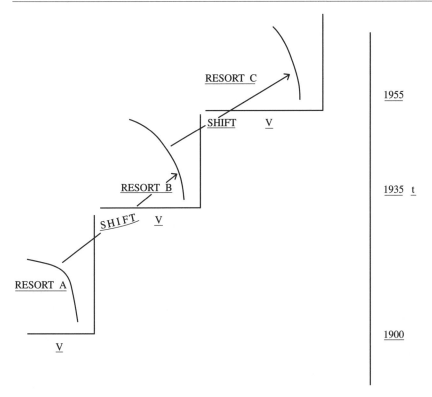

Figure 2.2 Modelling resort development in space and time

greatest contributors to theory in geography, it gave added gravitas to a tentative paper in a fledgling subject by young researchers.

Of equal importance in the development of the 1980 article was the frequently cited paper by Plog (1973) on the psychographics of tourists. It was titled 'Why destination areas rise and fall in popularity', and again, the title of this article does not really reflect the empirical work on which the article was based. This was a survey of American travellers to determine why some people were prepared to fly and others not. Perhaps ironically, it had been presented first at a meeting of the Los Angeles chapter of the Travel Research Association the preceding year, the same time and to the same association as the Brougham and Butler article had been presented. What made Plog's article of particular relevance and importance to the TALC model was that it put forward a suggested model describing how changes in the tourist market were related to subsequent changes in the destinations visited. It also included Plog's oft-quoted statement about destination areas carrying with them the seeds of their own destruction, making it one of the few articles at that time to even raise the topic of the decline of destinations. The points made in Plog's article fitted in extremely well with the ideas germinating from the 1972 paper and with Christaller's description of changes in visitors to destinations over time.

Three other papers were of particular relevance also. The first (although last in chronological order of publication) was Stansfield's (1978) article in the then recently established *Annals of Tourism Research*, titled 'Atlantic City and the Resort Cycle'. In this paper Stansfield discussed and analysed the rise and decline, and then rebirth of Atlantic City through the legalisation of gambling there. In doing this he supplied support in the academic literature for the concept of a cycle and a convincing example of the process of rejuvenation of a tourist destination. Stansfield has been one of the major contributors to the literature on resorts, and his earlier articles (1972) on the Recreational Business District (1970) were both highly insightful and innovative.

A second paper of considerable importance was that by Doxey (1975), yet another paper that was first presented at a meeting of the Travel Research Association. His well quoted 'Irridex' proposed a process of change in resident attitudes towards tourists in destinations. It suggested, in line with the adage 'familiarity breeds contempt', that over time residents of tourist destinations would move from a positive to a negative attitude towards tourism. While it has been argued (Butler, 1975) that such a view is probably too simplistic, the overall proposition of the article, that destinations and the attitudes of their residents change as tourism development takes place, clearly complemented well the other literature on resorts available at the time. Subsequent research on resident impacts (see, for example, Johnson and Snepenger, this volume) has shown how much more complicated this subject is, but such research was not available in the 1970s.

Finally, the third paper, which helped throw additional light on the process of change in tourist destinations, was one of several invaluable publications by Roy Wolfe (1954). Acknowledged as the 'Dean' of Canadian, and perhaps North American researchers in the 1950s and 1960s in outdoor recreation and tourism, Wolfe and his contributions are far less cited and well known in the tourism literature than they deserve to be. His epic study on second homes in Ontario (1948) provided a key link between 'old' and 'new' studies of tourism, and his works with the Ontario government on highway travel models are far in advance of most academic work in this area being published at that time. Wolfe's article on Wasaga Beach (1952), the classic Canadian 'honky tonk' resort, discussed its 'Divorce from the Geographic Environment' and traced its development from a quiet second home location to the major tourist and recreation destination in Ontario. In this he confirmed the importance of location, the way that development changes the role and importance of natural features in a destination's attractivity, and the influence of exogenous factors on tourism patterns. It was published in *The Canadian Geographer* almost three decades before the original TALC article.

To this rather limited number of references on resort development processes and related research should be added an even shorter list of writings that pertain to the other 'leg' or foundation of the TALC, that dealing with wildlife ecology and populations. This literature and its influence were not, in fact, cited in the 1980 article, although they have been referred to in subsequent discussions of the TALC (Butler, 1990, 2000), and Haywood (1986) also drew attention to such an analogy with wildlife population cycles. The comparison with wildlife populations was key to the development of the asymptotic curve in the 1972 article discussed earlier but the links were somewhat more tenuous and less profoundly academic than might be imagined. Again, my personal background intervenes. I had for a long time been a keen bird-watcher, and thanks to an excellent school library, had become familiar with the writings of the late Frank Fraser Darling, a naturalist and scholar. His books *Island Farm* (1943) and *Island Years* (1941), read in lieu of assigned school material, encouraged me to read more of his work, including *A Herd of Red Deer* (1936) based on his PhD research. Some of my apparently misspent afternoons in the school library proved useful eventually, and Darling's comments on the population fluctuations of 'his' herd of deer obviously remained in my memory. When writing the 1972 paper and looking for support and assistance in drawing the development curve, his comments proved invaluable:

> Mathematicians have helped ecology enormously by their analysis of data of experimental animal populations... We know now the nature of the asymptotic or S curve applied to animal populations, that after a slow start of increase in a population in an ample habitat there is a sharp rise in increase or productivity until near saturation of the habitat, whereafter the curve flattens out, making the numbers of the population more or less static. The animal manager gets ready for a catastrophic fall if he has read the signs. (Darling, cited in Thompson & Grimble, 1968: 47)

The analogy to a tourist destination, growing rapidly, without apparent regard for the future or the preservation of its resources, of a wildlife population increasing with a natural lack of regard for the future and the ability of the environment to sustain the increased population was a strong one to us, even if a little peculiar to others at the time. It has been interesting to read of support from others for an analogy between TALC and wildlife ecology and natural systems (Haywood, 1986;

Ravenscroft, other volume), especially as this was not discussed in the 1980 model.

Final Comments

This chapter has been intended to provide more detailed background to the development of the TALC model than had hitherto been available in order to provide a context for the chapters in this and the other volume. It may be pretentious to argue that the old generation have an obligation to interpret the past for future generations, but it is surely better for those who were working in the past (even if we occasionally appear to still live there) to take on that task rather than to leave it to those who were not. Admittedly we may at times be guilty of putting a more favourable gloss on developments and processes to hide our ignorance and embarrassment, but we are the only ones in a position to know how and why particular ideas emerged at specific times and others did not. What we cannot do is explain *why* particular ideas take hold and remain popular when others disappear.

There remain a few items to address. One is why a tourism article should appear in a journal such as *The Canadian Geographer*, which did not have a strong record of publishing articles on tourism. Excellent journal though it is, its relative obscurity outside the field of geography and thus absence from libraries in institutions that do not offer geography (the author's current university is a case in point!), mean that increasing numbers of students and others working in tourism do not have easy access to the original article. It is clear from citations appearing in the literature that some writers citing the TALC are doing so 'second hand', and its all-too familiar curve is taking on more variations than Paul McCartney's 'Yesterday'. This inaccessibility of the original publication was one of the reasons for reproducing it in this volume, and I am most grateful to the Canadian Association of Geographers for giving permission for this. *The Canadian Geographer* was the vehicle of publication because the original paper was presented at the annual meeting of the Canadian Association of Geographers in Vancouver, 1980. At the urging of Peter Murphy, for the first time in its history, the journal produced a special issue, one devoted to tourism and recreation, containing some of the papers presented at the annual meeting, reviewed and edited by Murphy.

A second point that needs addressing and is much more difficult to explain, is why the TALC has received the continued attention and application that it has over the past two decades. It is unusual, as all academics know, for any article to remain popular and apparently relevant for two decades, especially in social science. One of the authors in this volume, on being asked to contribute a chapter based on an

article he had written, commented to the effect that he was somewhat surprised to hear from someone who had actually read the article
as he never took it for granted that one's journal articles were actually
read (Snepenger, personal communication, 2001), a feeling I imagine
most academics share. One might conclude that the TALC has remained
accepted because, as Wall (1982: 18) commented, it is 'elegant and useful'.
But long-time friend and colleague though he is, he did go on to note
a number of difficulties and gaps, some of which have since been
addressed, but many of which are still causing researchers problems, as
noted in many of the chapters in these two volumes. The reasons
probably lie in a few simple realities including that noted by Lundgren
earlier. First, the model is simple and easy to use, and able to accept
a variety of forms of data. It is intuitively appropriate and provides a
conceptual 'hook' on which case studies of specific destinations can be
'hung', a rather valuable aid, especially to students undertaking thesis
research and to other researchers examining a specific location. Second,
it appeared at a time when concepts and models were lacking but
being eagerly sought in tourism as research in the subject moved beyond
simple description towards interpretation and analysis. Finally, it has
proved capable of modification and adaptation, as shown by the chapters
that follow, and as discussed later (Butler, other volume) still has
some relevance in the context of concepts such as sustainable tourism
and appropriate development.

Postscript

Although it may appear from the previous discussion that Brougham
and Butler (1972) coined the term 'resort cycle' before Stansfield (1978),
the concept of a consistent process of resort development and change,
with recognisable phases or stages, is in fact almost a century older
at least. In 1990 I received copies of several articles and letters from
Dr Bill Clark of the Graduate School of Geography at Clark University
in Massachusetts. They ranged in date from 1883 to 1914 and are rather
devastating in terms of their implications for supposed academic
originality! While too long to reproduce in their entirety, some selected
quotations are revealing. The earliest piece, and the initiator of the
correspondence which followed, was, according to Clark (personal
communication, 1990) an editorial in *The Nation* on July 19, 1883, entitled
'Evolution of the Summer Boarder' by E.L. Godkin, the editor of the
paper (Godkin, 1883: 47–48). Godkin notes that 'The growth of
the American watering place, indeed, now seems to be as much
regulated by law as the growth of asparagus or strawberries and is
almost as easy to foretell. The place is usually first discovered by
artists...or a family of small needs in search of pure air...'. He goes on to

describe a process of development beginning with the provision of informal accommodation, followed by advertisement, the conversion of farms to hotels and boarding houses (a stage lasting up to 30 or 40 years according to Godkin), followed by visitation by 'crowds of people'. After this comes the 'cottager' (second home owner), building on land sold by the original farmer, and the boarder moves on to find other 'unsophisticated' farmers. Godkin talks of the 'great summer tragedy of American life', referring to the loss of opportunity for the lower income boarder because of the development of cottages by the more affluent second home owners.

His editorial clearly hit a nerve among residents of the northeast of the USA. The following month a reader sent a letter (C.P., 1883) arguing that Godkin's process was based on a fallacy and that 'The evolution of certain perfidious boarders into the baleful cottager is merely a phase of the phenomenon of this annual migration. The evolution of the summer resort is not necessarily toward cottage life. Saratoga is, quite as logically as Newport, the outcome of this evolution' (as Wolfe, 1952 noted). C.P. goes on to state that 'The tragedy, the phenomenal fact, is the influx of large numbers into all the secluded summer nooks, and the consequent destruction of their rural picturesque aspects.' Dislike of the second home owner was stated again in a letter a week later by A.R. (1883) from Bar Harbour, who wrote, on the habit of locals selling property to cottagers, 'each is so busy frying his own little fish that he does not see that the fire on which all depend is already going out.'

The discussion begun by Godkin continued for several years in the pages of The Nation, as evidenced in a letter by A.G. Webster in 1914. He wrote in support of Godkin's description of the evolution of resorts, noting that 'The original discoverers have long since had to move on because of the rising scale of prices and the original simplicity of the place is lost...different villages on the island are now showing the successive stages of the development of Bar Harbour.' He discusses the declining fortunes of such settlements, ending with 'automobile weekenders or extreme transients' and concludes that 'while Bar Harbour is in its senescence, Northeast Harbour is in its full maturity.' A few years earlier George Street, in a publication *Mount Desert – A History* (1905: 328) pointed out that 'The development of popular summer resorts on the New England coast has followed a curiously uniform law', supporting the description of Godkin. Finally, in 1915, in an article in the *Worcester Magazine*, Conrad Hobbs (1915: 35) began with the statement 'Lake Quinsigamond is now passing rapidly through a history of gradual degradation, which has been the lot of many similar pleasure resorts owned by private individuals and subject to no comprehensive scheme of control.' Hobbs comments that 'the evolution of all the other pleasure resorts of the State confirms me in this belief' (p. 35).

He describes this process in this manner:

The story of each is roughly, this:

(1) Quiet enjoyment by a few.
(2) Increasing popularity and the appearance of symptoms of abuse.
(3) Rapidly increasing abuse and degradation, leading to
(4) a fuller appreciation of its latent but diminishing value and a public demand for its conservation, which, if strong enough and persistent enough, ends in
(5) its final reclamation and protection under strong and efficient control. (Hobbs, 1915: 35)

It is both encouraging and depressing to find such statements. Encouraging because they provide evidence and support for the ideas expressed in the TALC about the nature of the process of resort development, the idea of stages, of a consistent pattern or trend, and the inevitability of this process without the intervention of control and regulation. Depressing, or at best, salutary, in the sense that ordinary observant individuals had noted and recorded in print the same process that academics assumed to be their own discovery some half to a full century later!

Postscript to Postscript

In concluding this volume I reviewed the literature cited one last time and to my embarrassment realised that the idea of a pattern of development of tourist resorts is even older than the postscript above suggests. In their article *A Theoretical Approach to Tourism Sustainability*, Casagrandi and Rinaldi (2002) refer to Gilbert's (1939) article on English holiday resorts. They note that Gilbert cites an article from *The Times* dated 1860 discussing the process of resort development:

Our seaport towns have been turned inside out. So infallible and unchanging are the attractions of the ocean that it is enough for any place to stand on the shore. That one recommendation is sufficient. Down comes the Excursion Train with its thousands – some with a month's range, others tethered to a six hours' limit, but all rushing with one impulse to the waters' edge. Where are they to lodge? The old 'town' is perhaps half a mile inland and turned as far away from the sea as possible...But this does not suit visitors whose eyes are always on the waves, and so a new town arises on the beach. Marine Terraces, Sea Villas, 'Prospect Lodges', 'Bellevues', hotels, baths, libraries and churches soon accumulate, till at length of the old borough is completely hidden and perhaps to be reached by an omnibus.

Perhaps fortunately for me the author of *The Times* article did not discuss further development and relocation of resorts, and I end this introductory chapter before I discover how the Romans developed their coastal resort settlements, no doubt following the pattern of the ancient Greeks!

Chapter 3

The Application of the TALC Model: A Literature Survey

RICHARD M. LAGIEWSKI

Introduction

This chapter categorizes and documents a selection of major works relevant to Butler's 1980 article on the TALC. The goal is to present a simple, yet informative chapter that helps scholars find and select appropriate works and commentary pertaining to the TALC model. It is important to note that this chapter is not meant to be a literature 'review' of the original 1980 article, but rather a literature 'survey' that documents the works of others who have solidified this work as an academic classic in the field of tourism. This chapter does not take into consideration the new contributions to the volume in which this chapter is found, but rather looks back in order to document previous literature. The author has made every attempt to include a bibliography for this chapter that contains all works pertaining to the 'application' of Butler's concept of a tourism area life cycle. These works were generated between the year 1980 and 2002. Because of the nature of the volume in which this chapter appears, it is the author's judgment that it would be redundant to include a review and description of Butler's original work and its origins, as it can be gained from the previous chapter in this text. Again, this chapter is meant to be a resource based on works addressing Butler's destination life cycle model and judgments of the usefulness and appropriateness of such works are left for the reader to assess.

For the sake of clarity, the concept described in Butler's 1980 work will be referred to generically throughout this chapter as the 'Tourism Area Life Cycle' (TALC). The length of coverage of any one piece of research covered in this chapter should not necessarily be correlated with the relative importance of either the work covered or this author's personal interest. Rather, the depth of coverage reflects the amount of information deemed necessary to provide those interested in Butler's destination life cycle model with the right background, understanding, and direction, so they may choose and explore these original works further as they apply to their current interests and needs.

All of the works covered here clearly provide much more value when read in their entirety, yet the mission here is not to tell their whole story

27

in detail, but rather to lead the reader in the direction relevant to their current interest in the TALC. While Table 3.1 attempts to capture the majority of major works and authors concerning the TALC, the text that follows can only provide a glimpse into these works and authors that have challenged, supported, and expanded Butler's work over the last 20 plus years.

How to Categorize and Divide the Works

How to provide a useful overview of the literature pertaining to works surrounding Butler's original work is not an exact science. One could just discuss each work as it appeared over time. Works could be split between those that support the premise and those that do not. Additionally, works could be broken down by methods employed or stages of the cycle addressed. One could also look at simplifying access to the major works visually. Argwal (1997) proposed that research into the TALC should focus on either one of two aspects: assessing the applicability of the model; and redeveloping the model to incorporate different issues. In the end, a combination of these strategies, along with a broad division of the work based on broad themes is used.

Literature Survey

'The first test and the first proposed changes'

Gary Hovinen's (1981) work on Lancaster County, Pennsylvania is likely the first use of Butler's model. In using Lancaster County as a 'test case', Hovinen (1981, 1982) concluded that the destination departed significantly from the TALC in the later stages, yet the model does remain useful. Two critical conclusions arise from Hovinen's (1981, 1982, 2002) work on Butler's TALC (see also Hovinen, this volume). The first is that his case site (Lancaster County) is characterized by the coexistence of growth, stagnation, decline, and rejuvenation – a stage he terms 'maturity'. The maturity stage begins when rapid growth in the number of visitors has ended (Hovinen, 1982: 573). According to Hovinen, during this stage a diverse destination will see a complex coexistence of the consolidation, stagnation, decline, and rejuvenation in and among the tourist attractions and services. At this point he noted that outside investors invest in new ventures, while original enterprises decline. Some attractions begin to lose their drawing power while new attractions flourish. The issue here is that Lancaster County is deemed a diverse destination where the tourism product is not 100% comprised of a single tourist resource.

This leads into the second outcome of his application of Butler's model concerning the decline stage. While carrying capacity is Butler's premise for decline, Hovinen poses three 'interrelated factors': relative

Table 3.1 Summary of major tourism life cycle studies following Butler's model (modifications and update of Table 2-1 from Berry, 2001)

Author, date	Region	Aspect tested/method/ special emphasis	Results
Hovinen, 1981	Lancaster County, PA	Butler's theory in total. Uses visitor numbers, otherwise a perceptual/historical approach.	Substantially consistent with model. No sign of a decline in region.
Oglethorpe, 1984	Malta	Uses visitor numbers, number of beds, hotels and % foreign ownership. Emphasizes dependency on foreign tour operators.	Accepts relevance of TALC and makes the point that dependency has led to rapid decline in the tourism industry.
Brown, 1985	Weston-super-mare	Historical account, perceptive approach.	Rejuvenation attempted.
Meyer-Arendt, 1985	Grand Island, Louisiana	Emphasis on cultural processes and environmental degradation. Uses building activity, maps at 5 different stages visitor-days, & capacity.	Strong support for TALC which indicates onset of 'decline' stage.
Butler, 1985	Scottish Highlands	Historical account from early 1700s to early 1800s. Emphasis on fashion, tastes and transportation improvements. Uses maps and historical evidence.	Complies with TALC model.
Keys, 1985 (Masters thesis)	Some Queensland resorts compared, with Noosa in depth	Comparative, cross-sectional study of a number of Queensland resorts using TALC as an analysis framework and a time series study of Noosa. Data used is from Australian Bureau of Statistics, Queensland Travel and	The Noosa case substantially complies with Butler's model with some outstanding differences. The comparative study of the other resorts showed that they are at different stages of development.

Author, date	Region	Aspect tested/method/ special emphasis	Results
Table 3.1 (*Continued*)			
		Tourism Commission, press reports, interviews and observation.	
Haywood, 1986	Not region specific	Emphasis on making Butler's model useable by suggesting more rigid criteria & a method involving the use of standard deviation for stage identification.	Concluded the TALC model was not sufficient *on its own* to use for planning and marketing purposes even with the proposed changes.
Richardson, 1986	Galveston & other urban water fronts	Emphasis on revitalization of historic buildings and the use of product life cycle models as tools for managing resort evolution. Uses tax receipts, employment, population and dollars spent on works.	Using TALC theory, Galveston is in 'decline' stage but it may be possible to rejuvenate using historic buildings as an attraction. Work is being done in the area.
Wilkinson, 1987	Caribbean islands of Antigua, Aruba, St Lucia, & US Virgin Isles	Focuses on the later stages of Butler's model and Lundberg's (1980) model.	Essentially a comparative analysis, which found a high level of compliance with both models. Other conclusions related to the tourism industry rather than the TALC model.
Keller, 1987	Canada's NW Territories	Emphasis on importation of capital and management leading to possible dependence on non-locals. Leakage of tourism dollars back to core regions. Uses arrival types (business, fishing, sightseeing,	Does not question the applicability of TALC and concludes that no further development possible without large injection of outside capital.

Table 3.1 (*Continued*)

Author, date	Region	Aspect tested/method/ special emphasis	Results
		education etc) and where from. Also uses staff turnover in tourism.	
Strapp, 1988	Sauble Beach, Ontario	Emphasis on the transition from a tourism resort to retirement center as previous holiday makers buy holiday homes and then retire there. Uses visitor numbers.	Proposes using 'average length of stay' to calculate 'total-person-days' rather than visitor numbers to overcome the change of status of tourists who eventually become retirees.
Cooper and Jackson, 1989	Isle of Man	Butler's theory in total. Visitor numbers and other tourist statistics going back 100 years.	Exemplifies the utility of Butler's model, emphasizing dependence on management decisions and resort quality. Also introduces some suggestions for rejuvenation of region.
Cooper, and 1990	Isle of Man, European 'cold water resorts'	Uses passenger arrivals etc.	Most resorts in this category are in serious decline.
Debbage, 1990	Paradise Island, Bahamas	Combines the use of TALC with Markusen's (1985) 'profit cycle' and the influence of oligopolistic tourist suppliers.	Concludes that Butler's model does not take into account organizational behavior as the cycle matures (i.e. mergers and acquisitions).

Table 3.1 (*Continued*)

Author, date	Region	Aspect tested/method/ special emphasis	Results
Martin and Uysal, 1990	No specific region	Expands the concept and importance of carrying capacity for the TALC.	Each stage will reveal different carrying capacity levels and require separate policy responses.
France, 1991	Barbados	Mainly a perceptional approach but also uses visitor numbers, number of establishments, number of rooms, etc.	The Island is split into different market segments, which are at different stages in TALC. One area is in decline, another is still in the growth stages.
Weaver, 1988, 1990, 1992	Grand Cayman and Antigua	All aspects of TALC but emphasis on outside ownership and control, particularly in Antigua. Grand Cayman has little outside ownership and control. Uses arrivals, cruise ship statistics. Emphasis also on planning. Uses arrival numbers, building, bed numbers and Tourist Board Budget.	Found substantial compliance with Butler's model. Concluded outside ownership & control affected stability of cycle. Grand Cayman is planned and has low outside ownership and is stable but Antigua is unplanned with high degree of outside ownership and control and is in danger of decline. Referred to as a new type of plantation economy (dependency).
Cooper, 1992	Coastal resorts	Talks about the three uses of TALC (as a conceptual framework, for forecasting and strategic planning) and then goes into detail about the strategic planning process.	Strategic planning process consists of: defining the mission statement; business portfolio analysis; and growth strategies. Also talks about types of growth strategies.

Table 3.1 (*Continued*)

Author, date	Region	Aspect tested/method/ special emphasis	Results
Ioannides, 1992	Cyprus	All aspects but emphasized the role of government and dependence on foreign tour operators. Used visitor numbers, number of beds, type of accommodation, tourism receipts, tourist type, arrivals.	TALC used to make the point that govt is steering towards 'consolidation' (intentionally) and that destinations follow a predictable cycle through identifiable stages.
Getz, 1992	Niagara Falls	Examines carrying capacity and planning aspects. Uses historical data, existing statistical data, interviews, field observations, maps and questionnaires.	'Exploration' and 'involvement' stages correspond partly with Butler's model but there are many points of divergence and no dating of stages is possible. Niagara Falls appears to be in a long 'maturity' stage similar to Lancaster County.
Johnson and Snepenger, 1993	Greater Yellow-stone region	Variables used are visitation trends, the growth of the service economy, host resident's perception of current tourism development and current biological indicators of the ecosystem.	Tourism in the region is more intricate than the TALC theory suggests and the region is at no specific stage of the cycle. The TALC concept incorporates alternatives for future directions within the Yellowstone region.
O'Hare and Barrett, 1993	Sri Lanka	Considers the effect of the civil war on tourism using tourism numbers. Also discusses the effect of cheap airfares based on stop-overs in Sri Lanka.	Accepts relevance of TALC and concludes that there have been two distinct cycles in the country, one before the civil war and one after.

Table 3.1 (*Continued*)

Author, date	*Region*	*Aspect tested/method/ special emphasis*	*Results*
Choy, 1993	Pacific Island destinations	All aspects of Butler's model, but only with reference to visitor numbers.	Very little compliance with Butler's model reported. 'At best the model can be used after the fact as a diagnostic tool'.
Williams, 1993	Minorca, Spain	All aspects but emphasis on dependency theory through external ownership and control. An 'expanded' model of 8 stages was suggested. Uses tourist numbers, employment, number of hotel rooms.	High level of external ownership and control. Existing industries declined as tourism expanded. The region has yet to reach its peak.
Wang and Godbey, 1994	Lancaster, Poconos, America's Ind. Heritage Project (AIHP)	Emphasis on measuring growth in tourism activity and what is the ideal rate of growth to year 2000 using surveys and expert perceptions of future growth.	AIHP is in the early stages of TALC. Lancaster is in the mature stages and Poconos is in decline.
Cooper, 1994	Not applicable	Overall review of the TALC body of knowledge to date.	Found Butler's model to be a useful framework for analysis and stated that with every study the body of knowledge increases suggesting further re-search. He suggested some more criteria.
Bianchi, 1994	Not applicable	Compares TALC and a number of other theories and models.	TALC fails on many grounds and what is needed is a concept of tourism development which is integrated into a sociological framework.

Table 3.1 (*Continued*)

Author, date	Region	Aspect tested/method/ special emphasis	Results
Agarwal, 1994	UK generally. The resort cycle revisited	Discusses the usefulness of TALC for analysis and planning using anecdotal and perceptual methods.	Suggests that TALC be modified to include a 'reorientation' stage before 'decline/ rejuvenate'. States that as it stands, TALC cannot be usefully applied.
Prosser, 1995	Not applicable	TALC in general. Progress and prospects as well as some suggestions for future research.	Finds that TALC is a handy framework for analysis.
Opper-mann, 1995	Not applicable	Life cycle concept used to analyze the travel life cycle of individuals.	Successful application of general life cycle theory to individual's lifetime travel patterns.
Harrison, 1995	Swaziland	Used Butler's TALC as an 'ideal' or 'expected' model and analyzed the difference between it and the situation in Swaziland.	The cycle in Swaziland consisted of 'exploration', 'inactivity', 'transition', 'truncated development' and 'decline & attempted rejuvenation'.
Braunlich, 1996	Atlantic City	Success of rejuvenation program using casinos. Statistics include amounts invested, tax receipts, social services for the elderly, urban redevelopment.	TALC accepted as an appropriate framework for analysis. Atlantic City has successfully entered the 'rejuvenation' stage.
Russel, 1996	Coolan-gatta	All aspects of Butler's model, uses visitor numbers & a perceptual/historical approach for the period of the resort's existence.	Found substantial compliance with the model. The region was found to be in the 'decline' stage.

Table 3.1 (*Continued*)

Author, date	*Region*	*Aspect tested/method/ special emphasis*	*Results*
Meyer, 1996	Waikiki	Emphasis on rejuvenation plans. Uses reports etc.	Concludes that the area is entering the 'decline' stage and suggests rejuvenation.
Agarwal, 1997	Torbay region (Torquay, Paignton and Brixham)	Tests the validity and applicability of TALC. Justifies this work by stating that the universal applicability of TALC is not yet proven. Among other things, the author stresses the importance of the 'unit of analysis'.	The application of TALC is reasonably consistent with Butler's (1980) model except for the post 'stagnation' stage which requires more research. The author assumes that the original model specifies that 'decline' is inevitable (p. 72).
Prosser, 1997	Gold Coast, Coffs Harbour (NSW)	Uses time series (census) population figures, employment in tourism, unemployment etc. Also relies on a perceptual approach.	Both regions are at different stages in TALC. Finds that TALC is a handy framework for analysis.
Douglas, 1997	Melanesia, (PNG, Solomons & Vanuatu)	Historical picture using Butler's model as a framework. Uses largely perceptual methods.	Each country is at a different stage. A major influence is the colonial past of each country.
Tooman, 1997	3 regions in the Greater Smoky Mountains	Emphasis on the long-term, from 1900 to present and socioeconomic effects using unemployment and food stamp figures etc. Also looks at the number of 'Mom & Dad' hotels and motels verses chain companies as an indicator.	Concludes that TALC can be used to avoid the negative impacts of tourism.

Table 3.1 (*Continued*)

Author, date	Region	Aspect tested/method/ special emphasis	Results
da Conceição Gonçalves and Roque Águas, 1997	Algarve, Portugal	Analysis using TALC with demand, supply, distribution and competitors within each stage. Fits a 3rd degree polynomial to overnight data.	Identifies stages and links them to regional strategies (cause and affect). Concludes area should plan for a long period of stagnation and stabilization.
Russell and Faulkner, 1998	Coolan-gatta	All aspects of Butler's model, also use of visitor numbers & a perceptual/historical approach.	Found substantial compliance with the model.
Priestley and Mundet, 1998	Catalan Coast, Spain (3 resort towns)	Assumes away the early stages of TALC and concentrates on the poststagnation stages in response to Agarwal's (1994) challenge that there is not enough work in this area.	All three resorts (Lloret de Mar, L'Estartit & Sitges) are in post-'stagnation' stage and have implemented 'reconstruction' strategies in an attempt to rejuvenate. Uses hotel capacity as core data.
Opper-mann, 1998	No specific region	Main thrust is to attack Agarwal's (1997) article on Torbay. Says there has been too much testing of TALC.	Finds Butler's model good but suggests that there should be more testing of other models and theories.
Agarwal, 1998	No specific region	Defends her 1997 article against Oppermann's 1998 attack.	States there is a need to apply TALC to different tourism products in a variety of contexts.
Baum, 1998	No specific region	Proposes the idea that abandoning tourism altogether can be a theoretical extension of TALC.	Abandonment can be seen as an Exit Stage when tourism becomes impossible to sustain.

Table 3.1 (*Continued*)

Author, date	Region	Aspect tested/method/ special emphasis	Results
Knowles and Curtis, 1999	European mass tourist destinations	Study of second generation (Mediterranean but mainly Spanish) resorts. Ultimately, there is no avoiding decline for these resorts.	The authors generally find that the TALC model is a good fit up to the post 'stagnation' stages after which they postulate three new stages.
Johnston, 2001	No specific region	Integrates ontological & epistemological elements into the TALC debate.	That 'we have not yet learned everything' there is to know about the TALC.
Lundtorp and Wanhill, 2001	Data sets from: Isle of Man & Danish island of Bornholm	Uses mathematical process to form the 'ideal' TALC.	The TALC curve can only be representative if all tourist arrivals are repeat tourists.
Agarwal, 2002	Three mass tourism coastal resorts: Minehead, Weymouth, Scarborough	Integrates the theory of the TALC and the restructuring thesis.	Relating the two concepts provides insights into destination decline and a more in-depth understanding is needed of resort restructuring.
Hovinen, 2002	Lancaster County, PA	Revisits his early work and also considers chaos/complexity theory as a complement to the TALC.	TALC would be more useful by recognizing a "maturity" stage. Also the model has value by its premise that without appropriate planning, management & development, destinations will see decline.

location, diversity of the tourist base, and effectiveness of planning to alleviate problems that arise. The first two factors point to why the decline stage may be less significant at the time of Hovinen's first work on Lancaster County. The first is that the destination's close proximity to major cities in the eastern USA give it the ability to draw from a large population base. Additionally, the reasons for visiting the county are not solely reliant on the Amish community, but rather are supported by other cultural aspects and attractions, like the rural landscape itself.

In Hovinen's (2002) article in which he 'revisits' the issue of the TALC in Lancaster County, he proposed that the 'chaos/complexity theory' provides a useful alternative and complementary perspective to Butler's life cycle model. This is based on Russell and Faulkner's (1999) idea that changes in tourism at a destination can be 'viewed in terms of tension between entrepreneurs (who are agents of change) and planners (who seek to control change)'. In this hypothesis, entrepreneurs are the chaos makers while planners seek to establish certainty and predictability (see Russell, other volume). It is argued that entrepreneurial instincts are crucial, because to avoid the decline stage, innovative responses are needed to meet the complexities that a destination faces as it reaches this stage. Overall, his early work on Lancaster County is likely most recognized for proposing the idea of a 'maturity stage' to the TALC.

'Major criticism or major advancement?'

Haywood's (1986) work, 'Can the Tourist-Area Life cycle be made operational?' is often cited as being critical of Butler's tourist-area life cycle model, yet it has likely done the most to make the tourist-area life cycle model an operational research concept. Haywood's (1986) 'test of importance' for Butler's TALC is, 'its possible use as a tool for planning & management of tourist areas'. Six issues or questions are raised as requirements to make Butler's model a useful tool in destination planning. Many of the answers to these issues have gone on to provide a framework for researchers as they applied Butler's model (see also Haywood, this volume and the other volume). The following are considered operationally important for the usefulness of Butler's model (Haywood, 1986: 155):

- unit of analysis;
- relevant market;
- pattern and stages of the TALC;
- identification of the area's shape in the life cycle;
- determination of the unit of measurement;
- determination of the relevant time unit.

The first issue revolves around defining the tourist area under question. For example, is the tourist 'area' a town, a hotel, an attraction? Haywood (1986) states that defining the unit of analysis for the 'tourist area' is the crucial first step in using Butler's life cycle model. The next point addresses the issue of the number of tourists used as the 'Y' variable in the life cycle curve. The concern presented is that the total number of tourists over time may represent different markets, and it may be more helpful to consider them by different market segments. The reason is that a different market type, say 'domestic versus international tourist', may interact differently with the tourist area.

In the third operational requirement, Haywood (1986) questions whether the pattern of the s-shaped logistic curve is the only useful curve and suggests looking at other evolutionary curves. The fourth operational requirement is determining the stage of a tourist area and when an area has moved from one stage to another. He then questions whether using the change in the number of tourists to determine these changes will provide appropriate answers. Haywood (1986) provides one possible approach based on the total number of tourists occurring at the tourist area on a year-to-year basis and then plotting these changes as a normal distribution with a zero mean.

Based on the premise that as the number of tourists grow they negatively impact the carrying capacity, Haywood (1986) suggests the need for a clear unit of measurement. This is due to the fact that not all tourists have the same impact on the carrying capacity of the tourist area they are visiting; not all tourists are created equal. Some stay longer, some visit in different seasons, and some are more and some are less conscious of the local cultural and natural traditions. Therefore, the use of pure arrivals as a determinant of a tourist area carrying capacity is questioned along with whether there exists one variable that represents carrying capacity for the whole tourist area.

The last operational question is whether the traditional use of annual data to track tourists over time is necessarily the best relevant time unit. Here Haywood (1986) notes that if there is a 'major shortcoming' in the use of the tourist area cycle of evolution it is the 'lack of empirical data' available about the tourist area in question. Haywood (1986) also concludes that a 'natural use' of the tourist area is as a forecasting tool (see Butler, this volume; Manente and Pechlaner and Berry, other volume).

'Changes to later stages and the vertical axis'

As Hovinen's (1981) work first suggested, changes and discussion of the TALC's later stages has been a common theme in the literature.

Additionally, Butler's use of the 'number of tourists' on the vertical axis has also received great attention.

Strapp's (1988) study of Sauble Beach, Ontario, Canada contributes to the TALC through its recognition of second homeowners as tourists. The claim is that this type of tourism had been neglected by researchers in generating tourism models while Butler's model premises that without adequate planning, destinations are likely doomed to decline. In Strapp's (1988) work, 'conventional' tourism is showing a decline while 'residential development' and 'cottage conversions' are experiencing a revival. He suggests that this refinement to Butler's decline stage be termed a 'stabilization reaction'. Therefore, after stagnation, tourist areas may experience growth in a nontraditional tourism market, thus stabilizing an otherwise anticipated decline in the number of visitors. Strapp also provides two interesting 'discrepancies' or proposed departures to Butler's original model. These are that population and community changes are just as crucial as a tourist change in the resort cycle, no matter how dominant tourism may be as a segment in the local economy.

Here it is proposed that instead of measuring pure numbers of visitors over time, the use of a 'person-day' concept be used. The idea is that the person-day concept takes into consideration visitors and residents and their length of stay. This leads to the proposal that the most 'appropriate way' to 'graphically portray' Butler's tourist area curve is to use the average length of stay instead of the number of tourists. (See Figure 3.1) Using this model, Strapp (1986) proposes an illustration where in the early stage of Butler's TALC the length of stay is at its greatest and declines toward the stagnation stage over time. This argument, based on Sauble Beach, is that early in the life cycle of a tourist area it is difficult to access the destination, therefore it 'necessitates a long stay'. Strapp (1986) states that, 'as development increases, improvements in access makes shorter trips possible and overall length of visits decline'. Within his case, the ease of potential day trips increases near the stagnation stage.

Three options are presented at this point. The first is the length of stay declines to the point where the tourist area basically 'becomes more of a recreational area or rest stop'. The next option relates to rejuvenation. By exploiting or developing the area's resources, 'visit time regains its length'. The last option pertains to the evolution of a year-round community based on his case in Sauble Beach. Here a tourist becomes more like a resident. As tourists transition to homeowners, the tourist season increases beyond its traditional confines.

In Foster and Murphy's (1991) work on the connection between the TALC and retirement, they construct a case study of Parksville and Qualicum Beaches located on the east coast of Vancouver Island, Canada. Their goal was to determine if these destinations follow Butler's premise and whether retirement is a 'successor or parallel activity with regards to

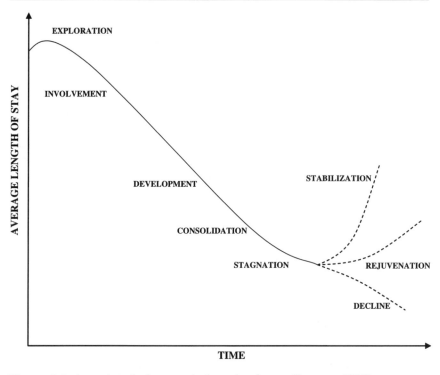

Figure 3.1 Associated changes in length of stay (Strapp, 1988)

tourism'. They conclude that their research supports Hovinen's (1982) suggestion that Butler's stages of consolidation and stagnation be replaced with an extensive maturity stage. In terms of retirement, Foster and Murphy (1991) provided a mixed review of its connection with Butler's later stages. They also point to the bias that the TALC has toward the supply-side characteristics of the market. Specifically, this pertains to the use of data of the supply of accommodations versus the use of actual visitation numbers (demand). This issue supports the critical challenge of applying the TALC; the lack of actual long-term visitor data over the life of a destination.

Douglas' (1997) application of Butler's life cycle model addresses its ability to explain tourism development in colonial and postcolonial societies. Specifically, she uses the model to develop a comparative study of tourism in three island nations: Papua New Guinea, the Solomon Islands, and Vanuatu. These tourist destinations are collectively known as Melanesia. Through this case study, the rate of tourism development is said to be significantly influenced by the pre- and postindependent government of the three island nations. Another contribution to the destination life cycle model concerns the use of the term 'locals' and

Butler's premise that in the involvement stage, contact between visitors and locals will remain high. The assumption is that while Butler didn't specifically define locals in his concept, the implication is that he was referring to persons indigenous to the tourist area. In the historic development of tourism, these former colonies' expatriates have often played the role of 'locals'. Specifically, Europeans visiting these tourist destinations preferred to interact with the European expatriates and not necessarily with the Melanesians.

Douglas (1997) also addresses three types of visitors who have influenced tourism development in the colonial period of these islands: 'excursionists', 'pilgrims', and 'planners'. Excursionists refer to the early cruise passengers and later air travelers who arrived seeking sun, sand, and sea. The 'pilgrims' were the Allied and Japanese soldiers who established the foundations of both the tourist attractions and later on the attractions in the form of military cemeteries and battlefields. The last group, the 'planners', refers to the organizations that attempted to establish the institutional foundations to manage the tourism system. These included all of the various tourism marketing and promotional boards, along with the chambers of commerce.

In the article, *The Resort Lifecycle Theory Generating Processes and Estimation*, Lundtorp and Wanhill (2001) examine the theory behind use of the number of tourists as the 'measure of the time path' of the destination. The authors formulate a demand model of the resort cycle that considers the segments of various tourist markets and their levels over time, related to Butler's tourist area life cycle. Specifically, two general types of tourist are considered: 'repeat' and 'non-repeat'. Using the logistic curve to model the relative demand at each stage, the authors conclude that the life cycle curve can only be representative of the destination if all visitors to that destination are 'repeaters'. By adding data concerning nonrepeaters (those who only visit a destination once but never visit again), the life cycle model becomes only an 'approximation or caricature' of reality. According to the authors, as more and more market segmentation occurs in the tourist data, the observed effect will result in a scatter diagram, 'from which it might be impossible to discern anything'.

Lundtorp and Wanhill (2001) present a mathematical process and formula to formulate the 'ideal' expected tourist volumes over the stages of Butler's model (see also Wanhill & Lundtorp, other volume). They test this concept on a data series for the Isle of Man in Britain and for the Danish Island of Bornholm. They find that Butler's concept fits the destinations 'tolerably well' during periods when domestic tourists dominate the market and return year-after-year. Therefore, for the data to support Butler's model it must be made up of repeat visitors. In later years, in the tourist area evolution they point to 'too many shift factors'.

That is to say new markets are drawn to visit the area while old tourists are drawn elsewhere. Demand or decline in demand to visit the destination may not be so much a function of exceeding a 'carrying capacity', but rather because 'the market is exhausted, as all tourists wishing to visit the resort "have been"'.

Getz's (1992) case study of Niagara Falls, Canada–US is considered unique in that this destination 'has evolved into a permanent state of maturity in which aspects of consolidation, stagnation, decline, and rejuvenation are interwoven and constant'. It is acknowledged that Hovinen's (1982) conclusions about Butler's later stages is a more appropriate way to view a destination's later life. The author states that for old destinations like Niagara Falls, the maturity stage will likely be a permanent condition. The rationale is that those in charge of resort areas will never allow tourism to disappear and will use every attraction they can to maintain it. Getz (1992) concludes that the destination life cycle does not fit Niagara Falls and therefore has very little usefulness for local tourism planning. Another departure from Butler's original model pertains to carrying capacity. Instead of carrying capacity being linked to a destination's ability to sustain change without environmental decline and loss of attractiveness, Getz sees it as a planning and management concept. This idea of capacity in a 'mature' destination is based on a tourist area's constant practice of mitigating the adverse effects of tourism while also pursuing destination enhancements. Agarwal (1994), like Getz (1992) and Hovinen (1982), suggests that the later stages of the TALC need modification. Her issue pertains to poststagnation, specifically 'decline'. She argues that dramatic and total decline of tourism is likely unacceptable both economically and politically. Therefore she proposes a 'reorientation stage' (see Agarwal, other volume). In this stage one would observe the constant efforts a destination makes to adjust to changes before decline occurs.

'New contexts and variances'

Much of the literature over the last 20 years has attempted to apply the TALC to new destinations to test its relevance. Additionally, many works point to particular departures from Butler's original TALC. Weaver (1990) states that his empirical research on Grand Cayman Island 'largely conforms to the stages' of Butler's TALC. He discerns one 'significant deviation' from Butler's original work. In Butler's TALC, it is stated that over time local control and ownership will shift to nonlocals. However, in viewing Grand Cayman, 'a non-plantation culture', and Antigua, 'a plantation culture', Weaver (1990) concludes control has been maintained by locals in the development of Grand Cayman's tourist sector (see Weaver, this volume). However, Antigua's tourist sector suffers from a high degree of external control associated with its former plantation economy.

Tooman (1996) uses Butler's model as a framework to explore the economic impact of tourism in the Smokey Mountain region of Tennessee and North Carolina. Specifically, he looks at first-, second-, and third-order economic effects. This discussion is based on tourism's roll as an economic development tool. From this perspective, Tooman (1996) discusses the theoretical economic outcomes that would be expected throughout Butler's life cycle stages. The author concludes that tourism is likely to be most beneficial from the economic perspective if it is not the dominant sector of the economy. Tooman (1996) points out that according to Butler's TALC, tourism should not dominate until the consolidation stage. However, in his case study, one local economy was dominated by tourism in the development stage and another in the involvement stage.

According to Tooman (1996), 'under conditions where tourism becomes the dominant economic sector (regardless of the particular stage), social welfare indicators failed to show significant improvement'. From the context of tourism and the economy, the involvement stage (where tourism does not dominate the economy) can produce desirable effects. These benefits have the potential for greater local economic linkages, economic diversity, and more time to establish the utility to manage the growth of the tourism sector.

Wilkinson (1996) supports Cooper's (1994) conclusion that while the life cycle concept has weaknesses, it does provide a useful tool for comparing tourism development among different destinations and provides one with an organizing framework to do so. Wilkinson selects six destinations in the Caribbean (Anguilla, Bahamas, Barbados, Cayman Islands, Dominica, and St. Lucia), to compare using the life cycle model proposed not by Butler, but de Albuquerque and McElroy (1992). This version of Butler's model proposes three general stages of tourism growth: (1) emergence or initial discovery, (2) transition to rapid expansion, and (3) maturity.

Another unique context for the application of Butler's TALC is by Johnson and Snepenger's (1993) to a 'federally managed resource'. In examining the Greater Yellowstone Region, the authors concluded 'that development is a not a specific stage in the cycle'. This work is based on the use of four factors to track the tourist destination over Butler's TALC: visitation trends, growth of the service economy, resident perceptions (see also Johnson & Snepenger, this volume), and ecosystem indicators. This work is based on the reconceptualization of the life cycle carrying concept by Martin and Uysal (1990). Their concept is based on the notion that there are many components that make up the resources in a tourist area. Within these different components, differing destinations will likely have different carrying capacities. For example, the physical infrastructure of a tourist area may have one carrying capacity while the environmental resources may have another. Martin and Uysal (1990) contend that this will require 'distinct policy responses' for each resource capacity. This being the case, Johnson and Snepenger concluded that, in fact, different resources in the Greater Yellowstone Region exhibit characteristics of different stages concurrently, depending on which resource is being measured.

'Destination drivers'

In Butler's original work, changes within a destination were attributed to 'preferences and needs of visitors' and the 'gradual deterioration' of manmade and natural attractions and services. Many authors applying the TALC as a framework for analyzing a destination have identified other issues that drive change within a destination and thus influence the 'evolution' of the resort.

In Klaus J. Meyer-Arendt's (1985) work, *The Grand Isle, Louisiana resort cycle*, he explores the issues pertaining to the factors causing the barrier island of Grand Island, Louisiana to move through all of the stages, ending in the stagnation stage. These issues relate to settlement patterns, changes in environmental perceptions, and efforts to fix a dynamic shoreline. Special emphasis is placed on the settlement patterns of residents over time to this coastline and the natural and manmade impacts on the shoreline. Here, the model is considered from the perspective of resident population growth over time versus Butler's growth in number of tourists (see also Martin, this volume). Therefore, Meyer-Arendt (1985) concluded that the settlement of Grand Isle and the manmade battle to secure the natural resource against storms and erosion help demonstrate the evolution of this resort through the stages of Butler's TALC.

Cooper and Jackson (1989) emphasize that the TALC provides, 'a useful descriptive tool for analyzing the development of destinations and the evolutions of their markets'. In their use of a case study on the Isle of Man, UK, they conclude that the TALC is, 'dependent upon the actions of managers and the settings of the destination'. The authors address Butler's model from its utility as both a prescriptive and descriptive tool. They conclude from the prescriptive point of view that the model encounters many problems, and that, 'Butler's original conceptualization of the tourist cycle did not envisage its use as a prescriptive tool'. However, as a descriptive tool, the life cycle is very useful in, 'understanding how destinations and their markets fall'. Their case study on the Isle of Man proposes that the unique setting of the island and the reliance on the UK market has presented challenges that have driven the destination along the life cycle curve. Additionally, the leadership decisions of private and public institutions, both directly and indirectly involved in tourism, have had substantial impact on the island's move through the tourist area life cycle.

Debbage (1990) provides an alternative to Butler's decline paradigm. Instead of decline being the outcome of a tourist destination exceeding its carrying capacity, thus resulting in the degradation of the resources in which the area relies on, he argued that outside influences destroy competitiveness. Specifically, stagnation and decline are influenced by oligopoly. This results in decline, because in this case, tourism suppliers are 'gaining market share' and maintaining 'competitive stability'. This is achieved at the expense of innovation and diversification. Debbage's (1990) argument, based on Paradise Island, Bahamas, is that declining visitor numbers were traditionally viewed as changes in tourism trends, and declining destination attractiveness may be better viewed as a result of the control and influence transnational corporations have at the destination level. Here, Debbage (1990) argues that Butler did not give appropriate emphasis to the role of imperfect competition and oligopoly, but put more weight on a detailed discussion of the internal dynamic of resort areas. This case is based primarily on the role of Resorts International in influencing both the tourist distribution chain and the composition of tourist products on Paradise Island.

Ioannides' (1992) case study of the island of Cyprus provides insights into the role the tourist area's government and external transnational firms have in destination change over the life cycle of a destination. Historical data for Cyprus demonstrated that the island's tourism area followed Butler's exploration, involvement, and development stages. During these earlier stages, the government played an important role in the growth of tourism. First there was the recognition that tourism should be used to increase foreign exchange earnings and to diversify the economy. That was followed by the government's efforts to stimulate tourism sector growth through economic incentives and loan programs. Additionally, the Cyprus Tourism Organization was formed to supervise tourism development. At this time, modern airport tourism facilities were also built.

During the development stage on Cyprus, the government helped the island recover from the 1974 War through Emergency Action Plans that gave a high priority to tourism (p. 721). The government also sponsored action plans in the late 1970s that provided financial incentives (low interest loans and free government land) to the private sector with the goal of making Cyprus an international tourist destination.

Besides identifying the influence of government on the TALC, the role of tour operators was also addressed. This influence of foreign tour operators from Cyprus's primary inbound markets (Britain, Germany, and Sweden) are acknowledged as supporting Debbage's (1990) point that dominant suppliers have a significant role in the TALC. In the case of Cyprus, this was shown specifically through the impact and influence of charter flights and preference for 'cheaper self-catering' accommodations, and inclusive tour packages targeting lower income mass tourism. These are seen as negatively impacting the environmental and cultural resources of the island. Additionally, the dependence on a few large tour operators has left Cyprus marketed as a 'could be anywhere' destination with little competitive market power. While Ioannides (1992) acknowledged that the growing power of foreign tour operators supports Butler's premise that external influences would increase over the life of a tourist area, he believes that the tourist area is not an actorless development path. The State was not only shown to have been a catalyst to developing tourism on Cyprus, but also to have reacted to its negative impacts. Specifically, the government enacted efforts to reduce the tourist growth rate and balance the geographic distribution of lodging development. Ioannides (1992: 731) concluded that 'Cypriot government has intentionally steered the island's resort cycle towards Butler's "consolidation" stage'.

'Theoretical foundations and integrations'

Agarwal (2002) relates Butler's TALC to the 'restructuring thesis'. Her motivation to 'inter-relate' these two works is based on the insights this would provide into the causes and consequences of destination decline. The 'restructuring thesis' referred to in this work pertains to the process of change in capitalist economies and societies, along with significant shifts in the strategy by which capital seeks expanded accumulation. Agarwal (2002) includes a discussion into the way in which industries have responded to competitive and consumption challenges. These are categorized into three main forms and strategies: product reorganization, labor reorganization, and spatial relocation and product transformation. These strategies are then defined as they relate to the 'structural process of change' in the context of tourism. Therefore, the key elements in the relation between the restructuring thesis and Butler's model are the application and insights into responses to decline. Agarwal (2002) acknowledges that a number of problems are associated with and encountered when using both Butler's model and the restructuring thesis to provide understanding into how destinations can respond to decline (see also Agarwal, other volume). However, it is concluded that that they do provide two useful theoretical links; both concepts may be related to the causes and consequences of resort decline, and to the responses of resorts to decline.

The premise is then discussed in the context of three English seaside resorts of Minehead, Weymouth, and Scarborough, all of which have been categorized as currently in the poststagnation stage. Here it is concluded that the integration of the restructuring thesis helps overcome the failure of the destination life cycle model to consider the role of external factors in the changes that occur at a tourist destination. The point being that decline in a destination is the outcome of interactions between internal and external forces. Thus, the responses to decline likely are responses to external changes.

While much of the literature has focused on the 'concept' of Butler's TALC model, Johnston (2001) has attempted to 'shore up the model's theoretical foundations'. His paper focuses on the ontological and epistemological aspect issues surrounding the model (see also Johnston, other volume). The methods used in this work were a modified form of 'grounded theory'. From this ontological and epistemological perspective of Butler's model, the author presents a redrawn version of the life cycle curve with two notable differences from the original (Figure 3.2). First, the original model is divided horizontally over time, by three eras. These are the 'Pre-tourism', 'Tourism-era', and 'Post-tourism era'.

Based on this discussion of ontological considerations, Johnston concludes that it would be reasonable to claim that Butler's model is based on a basic geographic process. He identifies a set of epistemological elements through a variation of the constant comparative method applied to four other types of process research. These elements are: human life

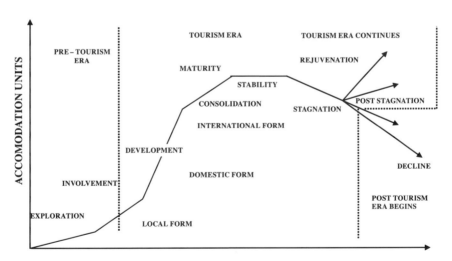

Figure 3.2 A revised version of Butler's (1980) 'classical' sequence of stages (Johnston, 2001)

cycle, product life cycle, port development, and ecosuccession. Following extensive discussion of the ontological and epistemological discussions, Johnston then revised the TALC, incorporating three eras. These are a pretourism era, from before the exploration phase extending into the involvement phase; a tourism era, which could carry through the maturity stage and may include a poststagnation phase; and a post-tourism era when a new institution dominates at the local level. Johnston also replaces growth in visitor numbers with growth in number of accommodation units. He applies this model (see Johnston, this volume) to the case of Kona, Hawaii (Johnston, 2002).

Final Comments

While not all the works cited below have been discussed in detail, every attempt has been made to include all relevant works pertaining to Butler's (1980) article in the bibliography. As mentioned in the introduction, works that pertained to the creation of Butler's original work have been listed, as they were important to the generation of Butler's concept, but only published works specifically using Butler's model have been discussed in detail. Works relating to the general theory of a product life cycle have been omitted (some are discussed at length in Coles, other volume, editor's note). Apologies go out to any authors whose works were not recognized in this chapter. This was not intentional; however, the literature survey was heavily biased toward both published works and works printed in English. Any and all errors pertaining to the representation of works covered here are completely unintentional and the fault of this author.

(Editor's note: Since the completion of this chapter yet another article using the TALC has been published (Moss *et al.*, 2003), and is included in the Bibliography.)

Chapter 4

Evolution of Tourism Areas and the Tourism Industry

K. MICHAEL HAYWOOD

Introduction

This chapter reviews some of the conditions and concerns necessary to make TALC studies and research of greater value to those individuals whose tasks and responsibilities necessitate the following: creating legitimisation for, and direction of, tourism development in specific areas or destinations; crafting and implementing industry policies and strategies; leading the development process; and managing destination management organisations or other types of tourism and hospitality enterprises.

As an industry paradigm, TALC has proven valuable in articulating the evolution of tourism region, and in confirming the mimicking of the predictable pattern of lifecycle stages – introduction, expansion, consolidation and contraction – associated with all forms of organisation – genetic, biological, cognitive, ecological, cultural and economic. As Butler (1980) and other tourism researchers seem to urge, a particular characteristic of a destination's evolution is that it is influenced and yet confounded by the nature, politics, demands, use and experience of place. Place gives substance and meaning to the tourism product being offered. Tourism is place-sensitive; not only are regional landscapes and cultures fragile and rarefied, but visitors and tourism developers are attracted to certain locales simply because of their attractiveness and appeal (a major and complex factor determining the growth and sustainable competitiveness of destinations). Tourism is also place-demanding and place-exhausting; that is, the development process and the usage of a locale (natural and cultural resources) by a typical, seasonal insurgence of users, mainly visitors, has a tendency to undermine attractiveness of an area if activities are not managed or if capacity limits become stretched or exceeded. Even citizens are susceptible. They grow weary of the stress, as characterised initially by Doxey (1975); and their behaviour may compromise a destination's hospitable characteristics if they are denied or do not realise promised benefits. If tourism's impacts are ignored and not acted upon, the movement into stages of maturity, and eventually decline, is exacerbated.

Identification of stages in life cycles of destinations with particular reference to the 'place' concept is concomitant with tourism development; that is, destinations are repositories of organisations in service to the needs of visitors. Because the speed, process and extent of tourism developments differ from one locale to the next, no two tourism life cycles are alike. The range and diversity of tourism developments (Bianchi, 1994), variations in growth patterns (Choy, 1992) and the scale of tourism developments (Gosling, 2000) have to be taken into account when determining the impacts of tourism development. The magnitude of tourism's impacts, however, has to be put into context. Consider the name – 'tourism area life cycle'. What actually constitutes a tourism area? A review of the literature suggests that it is any place that attracts visitors or represents a primary tourist gathering spot. It could be as large as a country and as small as a development site. Included are cities, rural areas, world heritage areas, parks, historic and cultural sites, fairs, theme parks, resort towns, and the like, as discussed in other chapters in this volume. Once an area is defined, then it is necessary to determine what constitutes a capacity limit for development, and/or for the number of users (not necessarily tourists) at one time or a prolonged period. This is a topic that has stirred considerable debate (Martin & Uysal, 1990; Prosser & Cullen, 1987), and determination of capacity limits for many tourism areas and the existing infrastructure remains a challenging and imposing task. Indeed tourism may be only one of many activities responsible for various impacts. It is inappropriate for the tourism industry to shoulder blame when other local industries, and normal commercial and resident behaviours, contribute significantly to the unattractiveness and demise of an area.

Fortunately an appreciation of the dynamic and diverse set of changes wrought by tourism on 'sense of place' (Hiss, 1990; Hough, 1990; Wilson, 1991) is beginning to awaken a sense of responsibility within the industry. As tourism destinations and organisations become 'place conscious', sustainable environmental practices – environmental codes of ethics, environmental impact studies and ecoefficiency programmes – are being considered and implemented. The determination and use of appropriate metrics and perceptual measures for measuring impacts is also moving forward. But should society be comforted by the current responsiveness and ways in which nature- and cultural-based resource issues are being addressed? There is doubt in some quarters as to whether transformational activities, and the ways in which they are currently conceived and implemented, are sufficient and appropriate. Hawkin *et al.* (1999) argue that conventional wisdom is mistaken when priorities in economic, environmental and social policies compete. They challenge industries, such as tourism, to find solutions based not on trade-offs or 'balance' between competing objectives, but on design integration, achieving all of them together at every level of the industry. Obviously, this challenge suggests that most destinations would have to alter the ways in which they think about and manage tourism. At the very least, more broadly based results-based objectives and strategies would have to be factored into the equations, while taking into account relations among the organisations responsible for tourism, the quality of tourism products and the dynamics of regional economies (Russo, 2002 and this volume).

Visualising the big picture or contemplating a different future for tourism is easily forestalled when destinations and tourism organisations operate on a demanding economic treadmill. Whether they are at the starting gate, capitalising on growth opportunities, or witnessing erosion of their success by successive tides of technological, demographic and regulatory change, the industry is in a constant state of anxiety, and sometimes flux. Hotels and attractions are examples of organisations with high breakeven points, and an inability to place products into inventory for sale at some future period. Fixed capacities have to be filled daily; hence preoccupation with marketing and the delivery of high-quality services. Furthermore, competitiveness problems are inescapable as increasing numbers of places hitch to the tourism bandwagon. In fact stagnant growth, declining margins and falling market share are not characteristic simply of the mature phase of the cycle, but of too much supply chasing demand or the not-too-uncommon disruptive phases of business cycles (Haywood, 1998). Factor in seasonality, climatic irregularities, market orientations, integration of global economies and the dynamic organisational interlinkages within the industry, and the complexities intensify. Regardless of which stage of the life cycle a destination might be in, the challenge is ever-present. Every destination and tourism organisation is being challenged to improve their understanding and anticipation of the underlying dynamics of change, not only within the industry, but particularly within the destination (Bianchi, 1994; Haywood, 1986, 1992).

While the study of life cycles in many destinations continues to provide interesting historical representations of cyclic activity (based on available, though often unreliable, statistical data), it is as if these studies examine tourism from the wrong end of the telescope: what is nearby seems far away, and so the details melt into amorphous blobs. Destinations viewed from afar can't help but succumb to the characteristic life/death pattern; yet when viewed closely the tourism organisations and the people could be observed making choices continuously. To be truly effective as a pragmatic paradigm, TALC studies must consider, not simply the existence of choice in reaction to change, but the conditions that both underlie change, and enlarge or restrict choice. Destinations and the tourism industry operate within a rich and nuanced world, full of surprises, a world that favours imaginative action. Tourism researchers must get closer to, and understand, the details.

Fortunately the life cycle can be employed in such a way as to explain some of the details associated with the emergence and development of tourism within a region; but serious gaps exist. For example, glimpses into the development of local entrepreneurship (Din, 1992) and small businesses (Beverland, 2001), and preconditions for urban destinations in determining investment and industry growth (van de Borg, 2000) provide useful information about the start-up phase, yet little is known about the activities and behaviours associated with the conceiving, incubator or predevelopment phase. This omission might not have occurred if methodological approaches for studying teleological (strategic) and dialectical (power) actions associated with developing a new industry had been employed. With literature on how to go about developing a tourism industry, particularly the importance of taking a community approach to development intensifying (Haywood, 1988), tourism leaders and decision makers need to know which processes work, or not, when, where and why. Wisdom and knowledge needs to be shared about the influencing factors inherent in the preformative years, and the ways in which tourism development needs to be legitimised – not only in this stage, but during every stage of the life cycle.

Early stages of development represent periods in which industry champions come forward (Weaver, this volume). Commitment from a community is sought. The enthusiasm of developers and their initial supporters and beneficiaries is infectious; promises are made; vision and goals are articulated; tourism master plans may be prepared; negotiations are entered into; feasibility and environmental studies conducted; sites selected; and projects designed. Gradually fantasies are translated into realities, and the inherent risks quickly translate into day-to-day responsibilities. Getting an infant industry and/or organisations started is an exhausting and emotional endeavour, so there is a tremendous need to understand the characteristics and behavioural patterns of young and emerging destinations. For example, what are the repercussions when destinations and tourism organisations are undercapitalised, and basic infrastructure lacking? Is inadequate planning, and development of appropriate systems and procedures problematic? Can the possibilities of premature death be avoided (the bankruptcy rate for many independently owned businesses is extremely high during the first few years of operation). What occurs, or doesn't, shapes the industry and affects the transition to subsequent stages in the life cycle for years to come.

Similarly, the factors that make the emergent and early growth phases of tourism development into a virtual honeymoon have not been explored in the TALC literature. Because the tourism development process is primarily supply-led, developers are courted and romanced, and investment incentives provided. Job creation is a high priority. As demand materialises, money pours in; everyone appears happy and content. But, misperceptions as to the benefits and beneficiaries abound. For example, profits and return on investment take considerable time to be realised. Sunk investment costs may not be recouped for decades (at which time, considerable reinvestment may be required), and demand may not be sufficient to exceed breakeven points. Attention, obviously, is focused on marketing and branding to build demand (fill capacities) and attract further investment. Yet, it is ironic that TALC researchers feel the urge to be extremely critical of developers and investors, and the focal relationship-building pursuit necessary to make the industry viable. Increasing numbers of visitors, tourist activity and large-scale tourism development projects are said to set the stage for decline. The ideal scenario is tourism without visitors and development! Given the improbability of this occurring, the notion that tourism activity may be merely symptomatic of problems, rather than being the underlying cause, needs further investigation.

Whether an organisation fulfilling its mission through capacity maximisation, or a tourism area protecting itself from reaching limits to capacity (see Boyd, this volume), there exist diverse views and interests in capacity research. The extent to which differing concerns about capacity utilisation are seen as overlapping, however, depends on the degree to which the dominating forces (natural, organisational, political, economic, etc.) can be unified and/or are seen as affecting each other's concerns, mandates or goals. Unfortunately, the impact that these forces have on each other, and on tourism within a destination as a whole, may not be readily apparent, to even the most knowledgeable of people. A primary reason is that insufficient time has been spent learning how destinations or tourist areas function from a structural point of view. TALC research needs to become better attuned to discovering the interplay of the dominant forces that cause a destination to advance or decline, particularly in respect to capacity management. Study of structural dynamics might reveal interesting information as to appropriate mixes or diversity of tourism segments, activities and programmes. Relationships among the various players could be better understood. The delicacy of managing the development and growth of the industry through the emergent and subsequent phases needs to be highlighted. The key questions are: how are destinations or tourism organisations being managed throughout the lifecycle, and what are some of the dominant characteristics of successful and unsuccessful tourism areas?

Some TALC studies characterise some destinations as being rudderless. Sucked in by the dogma of growth, and fuelled by a booster spirit and visions of 'bigger and better', tourism development is portrayed as (greedy?) economic salvation writ large. Multinational lodging organisations and tour operators become sought-after partners. Their brand power is considered catalytic in propelling growth. But what may not be appreciated is that many of these large, more mature organisations may be quite focused on linking their brand integrity with sustainable development. If, as corporations mature, they become more socially responsible (Swanson, 1999), then concern over growth-fuelled development may be ill founded. Inevitably, more knowledge is required as to how tourism organisations alter their values and behaviour over time. Certainly failure to meet a community's noneconomic needs is cause for considerable concern, but appreciation for the cause and effect relationships in relation to the evolution of the industry needs to be contextualised and improved.

Worrisome side effects and outcomes during phases of tourism growth suggest other concerns that need to be addressed. For example, there is misdirection lurking in commonly accepted measures of growth. Impact studies have revealed that growth is a complex, multidimensional process; therefore, visitation rates, visitor expenditures and market share may be inadequate measures in determining a destination's stage in a life cycle. Researchers might want to learn how astute corporations are building 'balanced scorecards' in order to align individual, organisational and community initiatives; achieve healthy growth; and broaden their base of leading indicators (Kaplan & Norton, 1996, 2001). Then there are the perils associated with forcing growth (for example, through tax incentives), and exacerbating the imbalance of supply in comparison to demand. Tourism areas, by focusing on a singular industry, are inherently vulnerable when they tie their fortunes to a cyclical industry. Moreover, ill-conceived development and improper management of the growth process can result in places becoming 'displaced' – out of favour commodities in an industry of sameness.

Achieving tourism growth has been characterised as a difficult, if not perilous, journey. For example, industry development can be either fostered or curtailed by numerous factors and influences – historical influences on development (Douglas, 1997); external events (di Benedetto & Bojanic, 1993); influence of business, investment and real estate cycles (Haywood, 1998); prevalence of market or state-managed capitalism (Bacon, 1998); relationships between travel personalities and destinations (Plog, 2001); the ability to satisfy visitors and build demand on repeat visitation (Oppermann, 1998); difficulties in branding and building awareness (Beverland, 2001); recognition that no local industry operates in isolation and that national institutions and transnational firms can foster or undermine development (Ionnides, 1992); involvement of both informal and formal sectors of local economies (Kermath & Thomas, 1992); proactive planning initiatives (Knowles & Curtis, 2000); the influence of corporate strategies (Debbage, 1990, 1992; Tse & Elwood, 1990); and the increasing complexity of decision making and investment at various life-cycle stages (Keller, 1987).

The importance of innovation and diffusion cannot be ignored, as they are instrumental in reinvigorating growth and diversity (Getz, 2000). The evolution of tourism's structural and dynamic properties over a lifetime cannot be ignored. For example, Schumpeter (1939) observed that after the introduction of a major product innovation, a strong 'band-wagon' effect often appears, followed by the entry of many new firms into the rapidly expanding sectors, attracted by the high profits associated with innovations (see Stansfield, this volume). However, the entry of new firms leads to an erosion of profit rates, and as the industry matures and its product becomes standardised, a shift to cost-saving (process) innovations then occurs. The exploitation of scale economies becomes important, and correspondingly this leads to a reduction in the number of firms in the industry. On the basis of these observations one might anticipate that future TALC studies could capture issues on the innovative efforts of destinations and tourism organisations, the importance of scale economies, and the shift from product innovations to process innovations. Klepper (1996) provides an appropriate general, dynamic model, and has explained why these and other parameters change over the life cycle of an industry.

While innovative behaviour is presupposed to occur during latter stages of growth, and during mature or stagnant states, in actual fact it can be prevalent during all stages of the life cycle. Most visitor-focused enterprises need to be rejuvenated every decade or less (Malcolm-Davies, this volume). During these times there can be major reinvestment in facilities and equipment. Similar changes also occur as hotel properties, for example, change brands or flags. Buildings that are poorly maintained decline in value and move 'down-market'. These might be replaced with new facilities, many incorporating environmentally friendly systems. While addition to the stock of tourism facilities may stem from corporate decisions, prudent or otherwise, they can also be spurred or denied through competing political priorities (Voase, 2002). So, there are multiple reasons and numerous actors involved in reconfiguring and restarting the cycle (Baum, 1998). Indeed, due to the fact that there are numerous types of tourism activities taking place within a tourism area, as well as variations or differentiation within a given activity or sector of the industry, it is possible to discover the coexistence of various stages of the life cycle within a destination (Hovinen, 2002). While this reinforces the notion that there can be numerous variations in the dominant design or states of tourism development (Weaver, 2000 and this volume; de Albuquerque &

McElroy, 1992), it challenges the ease in which stages can be identified and measured.

The possibility of dominant designs of destinations and/or organisations in accordance with various life-cycle stages is also worthy of investigation (Weaver, 2000). In the business world Abernathy and Utterback (1975, 1978) have made important contributions in studying relationships among firms. In a similar vein, Miles and Snow (1978) classified corporate behaviours into four broad categories, which they labelled *defenders*, *prospectors*, *analysers* and *reactors*, each with their own unique strategies for relating to their chosen markets. Another example of dominant design research is represented by the work of Mintzberg and Waters (1982). They identified five stages in the development of a firm's strategies – development, stability, adaptation, struggle and revolution – and suggested that stages were sequenced in accordance with four main patterns – periodic bumps, oscillating shifts, life cycles and regular progress – and probed into the periods of major change in organisations. In moving this research forward, Miller and Friessen (1984) went on to identify archetypes of organisations, that is, states of strategy, structure situation and process, and transitions between archetypes, and thereby noted that strategic and structural change are quantum rather than incremental. In other words, there are benefits in tracking the behaviours (actions and outcomes), as well as thought processes (intentions and perceptions), associated with the leaders and managers of destinations and the tourism organisations. Our understanding of how they learn and drive strategic change is strengthened; and our ability to recognise stages or states of change is sharpened. If tourism areas go into decline then it becomes vital to understand why destructive strategies and structures emanate from constructive ones. In his book, *The Icarus Paradox*, Miller (1990) suggests that all positive trajectories suffer from built-in faults. So cycles of success and failure, growth and decline, seem to be an inevitable part of the natural, human and organisational condition.

The inevitability of stagnation and decline is a common occurrence for homogeneous products and services, and among organisations that fail to adapt. This inevitability of tourism area decline is also being manifest by a widening chasm between expectations for growth and its realisation. Economic and geopolitical problems always have the industry on edge. Add to this list recognition that some markets are increasingly mismatched with demand; that not all growth is healthy; that social disintegration, cultural degradation and exhaustion of resources are possible outcomes; and the obvious signs of decay become worrisome. In any event there is a need to appreciate the options when growth prematurely halts or when nongrowth occurs. What does rejuvenation entail? is it possible? how can it be accomplished (see Cooper, other volume, editor's comment)? Life-cycle research has made some inroads, but the greater attention has to be focused on belief and behavioural change.

During the so-called saturation or mature stage, tourism areas cannot help but face an age of triage (Rubenstein, 1983). Successful tourism areas will be those that can deal with the threats (internal as well as external), and sift out genuine opportunities from the illusory. Important questions concerning management in nongrowth situations will have to be answered. Indeed, survival and sustainability for all tourism areas and organisations may hinge less on the possibilities of rejuvenation, and more on learning to recognise and avoid the traps waiting to ruin destinations and organisations that make desperate grabs for growth that should never happen in the first place (Knowles & Curtis, 1999).

Configuration and Transformation of Changing Tourism Areas

Sustaining the economic, environmental and cultural vibrancy of tourism areas are primary goals of every industry stakeholder. If the life-cycle concept is to gain validity and relevance as an evaluative framework, with mutually dependent goals in mind, it must become a more effective learning model capable of (1) discovering and representing the dynamic and inter-related qualities of the industry, those that are both self-reinforcing (for example, reinforcing development) and self-correcting (for example, limiting development due to imbalance with carrying capacity), and (2) facilitating evaluation of the consequences of new policies, strategies and structures that might be proposed. Legitimisation of the life cycle cannot occur, however, until a stop is put to attributing the demise of the industry solely to individuals and organisations, rather than recognising that systems structure is the prime shaper of behaviour. By discovering the leverage points brought about by system structure redesign, particularly if each stage of the life cycle has its own structural and dynamic qualities, researchers will become capable of identifying the actions and behaviours that lead to significant, sustained and beneficial improvements to industry and organisational performance.

Most attempts to identify the imminent change as reflected in the TALC have been based on sequential, open-loop views of change. As such suggestions as to how to make the lifecycle model useful and operational required addressing major conceptual and measurement concerns such as unit of analysis, relevant market, pattern and stages of the tourist area lifecycle, identification of the area's shape in the life cycle, determination of the unit of measurement and determination of the relevant time unit (Haywood, 1986). Tourism systems, however, react to development and to the interventions of all players. The resulting feedback defines the situations to be faced in the future, given the inadvertent time delays, the accumulation, usage and dispersal of tangible and intangible resources, attribution errors and false learning. In overcoming the limitations of the lifecycle in accounting for change, and based on the assumption that the lifecycle could become an appropriate nest for alternate theories of change resulting in the configuration and constant transformation of tourism areas, it is now recognised that a broader set of issues need to be resolved. Each of these is introduced under a label, by a question, and as a dilemma.

Unit of analysis

What is the appropriate unit of analysis – the tourism area, or change itself? If it is the 'tourism area', how is it defined? Tourist area life cycle research focuses on regions in which tourism is considered to be the prime activity or industry. But what constitutes 'prime' if tourism represents only, let's say, 25% of a region's gross product? Because life cycles of regions are influenced by a multitude of commercial, government, human and other activities, attributing cause and effect just to tourism seems foolhardy and misleading.

Just as confusing is: What constitutes tourism activity? As a modern phenomenon, tourism is in a constant state of evolution through the 'convergence of industries', and the growth of varied leisure activities pursued away from home. New relationships between tourism, recreation, cultural, educational, leisure and even work activities are developing constantly. Not only is there a merging of industries, but a merging of consumer groups or markets in search of 'experiences' (Pine & Gilmore, 1999). Many businesses find it virtually impossible to differentiate between local residents and visitors. Despite the prevalence of definitional distinctions, the current state of tourism market research and visitation and activity data in many locales may make the distinction moot.

Determining the unit of analysis is also confounded by the fact that life-cycle theories are only considered relevant to single, rather than multiple entities. If a defined geographic area is considered as a singular entity (a cluster or network of organisations in a defined space), then it seems appropriate to suggest that its development and growth (the function of potentials that are likely to occur within a given territory) is beyond the control of a single entity. That is, development decisions are made by a multitude of different organisations, each responsive for and to their own lifecycles. For example, if tourism is largely based on convention activity, the rejuvenation of conference and meeting facilities may not occur unless hotels participate in the process. A supply-side appreciation of those organisations that comprise and affect the industry, and their relationships with each other, is crucial in determining the industry's health and wellbeing. Indeed, a community-based approach may be totally ineffective in determining life-cycle changes if so-called destination management organisations are concerned only with marketing. Even government organisations that provide necessary infrastructure, or control over the development process, may be ineffective in managing the life cycle if they have limited appreciation for the dynamics and intricacies of tourism.

The fact that the TALC concept has been strongly based on product life-cycle research is quite evident as market performance measures dominate. Usage of visitation rates and the associated expenditure levels suggest that researchers consider the industry life cycle as being market-driven, rather than organisationally driven (Simon, 1991). As tourism areas are 'place-based', it seems reasonable to require that performance during the life-cycle periods be determined on the basis of sustainability measures. If the essence of a tourism area is its attractiveness, scenic beauty, natural and cultural heritage, then these attributes should be taken into consideration. There are a wide variety of industry stakeholders interested in place-based performance, but they need the requisite information to detect problems and progress, as well as institute preventative measures. Indeed, it can be argued that the creation of tourism's economic value is a process that involves the best or most appropriate, combinational use of all resources.

Being precise as to delineation of what constitutes a tourism area or geographic region also presents a conundrum. Tourism areas tend not to conform to jurisdictional boundaries; sometimes they are better determined through typical patterns of visitor or tourist activity. Even when the subject area is proscribed – a national park, for example – consideration should be given to visitation and development activity in peripheral areas (see Boyd, this volume). The 'park gate syndrome' represents distinctive and dense forms of development that may have profound impacts on tourism areas even though they may not be precisely located in the region under consideration. Another concern is the possible expansion and contraction of tourism areas over time; when this occurs it confounds and destabilises the notion of carrying capacity.

Particular attention also has to be given to those regions that are on the verge of becoming tourism areas. Sometimes tourism is introduced as a benign industry capable of overcoming place-related damage caused by other industries (usually in decline), or as a preferential form of industrial development. Then there exist those resource-rich tourism/recreation areas recognised for their potential, but which have yet to be developed in accordance with their potential. In each case the challenges associated with tourism development and growth need to be better understood. The obstacles to overcome are decidedly different if development and growth are to succeed.

As discussed in detail elsewhere (see Haywood, other volume, editor's comment), there is considerable merit in moving beyond discrete tourism areas as units of change, to the unit of analysis becoming change itself. If, as suggested, there are different explanations for stability and change then it becomes important to determine the degree to which these explanations are nested in each other. Research is required to determine the relationships among these explanations, the macro–micro links, their timing, temporal shifts and degree to which they complement each other.

Unit and mode of change

Is tourism development a linear or cyclical activity – a biological progression of life-cycle events? The tendency has been to treat seemingly random patterns as stochastic processes. Observed change and development processes within tourism areas, however, are more complex than the life cycle suggests. As such, conditions may exist to trigger interplay among several instigators of change and produce interdependent cycles of change. For example, change and development goes on at multiple and hierarchical levels – a geographic level (place and space), an industry level (groups of organisations), organisational levels, stakeholder group levels and individual levels. This classification suggests that there are two different angles for studying development and change – the internal processes of change, adaptation and replication of individual entities, and the interactive processes of competition, cooperation and conflict among entities (Baum & Singh, 1994).

Application of life-cycle theory to explain change and development has made occasional reference to teleological theories, either in attributing blame to tourism organisations or in proposing positive or ameliorating mechanisms (policy making or tourism planning) through government or nongovernmental organisations. Because the dynamics of tourism systems arise from the interactions of all these organisations, the impact of their relationships needs to be better understood. With evolutionary and dialectical theories operating at the level of multiple entities, their application in this regard should be invaluable.

Different approaches for examining and explaining development and change in tourism areas also require that recognition be given to variations in the sequence of change events. For example, sequencing could be either prescribed *a priori* by either deterministic or probabilistic laws, or could progress and emerge in a constructive manner as the change process unfolds. Lifecycle and evolutionary theories of tourism area development rely on the prescriptive in that the imminent form is realised through steps or stages that provide an underlying continuity of form. Appearance of radical or sudden change is extremely rare, and in reality tends to be explained as a statistical accumulation of small individual events that gradually change the nature of the tourism area or industry. Radical change or breaks with the past, however, are identifiable within the industry and in tourism areas. The accompanying change based on new goals (teleological) and resolution of conflict (dialectical) tends to be described as constructive as it produces unprecedented, novel forms that, in retrospect, are discontinuous and unpredictable departures from the past.

With tourism areas developing and changing over space and time, it is likely that more than one of the theories will come into play on any occasion. The development process is influenced by different organisations and individuals. The spatial dispersion of organisations and individuals also means that different influences may be at work simultaneously, each imparting their own particular momentum to the development process. Development and change also take time to occur, and may not exert any influence until noticed. In other words the patterns and impacts of tourism development and change processes is multilayered and complex.

Unit of measurement

If the health and wellbeing of tourism areas are of fundamental concern in TALC studies, why are visitation and expenditure data pre-eminent in determining the progression of cyclical stages? Understandably destinations or tourism areas are dependent on visitors, but should the inherent stages of the life cycle be determined and based solely on growth trends associated with the number of visitors and their expenditures? Furthermore, if these are measures of growth, are they not rubber yardsticks – uncertain indicators of that which is being measured? As TALC studies point to growth as a highly complex social, economic and environmental process, why is growth not considered more often from a multidimensional perspective?

In industry circles the growth drumbeat is so pervasive that it is hard to imagine tourism development without growth. But not every kind of growth leads to development, let alone progress. Not only has the management guru Peter Drucker (1973) admonished growth as an objective, but the ambiguities of growth prevent various definitions and measures of growth from serving as valid indicators of achievement. In fact most constituencies within tourism areas have their own preferences as to which measures of growth (development) should be emphasised. Arbitrarily imposed growth targets and rates, however, are likely to favour the interests of some constituencies in the short term at the expense of other constituencies over the long term. And here is an intriguing paradox. Of all the stakeholders, visitors not only have the least interest in any form of growth, but may avoid places where growth is rampant and destroying the essence of place. As such, some tourism areas and industry partners are learning that performance can be enhanced by actually catering to fewer visitors.

Because tourism areas pursue tourism development to accomplish societal purposes, not solely economic ones, progress and performance need to be measured in aesthetic, environmental, social, cultural, as well as economic and monetary terms. To date, measurement has been narrowly focused on traditional performance areas, which tend to look at visitation and expenditure data. These measures are quantitative, relatively abundant and precise, though historical or lagging in nature. Present and future requirements, however, require non-traditional, less well defined and emerging measures. These measures need to be more predictive in nature and sufficiently robust to deal with today's changing marketplace and resource environment. However, if researchers are to answer sophisticated measurement questions as . . .

- How can measures be identified that are linked to critical success factors, to industry/business risks, and to policy and strategic objectives?
- What are the key predictors of performance that relate to policy and strategic objectives; programmes, outputs, initiatives and limits; and contributions to desired results?
- How are the cause and effect of policy, strategic and other decisions to be measured?
- How do you benchmark a tourism area's ability to adapt to changing industry/business decisions or social/cultural/environmental conditions?

. . . there should be knowledge and awareness of key objectives, policies, strategies and capacity limits. This may be a challenge in that few tourism areas have a clear idea as to tourism's mandate, the strategic approaches used to operate effectively in the tourism industry or marketplace, and how value is created now or into the future for visitors and other stakeholders.

Because tourism policies and strategies set direction, measures are required to stay on track. By linking measurement to policy and strategy, researchers can identify and implement measures in the context of where tourism is headed, or what is expected from its development (leading indicators), rather than simply on where it is today, where it has been, or what has occurred (lagging indicators) (see Berry, other volume, editor's comment). This differentiator is critical in resource and community settings in which tourism challenges sustainability. Moreover, tourism areas and organisations that remain nimble and alert to the need to change their policies and strategies (and thus their measures) to meet evolving needs and requirements are more likely to be successful in environments increasingly characterised by change. The expanding use of nonfinancial and intangible measures, such as the Balanced Scorecard (Kaplan & Norton, 1990, 2001), environmental and community sustainability indexes, and quality of life measures, is indicative of a desire to find ways to enhance industry and corporate governance, meet stakeholder requirements, and reflect community and visitor value to be derived from tourism.

A tourism area's ability to optimise its return from tourism ultimately depends on whether it has the trust of its stakeholders. A key challenge is to identify which issues different stakeholders care about and to develop mechanisms for communicating with them in a timely manner. The goal is not to report on what stakeholders currently demand; it is also to supply information they need if they are to gain a better understanding of the area's strategy and performance. Promoting dialogue and engagement with stakeholders will help the tourism area obtain the information it needs in order to become more effective in managing through various lifecycle stages.

Cycle and pattern determination

Sustainability, defined in its broadest sense, is predicated on the clear expression of societal (community, organisational, individual) choices regarding the management of tourism areas and organisations for their intrinsic values, and tangible and intangible benefits they confer. Given the dynamics of change, varying spatial and temporal scales, and lag effects, the critical question is how can the TALC analysis become more useful in achieving goals and objectives, while anticipating and avoiding the inevitable barriers, behaviours and mistakes in achieving sustainability? Are there particular forces that influence the complex development process in tourism areas during different times? What are the typical characteristics and behaviours associated with various stages in the life cycle, and can these be determined *a priori*?

Acceptance of deterministic modelling of change is currently being critiqued as managers and planners broaden their utilisation of both prescriptive and constructive models to explain the patterns of stability and change in tourism areas and organisations. Improvement in learning about and managing such complex systems as tourism areas requires tools capable of capturing all the sources of dynamic complexity. Such tools as causal mapping and simulation techniques (made accessible through modern system dynamics modelling software) could be of tremendous value in capturing past events or in anticipating future events (Morecroft & Sterman, 1994). Their application to life cycles, as nests of change, could be profound if tourism areas and organisations are to influence the speed and means of the evolution they set in motion.

A first order priority is to pay attention to changing patterns of behaviour. It has been proposed that growth and ageing of organisations are primarily manifested in the inter-relationship between two factors, flexibility and controllability (Idizes, 1988). This observation runs counter to the importance *size* and *time* are afforded in TALCs. In other words, young tourism destinations or organisations tend to be quite amenable to development and change, although what they may do is likely to be unpredictable because there is little controllability. On the other hand more mature tourism areas and organisations tend to be far less flexible and pliant when it comes to change or managing transitions. This is due to a greater degree of calcification or controllability of behaviour. Understanding the differences in behaviours during cycles of change adds to the poignancy of intensified commoditisation among tourism areas and organisations, increased competition, product obsolescence and customer power. Recognising that there is no such thing as long-term sustained competitive advantage, and that operating margins are constantly being squeezed, tourism areas and organisations are anxious to learn how to manage through the necessary transitions; that is, they must demonstrate the most effective actions and behaviours.

Typically the inflection points in TALCs have been associated with significant increases or declines in tourism volume, thereby giving credence to the rather outmoded importance of market share as the driver of profitability. Paradoxically, TALC studies, while recognising that volume growth is important, have emphasised that *how growth is achieved* is much more important. Yet lacking are the convincing studies that point to why, when, where and how high growth, with poorly conceived tourism designs, destroys value and profitability. With fundamental shifts occurring in both business and tourism area land-scapes, there is a need for tourism life-cycle research to improve understanding of how and when tourism areas and organisations, if they are to remain sustainable and profitable, must change their designs so that, as living entities, they can continue to function in coherent and mutually reinforcing ways over time. So, if the inflection points are to be anticipated, they need to be based on a new set of metrics associated with value capture and value loss using a Balanced Scorecard approach (Kaplan & Norton, 1990, 2001), and market, financial, social and environmental measures or performance data must be incorporated.

Determination of life-cycle stages, therefore, requires a multicompo-site set of leading and lagging indicators that will identify value migration patterns of importance to key constituents in the tourism area – citizens, businesses, governments, NGOs – and throughout tourism's value chain or network/constellation (Norman & Ramirez,

1998). As life-cycle patterns really are graphic portrayals of the realisation or destruction of value, it can be argued that life-cycle stages need to be represented through value configurations. Based on Porter's value chain framework (1985), which is presently the accepted language for representing the logic of organisation-level value creation, it is possible to configure tourism areas (the unit of analysis) as value networks – the creation and reinvention of value achieved through the relationship of organisations within and affecting the sense of place. Subjecting this value network/constellation to analysis would then require decomposing tourism areas into a range of strategically important activities and then measuring and understanding the impacts of these activities in terms of cost and value (creation, capture or loss). If the unit of analysis were to be a tourism organisation, however, value configuration could be based also on the value chain (the creation of value through the transformation of inputs into performances, products or services). At a lower level of hierarchical analysis the notion of value shop could be employed (the creation of value by mobilising resources and activities to resolve particular problems associated with visitors or particular interest groups) (Stabell & Fjeldstad, 1998). For example, work is already proceeding in developing environmental chain analysis (Ishii & Stevels, 2000); the relevancy for tourism areas is significant.

Because tourism areas are configured as networks/constellations, value creation, capture and loss will need to be derived from a mix of activities, capacity levels and opportunities. Unfortunately, little work has been conducted, to date, in identifying and modelling these activities, and in measuring value, or changes in value, over time. Likewise, identification of corresponding life-cycle stages has yet to be determined. However, as previously stated, these stages should be in accordance with goals, capacity limits and boundary constraints that need to be identified *in situ*. As such, much of what is currently known about the pattern and stages of tourist area life cycles needs to be rethought.

The complexity of achieving truly sustainable tourism areas is in balancing various demands that reveal themselves at different points in the evolution of tourism areas. Supply-side and resource-based considerations definitely need to play a predominant role in value determination, as do behavioural patterns. For example, as organisations age they tend to become oblivious to the incompatibility of their current business models with changing operating conditions (Slyworthy, 1996). Different stages of the lifecycle also alter the resource requirements of organisations and the responsiveness to the demands of various stakeholders if they are not considered critical to their survival or needs at a given time (Jawahar & McLaughlin, 2001). On the demand side, visitor value can be compromised if ignored or if competing demands from other stakeholders take precedence. The result: repeat visitation and the development of loyal, visitor-centric relationships may not be realised; growth in tourism arrivals may cease; length of stay may diminish; and the TALC may prematurely slide into decline.

Conclusion

TALC research typically has been dominated by interesting, though synoptic, accounts of change and patterns at different points in time that normally escape perception. The industry, however, requires more sophisticated performance accounts of change, simply because they are more directly connected to the 'lived experiences', and actions and behaviours of practitioners. Indeed change, which is synoptically explained *ex post facto*, is experienced in tourism areas and organisations as an unfolding process, a flow of possibilities, a conjunction of events and open-ended interactions occurring in time. To understand how change is actually accomplished, it must be approached from within, not as an abstract concept, but as performance enacted in time.

As a nested theory of change, for example, the life cycle has the potential, not simply to clarify exogenous influences, but to further our awareness of how tourism areas and organisations respond to these influences. It is the endogenously conditioned responses, however, that cannot be anticipated. There is a world out there that causes tourism authorities and managers to respond, but the pattern of response depends on self-understanding – the historically created assumptions and interpretations of the community, the organisation, and the individuals, along with the perception of place, the importance of the environment, and the visions, goals and limits that exist for the industry. The responses to exogenously generated pressure over time are complex, multilayered and evolving, rather than simple, fixed and episodic.

The relevancy and pragmatism of TALC studies, therefore, will be enhanced when more is known about the motors of change – the degree to which they are nested at different stages of the life cycle, and whether they act simultaneously, at different times and complement each other. While the complexity of the theoretical relationships between constructive and prescribed motors of change is likely to play a major role in explaining patterns of stability and change in tourism areas, there will be a requirement to develop more dynamic systems models. If sustainability of tourism areas is the ultimate goal, then TREC studies need to focus on gaining a better appreciation of each of the major stakeholders, their beliefs and habits of action in response to local circumstances, and pressures to survive; as well as the influence and interventions of these stakeholders into the stream of actions that are manifest in various stages of the TALC.

As living entities and clusters of tourism-focused enterprises and human action, tourism areas are subjected to a barrage of change. The view expressed here is that if TALC researchers avail themselves of the opportunity to capture and make sense of the dynamics of this change, the myriad of issues and questions regarding sustainability have a greater chance of being resolved. In the process, TALC research needs to become more theoretically integrative, as well as demonstrate its relevance to practitioners, who require the knowledge and tools to (re)configure and continually transform tourism areas and their organisations in accordance with their independent quest for survival and their mutually dependent goals for enhancing the quality of the places or communities in which they live and operate.

Part 2
Implementation of the TALC

RICHARD W. BUTLER

This first section contains chapters that discuss the application and implementation of the TALC in rural settings in North America and the People's Republic of China. The first application of the TALC model appeared, as did the original article, in *The Canadian Geographer*, a year later in 1981, and was the first of three articles by Hovinen (1981, 2000, 2002), which have applied the TALC to Lancaster County in the USA. This is the setting made famous in the movie 'Witness', which helped to increase the visibility of the area and is partly responsible for making it more widely known to a more international audience. In the first chapter in this section, Hovinen discusses the process of the tourist development of this rural location and its distinctive cultural milieu. The changes brought about by tourism in this setting are perhaps, in some ways, more significant than in many other American tourist destinations because of the conservative and private nature of the Amish who populate this area. Hovinen notes how they have adjusted to tourism, utilising it in some situations and avoiding or minimising contact with it in others. He goes on to examine the TALC and tourism in Lancaster County in the light of attempts to move the tourism industry there to a more sustainable form, a topic which is discussed later in this volume by Marois and Hinch, and by myself in the final chapter of the accompanying volume.

The following chapter presents a second North American application of the TALC, in this case to another rather distinct cultural setting, that of the province of Quebec. While Quebec is predominantly French in language and to some degree culture, the Eastern Townships, the area to which Lundgren applies the model, is mostly English speaking. It has a long-established tourism industry as he notes, and one which has adjusted consistently to changes in transport innovations and accessibility. The tourism industry has taken several forms, including the traditional North American cottage development, winter sports (particularly downhill skiing), and most recently, a more varied focus on local community attractions, including festivals, art and gastronomy. Lundgren illustrates the cycles within cycles that affect a region and the way in which a region can constantly revitalise its tourist and recreational appeal.

The final chapter in this section, by Bao and Zhang, discusses the specific application of the TALC to tourism planning and development in the People's Republic of China. While China is relatively new on the international tourism scene, its massive population means that it has a large domestic tourism industry, and as general levels of affluence rise, it can be expected to emerge as a major player in international tourism in the years ahead. It is already a significant international tourism destination, and the 2008 Olympic Games will certainly increase its international visibility in tourism. Bao and Zhang's paper demonstrates a particularly pragmatic solution to some of the problems with applying the TALC, particularly the bounding problem noted by Johnston (see other volume) and others. They reveal how the decision to designate a specific feature as an addition to the attractions of a declining tourism destination can successfully, if possibly only temporarily, revitalise the appeal of, and increase the visitation to, the area. This is a theme returned to in the last section of this volume.

Chapter 5

Lancaster County, the TALC, and the Search for Sustainable Tourism

GARY R. HOVINEN

Introduction

Lancaster County, Pennsylvania, an important diversified tourism destination in the Northeastern USA, was the location of the first application of the Tourism Area Life Cycle (TALC) model (Hovinen, 1981). In a second, expanded article, Hovinen (1982) confirmed the general usefulness of the model while noting some of its limitations for this particular destination. A much more recent study (Hovinen, 2002) of Lancaster County revisited the TALC model after two decades of additional development and again evaluated its usefulness.

This chapter will first summarize the results of these previous applications of the TALC model. As the model emphasizes the potential for tourism destinations to experience significant decline if appropriate planning efforts are not undertaken, the author will then discuss the prospects for avoiding such a decline in Lancaster County. The county has in recent years begun to pursue elements of a sustainable tourism strategy. How has sustainable tourism been defined thus far and how may the definition be further refined in the future? What have been the successes up to now in the tourism planning approach? What setbacks have occurred and what challenges remain? Can a lasting form of tourism be devised which is economically successful while being judged by county residents as enhancing their quality of life? In the final analysis, how useful is the TALC model or suggested revisions thereof in assessing the future of Lancaster County tourism?

Previous Applications of the TALC Model to Lancaster County

The first applications of the TALC model to Lancaster County (Hovinen, 1981, 1982) dated the postulated exploration stage to the pre-World War II period. No organized tourist industry existed, visitor facilities were few, and the number of visitors was very small. Lancaster's highly accessible location meant that most early visitors were likely traveling through the county on their way elsewhere. An incipient cultural attraction was the large population of 'plain people', including the country's oldest settlement of Amish. By the 1930s these plain people, who had chosen to remain to a high degree culturally and socially separate from the rest of society, were becoming a curiosity to outsiders (Hovinen, 1982).

Butler's proposed involvement stage, characterized by local people investing heavily in tourist facilities and the establishment of a formal tourist organization, can be usefully applied to Lancaster County during the period from the end of World War II until about 1960. The Amish were the principal tourist attraction, so it is not surprising that tourist facilities developed rapidly to the east of Lancaster City in the direction of the major concentration of Amish. Heavy promotion of the Amish attraction by local businessmen and eventually by a formal tourist organization (henceforth called Visitors Bureau) helped generate growing awareness and resulted in a rapid growth of visitors from nearby urban centers along the Atlantic coast (Hovinen, 1982).

The development stage of Butler's model clearly characterized Lancaster County from 1960 to about 1975. The growth in the number of visitors was huge, and Lancaster County was being touted as one of the top tourist destinations in the USA. Although the Amish, with their horse and buggy transportation, distinctive conservative clothing, and homes without electricity, were certainly the principal attraction, the county was also becoming a more diversified destination. One example was the construction of the Dutch Wonderland amusement park with its castle façade along a major traffic artery east of the city. As Butler has suggested, the development period saw major investment in capital facilities such as motels and restaurants by external organizations, which had by now recognized Lancaster's business potential. The initial positive attitude of many local inhabitants and the media towards tourism, given its economic impacts, turned more critical during this stage. There was growing concern about garish commercialism as exemplified by Dutch Wonderland, about increased traffic congestion along the two principal tourist arteries, and regarding the perceived exploitation of the Amish as unwilling tourist objects. The Amish themselves complained about invasion of privacy. Two noted Amish scholars expressed concern that tourism was beginning to destroy Amish culture (Hovinen, 1982). Thus tourism had become much more controversial.

The next two stages in Butler's model, consolidation and stagnation, are difficult to apply to Lancaster County's tourism cycle as the tourist industry has become ever more diversified and the conditions of tourism ever more complex since the mid-1970s. For example, Butler's assumption in 1980 that few, if any, additional investments are made by franchises and chains from the consolidation period onward is contradicted by evidence in Lancaster County. A lodging and restaurant construction boom occurred in the 1990s, financed heavily by external chain and franchise organizations, during the same time that there was growing concern in some elements of the tourist industry about stagnation or even decline in visitor numbers and revenues. Lancaster County has never been a conventional resort destination and is now comprised of a number of different tourism elements with varying degrees of strength and weakness. Whereas the Amish were the principal attraction into the 1980s, that has not been true of the period of the 1990s and beyond. Instead new attractions such as factory outlet malls and theaters have come to the forefront (Hovinen, 2002).

The empirical evidence suggests that there has been no simple shift from a development stage to the postulated consolidation and stagnation stages in Lancaster County. Rather than a gradual slowing of tourism growth during a consolidation stage, there was an abrupt and dramatic decline in visitor numbers in 1979 because of a combination of internal and external factors (Hovinen, 1982). That decline was followed by a renewed growth of tourism through the mid-1980s, although possibly not to the level of the record high visitor numbers of the mid-1970s. The new growth was attributable partly to a brief renewed interest in Amish culture because of the impacts of a popular Hollywood film ('Witness'). By the 1990s, the Amish were no longer the principal attraction for a visit; instead shopping had become the single most important reason for coming to the county. Visitors flocked to large new factory outlet malls or to antique shops. Another example of a new and highly popular attraction was Sight and Sound, a theater that offered plays with religious themes. At the same time, owners of older attractions were complaining of stagnation or even decline and an air of crisis seemed to pervade the tourism industry (Hovinen, 2002). Thus there appeared to be a mixture of growth, stagnation, and even decline during the 1990s, making it difficult to discern a clear progression from Butler's proposed consolidation stage to stagnation and then decline.

Given the initial evidence used in testing Butler's model in Lancaster County, the author proposed replacing the consolidation and stagnation stages with a new maturity stage (Hovinen, 1982). Such a stage might be partly characterized by either a slowing of growth or the existence of stagnation, but also might have short periods of renewed growth or even decline. Further evidence from the 1980s and 1990s seemed to support this alternative maturity stage (Hovinen, 2002). Perhaps Butler's model is most successfully applied to certain conventional resort destinations that undergo cycles of evolution. A cycle is certainly discernible in Lancaster County, but the highly diversified nature of tourism that currently exists and the fact that there are different elements of the tourist industry which are at different stages of the cycle makes it difficult to distinguish between consolidation, stagnation, and decline. Growth, stagnation, decline, and even revitalization through new investment may in fact coexist (Hovinen, 2002).

Table 5.1 sheds further light on the growing complexity of tourism trends in the county. It includes annual percentage change figures for either visitors or sales calculated for five individual large businesses. Operators of these businesses had records dating back many years from which the author was able to calculate annual percentage changes. Although not representative of the entire industry, a partial picture of long-term trends thus emerges. The author agreed to respect the confidentiality of the businesses whose operators agreed to supply figures.

The attraction represented in Table 5.1 is one of the longest-lasting features of the tourism landscape and thereby contrasts with the newer types of attractions that date from the late 1980s and 1990s. This earlier attraction experienced rapid growth in visitors during the county tourist boom of the 1960s and much of the 1970s period. In the major downturn in county tourism of 1979, the attraction suffered almost a 30% decline. The next year, however, saw an equally rapid percentage rebound. Most of the remainder of the 1980s and the beginning of the 1990s were also strong, but then five of the next six years saw declines in visitors. The attraction is somewhat representative of trends in the older parts of the attractions sector during the 1990s period and gave rise to a perception among operators of these businesses that county tourism was facing a crisis.

The two large restaurants and the lodging facility included in Table 5.1 provide a more complicated picture, as visitor total percent changes do not exhibit a consistent pattern of growth or decline in most years of the 1990s period. Only in 1991 and 1993 did all three of these businesses experience decline together. In every other year of this decade, one or two suffered decline while the remainder had growth. This variability in growth or decline in individual years was also apparent in the overall industry during the decade, as reflected in trend figures for a much larger sample of businesses surveyed by the author (Hovinen, 2002). In contrast to the development stage of county tourism, this 'maturity' stage is characterized by greater variation in success or failure among individual businesses rather than the earlier tendency of all to prosper or (on rare occasions) to suffer together in a given year.

Results for the large shopping facility included in Table 5.1 further confirm the preceding generalization. In contrast to the other four businesses, this especially well managed establishment experienced no declines (in sales) during any year of the past two decades. The manager of this shopping facility told the author in a meeting in June 2002 that a number of tourism operators succeeded in the boom years of the 1960s and 1970s 'in spite of themselves'. At that time, favorable economic

Table 5.1 Percent change in sales or visitors for five individual businesses

Year	Attraction (visitors)	Shopping (sales)	Lodging (visitors)	Restaurant (visitors)	Restaurant (visitors)
1960	596.5				
1961	51.8				
1962	36.1				
1963	22.8				
1964	1.7				
1965	22.0				
1966	3.4				
1967	2.9				
1968	4.7				
1969	8.5				
1970	24.2		10.1		
1971	12.6		6.6		
1972	− 1.9		5.6		
1973	12.2		0.9		
1974	− 2.1		− 0.9		
1975	5.2		10.5		
1976	− 0.7		2.9		
1977	3.4		7.3		
1978	− 5.7		− 2.2	4.8	
1979	− 29.4		− 10.5	− 12.3	
1980	29.3		2.6	7.2	
1981	9.3	25.0	1.8	3.4	
1982	− 2.0	11.0	0.0	3.6	
1983	− 6.8	9.0	0.4	− 0.7	
1984	6.2	14.0	2.8	− 2.0	
1985	5.6	20.0	2.6	− 0.7	9.6
1986	1.7		1.3	0.5	1.9

Year	Attraction (visitors)	Shopping (sales)	Lodging (visitors)	Restaurant (visitors)	Restaurant (visitors)
Table 5.1 (*Continued*)					
1987	− 0.8	14.0	4.9	0.3	5.4
1988	2.9	14.0	− 1.2	0.7	0.8
1989	5.4	9.0	− 3.6	3.2	− 3.7
1990	10.8	5.0	2.5	− 3.4	1.0
1991	8.3	11.0	− 6.0	− 0.4	− 10.3
1992	− 4.2	5.0	1.3	− 2.7	5.3
1993	− 5.5	4.0	− 4.5	− 2.9	− 3.0
1994	− 10.7	4.0	− 0.1	2.0	2.3
1995	− 4.9	4.0	1.8	− 2.6	2.3
1996	4.2	5.0	− 0.3	6.0	8.2
1997	− 9.2	3.0	6.8	− 1.8	− 4.0
1998	13.6	14.0	− 1.3	2.8	7.4
1999			0.5		

The large attraction included is one of 104 Visitors Bureau member attractions in the county
The large shopping facility represents one of 98 shopping members, accommodation one of 186, and restaurants two of 63

trends in the overall industry virtually guaranteed success. Now success or failure is influenced more by the management or business planning skills of the individual operator than was true previously. In a mature industry, how to prevent decline therefore becomes a greater concern.

The decline stage of the TALC model

One of the most useful aspects of the TALC model is its emphasis on the potential, if not the inevitability, of significant decline if appropriate long-range planning strategies are not pursued for a particular destination. The author's previous studies of Lancaster County have not shown any evidence of significant overall decline up to now, despite clear evidence of decline among some individual businesses, especially including older attractions. Nevertheless, the potential for future decline was a matter of concern among some tourism operators during the 1990s (Hovinen, 2002).

The 1990s saw the emergence of a new proactive and longer-range planning approach at the same time that the dominant approach of the

Visitors Bureau and individual tourism operators continued to be reactive and short range with a strong annual marketing emphasis (Hovinen, 2002). The first example of the new proactive approach, in the mid-1990s, was a new heritage tourism program financially supported by the state and county governments; it also involved a public–private partnership, as it was sponsored in part by the private Visitors Bureau and the National Trust for Historic Preservation. The partnership produced a heritage tourism plan for Lancaster County by the beginning of 1998. Then, in the year 2001 another state-supported partnership resulted in the creation of a new Lancaster–York Heritage Region including the neighboring county to the west of the Susquehanna River. A long-range management action plan was completed in 2001, prepared with the assistance of a heritage tourism consulting firm from the Washington DC area.

Theoretical alternatives to the TALC's decline and rejuvenation stages

Agarwal (1994 and other volume, editor's note) argues for a reformulation of the poststagnation phase of the TALC model with its suggested alternatives of decline versus rejuvenation. Restructuring efforts may be initiated before decline sets in. In contrast to Butler's suggestion in proposing the TALC model that rejuvenation to avoid decline involves a complete change in the attractions on which tourism is based, Agarwal contends that this may not be financially or politically acceptable. Therefore, efforts are concerned with renewal and with encouraging growth and market maturity rather than with accepting decline. She proposes a reorientation stage after the TALC stagnation stage and before eventual rejuvenation or decline to reflect these restructuring efforts. Such a reorientation stage has some relevance to circumstances in Lancaster County although there has been no clear stagnation stage for the overall industry. As one example where 'reorientation' may better describe current efforts at renewal than 'rejuvenation', no complete change of attractions in Lancaster County is likely as long as the Amish remain in the county as one of the continuing attractions.

In a study of restructuring theory, Agarwal (2002) points out that restructuring involves both product reorganization and product trans-formation. 'Specific product reorganization strategies include investment and technical change, centralization and product specialization. Product transformation strategies include service quality enhancement (improving the quality of service delivery), environmental quality enhancement (improving key areas of the resort), repositioning, diversification, collaboration, and adaptation.' (Agarwal, 2002: 36–37). Some of these strategies are part of Lancaster County's restructuring efforts as will be evident from the discussion of further trends.

The Search for Sustainable Tourism

The potential for a tourism destination to avoid the decline stage can also be related usefully to the theme of sustainable tourism. Butler (1998b) has previously noted how popular this theme has become in the academic discipline of tourism. From the perspective of managers in the tourism industry, economic sustainability of tourism is without doubt the primary interest. But sustainable tourism is also defined on the basis of environmental, social, and cultural considerations. Butler (1998b: 28) has argued that 'it is clearly illogical and unrealistic to contemplate sustainability in any one sense alone, such as economic sustainability.' Furthermore, according to Butler (1998b: 29), 'calls for sustainable tourism to be developed irrespective of whether other, interrelated, segments are to be sustainable or not is inappropriate and contradictory.' That is, the tourism sector is related to and dependent upon other sectors of the economy and society, so any definition of sustainable tourism must consider the overall system and not simply tourism alone. The difficulty of implementing sustainable tourism therefore becomes apparent. Perhaps it is best to view sustainable tourism as a set of idealistic principles that may be useful as a basis for long-range planning rather than a condition ever likely to be fully achieved.

The first consideration of sustainable tourism principles in Lancaster County occurred as part of the preparation of the 1998 Heritage Tourism Plan. A basic premise of the heritage tourism program was that there is a need to maintain a strong balance between the economic benefits of tourism and the preservation of natural and cultural resources. After discussion and input from county tourism and development representatives, the following eight principles of sustainable tourism were adopted for the plan.

(1) The natural and cultural environment has intrinsic value, and its protection and preservation is [sic] essential to the long-term success and viability of tourism in Lancaster County.
(2) The relationship between tourism and the environment, both natural and cultural, must be managed so that it is sustainable in the long term.
(3) Tourism should enhance and complement the unique natural and cultural features of Lancaster County.
(4) Tourism activities should respect and accurately reflect the scale, nature, and character of Lancaster County's unique places.
(5) Carrying capacity should be a prime consideration in managing and protecting the natural and cultural heritage of Lancaster County.

(6) A balance should be sought between the needs of the visitor, the place, and the residents of Lancaster County.

(7) Tourism should communicate appropriate cultural and environmental sensitivity.

(8) Local involvement in sustainable tourism planning processes is essential in promoting harmony between tourism and the residents of Lancaster County. (Lancaster County Planning Commission, 1998: 18–19)

Development trends and issues in the county

Sustainable tourism, most appropriately defined, depends not only on achieving positive impacts from tourism itself, but also on what happens in other sectors of the economy and society. Therefore, it is necessary first to consider briefly some of the broader development trends and issues in the county that have implications for the success of sustainable tourism.

In 1998 the Hourglass Foundation, a private nonprofit citizens' group in Lancaster County, hired the Polk-Lepson Research Group of York to do a random scientific telephone survey of the Lancaster County population. The research firm asked a variety of questions about issues affecting the county, including what respondents considered to be the biggest threats to the quality of life in the county. Over one half of the sampled population cited overdevelopment, urban sprawl, loss of farmland, or unlimited growth as the biggest threats to the quality of life in Lancaster County; a much smaller percentage mentioned environmental concerns or traffic as the chief threats. Furthermore, a large majority of respondents said they considered sprawl a serious problem rather than a minor problem or no problem and agreed that something should be done to stop or slow down sprawl (Rutter, 1998).

The Hourglass Foundation commissioned a second survey of the county population by Polk-Lepson, with an even larger sample, in the year 2000. Results revealed that what more than half of respondents liked best about Lancaster County was the countryside, farmland, open space, and the rural way of life. This survey revealed an even greater concern with perceived threats of overdevelopment, sprawl, and loss of farmland to quality of life than found in the previous survey. Furthermore, a third of respondents said they felt the quality of life in Lancaster County was worse in 2000 than it had been five years earlier (Hourglass Foundation, 2001).

As further reflections of the challenge that sprawl development presents to quality of life in Lancaster County, the county has been designated on two different endangered places lists. In September 1997 the World Monument Watch included Lancaster County on its list of the 100 Most Endangered Sites in the world along with the Taj Mahal and

Angkor Wat. This listing was effective for the period 1998–2000 and later was renewed for the period 2000–2002. In a separate action, in June 1999 the National Trust for Historic Preservation designated the county as one of the 11 Most Endangered Places in the USA. The latter listing generated a great amount of discussion and debate in the county, and both the Pennsylvania Builders' Association and the National Association of Home Builders expressed objections and mounted a public relations counteroffensive.

Efforts to restrain sprawl development and to preserve farmland and the rural countryside for the future enjoyment of both residents and visitors are reflected in the goals of the Lancaster County Comprehensive Plan that dates from the 1990s. To implement the goals of the plan, the county has used such techniques as the establishment of urban and village growth boundaries and the purchase of easements on farmland. Despite the partial success of these and other techniques, sprawl development continues to be a problem in various parts of the county.

Whereas the UK and other European countries have a top-down planning system that gives government considerable authority over private land use decisions and makes it easier to prevent unwanted sprawl, the US system reflects more individualistic values and also emphasizes more of a bottom-up planning approach. Therefore, in order to implement the county comprehensive plan, county government must depend heavily on the cooperation of local governments, which have zoning and subdivision authority, and of private organizations, businesses, and individuals. Consensus building is an inherent part of successful implementation of a plan.

In 2001 Lancaster County announced a new Smart Growth initiative to help build the necessary coalition for implementing further the goals of the comprehensive plan. Smart growth is defined by the county government as growth that sustains the local economy, that enhances the livability of the community, that maintains or improves the quality of the environment, and that thereby enhances the quality of life. One of the stated themes of the Smart Growth initiative is the reduction of the sprawl development that is causing concern among many county residents.

Sprawl, overdevelopment, and loss of farmland were also mentioned as concerns in the author's late 1999 survey of tourism operators as well as in follow-up focus group meetings (for further discussion, see Hovinen, 2002). Although tourism development has contributed to overall development and to loss of farmland, it is clear that most of the sprawl and other development has taken place in other sectors of the economy. Nevertheless, if limits are not placed on such development, one of the principal reasons for visitors from large nearby metropolitan areas to choose Lancaster County as a destination will be diminished and tourism might suffer in the long run. In discussing sustainable tourism, one must therefore recognize the relationship between tourism and other sectors.

The transformation of the Amish attraction

In a diversified county tourism industry, the Amish are no longer the principal attraction as they were into the mid-1980s period. Most people who now visit on short getaway vacations or on day trips from nearby metropolitan areas have been to the county before and have experienced the Amish already. Nevertheless, the Amish and a pleasant rolling countryside of small farms still comprise important elements of the county image. The Amish and rural scenery are parts of the general environmental context of the tourist experience even as tourists today primarily undertake other activities, such as shopping, attending theater performances, and dining.

During the tourism growth years of the 1960s and 70s, there was much concern expressed about the exploitation of the Amish as unwilling tourist objects and the harm this might do to their conservative culture (Hovinen, 1982). In the past, some Amish religious leaders also expressed concern about tourism's potential to undermine authentic Amish agricultural heritage (Hovinen, 1995).

One tourism strategy that eased some of the pressure on the Amish themselves while providing opportunities for mass tourists to satisfy their curiosity about Amish lifestyles was the establishment of staged attractions such as the Amish Farm and House and the Amish Village along the main highways. These attractions gave many tourists a quick front stage experience of some aspects of Amish culture without the Amish themselves being present. They were criticized by scholars, however, as violating standards of authenticity (Hovinen, 1995). One staged attraction, the Amish Country Homestead in Bird-in-Hand, did win approval as an authentic heritage site in the 1990s county heritage program. Although the house tour does not use a building constructed or ever owned by Amish, a member of the Amish community verified that the interpretation provided an accurate view of how Amish now live. By contrast, the Amish Village is a particularly egregious example of lack of authenticity, as the Amish do not live in villages.

Even with these staged attractions helping to separate many tourists from the Amish, other tourists engaged in insensitive and offensive behavior on guided bus tours, while roaming the countryside in their own cars, or on encountering Amish conducting business in communities such as Intercourse. Not surprisingly, many Amish developed an aversion to tourism. It is therefore ironic that growing numbers of Amish in the main tourism district have not only accommodated themselves to the realities of tourism but have become active participants in it during the period of the 1990s on. Their psychological carrying capacity towards tourism has in effect been altered. Although the preferred Amish occupation is still agriculture, the shortage and high cost of land together with the natural increase of the Amish population has forced some Amish out of economic necessity to select nonagricultural occupations. Producing and selling farm products and craft items to tourists has become a means for some Amish to earn a livelihood and to remain in Lancaster County. These Amish, who generally practice a boundary maintenance strategy towards the outside world, have been pragmatically experimenting in recent years and have been cautiously shifting the boundary line in order to survive economically. Nevertheless, more conservative Amish outside the main county tourist district cling to the preferred agricultural lifestyle and frown on practices of their more liberal brethren elsewhere. What the ultimate outcome will be for tourism and for the Amish culture remains unclear (for further discussion of this issue, see Hovinen, 1995, 2002).

Some visitors to Lancaster County desire a more authentic backstage experience with the Amish, and the increasing Amish participation in tourism has accommodated them. In addition to interacting briefly with Amish children or adults selling fresh farm products or craft items such as quilts at their farms, tourists may be able to eat home-made ice cream on Amish farms or even to partake of a meal in an Amish home for a cash 'donation'. Some tourism operators and local elected officials regard eating in an Amish home as an important cultural exchange opportunity, especially for foreign visitors. In early 2002, one Amishman estimated that about 15 local Amish families provided such meal services in their homes (Smart, 2002). Often operators of bed and breakfast establishments arrange for such in-home experiences, and demand for them is growing. Certain Amish bishops have given the practice a tentative endorsement as a way for Amish farm families to supplement their income. However, state health authorities have pointed out that Amish families must be licensed to serve such group meals, just as regular restaurants are. To receive a license, an inspection of kitchen conditions must occur. Amish are unwilling to subject themselves to such government authority and intrusion of their privacy. So generally such arranged meals have been handled rather secretly. The issue came to a head in the summer of 2001 when a group of tourists who had just left Lancaster County became ill and some had to be hospitalized with a bacterial infection. To avoid a major fine, the Amish family in question had to promise not to serve home-based meals again. Despite this, some local elected officials argue that in general Amish kitchens are very clean and that the importance of the cultural exchange is a strong argument for excluding the Amish from the licensing requirements (Smart, 2002).

The tourism industry and sustainable tourism

In order for a tourism destination to remain competitive and thereby to support the goal of achieving sustainable tourism, the tourism industry should emphasize unique attractions rather than relying mainly on standardized and 'artificial' attractions imported from the outside. One long-term strength of county tourism has been the unique Amish population with their distinctive culture. But to sustain tourism at a high level of visitation it is necessary to develop additional unique attractions. This has been one of the goals of the Lancaster County heritage tourism program since its inception in the mid-1990s.

Two recent examples of attempts to foster new unique heritage attractions may be noted. The first involves rediscovering Lancaster's role in the planning of the Lewis and Clark expedition across the North American continent from 1803 to 1806. The second involves the proposed designation of a new historic site in the center of Lancaster City to emphasize the role of a prominent pre-Civil War era congressman as an early civil rights advocate. Neither one alone is likely to make much difference in county tourist numbers or revenues, but together with other existing and potential attractions each could help sustain tourism. The Visitors Bureau has been invited by private nonprofit organizations, as part of an evolving public–private partnership arrangement, to help promote the first of these initiatives, whereas a private nonprofit organization is the sponsor of the second.

Captain Meriwether Lewis, an aide to President Thomas Jefferson, spent three weeks in Lancaster in the spring of 1803. In Lancaster he received training form Andrew Ellicott, Secretary of the State Land Office and one of the country's foremost mathematicians, astronomers, and land surveyors, in the use of scientific instruments for accurately determining latitude and longitude on the journey of discovery to the Pacific Coast. Lancaster was the capital of Pennsylvania at this time.

The Bicentennial of the Lewis and Clark expedition will be held from 2003 to 2006 and will involve communities from the Atlantic to the Pacific. Given Lancaster's important role in the initial planning of the voyage, a public–private partnership of organizations is planning a series of exhibits and events, including one in the house where Lewis and Ellicott worked. By publicizing the planned activities in brochures and on a web site, the Visitors Bureau and the county government hope that visitors will come and learn more about this colorful part of American history. At the same time, they may also be exposed to the variety of other heritage attractions that the county has to offer.

The proposed Thaddeus Stevens and Lydia Hamilton Smith historic site in the center of Lancaster would educate visitors about an abolitionist attorney and later congressman who helped finance a spy network to infiltrate slaveholder groups that tried to track fugitive slaves escaping the South. His housekeeper and confidante, who lived in an adjoining house to the Stevens law office (both proposed for restoration), assisted escaping slaves. She also encouraged Stevens' efforts as a congressman to ratify two important amendments to the US Constitution granting full rights of citizenship to newly freed blacks after the Civil War. The Historic Preservation Trust of Lancaster has commissioned an economic impact study that estimates annual visitation to a proposed museum and revenues that it might generate. As of September 2002, the Trust anticipated that the historic site would complement a planned convention center adjacent to it and would generate some visitors therefrom. In 2001 the Lancaster County Convention Center Authority, which is planning the convention center, had thought it easier simply to remove the historic buildings in question from the site. However, the Historic Preservation Trust eventually succeeded in signing an agreement with the convention center authority to preserve the historic buildings. In September 2002 new plans for the convention center were in preparation, emphasizing respect for the existing streetscape and incorporation of historic structures. An architectural design firm also hopes to incorporate elements of the indigenous architecture of downtown Lancaster into the appearance of the planned convention center facility.

The planning process for the new Lancaster–York Heritage Region can also help make tourism more sustainable. One of the most important heritage resources of Lancaster County and neighboring York County that tourists find attractive is their agricultural landscape and the related farming activities. Of five heritage themes identified in the plan for the two-county heritage region, one is 'foodways: from farm to table' (Mary Means & Associates, 2001: 28–37). A grant from the state of Pennsylvania and contributions from the two counties' visitor bureaus are helping to finance an agritourism initiative. The Lancaster County Planning Commission is coordinating the effort. In August 2002 representatives of public and private organizations from both counties, working in a collaborative partnership, approved plans for a regional interpretive and informational guide and corresponding website. The guide and website were completed by 2003 and interpret regional agricultural heritage and list farm markets, historic downtown markets, roadside market stands, pick-your-own operations, wineries, and other sites where homegrown fresh or processed food can be purchased directly from the farmer.

Agarwal's (1994, 2002) proposed reorientation stage and restructuring alternatives are relevant to the tourism planning efforts noted above. There is recognition in Lancaster County that tourism is a mature industry and that a certain amount of renewal is necessary to prevent overall decline and to sustain moderate growth. Restructuring alternatives evident in the efforts discussed so far include new investment and product specialization (proposed downtown Lancaster convention center), repositioning by emphasizing unique heritage and environmental attributes, further diversification, preservation of the built and natural environment, and collaboration (initiation of joint public–private sector ventures).

In contrast to the aforementioned state-supported heritage planning programs where the initiative for a public–private sector venture has come mainly from government, the impetus for yet another potential tourism planning effort has come from within the tourism industry itself. As this is the first time a proposal for a long-range proactive planning process has originated from within the tourism industry, it is especially significant.

In early 2002 a secret task force, consisting of a half dozen members of the tourism industry with a long-range perspective, emerged. The task force was initiated by a local tourism operator who is very familiar with the TALC model and who is concerned with the potential for future decline in county tourism if strategic long-range planning and restructuring do not occur. This businessman contacted one of the elected county commissioners to attempt to gain his support for a collaborative tourism planning effort.

In June 2002 the author was invited to attend a meeting of this task force to discuss the TALC model and the need for long-range strategic planning. One prominent topic discussed at this meeting was how to achieve a more sustainable tourism. The author presented various ways of looking at sustainable tourism and tourism planning and advocated a planning approach based on broad-based community input and recognizing the interdependence of the tourism sector and other economic sectors. Members of the task force, including the county commissioner and the president of the Visitors Bureau, generally expressed support for the ideals espoused at the meeting. In a succeeding session held in July 2002 a tourism consultant from outside the local area met with the task force to help lay the groundwork for a tourism planning effort.

At the time of this writing, the success of this venture is uncertain. There are considerable political and economic risks to such a plan. The current intention of the task force is to announce the proposed tourism plan to the media and to members of the Visitors Bureau at a later date. It is possible that some tourism operators might then question the need for such a tourism plan. Overall political support for the plan from within the tourism industry and from other sectors of the economy would be important, as would be some financial support from the county government. Considering the county government recently announced cutbacks in budgets for 2003, whether it will be able to provide the financial support desired is questionable. Other sources of funding will have to be explored, including the willingness and ability of the Visitors Bureau to finance part of the planning effort.

Obstacles to sustainable tourism within the tourism industry

Despite the evidence that parts of the tourism industry have begun to show support for long-range tourism planning efforts, major obstacles to sustainable tourism remain within the industry. Most tourism operators have little understanding of the role of long-range tourism planning and remain focused on their short-term business operations supplemented by the Visitor Bureau's annual marketing campaigns. The author's study of Lancaster County tourism at the end of the 1990s (Hovinen, 2002) revealed considerable divisiveness within the industry. Tourism owners have widely varying viewpoints about a number of issues affecting tourism growth. Owners often disagree with Visitors Bureau staff about the causes of stagnation or decline of individual businesses. The former tend to blame ineffective marketing and promotion by the Visitors Bureau, whereas the latter point to the reluctance of many operators to reinvest in new products or in improved facilities and service quality. Therefore, developing a consensus within the industry for a long-range tourism plan will be a major challenge.

A recent example of bitter divisiveness within the tourism industry is the legal battle between 11 hoteliers and sponsors of a new Marriott Hotel and associated public convention center in downtown Lancaster. The proposed hotel–convention center project is an example of a public–private partnership in an attempt to revitalize the city's downtown and to make the city and its important heritage resources a stronger tourism destination. Plans call for the hotel to occupy space in a former department store and thereby preserve century-old architectural heritage. Sponsors hope the project will attract a new, more affluent market segment of convention visitors to spend money in the city and become aware of its attractions. The Visitors Bureau has officially supported the project, which is financed in part by a new hotel/motel room tax that began in January 2000. The Visitors Bureau and its members had for many years opposed such a tax, but a portion of the tax collected now helps support the Bureau's annual tourism marketing.

In March 2000 the 11 hoteliers began a legal challenge to the fairness of the tax, claiming that it in effect subsidized their potential competitors. The Marriott Hotel that would be developed by a consortium of three private businesses would share some space and facilities with the public convention center financed by the room tax and a potential $15 million state grant, lawyers for the hoteliers have argued in court. Therefore, they maintained, the private hotel would in effect be subsidized with public funds and would compete unfairly against hotels and motels in suburban locations. The fact that several of these suburban hotels had conference facilities was the basis for another claim of unfair public subsidies of a public convention center that would compete against private facilities.

The complicated and often bitter legal battle has dragged on for 2½ years. Sponsors and supporters of the public convention center project have often complained in the local media that the hoteliers who have filed legal challenge after challenge are simply trying to kill an important project. The Marriott Corporation has threatened to withdraw from its agreement to manage the privately built hotel if construction cannot begin by March 2003. The large state grant for construction of the convention center cannot be tapped until the legal challenges are resolved. In July 2002 the Pennsylvania Supreme Court rendered an important decision in favor of the public convention center by declaring that the disputed room tax for financing the convention center was constitutional. Such room taxes for public purposes are in fact common in the USA. The Supreme Court sent two other issues of fairness back to a lower state court for resolution, and lawyers for the hoteliers filed additional arguments against the project shortly thereafter. So the future of this project, which exemplifies several of Agarwal's (2002) suggested restructuring alternatives, remained unclear at the time of writing.

Conclusion

This case study has shown that a tourism cycle has been progressing in Lancaster County, although not always in the ways Butler hypothesized in his 1980 TALC model.

Earlier stages of exploration, involvement, and development with many of the characteristics suggested by Butler in his 1980 formulation are clearly discernible. But the county tourism industry is now mature and highly diversified, and problems arise when trying to fit the tourism trends of the past quarter century to Butler's assumptions of a progression to later stages of consolidation, stagnation, and then either possible decline or complete rejuvenation.

In the diversified and essentially culturally based tourism destination of Lancaster County, different sectors of tourism (older versus newer attractions, variety of accommodations, shopping alternatives, chain versus local restaurants) have combined to create what is now a mature industry where growth, stagnation, decline, and revitalization through reinvestment or new investment coexist. One tourism sector, or a portion of a sector, may have results in a given year that contrast with those of another sector. The different elements of tourism can be said to have their own individual life cycles. Some individual businesses thrive in a given year while others stagnate or even decline. An owner of an accommodations facility, for example reported to the author record results for the first six months of 2002 at the same time that some traditional attractions experienced stagnation (personal communication, August 2002). The overall industry may exhibit fluctuating growth patterns year to year based on a complex combination of internal and external factors. A temporary decline, for example, may be followed by a growth spurt as happened when the major attraction Sight and Sound was destroyed by fire and then rebuilt. A number of county tourism businesses apparently benefited in the first half of 2002 from the tendency of many Americans to prefer destinations that they could easily drive to in the new age of terrorism. Such are the characteristics of what the author has termed the 'mature' stage of county tourism.

Butler's TALC model suggests the potential for overall decline of a tourism destination exists if effective long-range planning to address problems and competitive challenges does not take place, thus the prospects for creating a more sustainable tourism in Lancaster County through long-range planning have been discussed in this chapter. The creation of several existing or potential public–private partnerships for long-range planning since the mid-1990s suggest the partial applicability of Agarwal's (1994) proposed reorientation stage as well as at least one of her proposed restructuring alternatives. However, the possible emergence of such a stage in Lancaster County has not followed a clearly defined stagnation stage as Agarwal suggested.

Chapter 6

An Empirical Interpretation of the TALC: Tourist Product Life Cycles in the Eastern Townships of Quebec

JAN O. LUNDGREN

Introduction

Tourist development has been a major focus of scholarly research for over two generations. Contributions have come primarily from environmental and social sciences, basically starting with W. Hunziker's famous, and interdisciplinary 'Tourism Doctrine', published in 1942, and W. Christaller's 'Beiträge zu einer Geographie der Fremdenverkehr' in 1955. Over the decades since, the writings have become both more voluminous and diverse, hardly surprising considering the consistent and vigorous growth in tourism after 1950. Some 60 million international tourist arrivals were recorded in 1960. Today, at the start of the Second Millennium, international travel volume stands at around 700 million, an 11-fold increase (WTO, 2001). In addition, recognising the dominant and massive domestic tourist travel volumes predominantly found in the countries of the Western world pushes the aggregate annual global (tourist) travel volume to levels between 2.5 and 3.0 billion.

Given the above, there is no surprise that the relationship between aggregate tourist travel demand/tourist destination area system (TDAS) is often strained, resulting in detrimental impacting consequences for many TDAS (Turner & Ash, 1974), and, more importantly, to their respective tourist attraction(s) – the geographically definable tourist product (Smith, 1994). The saying '...die Zerstörung der Turismus durch Turismus...' (Krippendorf, 1975), coined in the mid-1970s, when tourist travel volumes were much smaller, still holds.

Placing the Tourist Development Process in a Conceptual Context

Negative environmental consequences of modern tourism were recognised in the early 1970s – in overvisited national parks and popular nature reserves, mushrooming seaside resorts along the Mediterranean coastline (Ambio, 1977), in packed winter resorts – especially in Europe, and in popular small resort islands, notably in the West Indies (Ambio, 1981). Through the skilful pedagogical conceptualisation of TDA development dynamics by Butler (1980), the implications of unfettered tourism-based TDA development were brought to the forefront of the debate and the 'Tourism Area Life Cycle' (TALC) model was born (Figure 6.1).

Simplified, the TALC model pits two principal variables against each other: the open-ended, market-driven 'growth' factor, slowly rising, then quickly accelerating, but eventually stagnating *a la* W. Rostow's stages-of-economic-growth concept (1960); or the typical marketing/product life cycle (Kotler & Turner, 1993). The 'exploitation-of-limited-resources' variable demonstrates how the development reaches a 'critical range of elements of capacity', which initiates the decline in the capability of the TDA to 'handle'/'absorb' additional tourist influxes (Butler, 1980). This stage often activates secondary and third-rate under-used attractions, which invariably set the TDA on the road toward an increasingly destructive marginality. As the aggregate TDA components face diminishing returns, the development grinds to a halt and usually enters a stage of decline.

The critical factor in the TALC model centres on tourist resource depletion through excessive use. Viewed in the context of today's debate on the pros and cons of tourism-based development, it brings us to concepts not properly parlayed by scholars in the early 1980s. 'Sustainable (tourism-based) development', as emphasised in the Brundtland Commission report on Our Common Future (1987), and 'ecotourism' or

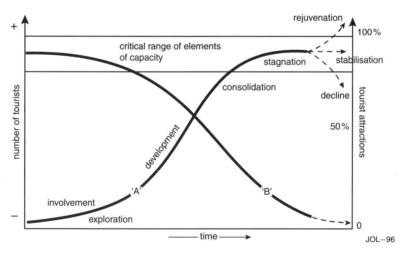

Figure 6.1 Tourist area cycle of evolution (modified from Butler, 1980)

'soft' tourism development were concepts still waiting in the wings (Smith & Eadington, 1994; see also Butler, this volume).

Product Life Cycles and their Spatial Consequences

Butler's model is not a complicated conceptualisation, and therein lies its beauty. Almost a quarter-century old, the TALC is still applied in tourism development case studies, sometimes as a benchmark device, sometimes as a conceptual framework for a more detailed tourism development study, invariably resulting in further fine-tuning of the model, or adding new aspects to the original. The model can easily be complemented with the notion of sequential tourist product (TP) developments (Figure 6.2), which would better reflect the innovative spirit of emerging 'new products', which is frequently stressed in marketing research (Kotler & Turner, 1993; see also Coles & Hall, other volume, editor's comment). In the typical physical production enterprise an 'older', well established on-line product (1) and a 'nascent' new product development cycle (2) often operate side by side. The dynamics of the auto industry, the fashion industry or the hectic consumer electronics company provide examples of this 'parallel' strategy of continuous product development/marketing and ongoing, new product development. Overlapping product cycles interact (Figure 6.2), with the activation of Product 2 dependent upon the duration of successful sales/profit performance of Product 1.

The 'product parallelism' described above also happens in tourism development, where new TDA complementary 'attraction products'

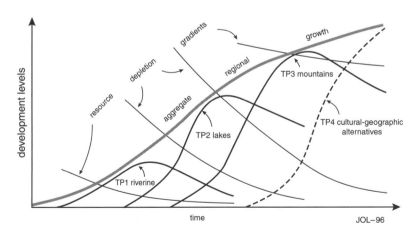

Figure 6.2 Multiple tourist product evolution/exploitation cycles (modified from Kotler & Turner, 1993)

often are grafted onto a well established older one. This has been the case at alpine ski centres that often broaden their market appeal by providing for cross-country skiing, as can be seen at Mt. Orford (Quebec), Stowe (Vermont) or Jasper National Park (Alberta). In a similar vein, the recent construction of a snowboarding 'half pipe' at Owl's Head and many other ski resorts may attract more of the younger snow boarder market clientele. Adding mountain biking during the summer season would obviously represent a 'third' TP cycle, thus making the same mountain destination a profit source even during the hitherto quieter summer season.

Objectives of Study

Sometimes, however, completely new, extra-regional 'tourism products' having little, if any, obvious local affinity with existing tourist attractions emerge, sometimes by accident, and succeed over time in countering stagnating trends experienced by the older attraction. The new TP often has different location characteristics, and therefore produces major shifts in the region's overall tourist geography. The phenomenon of successive new TP cycles in the Eastern Townships (ET) region of Quebec constitutes the principal focus of this review, especially as they relate to the modified TALC model (Figure 6.2). Thus, within the overall regional tourist development, we should be able to observe sequentially layered product cycles *a la* Kotler and Turner, representing diverse, new forms of tourism entering the region.

As a consequence of the introduction of new products, we should also be able to observe a successive and healthy regional TP diversification, which in turn should strengthen regional economic stability, reduce seasonality and partly lower excessive visitor pressures at already developed TP destinations. A final aspect relates to the layers of spatial impacting brought about by the new product cycles that tend to be much less dependent upon specific landscape features. Instead of a TDA having a comparative competitive advantage based on the effective verticals in the topography – typical for alpine ski hill sites – the 'new products' may rely upon completely different factors – unique individual talent, person-to-person interaction, idyllic geographic settings with local ambiance, cultural appeal, a sense of place, local history or combinations thereof. Consequently, to anticipate impacting patterns of new TPs becomes difficult, as they usually are spontaneous rather than planned creations.

Geographical Characteristics of the Study Region

Before analysing the specifics of the different TP life cycles, we must recognise some general landscape characteristics. Basically, the area being discussed is a subregion of the ET in southern Quebec, which broadly encompasses a west-to-east rectangular area. It is bound in the West by the Richelieu River, in the South by the USA/Canada border, and stretches some 100 km eastward to the Sherbrooke–Coaticook–USA border line. The northern limit follows the 140 km long Eastern Townships Autoroute (Figure 6.3), the principal road artery linking Montreal (3 million) to the City of Magog (15,000) and Sherbrooke (100,000).

The region features a gentle downward tilting, northbound extension of the US Appalachian mountains consisting of parallel mountain ridges separated by valleys and elevated plateaus. Starting east of Farnham, the terrain softly rises from the St. Lawrence Plain and becomes more dramatic. CLICOR (Canada Land Inventory Capability for Outdoor Recreation 1971) diligently registers this in the identified landscape scores, that stretch from an omnipresent Class Six (Low Capability) on the Plain via typical Class Five (Moderately Low) to more numerous patches of higher scores, Class Four (Moderate Capability), eventually reaching terrains with Class Three (Moderately High Capability) as well as a few Class Two/One (High/Very High) sites.

Three top-scoring locales demonstrate distinct tourist potentials: the Mt. Sutton and Mt. Orford Station-de-Ski areas and Provincial Park, and the spacious beach strip west of Magog; all are Class One. Impressive mountain topography (800 m elevations) and stretches of fine lakeshore

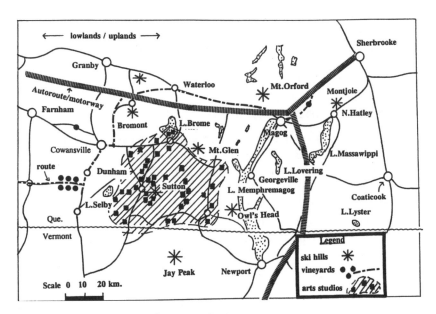

Figure 6.3 Eastern townships tourist resources

always produce top scoring sites – and attract developments. The central part of the study region features numerous mountain peaks with the essential effective verticals of 400–500 m, which would automatically condition their present vocation as alpine ski centres (Figure 6.3).

The climate is 'typical' for southern Quebec – continental, with pleasant winters in its more easterly part, notably east of Granby-Bromont-Cowansville-Dunham, where the 'stable' snow line begins. This guarantees good ski conditions for the seven alpine ski centres (see Figure 6.3), with a business season starting around Christmas and closing in early April. Summers are warm with July day temperatures in the 20–25°C range, usually including two or three week-long heatwaves with temperatures around 30°C. Cooler night temperatures compensate for the daytime heat.

The landscape characteristics also relate to settlement history. The study region has a long settlement history dating back to the 1790s, when United Empire Loyalists moved north, away from republican USA, settling most of the region (Bullock, 1926). This has ensured a particular regional distinctiveness: substantial forest areas alternate with extensive tracts of rolling meadows and cultivated lands; rural New England styled villages and farms invitingly dot the landscape; small but diverse industrial (mill) towns at the edge of rivers with manageable, modest waterfalls offer an interesting industrial cultural heritage; the original predominance of English-speaking settlers and their descendants has diminished in the past century – today's regional population is mostly francophone, but the historical anglophone ethnic/cultural heritage is strong and comes through as a distinct tourist attraction; the region is uniquely and comfortable bilingual, the latter further reinforced by cross-border interaction with neighbouring USA.

Development Characteristics

The background to this review rests on observations by those that have closely followed the region's tourist history. In principle, the traditional bases for early tourist development were in most cases more or less fully exploited, in an accelerating tempo, only in the last 25 years (Fritz-Nemeth & Lundgren, 1996; Lundgren, 1988; Nadeau, 1989). However, reviewing the historical and regional application of the modified TALC tourist development concept, one can observe a clear succession of distinct TP life cycles. It is this regionally based spatial TP succession that constitutes the interpretative part of this study. Thus, below follows a discussion of the TP life cycles experienced by the region, and the extent to which their respective development dynamics relate to the TALC model.

Traditional TP cycles: Riverine and lakeshore tourism developments

Certain types of tourism were responsible for carrying the overall development process over long periods of time. Among these, riverine- and lakeshore-based tourism were early initiators, with their cycles starting in the 1840s, when transport access saw some improvement, but also when a more substantial wealthy urban market segment started to emerge in major urban tourist-generating locales – Montreal in particular. Steamship services along the Richelieu River corridor in the West already operating in 1845 helped to bring in the first tourists. This aided both riverine cottage development and the establishment of commercial tourist resort operations in the foothills of Mont St. Hilaire and at the Fort Chambly rapids (Tulchinsky, 1977). The Lake Memphremagog basin, some 110 km further east, an area hardly accessible at all until the arrival of the railway in the 1850s (to Sherbrooke) and the early 1860s (to Newport, Vermont) also saw major facility developments. The lakeshore Mountain House Hotel at Owl's Head Mountain (1847) catering to the US market was followed three years later by the private Hermitage Club located halfway between Magog and Georgeville on the eastern shore – still thriving 150 years later.

Steamship services gradually integrated otherwise small lakeshore settlements more effectively (Story of Magog, 1951) starting already in the 1850s, with major economic consequences. Thus, both the resorts above, and the two principal urban centres on the lake, Magog, Quebec at its northern tip, and Newport, Vermont in the South, became hubs in a dynamic 'lake economy', with tourism traffic being an important, albeit seasonal, component.

However, a more modern transport infrastructure was needed before the lakeshore-based cottage TP2 cycle (Figure 6.2) could take off. The main bottleneck problem disappeared with the 1859 inauguration of the Victoria Bridge, spanning the St. Lawrence from Montreal, plus an energetic eastbound railway construction programme (Booth, 1982; Briere, 1967). The 1870s saw strategic southbound rail connections effected with the New England rail network (Meeks, 1986, see Figure 6.4). As a result, the US market emerged as an important player in Eastern Townships' tourism development. Thus, well before the turn of the century, the tourist development could forcefully converge upon numerous appealing lakeshores – Brome Lake and Selby Lake, the Mt. Orford Lakes, Lake Massawippi further east – but above all, upon the magnificent Lake Memphremagog.

For each lake, where rail access played an important role, a powerful market-driven 'lake shore cottage subdivision encirclement process' was initiated (Bullock, 1926), a linear land/cottage occupancy process similar

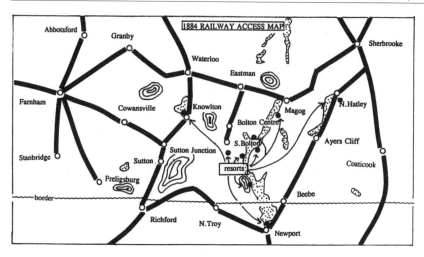

Figure 6.4 1884 Railway access map

to modern urban sprawl roadside subdivisions. It started in earnest in the 1870s but reached its conclusion a century later, between 1975 and 1990 (see Lake Memphremagog 1:50,000 Topographic Map Sheets, 1917–2000 editions). With the final stage in the lakeshore cottage exploitation concluded, the encirclement had succeeded in effectively closing the earlier informally functioning para-public lake access for the larger year-round residential populations. Only occasional fortunate compensations partly remedied the situation, notably for the City of Magog, which in the 1980s secured land for an extensive, new municipal public beach complementing the older public town beach. However, for most lakeshore municipalities, public access to their lakeshore was usually reduced to a few points around the lake. The most popular of summer pastimes – 'going to the public beach' – was practically history. The same extra-regional tourist demand resulted in the advent of steamship services on the lake. Influential outsider Sir Hugh Allen of Allen Steamship Line of Montreal initiated this crucial enterprise, which more than any other transport provision contributed in integrating the 'lakescape' as a major tourist attraction (Potton Heritage Association, 1993, North Troy, Vermont, Public Library Historical File).

As a consequence, small and large commercial lakeshore resort facilities sprang up in strategic locations, sometimes in beautiful lakeshore sites, and sometimes near the two major urban centres on the lake (Wall & Marsh, 1982). Time and fire, however, seem to have been the common destructive agents at work for many of these large wooden encampments. With few exceptions they are now all gone. What remains in terms of concentration of resort facility development can best be seen at the North Hatley end of Lake Massawippi, which to this day retains a reputation as a high-quality resort tourist village, probably one of the most idyllic in Quebec, and gastronomically one of the finest. Hatley Inn, Hovey Manor and Ripplecove Inn are principal magnets for this part of the region.

The final stage of cottage-derived market pressures occurred quite late in the development cycle, primarily in the 1980s and early 1990s, with the introduction of major capital-intensive 'high density' lakeshore cottage/condominium projects. These exploitations often originated with discreet partial acquisitions by the developer of agricultural properties with substantial shoreline frontage, which, after zoning bylaw modifications had been secured, were developed in a large scale. Villa de l'Anse on the eastern shore of Lake Memphremagog, halfway between Magog and Georgeville, as well as the Owl's Head condominium and hotel project on the lake's western shore, are typical. Similar high density projects are common elsewhere as well: outside Magog, adjacent to the large Plage Municipal, also with a wide range of direct and indirect impacting consequences; and at other lakes in the region, notably the Inverness development on Brome Lake.

Presently, the cottage-based lakeshore TP life cycle has reached its physical carrying capacity limits on most lakes as the encirclement process has run its course. The rate of exploitation has dropped. However, lakeshore property is frequently changing ownership, which often triggers large-scale urban-styled rebuilding projects of older, quaint cottage residences, which suggests that lakeshore cycle dynamics are not completely dead.

Nodal tourist resources: The mountain locales

In contrast to the lakeshores, the TP3 life cycle is based on site-specific characteristics in the physical landscape – the 'mountainscape' and its topographical dimensions. Thus, we deal with a nodal resource, both in appearance and in touristic usage. The Clawson and Knetch (1966) classification of outdoor recreational lands comes to mind, with its differentiation between 'user-oriented resources' and 'resource-based' outdoor recreational areas. The former defines multipurpose outdoor recreation terrains such as sports fields or certain types of (urban) parklands while the latter tends to rely upon some outstanding physical landscape attributes that predetermine one or two kinds of specific outdoor recreational usage. 'Landscape specificity', then, is the key. This gives the TP3 cycle a good fit with the 'ski hill development process', a relatively late arrival on the tourism scene, in the early 1960s.

The CLICOR (1971) landscape differentiation of the study region identifies numerous 'above average' mountains with adequate slope angle, good orientation and effective verticals (calculated from base elevation to mountain summit), that usually have attracted ski hill developers and the establishment of fully fledged alpine ski centres. The existence today of seven ski hill operations – eight including nearby Jay Peak in Vermont – attests to the excellent site potentials for such developments (see Figure 6.2). The cycle as such, however, hides a much longer incubation time than that which meets the eye.

Prior to the advent of modern alpine skiing, which developed around 1930 in the Austrian Alps, Canadian mountain tourism was a summer pastime involving fresh air, nature discovery, hiking and mountain climbing. Any change over to ski-based mountain winter tourism required, out of necessity, a lengthy introductory learning stage, as skiing hardly was an indigenous winter sport. Therefore, even with the first integrated alpine/downhill ski centres opening up and demonstrably being successful in the mid 1930s in the Montreal Laurentians, it took time to activate the market. In fact, the ET region was 30 years *behind* the Laurentians in discovering and launching alpine skiing. This delayed start is remarkable and can only partially be explained by the fact that the Laurentians had access by autoroute and passenger rail services around 1960, however, the first alpine ski centres were established already before WWII, even the least accessible of them all, Mt. Tremblant, which opened for the winter season of 1938/39. The ET region had good access, with railways crisscrossing the landscape well before WWI (Railway Access Map, 1884), to no avail for ski resort development, which did feature early, but hardly in a commercially viable form (an alpine ski facility was established at Mt. Orford in 1938 (Nadeau, 1989).

The true start of TP3 and the full-scale commercial alpine ski development cycle is well known. The year was 1959 and the place was Sutton. The reason was to develop a complementary winter season income for the Belanger family's very seasonal dairy business. The rapid succession of ski centres that followed was remarkable: Mt. Orford (1962), Mt. Glen (1963), Bromont (1964), Mt. Echo (1964), Owl's Head (1965), Jay Peak, Vermont, USA (1956) – the latter functioning with its own, unique cycle – an overall almost explosive regional capital investment and development sequence within a geographically quite confined area; the centres are a half hour's car drive from each other. Except for Mt. Echo, all centres still operate, admittedly sometimes saved through opportune refinancing actions. By virtue of survival, they have now for over 40 years been impacting both their respective mountains and their surroundings, physically, economically and socially. To the above seven should be added two modest places – the recently renovated Montjoie ski centre outside North Hatley, and the equally neighbourhood-oriented centre at Shefford Mountain across the autoroute from Bromont, equidistant between the towns of Granby (45,000 inh.) and Waterloo (5000 inh.).

The convergence of major tourist traffic flows toward the centres have resulted in major local impacting due to the service multiplier factor, almost immediately triggered in order to make each centre properly equipped to meet the service demands from the ever-increasing visitor volumes (Nadeau, 1989). These include trail maintenance and artificial snowmaking, base lodge facilities with food, beverage and after-ski services, ski rentals and ski schools, sports boutiques, and, given the above-average site quality, diverse accommodation: hotels, condominiums, chalets and smaller pensions.

Further, if locations possess summer potential, the opportunity has existed for 'diversifying out' of winter season dependency by converting the locales into year-round resort operations. This has been done at Mt. Orford with the lakeshore city of Magog and its waterfront a 10-minute drive away, and at Owl's Head, with its all-important lake access, apartment hotel and an 18-hole championship golf course. But places deficient on the important point of lake access have diversified also – Bromont and Mt. Sutton today offer mountain biking, tennis, golf and spa services, while others such as Montjoie (North Hatley) and Mt. Glen (Knowlton) benefit from nearby, picturesque village services. The same applies to a degree also for Mt. Sutton with Sutton village in the valley below.

Since 1959 the TP3 cycle has run its course, responding to the seemingly inexhaustible alpine ski demand generated by the metropolitan Montreal market area, and the more distant Lake Ontario urban conglomeration, as well as smaller local towns on both sides of the Canada/USA border. Today, little remains in terms of expansion potential of the basic TP3 phenomenon, although mountains with the essential effective vertical minimum of 500 m still exist. However, the increasingly unreliable winter season may make investor-developers hesitant. Extra-regional competition is greater – from the Laurentians in the North with Intrawest's massive Mont Tremblant expansion, from the Canadian Rockies, and snow-rich Quebec City and Charlevoix in the East. Also, snow boarders do not necessarily need a big mountain-challenging obstacle – designed half-pipe courses do the trick. The threat of global warming might also drive the market northward to more reliable winter seasons (Wall, 1998). Also, the physical impact of mountain developments may be less acceptable in our modern era of environmental–ecological concern. Therefore, any new alpine ski centre developments in the region must be considered unrealistic. The growth dynamics of the TP3 cycle are over.

The Contemporary Era, New TPs, New Cycles

The break with past TP cycles and the injection into the region of new sets of TPs hardly occur at a revolutionary tempo. Rather than the gradual consolidation and stagnation of the resource-based TP3 cycle, regional economic restructuring and a quickening demise of more traditional regional economic sectors – agriculture, and the historically famous regional industrial sector with roots in the small-scale industry developed in the early 1800s – have assisted the easing in of the new. TP2 and TP3 were both spent forces lacking in dynamics toward the end of the 1970s. Hence, if any new tourist-derived regional dynamics were to occur in the TALC model (Figure 6.2), alternative tourism ventures had to emerge. Three new TPS have been selected for analysis in order to demonstrate how new TP cycles become reality and how they differ from the older, more resource-dependent cases discussed so far.

Institutional facilities as tourist attractions

Some embryos for new tourism and new TPs have been regionally rooted for many decades, but their presence was on a very minor scale – diverse cultural institutions, often historical museums, usually supported by enthusiastic local historical societies. The official 2000 Eastern Townships Tourist Guide and the Repertoire de la Societe des Musees Quebecois list some 15 museums, among which the historical museums stand out as the most serious and most resilient enterprises, some not even new, as they date back to the 1920s.

Mississquoi Historical Society Museum (in Stanbridge East), Brome County Historical Society Museum (in Knowlton village) and the Stanstead Historical Society's Colby-Curtis Museum in Stanstead belong to the historical group, all three located in quaint villages. Geographically, their locations are interesting as no deliberate act of planning has been at work, but rather individual local initiatives – and 'luck'! Hence, they can only benefit from proximity to other, popular tourist attractions: near Dunham's popular vineyards ('the Mississquoi'), in idyllic and historic Knowlton village ('Brome County'), and in the urban core of well established and historically stylish Stanstead next to a very busy US border crossing. In contrast, and in addition to the 'historical' institutions, is the modern entrepreneurial/industrial snowmobile inventiveness, the forte behind the Musee Bombardier in off-beat Valcourt, the birthplace of inventor Armand Bombardier, some distance north of the ET autoroute.

Industrial cultural heritage milieus (Fritz-Nemeth & Lundgren, 1996) have in many cases constituted a different basis for the development of outdoor attractions – The Gorge and waterfalls in downtown Coaticook, the renovated turn-of-the-century industrial milieu on the St. Francis river rapids section in central Sherbrooke, and the Stanbridge East mill pond complex are examples of how early regional industrialisation outside the major Canadian urban centres have been 'redesigned' into touristic lures.

The tourist attractions discussed above have very few linkages to the previously discussed TP1-2-3, except for the fact that they cohabit regionally, and consequently benefit from overall convenient access for the touring excursionist.

Rural agricultural attractions

The bucolic ET landscape is constantly referred to in guide books and in conversations with tourists as the principal tourist asset, offering distinctly different seasonal attractions. The rapid post-WWII development boom brought increased societal prosperity which boosted car ownership, which in turn improved spatial mobility for the population at large (CORD Surveys 1969–72). In a regional context, the role of the Montreal population as a tourist-generator and the upgrading of the road system increasingly benefited the whole of the ET region. Touring and day excursion travelling into the region is very much a function of the natural assets. These include apple blossom trips in springtime toward Freligsburgh on the US border, vineyards visits (see Figure 6.3) in Summer and Fall to the popular Dunham area and the recently promoted 150-km long vineyard route (Chemin des Vignobles pamphlet), popular back road bicycling, lake/beach outings in provincial parks, early-Fall U-pick orchard visits or glorious foliage tours, and in winter the design-sharp scenic winter landscape and winter sports.

In this multiseasonal way of recreational/touristic opportunities, the vineyards stand out, for two reasons. First, they represent the beginning of a distinctly new TP cycle, suddenly initiated in 1979, in the Dunham area, basically an apple orchard district south of Cowansville. Second, from at first being a seasonal (harvest-time) attraction, they have extended their appeal to most of the year, winter being the exception. With a three-season spread, the annual visitor volume has grown fast; today's estimate is close to 100,000 (conversations with Dunham vineyard owners, 2000), proof enough of the popularity of the Dunham area as a weekend- or day-excursion destination.

The economic impacting process is spatially very concentrated – the vineyard area is just a 3–4-km country road stretch offering a diverse range of visitor services, wine tasting, restaurant services, picnicking, food/wine boutiques, and crafts and souvenirs, with considerable vertical business integration. Calculating only the basic $5 expense for a wine tasting at the five or six establishments produces only some $500,000 in annual gross sales, but there is clearly more than bottled wines sold, such as foodstuffs and lunches. Economic leakages exist, but still a large portion of the first, second and third round of expenditures remain in the vineyards area and adjacent Dunham village. The vertical integration and local entrepreneurship assure this.

The vineyards seldom operate as a single destination; they are 'stops-en-route', together with many others, all often part of a systematically organised day of touring featuring historical museums, fine art exhibitions, a local summer festival or a theatre matinee, and walking tours.

The artist: A dispersed persona attraction

The fact that the landscape appeal of the ET has manifested itself in the Canadian arts world for almost 200 years leads to the most recent TP development cycle – the artist's studio/the artist's world/the artist's products. The famous historical landscape etchings by W.H. Bartlett date back to the 1830s and early 1840s (JETS, Spring, 1996). Thus, already then, the artist's visual sensuality had discovered the dominating grandeur of Lake Memphremagog with its string of quaint shoreline settlements. Later, in the 1870s, other Canadian painters like E.A. Edson and J.A. Fraser produced panoramic landscape art of still recognisable scenic vistas.

Thus, the artists' local presence is hardly a 'new' TP (Christaller, 1964). However, today's presence is not just of occasional artists, but of coteries of painters, who, together with skilful and talented arts-and-crafts professionals, represent an interesting case of a spontaneous, unstructured recent TP development. Through the formation of loosely organised associations, they have become major tourist attractions and have, jointly, instigated an intensive and vigorous new TP cycle.

The oldest coterie is that of the 'Tour-des-Arts' (TdA), started in 1988, with some 40 artist members (TdA 2002 pamphlet), all opening the doors of their studios/ateliers to the general public during a hectic 10-day period each July. The membership is spatially quite concentrated (Figure 6.3). With few exceptions, the TdA members, when moving into the region, have tended to avoid high-priced lakeshore locations. Rather they have tracked down more low-priced rural cottages, old farm buildings and adjacent barns in back road locations, in the foothills of mountains, or in unassuming locations in the outskirts of villages. Thus, they have successfully avoided areas where property and land have become more directly affected by local tourism development. TdA members also have the privilege of being the first 'past the pole' each Summer (TdA 2002 pamphlet), usually a 10-day period in the second half of July each year, nicely timed for the peak of the tourist season. The financing of the summer programme comes from the membership and local sponsors. The other two organisations – the Circuit-des-Arts (CdA, 1993) centred on Magog and the northern end of Lake Memphremagog, and the Freligsburgh Festiv'art (1996) south of Dunham – are more recent and they also function differently. The CdA usually mobilises over 100 artists, half of them being local and seasonal Fine Art practitioners, for a 10-day summer exhibition programme starting at the end of July, combining open-house studio visits for the public with indoor art shows in strategic locations – in Magog, Georgeville and the famous Elefant Barn, south of Georgeville (CdA 2002 pamphlet). In contrast, the Freligsburgh Festiv'art is an outdoor Fine Art village street market with some 150 participants (culled from 300 applications but including only a few local resident artists. The majority comes from a wider region, particularly metropolitan Montreal, only an hour's car drive away.) Among the three, only the CdA receives government funding.

The aggregate impacting of the fine art TP is difficult to gauge. Visitor statistics for the individual studios are notoriously unreliable. However, a 1995 TdA survey of studio guestbooks recorded 20,000–25,000 visitors. The 2002 Freligsburgh Festiv'art supposedly attracted over 50,000 during its Labour Day weekend programme. Close proximity to Montreal is a vital factor behind the large number (Lavasseur interview).

Given the above, the economic multiplier is hard at work, and in the Freligsburgh case strongly concentrated on the village. Economic leakages are substantial, however, due in part to the many extra-regional artists participating. To the purchases of art objects can be added many other visitor expenditures, including parking, dollar expense among village-based service actors, which in turn pumps the tourist dollar back into the village economy. Studio visits, visits to exhibition halls or walks through a Fine Art street market represent the principal TP attraction, at least the pretext for the visit – while the intricacies of the multiplier are place created and offered beyond the Fine Art experience per se.

Summary and Conclusions

The purpose of this review has been to relate tourist-based regional development dynamics to the cycle concept expounded in the TALC model. Hence, the review covers a section of the ET area in southern Quebec well suited for the exercise, as the region has been exposed to tourist development dynamics over the past 150 years. This means that the region has experienced typical Canadian tourism development characteristics of both earlier eras and new, more recent TP cycles. Looking back on the empirical material presented, certain characteristics deserve emphasis.

First, apart from the recent and new attractions, one can undoubtedly recognise a chronological sequence of TP life cycles already beginning with the exploitation of the very first tourist resources, subsequently creating the distinct development cycles of the 1850–1900 period, and repeated with the activation of subsequent attractions. The successive TP cycles are an unmistakable reality and should be an equally realistic phenomenon in many other tourist regions.

Second, the duration of TP cycles is difficult to establish as is when they start, and when they have they run their full course. In these examples, beginnings can be undistinguishable, but endings finite. This is for instance the case with the TP2 cycle which starts as access improves in the 1850–60s, but does not seem to realise that by now it has reached its end as the prime lakeshore locations are fully occupied. Cottage and condominium development projects may still occur, but the particular lakeshore sitings of the past have now sometimes been replaced with manmade attractions – golf course developments and locations along ski runs up the ski hills, both locations appealing to the active sportsperson and to the active retired individual.

Third, TP cycles often start 'with a bang' – as the ski hill development did. In less than a decade the development cycle, in terms of facility investment, was completed. The cycle still contains dynamics which keep it going, and which should also maintain the cycle on a fairly stable business level for years to come – unless global warming makes the operations uneconomic.

Fourth and finally, modern TP cycles can be quite unpredictable phenomena. In this study, this is true both for some museum-related developments and for the vineyards – but above all for the Fine Art phenomenon. To predict their beginnings is hard, to simulate their development likewise. When their developments start, they are explosive, and location patterns are quite accidental. No tourist development expert working in the 1950s or 1960's ever foresaw their true beginnings and growth, but this may be a common problem in many tourism destinations.

Chapter 7

The TALC in China's Tourism Planning: Case Study of Danxia Mountain, Guangdong Province, PRC

J. BAO and C. ZHANG

Introduction

Danxia Mountain, located in Guangdong, China, is one of the important scenic spots designated by the central government in 1982. Well known for its temple, it is also one of the four famous mountains frequented by tourists in Guangdong. In the early 1990s, the resort experienced a decline in the number of visitors. Tourism experts were invited to tackle the problem in 1993, and they agreed that the resort had fallen into the decline stage of its life cycle because of the declining image of Danxia Mountain. Applying the life cycle model (TALC), they planned a new attraction, Yangyuan Scenic Spot, in order to rejuvenate tourism at Danxia Mountain. Five years later, the mountain came to the rejuvenation stage. In the mean time, some new problems arose. This paper studies and applies the life cycle model theory to this case.

Literature Review

Since the life cycle model was put forward by Butler in 1980, it has been widely accepted around the world, though many arguments have arisen at the same time (Haywood, 1986; Prosser, 1995; Wall, 1982). Different case studies show that different tourist destinations have different characteristics at different stages of their life cycles, especially at the stages of decline and rejuvenation. Nevertheless, Prosser concludes in his review of empirical case studies that the concept of the life cycle provides a useful framework for research that seeks to enhance under-standing of development processes and their implications, but the model is not operational enough (Haywood, 1986; Oppermann, 1995). Some scholars argue that these case studies are not credible because the data used for research did not exhibit the properties of uniformity and replication of tourists (Lundtorp & Wanhill, 2001). Moreover, another method for analysing the tourist area's stage of life cycle, the Travel

Balance Approach, was discussed with the aim of replacing Butler's life cycle theory (Toh *et al.*, 2001).

The life cycle model was first introduced to China by Jigang Bao in 1993. Since then, various scholars have used it as a descriptive tool for specific case studies. For example, Bao (1994, 1995) analysed the life cycle of large-scale theme parks and karst caves. He found that a karst cave has no obvious exploration and involvement stages, and that shortly after its development stage, visitation to such a cave will decline. Lu (1997) took the famous Huangshan Mountain as an example to examine the life cycle of the mountain resort. He found that most famous mountains had already moved into the development stage, and action was needed to be taken in order to avoid a decline in popularity.

The first application of the life cycle model in tourism planning in China, as noted above, was by Jigang Bao in 1993. He found that Danxia Mountain was in the stagnation stage, and considered that the best way to solve the problem was to develop a new tourist attraction there. After all related factors had been considered, Yangyuan Stone Scenic Spot was chosen as the new attraction and subsequently developed. Danxia Mountain was quickly rejuvenated. Bao (1998) also discussed some other issues of the life cycle, taking the Summer Palace and Seven-star Cave as examples.

As Western scholars had done, Chinese scholars questioned and refuted the theory of the tourism life cycle when it was introduced. In 1996, a paper entitled 'Doubts About the Life Cycle Theory' was published in the journal *Tourism Tribune*. The author (Yang, 1996) argued that the life cycle model was neither convincing in theory nor operational in practice. Yang's discussion was followed by a series of discussions in the academic circle. Yu (1997) put forward a double cycle theory, the long cycle indicating the decline process, the short one indicating the fluctuation caused by external factors. A number of other scholars also contributed to the discussion (Chen, 2001; Li, 1997; Xu, 1997; Yan, 2001).

Based on the analysis of the stage variation in a tourist area, Xie (1995) suggested approaches for controlling the fluctuation of the life cycle curve. Other scholars have used the system dynamic approach to demonstrate the theory of the life cycle model (see, for example, Xu, 2001). The descriptive function of the life cycle model theory has been widely accepted in the West, but some scholars argue that the true test of any theory in applied social sciences is whether it is operational. The main argument is that the criteria for stage identification and criteria for turning points are difficult without hindsight, and different units of analysis lead to different results because of the problem in market homogeneity (Cooper, 1994). The situation is different in China: the data used to analyse the life cycle in a tourist area are the numbers of admission tickets; therefore, the geographic boundary of the research is clear and market homogeneity is guaranteed. This makes study of the life cycle relatively easy in China.

Different Types of Life Cycle Models in China

Life cycle of theme parks

Because the history of theme parks is short in China, it may be still somewhat premature to discuss the life cycle of theme parks now, however, some characteristics of theme parks' life cycle can be concluded (Bao, 1998).

Large theme parks usually need big investment and mass advertisement. Tourists are normally given massive amounts of information about a new theme park and become anxious to see it for the first time. As a result, thousands of tourists tend to swarm into a newly opened theme park. According to a market survey (Bao, 1996), about 30% of the tourists visiting a certain theme park during its opening period had their entrance tickets paid for by their own enterprises or companies. All they wanted was to have 'the first look' and to see 'something new'. Thus the theme park reaches the culmination of its visitation in the first year, and its business slows down from the second year on.

This phenomenon has been demonstrated by many theme parks in China. Generally, the number of visitors at a theme park will fall to the lowest level within 2–5 years. Although it is not convincing to say that this is the decline stage of a theme park, it has been true that a theme park will have to close soon if no new product is developed.

Karst caves

According to many cases studies (Bao, 1995), the life cycle of a karst cave is very special. They usually have no exploration and involvement stages, and their first stage is usually the development stage. Normally, caves isolated from other tourist destinations go directly to the development stage after they are open. They then will experience a short consolidation and stagnation stage, and subsequently come to a close soon afterwards. If a cave is close to a famous tourist destination, the situation will be different.

Because it is dark and dangerous in the karst cave before it is open, only a few local residents would go to it after its initial discovery. When it is better known, tourists tend to flood in. Because there are so many karst caves in China, they can only attract tourists from nearby. The number of tourists normally falls quickly after the initial influx, as shown in the cases in Guangdong and Yunnan Provinces (Bao, 1995). However, if the cave were close to a famous tourist destination, such as Ludi Cave in

Guilin city, tourists to such caves would fluctuate in numbers with those going to the famous tourist destination.

International Level Tourist Destinations

Tourist destinations that attract international tourists usually enjoy very long consolidation and stagnation stages. The Summer Palace can be taken as an example. It has one of the best royal gardens in China, and has been listed as a World Heritage Site since 1998. It is considered to be a must-go place for international tourists. From the available data (the entrance tickets), the number of tourists fluctuated with the economic development of the country during the period 1949–2001. After 1985, The Summer Palace entered into its consolidation stage, but because it is irreplaceable, it will stay in the consolidation stage for a very long time. Similar cases are Huangshan Mountain and The Great Wall (both also World Heritage Sites) (Bao, 1998).

These kinds of international level tourist destinations usually enjoy good business under the right economic circumstances. All the manager has to do is to control the carrying capacity and maintain their images and quality to ensure sustainable development.

Applicability of the Life Cycle Model in China

Stage identification

Although tourism in the modern sense only began in China no more than 30 years ago, the phenomena of travel and sightseeing have been around for more than 1000 years. There was some government involvement in tourism, and although the number of travellers was not recorded, aristocrats and politicians did travel a great deal at the public's expense in historic times. However, virtually all industries, including tourism, were destroyed during the last 100 years in China; therefore, taking this period into account would be irrelevant to life cycle research. It was only after 1949 that China's economy began to prosper and the tourism industry started growing.

After the major political, economic and social reforms in 1978, the government began its involvement in scenic spot development. This marks the development stage in the current research. During the late 1990s, most of the scenic spots in China were crowded with tourists. Some of the facilities were in very poor shape, and their environment was spoiled. These are indications of the stagnation stage and the decline stage. However, mass tourism was only in its early stage, with demand increasing rapidly from the market. Therefore, the stagnation stage in the Chinese context may be temporary and caused by external factors rather than internal developments or policy. Improving and strengthening the management of the attractions involved could rejuvenate them.

Data collection

Another issue with the life cycle model is that the theory is difficult to calibrate because of the lack of long-term data on visitor numbers and sales. Many of the studies in the past have been based on island tourism. The number of visitors was obtained from traffic tolls. This makes the data reliable but also causes a problem in market homogeneity. The tourists who reach an island by vehicle may go there for different purposes. Some may do sightseeing; some may be taking a holiday. In China, only the tourists who purchase a ticket can enter a scenic spot. For a very long time, a Chinese tourist's purpose in going to an attraction was to sightsee. As a result, ticket counts guaranteed both the accuracy of the number of visitors and market homogeneity. This makes the ticket count a reliable source of data for the analysis of a destination's life cycle. On the other hand, as China's tourism industry develops, the purposes of the Chinese tourists will become more varied, which will create a problem with respect to market homogeneity.

Unit of analysis

In terms of research on the life cycle of an attraction, the level of aggregation is problematic and must be clearly addressed. Geographical scale is of considerable importance for a tourist destination's life cycle, because in the Chinese context each destination has a single product rather than having different hotels and other facilities as well. Depending on the scale taken, a destination may be seen to be at a different stage in the cycle. The unit of analysis is, therefore, crucial. As noted earlier, some scholars argue that life cycle assumes a homogeneous market and a perfectly logical stance would be for different scales of a destination to contain different market segments. Some scholars argue that using different units of analysis will lead to different conclusions, and will affect the reliability of the life cycle model. In the case studies in the literature, some experts took a county as the unit of analysis (Haywood, 1989; Lundtorp, 2001), while others took an island as the unit of analysis (Cooper & Jackson, 1989; Weaver, 1990). Different scales may bring about different tourist products, and different tourist products may vary a great deal over the long term, making the life cycle model of a destination much more complicated (Hovinen, 2002), thus increasing the difficulty in research. However, in China, every scenic spot has a distinct boundary, and the number of admission tickets sold shows the number of visitors within that boundary, thus variations in the numbers sold reflect the real situation in that tourist area. This is a system that facilitates the life cycle research.

The Application of the Life Cycle Model in Danxia Mountain

Danxia Mountain and Red Stone Park

Danxia Mountain is one of the most popular scenic spots and geological parks in China. It is located in northern Guangdong province, 9 km south of Renhua County. It is 56 km away from Shaoguan City, its main area being about 180 km². Red stone and hills are typical characteristics of the Mountain. It is where the term 'Danxia Landform' originated, thus giving the developed tourist attractions in Danxia Mountain the recent new name Red Stone Park. Before the new attraction was developed, the area opened to tourists was about 3.5 km². About 1200 years ago, a temple was built in Danxia Mountain. Later, this became one of the most famous temples in Guangdong. As a result, Danxia became an important pilgrimage destination, as well as a place for sightseeing and watching the sunrise.

The decline and rejuvenation of Danxia Mountain

People started to visit Danxia Mountain as long ago as about 1000 years. For the convenience of this research, the period of the late 1970s is taken as the beginning of the development stage in Danxia Mountain. Inadequate management and competition from other resorts eventually caused visitation to Danxia Mountain to decline. The number of tourists stopped growing and overnight tourists decreased in numbers. Although efforts were made to counteract this trend (including sales promotion in Hong Kong and special express train service between Shaoguan and Shenzhen), the number of visitors remained low.

In 1993, Professor Jigang Bao was invited to work on improving the old tourist attraction in order to revive its popularity. Bao decided that the decline was the result of an image crisis at Danxia Mountain caused by poor management of the resource, and that the way to solve the problem was to plan a new attraction to improve the image of the Mountain and then rejuvenate it. Reflecting the situation of Danxia Mountain, and taking into account factors such as the state of the facilities, and the uniqueness of the resort, the planners chose to feature the Yangyuan Stone as the main attraction. The Yangyuan Stone is a stone that is 28 m in height and 7 m in diameter, and is in the shape of a phallus.

Red Stone Park includes both the old and new attractions in Danxia Mountain. It began to receive tourists in 1995. The number of tourists has climbed steadily since it was opened (Figure 7.1).

It should be pointed out that after the development of the Red Stone Park, the new scenic spot (represented by the Yangyuan Stone) and the

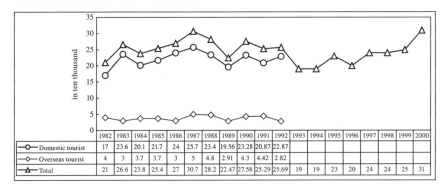

Figure 7.1 The number of tourists to Danxia Mountain (old scenic spot) from 1982 to 2000
Source: Danxia Mountain Administrative Bureau

old one (represented by the temple) sold admission tickets separately. Therefore, Figure 7.2 does not show how many tourists the new scenic spot brought to the old one. However, it does indicate that the increase of tourists to the old scenic spot is closely related to the new scenic spot.

A search was made on the Internet to examine the material and information about the destination in order to confirm the rejuvenation of Danxia Mountain. The tourism industry has been one the first industries in China to take advantage of the convenience of the Internet. Almost all big travel agencies, scenic spots and hotels have their own web pages. Most of the commercial websites have special columns to promote tourist products. In order to make the web page more attractive, the best part of a destination and the best designed products would be advertised. These become the selling points of the destination, and the key component of the destination's image, which can be taken to reflect the demands of the market.

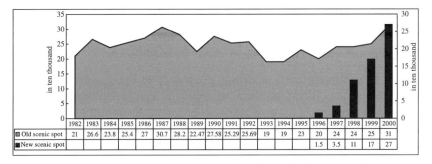

Figure 7.2 The number of tourists to the old and new scenic spots
Source: Danxia Mountain Administrative Bureau

Table 7.1 The selling points of Danxia Mountain on the commercial websites

Searching key words	Results	Percentage (%)
Tourism + tourist itinerary + Shaoguan + Danxia Mountain	497	100
Tourism + tourist itinerary + Shaoguan + Danxia Mountain + Yangyuan Stone	18	3.62
Tourism + tourist itinerary + Shaoguan + Danxia Mountain + sunrise	24	4.82
Tourism + tourist itinerary + Shaoguan + Danxia Mountain + Biechuan Temple	10	2.01
Tourism + tourist itinerary + Shaoguan + Danxia Mountain + sightseeing	77	15.5
Tourism + tourist itinerary + Shaoguan + Danxia Mountain + taking holiday	46	9.26
Tourism + tourist itinerary + Shaoguan + Danxia Mountain + meeting	46	9.26
Tourism + tourist itinerary + Shaoguan + Danxia Mountain + recuperating	8	1.61

Searching time 19:31– 19:47, 1 January 2002

A search of the Internet showed that the rejuvenated old scenic spot is still the most important selling point of Danxia Mountain. The new scenic spot is also one of the important selling points of the tourist area (Table 7.1), and this coincides with the authors' assumption. It is clear that the old scenic spot in Danxia Mountain is still favoured by tourists. It also explains the decline that was experienced in the 1990s: some factors negatively affected its image but it was rejuvenated after the image improvement through the development of the new scenic spot.

Conclusion and Discussion

Since it was introduced to China, the theory of the Tourist Area Cycle of Evolution has been applied widely. Its successful application in tourism planning in Danxia Mountain demonstrates that the right unit of analysis can identify the right stage of the tourist area if the admission ticket count is used as research data. The model can also be used for the tourism planning of an attraction.

When the theory of the life cycle model is used in China, it is inappropriate to take into account the period before 1949. The period after the reform and open policy in 1978 is a suitable point from which to benchmark the development stage for life cycle research. Recently, some scenic spots have begun to show signs of deterioration. This may be the result of the negative effects of an image crisis caused by external factors. Under these circumstances, the image of a tourism destination can be amended through exploiting new attractions that are appealing to tourists.

Resorts that are newly exploited are likely to come into the development stage quickly because their external condition is relatively mature, but they may soon face stagnation and decline if there is lack of good planning and management, confirming the original argument of Butler's model.

Part 3
The TALC in Heritage Settings

RICHARD W. BUTLER

As discussed earlier, the concept of carrying capacity was, from the beginning, an integral part of the TALC and the process of resort development discussed in the model. While all destinations have some inherent merit and warrant appropriate management, including even those created specifically for the tourism industry, for those destinations whose attractiveness is based on some aspect of heritage, the importance of operating within the limits of their capacity is particularly important. Not only does their existence as a tourist destination depend on the existence and quality of their heritage resources, but perhaps more importantly, the heritage resources themselves need to be safeguarded from overuse or misuse and subsequent degradation (see Butler, other volume). The importance of preserving the heritage aspects of destinations is crucial, whether these be natural or cultural in nature, and the chapters in this next section examine the application of the TALC in a variety of heritage situations.

Boyd discusses the issues involved in applying the TALC to national parks, using the specific case of national parks in Canada. Many of Canada's national parks are significant tourist destinations, none more so than the oldest park, Banff, and they provide good examples of how tourism use and development, over more than a century in some cases, can impact on the parks' natural resources and require continual evaluation of and changes in policy and management. The significant shifts in the policies practised by Parks Canada and its predecessor agencies are reviewed and the contemporary policies examined in the light of the processes outlined in the TALC and the concept of sustainable development. While Boyd's paper is not the first to discuss the TALC in the context of parks, it provides by far the most detailed and extensive discussion on this topic. (A discussion of the conceptual issues raised in applying the TALC to a wider range of protected areas is contained in Weizenegger, other volume.)

The second chapter in this section, by Russo, builds on his earlier work in discussing what he terms the 'vicious circle' of essentially negative feedbacks in the tourism development process in a variety of locations, whereby the negative effects of tourism upon destinations results in a reduction in attractiveness that in turn results in a range of other problems, ending in a downward spiral of investment and quality. He uses the case of Venice to illustrate this process, thus providing an example of the application of the TALC to both a heritage situation and a traditional urban settlement which operated for much of its life as a 'normal' urban centre. While Venice has a long history of attracting visitors, its rise as a modern tourism destination is relatively recent and the problems which Russo analyses can be seen as very contemporary in their nature and cause. The problems that Venice faces, an old infrastructure, a declining population, decreasing tax base and an increasing proportion of day to overnight visitors, are common to many historic urban centres. While Venice has unique problems in addition because of the physical nature of its setting, these are only compounded by the pressures of tourism. The implications which can be drawn from Venice have application to a considerable number of other tourism heritage destinations.

The final chapter in this section deals with the application of the TALC with respect to heritage sites and properties, and in particular with the issues of marketing such attractions in a manner that maintains both their heritage qualities and their tourist attractiveness. Malcolm-Davies discusses the basic problems resulting from the differences in approach to the marketing and development of heritage sites in the public and the private sectors. Whereas the private sector is willing to renovate and rejuvenate its product, the public sector is often either unwilling or unable to provide the necessary funds to allow the site to avoid a decline in attractiveness and quality to visitors. She reviews the marketing approaches and their relevance to the TALC process in the context of the future roles of heritage sites in tourism.

Chapter 8

The TALC Model and its Application to National Parks: A Canadian Example

STEPHEN W. BOYD

Introduction

This chapter differs considerably from the majority of chapters in this book as it addresses how Butler's (1980) Tourism Area Life Cycle (TALC) model can be applied outside of the tourism context. The focus of the chapter is on national parks, with a case study presented on the development of the Canadian national park system and how Butler's model may be applied in this specific context. While national parks are a relatively recent phenomenon compared to protected areas in general, it is well acknowledged that they are important spaces for leisure, recreation and tourism (Butler & Boyd, 2000). While their location remains constant, the purpose of use varies between those making use of national parks as a local recreation venue and those entering the parks as domestic or international tourists. In many cases, local recreation users make up the majority of visits, Banff National Park in Western Canada being a good example of this. Regardless of whether visits are for recreation or tourism, the concern that many parks face today is pressure from visitors and therefore the distinction between the nature of users becomes meaningless. An argument to be put forward in this chapter is that the TALC model has applicability as a useful guide to trace park development, measure the extent of development and to avoid overuse. The author, therefore, has undertaken three tasks. First, the extent to which the evolutionary elements of the Butler model can be used to describe how individual parks and entire park systems are developed is examined. Second, visitor data for Canadian national parks between 1993 and 1997 and information on impacts, threats and the condition of parks are used to locate individual parks along the curve of the TALC model. And third, a general discussion is presented that explains the mechanisms that are available for park management to avoid parks moving towards the latter stages of the model and numbers overreaching the zone of critical limits of capacity.

The Lack of Application of TALC to Other Leisure Environments

The TALC has probably been the most written about model developed within tourism research, and the contributions in these two edited volumes of works are testament to this fact. One of the reasons for its popularity is the relative simplicity of the model itself, demonstrating that destinations evolve, change and in doing so may pass through a number of identifiable stages (exploration, involvement, development, consolidation, stagnation, decline or rejuvenation). Based on two very different principles, those of the product life-cycle and animal population growth, the pattern of development resembled that of an S-shaped curve where growth was finite and dependent upon recognition that there existed capacity limitations beyond which growth could not be sustained. It is argued that this capacity would vary according to type of setting and that stagnation or possible decline in tourism would result if capacity limitations were indeed exceeded (see Butler, this volume). The latter feature is often less discussed when the model has been reproduced and critiqued by other researchers. Butler himself, in a review of his model in 1990, noted that the majority of the discussions concerning the model had been focused on applying it in various locations from which the findings have been compared and contrasted with the original postulations made by Butler in 1980.

While the literature on the model and its application within specific contexts is vast, commentary has been generally supportive of the model. Wall (1982) and Haywood (1986) were perhaps the first to raise some issues such as the ability to identify actual stages of development as well as the use of the product life-cycle itself. Despite early criticism, the model has been applied and presented in case study form for destinations as diverse as Lancaster County, Pennsylvania (Hovinen, 1982), Canada's Northwest Territories (Keller, 1987), the Bahamas (Debbage, 1990) and the Grand Cayman Islands (Weaver, 1990), and has been the topic of update and review (Agarwal, 1994; Cooper, 1994). Butler (1990), in his own review, talked of the applicability of extending the model beyond that of a particular tourism destination to tourism development in a broad regional context and to applying the model to specific types of tourism in a region such as heritage tourism in a developing world destination (see Butler, 1997). While the model was developed primarily for tourist destinations and for tourism in a region in general, there have been relatively few applications in other leisure-oriented settings such as national and provincial parks, although the contributions by Eidsvik (1983) and McKay (1990) should not go unnoticed. This is relatively surprising, given the comments offered earlier in the chapter that national parks more than provincial or other parks are increasingly been sought out by tourists, and are becoming increasingly reliant on revenue from tourism to justify their existence. In many cases national parks, particularly those being inscribed with World Heritage status, are emerging not just as tourist attractions and part of the overall tourism experience but rather specific tourist destinations and the entire tourism experience in their own right. This latter development is a consequence of many national parks emerging as leading ecotourism and natural heritage destinations.

Historical Review of the Development of the Canadian National Park System: The TALC as Chronology Descriptor

National parks owe their origin to the emergence of a preservation/conservation ethic that permeated North American society in the mid-19th century and it is not surprising that Canada was one of the earliest of the New World nations to set aside tracts of land for its people (see Boyd & Butler, 2000 for a detailed discussion). Banff and the original area around its hot springs were set aside as Canada's first national park in 1885 to be free from sale, settlement or squatting (Lothian, 1977). While this would establish a precedent which other national parks would follow, Banff was to develop in an atypical manner compared to other parks that would be declared later, as it would become Canada's most 'developed' national park. According to researchers like Nelson (1982), Canada's national parks were developed on the basis of three threads of interest, first that of preservation; second, the potential that parks offered for tourism; and third the role that the parks may play as poles around which economic growth would occur. Alongside these three threads, there existed a myriad of institutional arrangements that would both encourage as well as prevent national park development from taking place. The historic chronology of national parks in Canada resembles a series of flows (or possible curves) when numbers of parks and park developments are plotted against time. And therefore in a relatively tangential manner, it may be loosely argued that the chronology of national parks in Canada resembles a Butler curve that repeats itself.

The 'exploration' stage could be summarised in the creation of other parks in Western Canada around Banff the following year (Glacier and Yoho) to be quickly followed by three more by 1907 (Waterton Lakes, Elk Island and Jasper). Many of these parks occurred alongside railroad development in Western Canada and the beginning of early forms of tourism to the parks and tourist-related developments in the parks. The early parks were individually managed but in many cases they were noted for their absence of management (Boyd, 1995). Only one national park was established in eastern Canada by 1907, namely St Lawrence Islands, established from federal crown land that had been initially under Indian ownership. Aspects of park development that could be labelled as constituting the 'involvement' stage comprised further national park establishment in both Western and Eastern Canada up until 1929, a date which saw the park count rise to 14 in total. As for institutional developments, the Dominion Parks Branch was set up in 1911 and became the world's first national park service. Established under the Dominion Forest Reserves and Parks Act, it placed all existing parks under the jurisdiction of park service, and in essence was the start of a 'national parks system' (Eidsvik, 1983). Its first commissioner was James B. Harkin, who was to hold the office until 1936. It was under his leadership and vision that the recreation and tourism potential within the parks was realised, balanced with the need to ensure preservation and a state of wilderness, but where the revenue to be gained from use within the system would provide the means to further develop the park system.

It is possible to argue that Canada's national parks entered the 'development' stage between 1930 and 1978. A stop–go policy existed regarding park establishment owing to legislation, which prevented the federal government having control over public land across the Prairie Provinces, allowing park creation in only Eastern Canada. The post-war years and subsequent travel and leisure boom that followed created a demand for travel for recreational purposes in natural places, supported by a new phase of park establishment between 1969 and 1972. This period saw 10 new parks being added to the existing system, both in the West, East (where parks were established to act as regional economic growth poles) and for the first time in the North. Park attendance was recorded to have increased threefold between 1960 and 1972 from 5 to 15 million, with the majority of that increase being absorbed by a few Western parks (Boyd, 1995). Towards the end of the 1970s it was clearly emerging that institutional arrangements were needed to safeguard parks from overuse and abuse. Early forms of institutional arrangements had developed as early as 1930 with the passing of Canada's first National Parks Act. The wording of the Act stressed 'unimpairment', 'enjoyment' and 'benefit' and was an early example of the principles of sustainable development. Other evidence to suggest Canada's national parks had reached the 'development' stage includes the first national parks policy tabled in government in 1964. While this had strong development-use tones, it helped greatly to establish the preservation of significant natural features in national parks as its 'most fundamental and important obligation' (Eidsvik, 1983). This was followed in 1970 by the development and approval of the first systems approach to national parks planning and development in Canada. An early iteration of the systems plan was based on broad physiographic regions (see Eidsvik, 1983). The systems plan approved by government was based around the concept of 'natural regions'. Canada was divided into 39 terrestrial (natural) regions based on biological, physical and geographic features, and it was based on these regions that further development of the park system would be developed to ensure that each region had national park representation.

In terms of features that could suggest a 'consolidation' stage, the following argument is made. Between 1979 and 1992 few new parks were added to the existing system. By 1993 Canada had 34 national parks, with new parks added in North and Eastern Canada. Visitation had levelled across the entire system to around 20 million. Institutional arrangements were well established with a revised national parks policy coming out in 1979 that introduced ecological integrity as the guiding principle in parks as a prerequisite to use. This development saw a formal amendment to the National Parks Act in 1988, which formalised the principle of ecological integrity. Other developments in this time period include the establishing and tabling of State of the Parks Reports and the establishment of a co-management agreement between the federal government and the Haida Nation over the management of Gwaii Haanas in 1993. An additional revision of national park policy in 1994 further stressed that priority be assigned to ensuring the ecological integrity of parks.

It would be difficult to establish a case that after 1994 a 'stagnation' phase followed. Rather it would be fair to suggest that increasing evidence was emerging that parks were coming under increasing threat and, if this was not addressed, could stagnate and become less attractive and lose their unique natural and commemorative integrity. This concern had been stated a decade earlier in a study undertaken on external perspectives and future strategies that Parks Canada (the title of the national park service then) should embark on up to 2001 (Nelson, 1984). But the first comprehensive study of human use in national parks would not be commissioned until 1994 when the Banff–Bow Valley Study was launched over concern about the montane region of Canada's first national park (Parks Canada, 1997). The study reported its findings in 1996 and brought into focus the need for ecological integrity to be established as the first priority. The implications of the study were to have a wider application to the entire national park system by establishing and making clear that the 'stagnation' threatening the system could be avoided in parks if integrity received priority over use (including tourism, which was a major component of use). Another action taken to avoid stagnation and decline was the announcement in 1998 of a moratorium placed on commercial development outside of park communities within national parks (Parks Canada website, 2002).

There is evidence since 1998 to imply that Canada's national parks have entered a stage of 'rejuvenation'. Much of the legislation that was passed since 1979 and the related institutional arrangements that were put in place were directed at attempting to keep use levels within the parks system within the zone of the 'critical limits of capacity' or at worst, to avoid capacity limits being severely overreached. The chronology of national parks since 1998 reflects concern over use levels and the pressures placed on parks by users. A report by the Panel on the Ecological Integrity of Canada's National Parks was released in 2000 and stated that the ecological integrity of the parks was under threat from many sources and for many reasons. Action that was taken included the passing of the Canada National Parks Act in 2001 that shifted priority to beyond just ensuring ecological integrity to maintenance and restoration of ecological integrity through the protection of natural resources and natural processes. The Act helped set new standards for park management plans where the primacy of ecological integrity is enforced. Other developments within the Act that could promote a base for rejuvenation were the requirement of legal designation of wilderness areas within parks and the placement of commercial development in national park communities. The Act heralded in the recycle of the cycle as it saw the establishment of seven new national parks. This was then followed up in 2002 when the government declared its intentions of establishing what it called the 'most ambitious expansion of national parks in over a hundred years' by aiming to establish 10 new parks by 2007, increasing the size of the Canadian national parks system by almost 50% (Parks Canada, 2002). In so doing, national parks will be present in all of Canada's 39 terrestrial regions and thereby complete the system. In addition, the 2002 announcement stated that action would be taken to restore the ecological health of all Canada's 39 existing national parks based on an integrated strategy. This strategy has three key elements: to improve understanding about what is changing in the parks, to understand why these changes are taking place and to take action to address the changes. The focus will be on scientific understanding of the parks, involving active monitoring and research into gaining a better understanding of human use of the parks and their surrounding ecosystems. Other efforts will include enlisting the help of Canadians as active partners through the development of partnerships to address stresses originating outside the parks, and encouraging and strengthening partnerships particularly with Aboriginal peoples. Such actions will go a long way to ensure that Canada's national park system will enjoy a rebirth or rejuvenation.

Application of the TALC to Individual Parks

Although the concept of sustainable development had not been 'coined' when Butler produced his model, implicit within the curve is the notion of limits and what possible scenarios may result if these are exceeded (see Butler, other volume). Figure 8.1a outlines the model as it was first developed in 1980 and how it may be modified to include issues of sustainability (Figure 8.1b), where a number of types or stages of sustainability may exist. These types or stages may be discernible on the basis of the ability of parks to cope with pressures, economic, environmental, or social, that are placed upon them from the mix of activities present and the various functions of the parks themselves. In the context of parks, the modified model implies that for both the 'exploration' and 'involvement' stages, initial sustainability is evident with an emphasis on maintaining ecological integrity (for an example of applying the TALC to other types of protected areas, see Weizenegger, other volume, editor's note). User levels are low and no noticeable impact occurs on the environment. Between the 'development' and 'consolidation' stages, it may be argued that conditional sustainability exists. More specifically, the nature of this sustainability is perceived as, first, moving in the direction of achieving economic sustainability with an emphasis on growth and, second, returning to maintaining ecological integrity as decreasing tolerance and stress placed on parks from both greater development (use) and continued high visitor counts may lead to exceeding the capacity limits of some parks. Parks placed between the

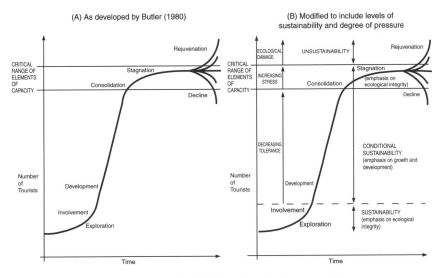

Figure 8.1 Modification of the TALC of evolution model

stages of 'consolidation' and 'stagnation', thus falling within the critical range of capacity, may be perceived as having a focus placed on maintaining ecological integrity as the increased stress, threats and impacts on parks may result in carrying capacity being exceeded. Parks found to be beyond the carrying capacity level may be perceived as being managed in an unsustainable manner.

Though this model is essentially conceptual, it was applied using the following data between 1993 and 1997: the length of time since the park was created, the physical size of the park, visitation counts over time (see Table 8.1), type of impacts (stresses/threats) facing parks and the ability of managers to address them (see Table 8.2) on the basis of the State of the Parks profiles over the time period. It may be argued that this range of information can provide, at best, crude indicators of the physical and environmental carrying capacities of parks, which in turn enable one to determine the general position of parks along the curve.

Given that these indicators provide at best a general impression of individual parks, each park's position is shown not as a specific point but as falling within a certain range (see Figure 8.2). For logistic purposes regarding visualising the findings and to avoid concealing regional differences, parks are presented on a regional basis with one curve being used to show parks in the Ontario and Quebec region of the overall parks system. Space does not permit a detailed explanation of where individual parks were placed on the curve, and so a number of case examples are drawn from Figure 8.2 as way of explanation for positioning.

For the Atlantic Region, all parks are plotted as falling between the 'development' and 'consolidation' stage, a fact not surprising given the range of park ages (Kejimkujik was established in 1969, compared to Cape Breton Highland in 1936). Further, a pattern of decline in visitation, increased threats and the lack of attention to external pressures on some parks may imply that the positions along the curve may be closer to 'consolidation' than to 'development'. A similar pattern is evident, albeit with some exceptions when parks in Ontario and Quebec are considered. For instance, Point Pelee is a park with an ecologically sensitive environment, a long history (established in 1929), small in size (16 km²), but one that has had to cope with development (cottaging) and seasonal variation in visitation (dramatic increase during the bird-watching season). With increased stress placed on the natural environment from overuse and pressure from outside interests, it could be argued that this park is between 'consolidation' and 'stagnation'. However, management actions and strategies within this park (including the establishment of boardwalks and the absence of motorised transport) may help to ensure that 'stagnation' is not reached. The Prairie and Northern Region may be

Table 8.1 Number of person-visits to Canadian national parks (1993–97)

Province	Park	1993–94	1994–95	1995–96	1996–97
Newfoundland & Labrador	Gros Morne	126,019	124,729	129,083	120,943
	Terra Nova	233,783	237,978	241,567	232,616
Prince Edward Island	Prince Edward Island	690,645	808,899	836,344	749,212
Nova Scotia	Cape Breton Highlands	594,384	598,474	379,894	379,894
	Kejimkujik	55,469	58,552	58,308	56,592
New Brunswick	Fundy	223,357	241,087	233,486	220,725
	Kouchibouguac	210,684	230,089	226,631	229,562
Quebec	Forillon	169,412	181,953	180,816	173,914
	La Mauricie	247,104	232,765	239,774	215,888
	Mingan Arch.	25,350	27,125	28,596	19,860
	Saguenay			421,452	377,382
Ontario	Bruce Peninsula	144,650	163,255	210,980	207,444
	Fathom Five	390,562	335,412	411,867	399,054
	Georgian Bay Is	86,589	86,720	72,954	69,252
	Point Pelee	448,655	500,282	439,196	384,682
	Pukaskwa	13,298	13,252	19,180	7940
	St Lawrence Is.	43,980	58,365	73,021	63,278

Table 8.1 (*Continued*)

Province	Park	1993–94	1994–95	1995–96	1996–97
Manitoba	Riding Mtn	286,574	360,165	368,886	353,134
Saskatchewan	Grasslands	2528	2796	5082	3451
	Prince Albert	178,523	184,346	171,669	172,194
Alberta	Banff	4,395,400	4,892,551	4,858,161	4,453,021
	Elk Island	302,023	264,214	217,395	152,852
	Jasper	1,511,853	1,587,402	1,605,941	2,100,089
	Waterton Lakes	349,393	351,990	456,507	330,939
British Columbia	Glacier	173,321	194,751	143,085	101,924
	Gwaii Haanas	1902	2768	2775	2077
	Kootenay	1,263,412	1,323,913	1,288,495	1,113,795
	Mt Revelstoke	203,751	205,916	163,687	163,687
	Pacific Rim	1,102,559	1,121,145	920,795	836,120
	Yoho	747,292	848,321	761,871	678,189
Yukon	Ivvavik	429	129	244	152
	Kluane	78,996	72,511	66,489	69,924

Table 8.1 (*Continued*)

Province	Park	1993–94	1994–95	1995–96	1996–97
Northwest Territories	Aulavik		151	20	20
	Auyuittuq	379	349	507	470
	Ellesmere Is.	451	454	462	462
	Nahanni	3793	3095	4551	4605
	Wood Buffalo	6251	6231	6444	6040
Total		14,312,771	15,322,135	15,246,215	14,451,383

Table 8.2 Internal and external threats facing Canadian national parks

Region	Park	Internal threats								External threats				
		A	B	C	D	E	F	G	H	I	J	K	L	M
Atlantic	Cape Breton Highlands			X	X					X				
	Prince Edward Island	X	X			X		X	X	X		X		
	Fundy	X	X							X	X	X		
	Terra Nova		X		XX		XX			X	X			
	Kejimkujik	X	X		XX	X	X			X	X			
	Kouchibouguac	X	X			X	X		X	X		X		
	Gros Morne		XX	X	X	X				X				
Quebec	Forillon				X	X				XX		X		
	La Mauricie	X			X					X	X	X		
	Mingan Archipelago				XX		X			X		X		
Ontario	St Lawrence Islands	X			XX		X			X		XX		
	Point Pelee	XXX			XX				X	XX		XX		
	Georgian Bay Islands			X	X		X			X	X	XX		
	Pukaskwa			X							X			
	Bruce Peninsula													

Table 8.2 (*Continued*)

Region	Park	Internal threats							External threats					
		A	B	C	D	E	F	G	H	I	J	K	L	M
Prairie/Northern	Wood Buffalo	X				XX				XX		X	X	
	Prince Albert	X	X						X	X				
	Riding Mountain		X	X			X		X	X		X	X	
	Kluane			X					XX	X				
	Nahanni		X					X			X			
	Auyuittuq			X				X						
	Grasslands	X				X			X					
	Northern Yukon						X			X				
	Ellesmere Island			X			X			X	X			
Western	Banff	X	X		X		X			XX		X		XX
	Waterton Lakes	XX	X							XX				
	Jasper	XX		X			XX			X				
	Yoho	X		XX	XX		XX		XX	XX		X		X
	Glacier			XX	XX		X		X	XX				
	Elk Island	XXX										XX	X	X

Table 8.2 (*Continued*)

Region	Park	Internal threats							External threats					
		A	B	C	D	E	F	G	H	I	J	K	L	M
	Mount Revelstoke								X	XX				XX
	Kootenay	XX		X	X		XX			X				X
	Pacific Rim		X		XX					X				X
	Gwaii Haanas	XX			X							XX		

X, limited; XX, major; XXX, extensive

Internal threats: A, natural threats; B, tourism and recreation related; C, waste management and services; D, heavy use/overuse of area; E, traditional activities/commercial activities; F, conflict between wildlife and users; G, modification of the physical environment of parks

External threats: H, removal of buffers around parks, foreign species; I, nonconforming uses outside park boundaries; J, climatic influences (e.g. acid rain); K, pollution; L, community development; M, accessing parks from areas outside parks

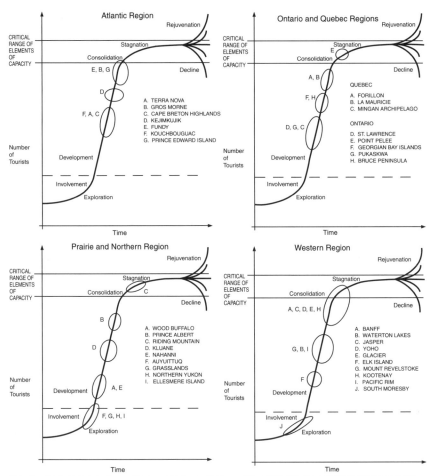

Note: the detailed labels for the modified model (diagram B, Figure 4.3) are left off to leave sufficient room to apply the model to the Canadian national park system. Given the data, it is impossible to accurately position each park on the curve. Therefore, the region of the curve considered most applicable to each park is shown instead.

Figure 8.2 Application of the modified tourist area cycle of evolution model to Canada's national parks

categorised into a number of divisions. First, Prince Albert and Riding Mountain National Parks, which have had a long history of recreation and tourism, with large visitor counts and severe external pressures, are plotted as approaching 'consolidation' and 'stagnation', respectively. Second, parks established in the North (Auyuittuq, 1974; Nahanni, 1976; Kluane, 1976; Northern Yukon, 1984; Ellesmere Island, 1988), where visitor counts are low, growth moderate and impacts minimal, are plotted between the 'involvement' and 'exploration' stage, with some approaching the level of 'development'. Wood Buffalo National Park is one park that resembles the pattern identified for the latter category, but with a number of differences, namely a longer history (established in 1911), being developed as an animal sanctuary, with the greatest impact coming not from outside the park from nonconforming land-uses but from the within the park in the form of an outbreak of disease amongst the bison herd and from indigenous uses.

The Western Region reflects parks that may be categorised as ranging between 'development' and 'consolidation', with the exception of South Moresby/Gwaii Haanas that has not advanced much beyond the 'involvement' stage given that it was only established in 1992 and is relatively inaccessible because of its location. Parks such as Banff, Jasper, Yoho, Glacier and Kootenay are seen as having reached or being close to 'consolidation'. With the exception of Glacier, these parks have continued to attract large numbers of visitors over time, but with the development of specific management strategies to address internal problems and the cooperative arrangements existing with neighbouring jurisdictions for many external issues, it may be argued that these parks have not yet reached the point of 'stagnation'. The large numbers of visitors and the conflicts between wildlife and visitors would suggest, however, that capacity limits have been reached and exceeded for some sections within these parks (e.g. Lake O'Hara in Yoho and the montane valley section in Banff). The Banff–Bow Valley study released in 1996 would support the latter argument. However, the history of tourism in specific parks (e.g. Banff), the attraction of recreation with a Rocky Mountain setting and the presence of a large urban market in the Calgary–Edmonton corridor, make it very likely that these parks will continue to receive large numbers of visitors.

Both axes in Figure 8.2 are produced as constants, but it may be argued that given the diversity of parks that comprise the system, the shape of individual curves would reflect a range of factors. These could include park history with respect to tourism, recreation and general visitor use, size, type of environment present, park location and management ability to redress internal and external problems. As such, it is possible to argue that the shape of individual park curves would fall between both scenarios presented in Figure 8.3, where scenario A depicts a park that is well established, popular, but increasingly facing stresses both external and internal, whereas Scenario B is reflective of parks that have been recently established, located within extremely sensitive isolated environments, where levels of visitation remain low. Regardless of whether graphs are plotted on axes that vary or are held as constants, the overall utility of applying the TALC model to Canada's national parks remains. Its application may reveal the extent of

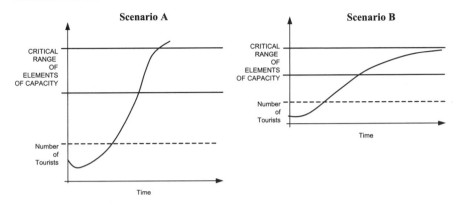

Figure 8.3 Alternative scenarios of park development

'development' that each park has reached, which in turn may be useful in indicating their potential to be sustainable landscapes.

Discussion

The focus in this chapter has been to illustrate the application of the TALC in a national park context. Attention now shifts to discussing how park management can redress the situation where parks have moved into the latter stages of the model, and what specific strategies can be employed to ensure that the 'critical range of elements of capacity' is not overstepped. Discussion is directed at specific policy developments that can shape individual park management plans as well as offering some comment on the extent to which partnership development, alluded to earlier in this chapter, is providing a new means of park management. In both cases, Banff National Park is highlighted as it remains the most visited and yet atypical park within the Canadian system, and if strategies can be employed here and be successful, then they have potentially wide utility across parks within the system as a whole.

National park policy, stemming from the 1930 Parks Act to the current policy released in 1994, can be compared to the analogy of a pendulum, swinging between development (use) and protection and ensuring ecological integrity (Boyd, 2000). At present, current Acts and institutional arrangements, previously discussed in this chapter, imply that the pendulum has clearly moved towards ecological integrity. The guiding principles outlined in the Parks Policy of 1994 (Parks Canada, 1994) place ecological and commemorative integrity as taking precedence with respect to acquisition, management and the administration of heritage places and programmes. The policy goes on to state that management decisions must be made on the basis of ecosystem-based management practices and sound cultural resource management, respectively. Other guiding principles and strategies include leadership and stewardship, new protected heritage areas, education and presentation, human–environment relationship, research and science, appropriate visitor activities, public involvement, collaboration and cooperation and accountability. These broad guiding principles, when translated into specific management plans at the level of individual parks, are applied by management which stresses ecosystem-based protection. In the case of Banff National Park, the current management plan was released in 1997 and provides a blueprint for action between 1997 and 2012. Sheila Copps, then Deputy Prime Minister and Minister of Canadian Heritage, in the foreword to the Banff National Park Management Plan (Parks Canada, 1997), states clearly that first and foremost, Banff is a place for nature in which ecological integrity is the cornerstone of the park as well as its key to the future, but that it is also a place for people, a place for heritage tourism, a place for community and a place for environmental stewardship. The plan is strategic, offering a clear and core vision shaped around a range of themes such as an integrated approach to decision-making, and that the parks tourism strategy shaped around heritage will serve as a model of integrated management. Specific strategic goals have been established for each section of the plan.

Much has been written about specific management strategies within the tourism heritage literature (see Hall & McArthur, 1998; Timothy & Boyd, 2003) and managing visitor impacts in general (see Garrod, 2003) and no attempt is made here to repeat familiar ground, other than to make the point that national park environments have often been the setting against which management strategies have been assessed. A strategy such as zoning regions based on their suitability for activity, for example, has a long history where national parks are concerned. The point to be made here is that a plethora of management strategies and procedures now exist at the discretion of park managers, and the history of park management would suggest that overall, they have been well used.

A recent strategy that has been commented on earlier in this chapter is that of building partnerships, and although the term is a relatively old concept, it is a relatively new one where tourism thinking is concerned (see Bramwell & Lane, 2000). In the case of Banff National Park, partnerships have emerged as one of the key components of the park's vision, namely 'people who live and work in the park will be a "community of communication", welcoming visitors and enhancing their understanding of the nature, culture and history of the park' (Parks Canada, 1997: 10). This thinking emerged as one outcome of the Banff–Bow Valley Study of 1996, which helped develop a heritage tourism strategy for the park (Parks Canada, 1997). The heritage tourism strategy has the following four goals:

(1) Create visitor awareness of being in a national park through fostering visitor appreciation and understanding of nature, culture and history of the park itself.
(2) Encourage and develop opportunities, products and services that are consistent with heritage values.
(3) Encourage environmental stewardship initiatives upon which sustainable heritage tourism could be based.
(4) Set up a heritage orientation programme with the express purpose of giving residents the knowledge base on which they could share their understanding of heritage of the park, both natural and human, with visitors.

It is the latter goal that attempts to foster a 'community of communication' by selling heritage through an orientation programme. Boyd (2003) commented that this education programme provides a new marketing approach, creating opportunity where heritage tourism is concerned, and that as a model has utility for 'educating' visitors as to the purpose, heritage or otherwise, of national parks and historic sites across Canada, and, indeed, more widely.

While this discussion has been limited, the point to be made is that the direction that national policy and specific management plans have taken and the initiatives behind building partnerships, for example, imply that national park management has the tools to avoid parks moving towards stagnation, indicated by their environments having overreached their capacity.

Conclusion

This chapter has presented an alternative application of the TALC model. National parks remain popular venues for leisure, recreation and tourism, and in many cases represent the majority of World Heritage Sites that were inscribed on the basis of natural criteria. It is therefore fitting and relevant to consider the merits of this popular tourism model in this context. As many of the chapters in this book will attest, the TALC model has moved well beyond the initial thinking around which Butler wrote of in 1980. Butler himself has noted that the model has utility beyond the level of destinations to that of tourism within regions and to specific types of tourism in general. Within the context of national parks, it is postulated here that the TALC model is applicable in broad terms as a descriptor of how entire park systems have developed, as well as offering utility in the placement of individual parks along the curve. The chapter provides yet another example of the difficulty of determining where individual cases may be best represented within the model. Despite this weakness, the modifications of the original TALC model provide the opportunity to think beyond the boundaries and justify the model's application to landscapes such as those found within national parks in a protected situation. A final point is that the importance of the TALC model and its application to national parks lies not in pinpointing the position of where parks lie along the curve, but rather in highlighting the need for good management of parks to avoid them reaching the latter stages of the model's cycle of development. National parks have a long history of management strategies and the ongoing application of these will be vital if national parks are to become and remain representative examples of sustainable landscapes.

Chapter 9

A Re-foundation of the TALC for Heritage Cities

ANTONIO PAOLO RUSSO

Introduction

Drawing on the example of Venice and similar congested destinations, this chapter looks at the way in which destinations have become overdeveloped or overused. It examines tourism development in the context of limited accommodation capacity and discusses the implications of the strategic responses from the market players, as well as alternative options which such destinations might adopt to bring their evolution to sustainable tracks. Cultural tourism is an important resource for cities and regions. It provides solid opportunities for growth that are not limited to direct employment and revenue generation. A visitor-friendly environment enhances the quality of life of a place – and consequently its capacity to attract new and strategic functions, contributing to general goals of urban development in the global economy (Russo & van den Berg, 2002). In fact, a culture-rich environment is not only attractive to visitors, but also to new citizens and firms. Apart from their ethical value, historical buildings, monuments and sights enhance the atmosphere of a city, providing prestige to the urban environment. Cultural attractions score high in the preferences of agents in the new service class (Dziembowska-Kowalska & Funck, 2000), and influence the development plans of companies and multinationals. This feeds a process in which tourism is the engine of economic regeneration.

For those reasons, an increasing number of cities invest in promoting their historical and cultural resources and making them accessible to residents and visitors. In doing so, however, they risk an unbalanced and short-lived development. The experience with tourism in many European cities suggests that the results of such efforts are often unsatisfactory (Russo *et al.*, 2001; van der Borg & Gotti, 1995). Tourism pressure grows unbridled in heritage and cultural destinations, with negative consequences in terms of costs and lost opportunities for cities as living and working locations. As a strategy for urban growth, is has been proved largely nonviable in the long term.

This is especially a problem for a city whose mass is small with respect to the flow of visitors that it attracts – such as the small and medium 'stars' of European urban tourism, Bruges, Salzburg, Toledo and Venice. Not only the socioeconomic profile of entire communities, for which tourism is far too often the only source of wealth, is at stake in this process. Perhaps even worse is the risk that as a result of the loss of competitiveness of tourism, the very opportunities for the protection of the cultural heritage are eroded. To the extent that this patrimony represents an element of the foundation of the civil society and the collective memory of the past, its loss would be disrupting.

The challenge for such cities is to develop as thriving and attractive places without missing the opportunities offered by tourism. Hence the need for an integral policy that prevents the worse effects of tourism development, allowing the urban economy to grow harmoniously, and preserves in the process the valuable assets on which such growth is based, according to the general principles of sustainability. Yet, few sound explanations have been given of possible undesirable outcomes. Urban tourism remains in a sort of 'scientific vacuum', which Cazes and Potier (1996) attribute to the difficulty of establishing disciplinary boundaries in the study of the phenomena. It is somewhat surprising to find that in the top journals in the field, for instance *Annals of Tourism Research and Tourism Management*, only a small number of articles have been devoted to urban heritage tourism in the last decade. However, any mayor of a historical city in Western Europe is likely to put visitor management high on the political agenda, together with closely associated issues such as economic regeneration, traffic and environmental control, and infrastructure development. Policy practice calls for more scientific elaboration, but science hardly responds.

This chapter addresses these issues, starting with a discussion of the shortcomings of the most current Tourism Area Life Cycle (TALC) conceptualisations and applications in explaining the unsustainable outcome of tourism development in heritage cities. It is argued that a specific approach to tourist cycles based on spatial issues should be considered in such contexts. A 'vicious circle' model of tourism development is then presented, which puts the interrelations between the spatial development of tourism and market strategies at centre stage. The long-term developments of this model and the necessary policy responses are also discussed. The fourth section illustrates the working of the model and its implications in the case of a world-famous heritage destination, Venice. Finally, the conclusions draw useful insights for a more effective comprehensibility and use of the TALC framework as an instrument for planning.

TALC as a Policy Tool for Heritage Destinations: Problems and Extensions

Cities and urban regions are complex systems; any change in their component parts is likely to have repercussions in other domains, influencing the welfare and quality of life of various groups of citizens, or the power and legitimacy of organisations. While the expectation is that tourism development makes a city as a whole better off, this is not always the case. In some cases, development processes take place outside the city. The costs generated by development would eventually outweigh the benefits, in a zero-sum game in which there are 'winners' and 'losers'. Whereas benefits may be gauged by simple multiplier analysis, the disenfranchised spatial and temporal nature of development costs makes their evaluation particularly hard; sophisticated, complex tools are required for this analysis.

One such instrument is the TALC model, which provides a framework to analyse tourism in an evolutionary context. The destination-cycle scheme is complementary to multiplier analysis as it provides a 'reduced form' of the dynamic relations that are implied in tourism development. It gives an idea of 'what to expect' from a certain structure of the tourist economy and its relations with the local context, be it economic, environmental or social.

Despite its widespread influence in tourism studies, the destination cycle has attracted criticism. Part of the literature argues that the 'deterministic' nature of the model does not leave room for a diversity of outcomes in the development process (Prideaux, 2000), or points the finger to the unclear consideration of demand–supply interaction (Haywood, 1986). Another problem is that most studies focus on applications regarding beach resorts and other 'new' tourist products (for instance, Debbage, 1990; Holder, 1991; Knowles & Curtis, 1999). Little attention has been given to urban tourism, and to heritage cities in particular (Garrod & Fyall, 2000). One reason may be that the late development of this form of tourism (compared to other forms of recreational and '3S' travel) does not offer many examples of complete cycles to be observed and analysed. However, heritage destinations do have peculiar characteristics that make the straightforward application of the TALC framework not as credible as in other contexts. Whereas we can rely on arguments derived from aggregate consumption theory (as in Towse, 1991) to explain the rise in popularity of heritage destinations, it is difficult to grasp how in practice a 'decline' in tourism could occur. The cultural assets inherited from the past are irreproducible and highly specific to the local historical and cultural context, hence the 'substitutability' between destinations is limited. The decline stage of the destination cycle, hardly observed in the real world, would not even be an expected outcome of tourism development. Though authors such as Butler (1980), Haywood (1986), Ioannides (1992) and Plog (1973) offer arguments that could be adapted to the problems in question, none of these is thoroughly convincing in the case of heritage cities and anyway their approaches have not been applied to these destinations. However, socioeconomic impacts from tourism on heritage cities are perceptible (van den Berg & Gotti, 1995). Cities like Venice and Bruges have tripled their visitor/resident ratios in the last few years and tourism is perceived today as a 'danger'.

Following on, the least attractive aspect of the destination cycle is its poor use as a tool for policy (Haywood, 1998). The simple description of the trend does not capture the nature of the linkages that make the cycle self-propelling. One major consequence is that while TALC theorists prescribe that policy should act proactively to smooth the fluctuations of the cycle and prevent decline, it is not clear how these objectives should be achieved, nor which variables should be the object of regulation at each stage. According to authors such as Martin and Uysal (1990) and Canestrelli and Costa (1991), the challenge for tourism managers is to keep flows under the threshold of carrying capacity. This is generally defined as 'the number of visitors that an area can accommodate before negative impacts occur' (Martin & Uysal, 1990: 329). Yet few authors manage to define precisely the link between carrying capacity violations and the life cycle. Is carrying capacity the point beyond which, if repeatedly violated, the visitors' flows start to decline? Or rather does it cause tourist receipts to perform a cyclic path, affecting the performance of the urban economy? That is completely unclear, and contradicted by empirical observation. In cities such as Bruges or Venice, visitor flows – both in the resident tourist segment and in the excursionist segment – are still increasing, even at sustained rates, but carrying capacity is violated for many days in a year (Costa & van der Borg, 1988). Martin and Uysal (1990) suggest that each stage in the cycle will reveal different capacity thresholds, and requires distinct policy responses. Hence, we are not in a position to give clear indications for a long-term strategic policy to tourist planners, based on the notion of carrying capacity alone.

We adhere to the remark made by Haywood (1992: 353): decision-makers need to know what strategic moves are appropriate in each specific situation, and the destination cycle has no immediate prescriptive implication unless it explicitly takes into consideration the characteristics of places and resources. A promising step forward in this sense is provided by authors who focus on the changes in the spatial organisation of the tourist system (Debbage, 1990; Gormsen, 1981; Miossec, 1976; van der Borg, 1991) and on the repercussions on the performance of the destination. The original TALC model can be extended by a qualitative element, that is, the kind of visitor that is attracted (van der Borg, 1991). A close scrutiny of the characteristic of the visitor flows in cities at different stages of their life cycle suggests that not only the absolute number of visitors is changing, but also their mix, with major consequences in terms of associated costs and benefits in the space. This interpretation seems appropriate to describe the situation of historical urban destinations, as it hints at a specialisation of the space in and around the city, induced by the peculiar structure of the destination area. In the upper part of Figure 9.1, this 'revisited' version of the tourist life-cycle scheme is presented. Each stage of the cycle can be associated with a specific distribution of the costs and benefits arising from the tourist activities (lower part of the figure). At the first stage, the area benefiting from tourism is different from the newly discovered destination. As development proceeds (e.g. with the building of hotels), the two regions almost coincide. Municipalities are able to cover the costs

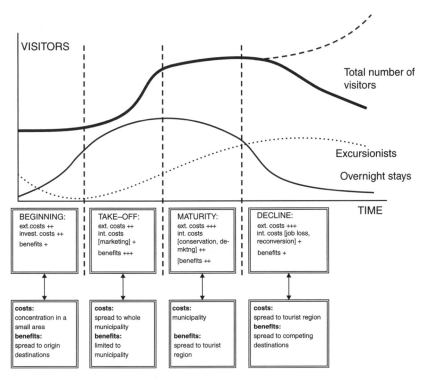

Figure 9.1 The destination life cycle reinterpreted: Visitor mix and spatial allocation of costs and benefits from tourism development in a site Adapted from van der Borg (1991)

generated by tourism with the receipts from tourism that at this stage
are concentrated in the locality. At a later stage, the tourist revenues are
diffused to the rest of the region as a result of the emergence of a tourist
region, while costs remain concentrated.

According to this view, the negative effects of development are
associated with the enlargement of the tourism region, pushed by the
emergence of a class of 'false excursionists': would-be tourists that, faced
with the high prices and the limited capacity of central facilities, choose a
peripheral site for their visit to the main destination. A conflict arises
between the centre – bearing the costs of tourism activity and retaining a
decreasing share of the benefits – and the neighbouring communities.
The latter enjoy as *free-riders* the advantages of proximity to the main
destination; the core, instead, is pushed to impose higher taxes, and the
budgets for heritage maintenance, cleaning of the city and marketing
become overstretched. In the end, the possibility to preserve and market
the cultural supply depends on the availability of external sources of
income, like special laws or governmental transfers, increasing the
rigidity of the context in which tourism policies operate. At the same
time, tourism imposes a new valorisation dynamic, with devastating
effects on the less competitive sectors of the urban economy (Sasson,
1995). The destination is transformed into a tourism monoculture and
lacks any other economic activity that might balance a possible decline of
the local industry. This 'spatial-economic' approach to destination cycles
paves the way to a thorough analysis of the inter-relations between
spatial development and changes in the competitiveness and performance of the tourist city. This insight may give arguments to policymakers to calibrate their policy. What factors may lead to a decline of
tourism in heritage cities? How can this process be redressed towards a
sustainable path? The next section proposes an analytic framework to
describe why tourism development in heritage destinations is likely to be
unsustainable.

Space and Market: The Tourist Region as a 'Strategic Space'

The 'vicious circle' model consists of a series of logical *steps*, leading
from the enlargement of a destination's Functional Tourist Region
(FTR) under the pressure of persisting demand increases, to changes in
the market structure and in the behaviour of visitors, and feeding back to
the competitiveness of the destination. The main assumption is that
visitors are attracted to heritage cities because they hope to enjoy a
'heritage experience', which materially takes place through the aggregate
consumption of a set of goods and services, among which are the
cultural assets. Such assets are virtually irreproducible and remarkably

concentrated in historical centres (HCs). The quality of the experience depends not only on the quality of the primary heritage assets, but also on the quality of the environment in which the act of consumption takes place.

Tourism may grow 'undisturbed' in a city until some critical level of tourist development is reached. Beyond that point, problems begin. This critical threshold is easy to detect. The first visible sign of excessive tourism growth is the saturation of the central accommodation supply, which implies the expansion of supply facilities in the FTR around destinations.

In historical cities, the socioeconomic carrying capacity is likely to be violated at lower levels than the physical. However, even before getting to the point of physical or 'economic' saturation, the complementary industry will start to grow more dispersed, particularly those activities for which centrality becomes increasingly costly, such as new hotels, recreation areas and transport facilities. Therefore, the first step of the 'vicious circle' springs from the incapacity of the heritage city to limit the growth of tourism in accordance with its physical resources. The complementary product is much more mobile than the primary assets, and the administrative boundaries of the city are to a large extent insensitive to these dynamics. The region involved in tourist production tends to become larger, overstepping the boundaries of the municipality, as in the classic scheme of Miossec (1976). However, if the city is a very attractive one – as is the case of principal European cultural destinations like Venice, Bruges or Salzburg – it might well exceed regional or even national boundaries. As a consequence, the share of day-trippers among the overall number of visitors increases (Figure 9.2A). Among these, the

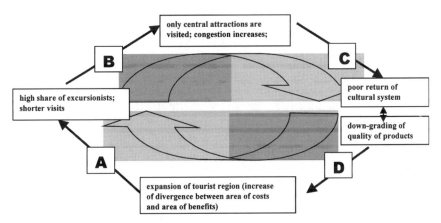

Figure 9.2 The 'vicious circle' of tourism development in heritage destinations

number of would-be tourists who turn into *false excursionists* because they cannot find a place in the city centre or because it is too expensive for their limited budgets, becomes higher and higher. (Van den Berg (1991) defines *real* excursionists as all those day-trippers who come to the visited city during the day from their normal place of residence and go back there in the evening: *indirect* excursionists are all those who visit the city during the day coming from and going back to another place that is the main destination of their journey; *false* excursionists are all those day visitors that spend the night in a different place from the city itself which remains the main destination of their excursion.)

This mode of visiting the city is remarkably less flexible than overnight-staying visits. On the one hand, day trips are typically more sensitive to weather conditions and 'special occasions', so that their seasonal pattern is more pronounced. On the other, visitors who commute have less time for retrieving 'tacit' information about the cultural and the complementary products. Consequently they tend to be (i) less aware of the qualitative content of the tourist goods and (ii) less reachable by traditional information tools. Therefore, they tend to concentrate in space, as the centrally located attractions are reached (and experienced) with a minimum level of information. This point is made by Towse (1991: 3–4). She assumes that visitors meet 'search costs' to gather information about the exact location, content and access of the cultural-tourist supply. In tourist gatherings around 'superstar' attractions, such costs are minimised. A further step in the vicious circle can thus be identified (Figure 9.2B). Day trips produce more congestion (and associated costs) than overnight stays, and their share of the total number of visits increases in the light of persistent demand pressure.

However, the imposition of costs on residents is not central to the present analysis. More relevant to this study is the impact of such an inefficient organisation of the visits on the quality of the tourist experience. Visitors now come from a wide (and widening) area and are therefore on average less informed about quality. Hence the suppliers of tourist goods in the city centre will be able to curtail the quality content of their products to increase their market share. This may happen with increased likeliness as the share of uninformed visitors increases. Pursuing this strategy, suppliers may lose some 'sophisticated' customers, but appeal to visitors less concerned with quality and much more sensitive to prices. In the end, in a typical process of adverse selection, only low-quality suppliers are left in the market. Whereas in the initial stages of growth the economic strength of tourism causes the displacement of other economic activities, at this later stage tourism tends to crowd itself out, replacing high-quality products with cheap standardised ones. At that point, the tourism space undergoes what is often referred to as 'McDonaldisation'. Not only is the capacity of products to match the demand of a certain segment of tourism compromised, but the whole aesthetic quality of the landscape and the system of cultural values embodied in the city is in jeopardy (Figure 9.2C).

The consequence of this decline in quality is a strong feedback to the very origin of such mechanisms. In the fourth and last step of the vicious circle, the regional dispersion of tourist activities has far-reaching implications on the sustainability of the development process. Visitors would set the cost of distance against prices and the quality of the complementary facilities, and find it more convenient to consume non-central facilities. The budget of visitors is reallocated between the goods in the tourist package in such a way that as many goods as possible are purchased outside the city, to save money and escape possible 'quality traps'. Indeed, more and more of those who still wish to visit the city will choose peripheral accommodation, thus feeding the dynamics of the vicious circle. The circle is now complete (Figure 9.2D). The expansion of the tourist region beyond the boundaries of the city centre, due first and foremost to the growth in demand, in the end causes that very expansion to continue.

Caserta and Russo (2002) analyse the process of quality downscaling in heritage destinations through a formal model. Utilising the reputation model toolbox developed by Tirole (1997) and applied to the tourist market by Keane (1997), they find that in order to continue to offer high quality, tourist suppliers charge a mark-up on prices. This depends on parameters such as the share of 'informed' visitors, which is most likely to be the resident tourists rather than the excursionists, whose learning capacity is eroded by time lost in commuting and compromised by lack of opportunities to compare or fewer contacts with informers. On this account, the widening of the tourist region is linked with the market behaviour of suppliers. As tourist regions become larger (due to persistent pressure from the world market), the conditions that are compatible with high quality are not sustained. Destinations are 'forced' to reorient themselves towards low-quality and low-budget visitors, those that are less likely to be struck by declines in quality. Caserta and Russo (2002) also discuss the full implications of this market change for the sustainability of tourism development in heritage destinations. To this aim they look at the effect on the performance and viability of the 'heritage industry' that is in charge of preserving the heritage and making it accessible to visitors and citizens. The combined effect of congestion and lack of information is that some cultural resources are underutilised while some others are overutilised. On the whole, far fewer visitors enjoy the cultural heritage than the city could afford. As a result, heritage attractions are less able to generate value. A larger share of the visitor budget comes to be spent on pricey tourist goods or simply leaks out of the destination to peripheral and unattractive places where better conditions are offered. To the extent that 'less sophisticated visitors' replace quality-sensitive tourists disaffected with the destination, the budgets spent on culture shrink.

In the end, this process affects the very competitive capacity of heritage cities. In fact, the resources needed for the maintenance of the heritage, for innovations in products, and for implementing information and marketing strategies cease, to a large extent, to be any longer in the control of the local institutions. That is particularly true in an era of decreasing transfers from central governments. Even if monuments and historical sites were subsidised, the conservation standards would be low and excessively rigid. In a 'user pays' approach, tourism should produce extra revenue to be channelled into heritage protection. If the tourist region around heritage centres is small, and/or it falls under the jurisdiction of an authority that can reallocate the tourist revenue generated in the periphery to the enhancement of the cultural assets in the core, then these mechanisms may operate. Yet, this may well not be the case, for two reasons.

i.   Despite any redistribution, the pressure for the enlargement of the tourist region will persist, leading to higher prices/lower quality than in competing destinations.

ii.   Frequently, tourist regions extend over regional or even national boundaries (as in the case of famous cultural cities such as Venice, Salzburg or Bruges), and then heritage preservation through fiscal mechanisms may be hard or impossible to enforce. Peripheral localities would *free-ride* on their proximity to the heritage centre until this loses its attraction capacity due to the changes experienced.

The 'vicious circle' provides a rationale for the decline of heritage destinations that one expects from a straightforward application of the TALC model. It emphasises that the maintenance of the 'place qualities' that make a destination attractive involve both direct maintenance and management costs and opportunity costs (like the 'information rents' captured by tourist suppliers). If tourism development does not generate in the process the resources that are needed to cover these costs, or leaks them out to a wider region, then this is not a sustainable process. The myopic, fragmented and preindustrial nature of the local tourist cluster (as analysed by authors such as Tremblay (1998) and Keane (1997)) ensures that such agents would not anticipate a foreseeable decline internalising the heritage conservation costs through responsible behaviour. A noteworthy element of this framework is the role of tourist regions, which present themselves as 'strategic spaces'. Tourist suppliers can relocate out of the city centre to escape physical and economic constraints, and in this way they produce spatial imbalance in the costs and benefits generated by tourism. In the same vein, visitors themselves may increase their utility by reallocating part of their time and expenditure outside the city, also contributing to a nonviable use of the heritage assets. The consequences for the wider issue of 'urban sustainability' can thus be discussed.

Though markets can substitute for one another, cities are not indifferent among them. First, declines in quality are reflected in worsening conditions for residents, whose demand base overlaps with that of tourists for many elements of the tourist package (e.g. food, public space, access). If the visitor/resident ratio is high, residents' welfare will be strongly eroded. That is commonly observed in tourist cities in which the residents have to turn to suburban shopping malls and non-tourist areas for their daily purchases, or relocate altogether as in the classical Tiebout (1956) scheme. Secondly, if a tourist city wishes to diversify its economy and become less dependent on a highly unstable industry like tourism, it needs to project an image of an attractive and convenient location that sells value for money (van den Berg & Braun, 1999). However, this option may not be available owing to the dynamics analysed in the model. What we find instead in heritage cities is a highly contentious environment where values are inflated by the pressure of the tourist economy.

A number of policy prescriptions follow immediately from the model structure. Each of the 'steps' that make up the vicious circle mechanism can be prevented from operating or its effects limited. First of all, the 'regionalisation' of tourism may be limited, by expanding the accommodation capacity of the city centre. When this is not an option anymore, the impact of dispersion on congestion can be eased through regional planning (for instance improving the connections between the core and periphery and favouring a 'compact' structure of the tourist region). Moreover, policy can play a role in preventing information asymmetries, for instance through information campaigns. The use of interactive Information and Communication Technologies (ICT) to inform visitors about attractions and itineraries, so that visits are as 'effective' as possible, is a promising alternative to unplanned, spontaneous visits. The incentives to cut quality can also be reduced if opportune regulating tools are deployed, like patenting and labelling.

Finally, the tendency to reallocate the budgets away from the cultural system (which would be typical of the last step of the vicious circle) can be counterbalanced through appropriate cultural policies. If the managers of heritage could turn its intrinsic qualities to account, generating the revenue needed for its preservation and promotion independently from central transfers and revenue redistribution within the tourist economy, then the HCs would remain attractive even in the face of a decline in quality in the tourist market. Moreover, there would ensue a self-selection of the visitor mix towards those high-paying, quality-rewarding visitors that are also the ones more likely to choose central accommodations for their visits. It would be an endogenous 'brake' to quality decline. However, the historical heritage, because of its characteristics as a merit good, is clearly the weakest link in the chain. Therefore, strategies that support an enhanced strong performance of the cultural assets of a city have to be diverse and complex. We may list the most promising:

- Strengthening the 'systemic' nature of the cultural sector. A coordinated marketing and communication strategy increases the efficiency in the provision of cultural products of different natures, addressing target markets in a coherent way.
- Diversifying the cultural supply. This would increase the city's appeal for visitor segments that at present are not attracted or less willing to pay for visiting the existing attractions, articulating the 'rejuvenation' concept in a heritage environment. Coupling heritage with other forms of cultural production could achieve desirable results.
- Increasing the quality and service levels in museums and other cultural resources. One good way to do this is to organise the supply of additional elements that are charged for at market prices: e.g. cafeterias, art galleries and bookshops, and electronic archive services around the core cultural supply.
- Increasing the capacity of visitors to interpret and assimilate culture. Visitors who are aware of the cultural and symbolic value of the heritage are more willing to reward it. The full comprehension of the role of specific cultural assets in the historical development of a place increases by association the curiosity towards other parts of the heritage, adding value to the whole system.
- Developing cultural attractions in strategic locations. Cultural attractions should be developed in the periphery of the tourist region, allowing for 'thematic' links with the main destination. In that way, the cultural function is also dispersed in space, following the dispersion of tourist facilities. Peripheral communities could be convinced in this way that they have something to gain from investing in their cultural attractiveness, participating in a regional system organised around many poles. From this point of view, the 'strategic role' of tourist regions could be turned from a source of problems into an opportunity for sustainable development.

Banal as these prescriptions may seem, they are more often the exception than the rule in real-word tourism policy. For years, cities have insisted on regulating the demand, trying to separate tourism from the urban economy rather than building the bridges and synergies that would make tourism a real engine of sustainable urban development. Demand regulation has often been directed at the wrong objectives – for instance, failing to discriminate between tourists and excursionists in visitor management policies – and has achieved poor results. As a consequence, today the pressure of tourism on urban centres and heritage assets is more critical than ever. A recent study on the 'sustainable use' of European heritage (van den Berg *et al.*, 2000) points out that the areas of 'crisis' for a sustainable use of the heritage are scattered throughout Europe. Among these, the heritage star attraction *par excellence* is the city of Venice.

A Case Study of the Vicious Circle Mechanism: Venice

The observation of tourist development trends in the city of Venice – possibly the most famous heritage destination in the world – may be a way to test the validity of the assumptions of the 'vicious circle'. Moreover, the sustainability of tourism development in Venice may be evaluated in the light of the prescriptions following from the use of that model.

Context

Venice is a well known international attraction. Yet, its HC in the heart of the lagoon is a 'problem area', whereas the mainland section of the city is well integrated in a booming regional economy. With young households pushed out by inaccessible housing prices and lack of specialised jobs, the population in the HC of Venice declined from 170,000 to 70,000 over the past half a century, and is still decreasing at a yearly rate of ca. 0.5%. The poor accessibility of the HC is one reason for workers to move outside to pursue jobs. The reoccurring floods generate economic instability. As a consequence, tourism is one of the few economic sectors experiencing full development left in the city. At the same time, it is seen by many as the main culprit of the irresistible decline faced by the city, because it produces all sorts of management and opportunity costs.

Visitors crowd the main attractions of the city – a sample of the best architecture spanning 13 centuries, inestimable collections and top cultural events. However, most visitors come for the city in itself rather than for any individual attraction. Its millenary history, its urban fabric, its atmosphere, the delicate interweaving of its water and built environment, suggest that the city as a whole should be considered a piece of art and a world heritage site, and it is deemed as such by international organisations such as UNESCO.

The visitors-to-residents ratio reached a peak of 50 to 1 in 2000 in Venice HC (175 to 1 if excursionists are considered as well, on the assumption that each tourist wants to visit the HC at least once during their vacation). Faced with this tourist pressure, which has increased further after the recent geopolitical changes in Europe and the rest of the world, Venice started a wide-ranging reflection on possible viable options for its development and on the role that tourism could play. One imperative was the necessity to quantify the tolerance of the city with regard to tourism, as it seemed clear that the costs of tourism could become unsustainable and compromise the endurance of the city's functionality and economic soundness. Canestrelli and Costa (1991) estimated the optimal level and composition of the visitor flow that is compatible with the full functionality of the different subsystems used by citizens and tourists alike (including transport, waste collection and access to cultural assets): i.e. the socioeconomic carrying capacity. This exercise indicated that Venice could absorb a total number of about 22,500 visitors, but only a maximum of 10,700 of these should be excursionists. This limit was surpassed in 1987 for 156 days in the year; the number of yearly violations has been increasing since then, despite any attempt to smooth the peaks through regulation and planning.

Analysis

Apart from its validity as a management prescription, this exercise made it clear once and for all that Venice attracts a flow comprised of very different types of visitors. Excursions represent by far the most popular way to visit the city, and have distinct profiles regarding their impact and management requirements. Moreover, even within the excursionist category, different types can be identified. Consequently, the territory involved in the delivery of the tourist product 'Venice' is much larger than the city itself. The FTR (the region where a substantial share of the visitors of the city is hosted overnight) has surpassed the provincial scale, extending to foreign countries like Austria and Slovenia, and has become specialised. Part of the territory surrounding Venice, whatever its (sometimes nil) intrinsic cultural richness, attracts a flow of visitors just because of its proximity to the city. In addition, another portion of the region, which is specialised in seaside tourism, generates a substantial share of 'indirect' excursions to the city that adds to the 'normal' tourist flow.

Though upgraded information is badly missing, it is today accepted that more than 80% of the daily arrivals in the HC are excursionists. On average, daily visitors spend less in the city than overnight-staying visitors (as a substantial part of their budget – an estimated 60% – is spent in hotel accommodations elsewhere) and have a distinct logistic behaviour that supports the assumption of the 'vicious circle' mechanism. Excursionists do not only spend less money in the city, producing a spatial mismatch between costs and benefits generated by tourism, but they also have less time and information, attributes that are needed to spend their budgets 'efficiently', as suggested by the model presented earlier.

A visitor survey of 1997 allowed reconstruction of the main directions of visitor behaviour in the city. A random sample of 1500 visitors over a one-year period was surveyed (the main results are summarised in ICARE, 1997). Sixty to seventy per cent of the daily flow of people (and vehicles) is concentrated in a couple of hours in the morning and another couple of hours in the afternoon. The average duration of a day trip to Venice is about eight hours, three-fifths of the visits being shorter. Moreover, the bulk of this flow approaches Venice through its only road/rail connection with the mainland, provoking congestion on the main routes connecting that terminal to the central areas.

The choice of the attractions to visit and the itinerary are consequently affected, supporting Towse's (1991) hypothesis about crowding to 'superstar' attractions as a result of trying to minimise search costs and time in situations of limited information. The resulting maps of visitor itineraries with different time budgets (Figure 9.3a–d) illustrates that for the biggest share of visitors, who stay in the city for less than 12 h, the number of attractions accessed is severely limited. Visitors are on the whole more likely to 'discover' attractions that they did not explicitly wish to visit before their arrival in Venice, the closer the locations of such attractions are to the main tourist routes. Location – and not intrinsic cultural motives – guides the visiting patterns, and that trend is reinforced as time is shorter and information scarcer. The impact on the cultural system is a serious mismatch between potential capacity and actual visiting on a territorial basis.

As a result of the combined effect of congestion and lack of information, some cultural resources – the most central ones – are overcrowded whereas others, slightly out of the main tourist corridors, are utilised below their capacity. On the whole, far fewer visitors are able to enjoy the cultural heritage than the city could afford. Data relative to the main attractions show that on average one out of 4.4 visitors buys a ticket to one museum and just one out of 55.7 enters a church when they have to pay for it. In aggregate, visitation rates decrease in time. Figure 9.4 describes the extent of the mismatch between visits to the city (grey bars) and visits to its main cultural institutions, such as the centrally located Doges' Palace, the Guggenheim collection and the Academia Art Gallery, possibly one of the greatest collections of Italian renaissance arts.

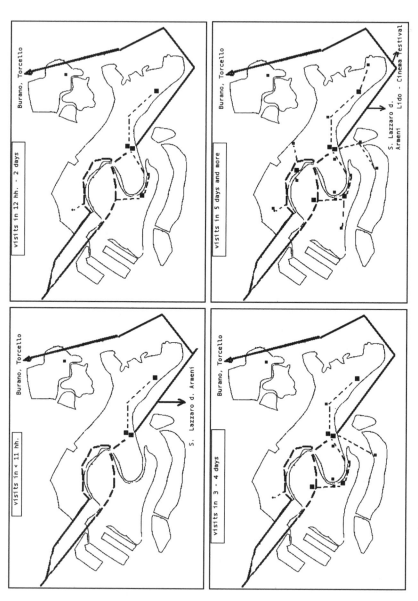

Figure 9.3a–d Time–budget analysis of cultural visits in Venice

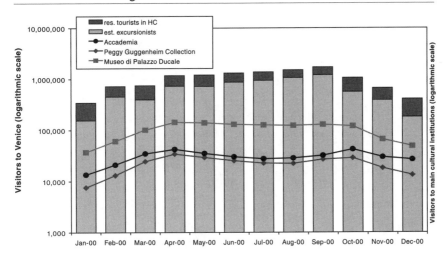

Figure 9.4 Visits to the city and visits to the main cultural institutions, Year 2000. Logarithmic scale.

However, as was argued earlier, primary cultural products are not the only elements to be affected in the vicious circle mechanism; more importantly, the very market structure for secondary or complementary tourist goods changes, provoking unsustainable effects in terms of consumption decisions of visitors. Unfortunately, it is rather hard to monitor the quality of the tourist goods on offer. The only sector for which reliable and comparable information is available is hospitality.

In Figure 9.5 the mapping of price-to-quality ratios (calculated as the average price of one star in a hotel room) shows that the priciest rooms are clustered around the main tourist gathering point of St. Mark's Square, where the first hotels were erected at the beginning of the 20th century. These hotels clearly count on a 'reputation rent' in fixing prices. Aside from them, one can see newer expensive hotels along the main corridors from the central station to St. Mark and in the proximity of the station itself. In these locations they exploit 'accessibility rents'. The same trends would be observed in relation to other tourist subsectors. For the sake of simplicity, the local tourist industry has been further divided isolating those activities called 'ancillary' by Jansen-Verbeke (1986), which in the light of the vicious circle models are more likely to seek the 'window effect', charging highest prices on account of imperfect consumer information. Among these are souvenir shops, street vendors and entertainment facilities. The concentration of these outlets in the most central areas (Figure 9.6) is again revelatory of an ongoing change in the tourist market. The location patterns of such subsectors reveal that whereas the traditional form of tourist crowding-out results in the substitution of a resident activity with a tourist activity, a new

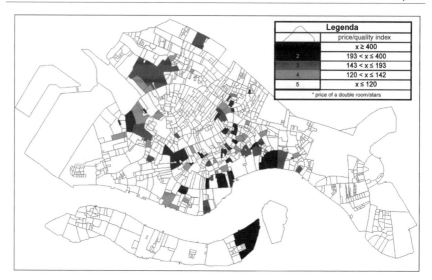

Figure 9.5 Price-to-quality ratios (av. price of stars) in Venice HC, Year 2001, census zones

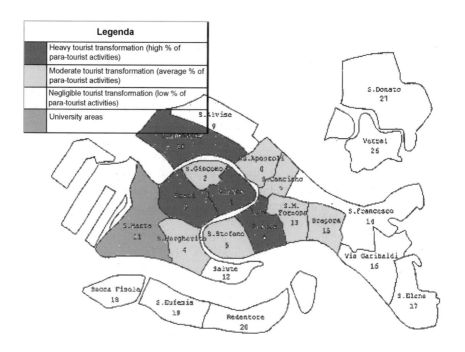

Figure 9.6 Tourist transformation in different areas within Venice HC

dimension is emerging today: the substitution within the tourist industry of high-quality with low-quality suppliers.

There are signs that in Venice the process of quality downscaling has in fact started to affect the consumption decisions of visitors, as foreseen in the fourth step of the vicious circle. Even on peak days, the hotel rooms in the upper categories are not fully occupied, and this occurs with increasing frequency.

The number of 'repeat visitors' is decreasing. Despite different interpretations in the literature (Darnell & Johnson, 2001), a decrease in interest from the 'traditional', high-paying segments and a simultaneous expansion of new origin markets does not suggest an improvement, as the new market segments have a lesser capacity to pay and a less sustainable logistic behaviour.

The share of 'group visits' in total tourism is increasing with respect to individual tourists. The most recent information estimates group visits at 32% of the total.

Tour operators are selling packages including daily visits to Venice that include overnight stays at increasingly distant locations. A number of interviews with local travel agents clarified that there is a relationship between the type of clientele and the location that is offered, especially to groups and other price-sensitive visitor types. This information should be read in conjunction with the analysis of Costa and Manente (1995: 67), who indicate that 'repeat' visitors are the most likely to spend the night in the hinterland of Venice: those who have already visited the city, on their return are likely to come as 'false excursionists'.

These 'clues' indicate that the prevalence of day trips as a means to visit Venice is less and less linked to the saturation of central accommodation, and more the result of a decision taking into consideration some of the perceived 'costs' of sleeping in Venice. As the concept of the vicious circle suggests, the elements of distortion in the tourist use of the city become self-feeding, creating further distortions.

Policy

Where is Venice going? Is tourism development in Venice proceeding relentlessly, as the main indicators would suggest, or might we expect a 'decline' in its life cycle? And what can the city do about it? The immediate suggestion from the data illustrated is that despite the richness and variety of the cultural system of Venice, both the heritage and the events, the capacity of this system to generate value is rather low. Moreover, the tourist market is not supporting a 'sustainable use' of that heritage. The price–quality spiral threatens to affect the reputation of Venice as a destination in the long term, to the benefit of its competitors. The very structure of the tourist region, where many of the benefits accrue to distant second-order destinations, is producing a 'fiscal crisis' for the maintenance of the heritage. The necessary funds, which depend on national transfers and international donors, are increasingly at stake. What is worse, this system is not inducing responsible behaviour on the supply side, which is oriented to rent extraction more than ever.

In other words, the developments conceptualised in the vicious circle model are largely present and the model seems to be developing to the full, requiring an integral policy response that addresses each of the steps of that mechanism. Hence, local policymakers should act to smooth the visitor pressure through effective tourism planning and management tools, but they also have to consider the market variables, reducing information asymmetries and controlling quality. They also have to bring forward an enhancement of the system of value generation from the cultural supply, in at least two directions: (a) intercepting a larger share of visitor expenditure and (b) becoming more diverse and spatially articulated.

The poor return from a policy approach totally focusing on demand regulation – perhaps hiding the lack of any approach whatsoever – started to be acknowledged by decision-makers and public opinion in the last few years. However, it would never have reached the top of the political agenda were it not for a series of unfortunate circumstances. First of all, there was a boom in day visits from former socialist countries in the late 1980s. These new flows spend practically nothing, have pushed congestion to the extreme, and produced a lot of waste, for which Venetians have come to pay the highest collection tax rate in Italy. The public resentment, misunderstood at that time as 'tourist racism', made it clear and very apparent that not all tourism is good, and that tourism may change for the worse if unguided. This argument was reinforced by two dramatic incidents. The first was the concert of Pink Floyd off St. Mark Square in 1989 – the event attracted a crowd of more than 200,000 without adequate facilities being set up for resting, sleeping or restoring, paralysing the city for days. The second was the fire that destroyed the city's prestigious theatre, La Fenice, in 1995. Another proposed mass event, the International Expo 2000, was finally turned down after the mobilisation of public opinion, supported by national and international organisations. It was then finally accepted that the management of tourism had to change, that the cultural heritage was a precious resource demanding preservation, and that tourism had to be a lever and not an impediment to other activities.

A number of new projects may finally trigger an appropriate process, as they are likely to improve the spatial and industrial configuration of various elements in the Venetian tourist system. On the marketing side, the promotion and commercialisation of most cultural assets as an integrated system (involving common ticketing, coordination of events, websites and the creation of a marketing agency) has been accepted, overcoming a long-lasting fragmentation in the management and ownership structure of cultural goods. Zago (1996) counts at least 10 institutions, public or private, directly responsible for the museums of Venice. Proactive cultural marketing is a new thing for a city that used to consider its international fame sufficient to attract a steadily growing flow of visitors. Moreover, an effort is being made to link the existing resources through advanced communication technologies, with the provision of online archival services and information facilities. Internal accessibility will be enhanced with the rationalisation of water transport, the diversification of access points to the HC and the creation of alternative itineraries and water routes. In the absence of such facilities as signposts or kiosks, this would result in a simple shift of crowds from one part to the other. However, the city is now convinced that the spatial management of the tourist flows must be pursued through an integral approach that also considers the accessibility and strategic location of the cultural supply.

Two management tools worth mentioning have been introduced recently:

(1) One is the ALATA partnership, a consortium of municipalities and provinces around Venice that got together to manage more effectively the incoming flows on the occasion of the Holy Year, 2000. A complex information system and a series of information points were set up to this aim. The rationale for this partnership is that the excess visitor flow expected in that year (approximately 6 million) would saturate Venice's capacity but would be attractive for peripheral destinations which are generally overlooked by tourists, starting a process of 'dispersion' of the flows in the tourist region of Venice.

(2) The second is the Venice Card, a pass (utilising 'contact-less' technology) to access a variety of facilities and functions. The Card is purchased by tourists when they send in the booking for their accommodation, and physically collected upon arrival at one of the city's terminals. The number of Cards issued is to be equal to the tolerance threshold, to be periodically determined. In that way, motivated cultural tourists get a better deal because they can more easily discover what is on offer, and then arrange their itineraries, expediently benefiting from free parking, access to limited-number events, reduced time in queues and reductions of transport fares. At the same time, the city is better off because it attracts relatively high-spending and well organised tourists.

Overall, these projects are fully consistent with the integral, complex and spatially inclusive policy approach dictated by the vicious circle.

It should be noted however that none of them was completely successful. ALATA collapsed when the 'business model' provided by the Holy Year extra-movement (and funding) was over. After the event, the peripheral sites in the tourist region of Venice found it again more convenient to play against Venice as free-riders. The Venice Card has finally been issued; however it is not the 'smart card' version originally planned, but a normal ticket, which is fine as a marketing tool but hardly achieves any of the logistic/management objectives. It is thus insufficiently flexible to manage different kinds of visitors in an interactive environment. That was due to the difficulty in getting all the stakeholders to participate in the system right from the start, and to the related delay in establishing the necessary infrastructure. The Venice Card's managing company has opted, therefore, for a 'low-profile' introduction, hoping to build up a consensus for the 'smart' version of the card. These partial failures are illustrative of the implementation difficulties faced by many heritage-city managers. Policy changes of this magnitude require a high 'organising capacity' through strategic networking and capacity building, as suggested by van den Berg and Braun (1999).

Conclusions and Implications for Life-cycle Models

This chapter has presented an original interpretation of the relations between space and market which supports the assumption of a cyclical development pattern in urban heritage destinations, for which relatively little evidence has been produced in the literature. The application of this model, however, can be extended to a variety of contexts, and in particular to those in which the local capacity is negligible with respect to the global dimension of tourism.

The vicious circle model should not be confused with the destination cycle; rather, it should be seen as an 'appendix' to it, providing a spatial–economic explanation for the decline stage of the TALC. It is argued that the reasons for decline have to be looked for in the inability of tourism to generate the resources that are needed to 'keep up' the quality of the destination, both for what is the market for tourist goods, and the heritage itself. We are not concerned in this study with the start-up process. In fact, it is assumed that tourism is a viable industry in the beginning, and attention is focused on the mature stage of the tourist industry, in order to better understand the determinants and the consequences of change within a region. Another point of distinction is that the time horizon of destination cycles is medium to long, whereas the four steps of the vicious circle model, while logically sequential, may in fact occur simultaneously from the moment of saturation of the accommodation capacity in the city centre.

One of the main difficulties with the operational use of the TALC has been in its 'tautological' nature (see, for instance, Martin & Uysal, 1990): the cyclical trend is likely to be perceived as a problem when the problem is already there. This springs from the difficulty of using it as a forecasting model. The underlying economic variables are not clearly identified, and neither is the dynamic mechanism; moreover the critical thresholds tend to be different in each context or type of destination. The TALC methodology may gain from the vicious circle conceptualisation, because this framework can easily be benchmarked through indicators that are valid in all circumstances and may anticipate the likely emergence of decline (see chapters by Berry and Manente and Pechlaner in other volume, editor). Policymakers may set up an apparatus to signal when any step of the vicious circle is critical, and act to smooth it. The 'economic nature' of these indicators makes it possible to calibrate policy tools accordingly. As long as the pressure from visitor demand persists, the circle will continue to operate, and when it is endogenously reduced as a consequence of the model's mechanism, the sustainable development of the destination is at stake. Hence policy should be integral in character, preventing the model from operating, and at the same time reducing the pressure factors at the relevant territorial level.

There is however another strong message emerging from the use of this model, one vital matter that has been largely left out of the destination-cycle literature: the fact that unsustainable tourism development may come not only from abuse of the heritage, but also from its insufficient use (van der Borg *et al.*, 2000). This idea underscores the fact that even though physical impacts must remain a focus of the management of sustainable tourism, there should be more attention paid to the question of how to link heritage preservation to an integrated and balanced tourism development. As Gartner (2002: 11) puts it,

> Whether one believes in product life-cycle to explain the rise and fall of consumer acceptance, or not, it is clear that demand for culturally-based tourism products, which is reported to have increased substantially in recent times, is still lower than the supply of products. In this situation, other factors such as service, value added, niche marketing take on greater importance.

Tourism management often seems to miss the point, treating tourism as a sector to be 'isolated' from other functions performed by a city, rather than as an engine of harmonious, synergetic regional development. The peculiar nature of the resources on which heritage tourism is based, and the extreme complexity of the environment with which tourism strategies have to cope, contribute to the incapacity of traditional policy approaches to fully grasp and govern the process.

Chapter 10
The TALC and Heritage Sites

JANE MALCOLM-DAVIES

Introduction

The democratisation of culture has permitted the British bourgeoisie to participate in ways previously reserved for the elite before the two world wars. Long before that, Napoleon sneered at the English as a nation of shopkeepers. Now, it seems, even the symbols of power – royal palaces, stately homes, ancient cathedrals – are in the hands of middle-class marketeers, desperate to attract visitors. Heritage sites are being redefined as products and this new perspective suggests that they are subject to the vagaries of the product life-cycle. It is the purpose of this paper to investigate whether this revolution is actually taking place and, if so, whether it threatens what it promises to preserve.

Heritage attractions, whatever their original functions, found themselves thrust into a highly competitive marketplace during the 1980s. There are myriad activities that offer alternative leisure experiences. There has been a growth in book sales and an expansion of networked entertainment services in the home in addition to walking for pleasure and sports or leisure centre activities (Davies, 1994: 23). The attractions sector itself has boomed. In the UK, the number of tourist attractions increased dramatically at the end of the 20th century – 47% of all existing attractions have appeared since 1980 (Middleton, 2001: 196). There is much evidence of a growth in heritage attractions in particular (Hall & McArthur, 1996; Hooper-Greenhill, 1994; Yale, 1998). It is difficult to think in terms of competition for attractions such as Notre Dame Cathedral, the Pyramids and Buckingham Palace because they are all unique (Swarbrooke, 1995: 49). But it is nevertheless true that Notre Dame is just one of many great cathedrals, the Pyramids one of many ancient burial complexes and Buckingham Palace one of many royal residences.

The competition phenomenon has not been confined to those places where the economics of the marketplace held sway: 'The number of museums in both western and eastern European countries increased substantially during the 1970s and 1980s ... Museum growth was also encouraged by Communist regimes in eastern Europe during the 1980s, although arguably with different motives from their western counterparts' (Richards, 1996: 10–11). With the collapse of the Soviet Union and the reunification of Germany, the last bastion of market-protected heritage bit the dust.

The test for success for cultural institutions can no longer be a purely aesthetic one. They must justify themselves in quantitative terms, such as the number of visitors or income generated. These performance indicators are equally important for institutions which operate in a wholly commercial environment and for publicly funded organisations which have to demonstrate the effectiveness of subsidy (Richards, 1996: 13). Improved access or display is now essential for a successful Heritage Lottery Fund grant in the UK (Heritage Lottery Fund, 1997). Much that has been written about these trends focuses on museums, which stand as representatives of what is happening in other heritage sectors (Davies, 1994: 24; Light, 1995: 118). Peter Longman of the Museums and Galleries Commission remarked in 1994: 'All museums now exist in a mixed economy. Very few can rely solely on the public purse... This means that they are subject to fluctuations in the economy, and prey to demographic and social trends in much the same way as any other industry' (Davies, 1994: 4).

The move to the marketplace has brought about fundamental changes in the management of heritage attractions. There has been a discernible shift from historical monument to heritage product since 1850 (Figure 10.1). Three successive management approaches are identifiable – preservation, conservation and heritage (Ashworth, 1994: 15). The 'heritage' phase is the one in which the resource is transformed into a product for consumption in the marketplace. In this transformation many managers and commentators ignore any distinction between the management of a historic site and a theme park, applying mass-market concepts to heritage attractions without a second thought (Swarbrooke, 1995; Walsh-Heron & Stevens, 1990). This belittles the real challenges facing fragile sites under increasing visitor pressure. Some authors are more sensitive to historic sites' particular concerns, noting that heritage attractions are, for the most part, concerned with the management of vulnerable resources (Richards, 1996).

Nevertheless, the stress now is on inviting people in, not tolerating them if they arrive. 'The balance of power in museums is shifting from those who care for objects to include, and often prioritise those who care for people' (Hooper-Greenhill, 1994: 1). These changed priorities are due in part to political forces. The withdrawal of state funding from the arts in general has forced heritage attractions to face up to the challenge of making money. Government-created quangos in the UK have been charged with making ruins (English Heritage) and redundant official residences (Historic Royal Palaces) accessible to wider audiences both physically and intellectually (HRPA, 1995). While public responsibilities have been shifted to the private sector, entrepreneurs

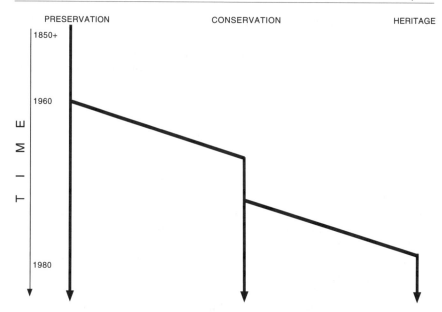

Figure 10.1 Phases in the evolutionary process: Historical monument to heritage product (Ashworth, 1994: 15)

have moved in on the same market: 'One striking feature of these recent developments has been the increased privatisation of the heritage/museum industry, with 56% of recently opened museums being in the private sector' (Urry, 1990: 107).

The theory of the product life-cycle, which is frequently discussed in relation to destinations (Cooper, 1992), is applicable to heritage attractions, although few authors note it. A detailed study of visitor figures to 16 ecomuseums such as Skansen in Stockholm, Old Sturbridge Village in Massachusetts, and the Museum of Welsh Life in Cardiff, demonstrated the classic product life-cycle despite geographical and economic differences (Figure 10.2). Having recognised the downturn in their visitorship, several of the ecomuseums set about rejuvenating their product. At Sovereign Hill in Victoria (Australia), a *son-et-lumière* experience was developed to rekindle interest in the site; while at the Museum of Welsh Life a competitively priced season ticket contributed to a recovery (de Haan, 1997: 26–27).

Rejuvenation

A Confederation of British Industry survey showed that 'mature attractions which recognised/anticipated changing market trends, had successfully developed to meet those needs, and experienced sustained

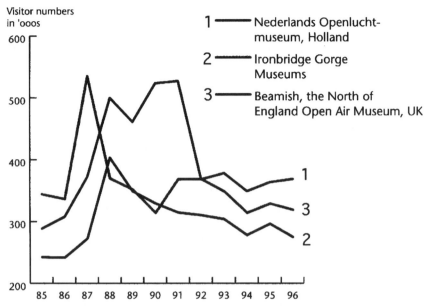

Visitor numbers in 'ooos

1 ——— Nederlands Openlucht-museum, Holland

2 ——— Ironbridge Gorge Museums

3 ——— Beamish, the North of England Open Air Museum, UK

Promotional activities and local events generate noticeable peaks in visits, but are rarely sustained

Figure 10.2 The product life cycle theory applied to ecomuseums (de Haan, 1997: 26)

growth as a result' (CBI, 1998: 20). The need for rejuvenation of resources as visitor numbers fall over time is recognised in the management of theme parks and addressed by the development of new and yet more thrilling rides, often costing as much as £1 million each (Gilling, 1995: 41). Heritage sites may introduce new methods of presentation or improved support services such as dining facilities in order to boost falling admissions, although usually at considerably less cost (Swarbrooke, 1995: 48).

In 1996, the Jorvik Viking Centre in York (UK) updated its static displays, added an opportunity for visitor participation and introduced costumed interpreters (Yale, 1998: 131). The introduction or retraining of front-of-house staff is a way of introducing novelty (Holloway, 1994: 144) and enhancing the visitor experience (Richards, 1992: 39), and thereafter, regular changes to their activities and presentations are cheaper than replacing technological systems of display (Binks *et al.*, 1988: 39). But even these relatively inexpensive ways of rejuvenating an experience are not without difficulties for the heritage sector. People are a bothersome business and few heritage organisations have the time or expertise to recruit, train, motivate and retrain staff in what can become a boring and repetitive job (Risk, 1994: 326).

Heritage sector rejuvenations are cheap, expedient solutions compared to those dreamed up by private attractions such as Camelot, Alton Towers and Blackpool Pleasure Beach where £3–5 million is spent on rejuvenation every few years (Davis, 2001: 26). Wigan Pier's *The way we were* heritage centre undertook a major overhaul of what it was offering in 1999/2000 when a Single Regeneration Budget grant permitted an investment of £2.2 million in Robert Opie's Museum of Memories. In its first year, the Opie collection attracted 260,000 visitors but in 2000/01 visitation fell back to 160,000 again. How often may a heritage attraction tap into such funds? One historic house owner reported that having received a government grant in 1969, he had been refused every application ever since (Williams & Bradlaw, 2001: 286).

If rejuvenation at heritage sites is not possible through major new projects, the facilities at heritage sites may be tailored to match the benefits sought by specific visitors in order to exploit a target market successfully (Swarbrooke, 1995) but it is not often that this happens. Manchester's Museum of Science and Industry published a marketing plan in 1992, which presented information on the current visitor profile and the potential for development in the main segments of that market with strategies to increase the existing customer base and attract new audiences (Hooper-Greenhill, 1994: 175). By the mid-1990s, *The way we were* recognised that most of its 160,000 visitors were schoolchildren. The management did something rare in the 'We're here for everyone' world of heritage attractions – it chose a target market and worked to produce specially tailored packages. It focused firmly on the educational market: 'Schools are our lifeblood', maintains the council's group marketing officer (Davis, 2001: 24–27).

Marketing Heritage Sites

The postmodern era has been marked by the emergence of new interest groups and specialised markets (Richards, 1996: 10–11). A heritage market segment may be identified by grouping all potential visitors with similar motivations and propensities towards particular types of heritage or visitor experiences (Hall & MacArthur, 1996). Social psychologists, market researchers and business forecasters have identified attitudes and lifestyles as important alternatives to the traditional classification of people by demographics and socioeconomic groups (Middleton, 1990: 29–31). Middleton argues that museums should target an 'inner directed' group which has been growing in significance (from 25% to over 40% of the population) over the past 20 years. This group is made up of 'people of all social groups and income levels, mostly educated beyond school leaving age and typically aged over 40, who have achieved the self confidence, maturity of personality and tolerance to be able to live easily with themselves and social contacts' (Middleton, 1990: 30). This is a significant alternative to more traditional segmentation approaches (Davies, 1994: 58). Another alternative is the 'values and lifestyles' framework, which identifies nine different types of consumer (Gunther, 1999: 119). This has been used to target adults most likely to visit museums (Mitchell, 1984: 8).

A further attempt to segment the London (UK) tourist attraction market in a different way (Figure 10.3) is based on a psychographic analysis of motivation (Plog, 1991). It puts the Tower of London on the itinerary of the psychocentric visitor and the Hayward Gallery on that of the allocentric (Richards, 1992: 7). The Canadian Museum of Civilization in Hull has segmented its market according to patterns of behaviour and designed exhibits to suit: visitors can be characterised as 'streakers', 'strollers' or 'students' (MacDonald & Alsford, 1989: 74). Both these approaches go some way to differentiating the visitors in terms of personality but their usefulness is questionable in a sector lacking the management skills to innovate and take risks (Graham & Lennon, 2002: 216).

Nevertheless, the application of mass marketing ideas to heritage sites has had the advantage of freeing some from old-fashioned notions of exclusivity. The shift from the traditional collection, care and conservation-centred approach to a concern for the visitors' welfare is analogous to the switch from a product-orientated approach to a

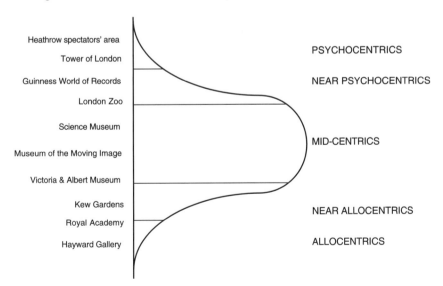

Figure 10.3 Psychographic positions of London paid admission visitor attractions (Richards, 1992: 7)

customer-orientated culture (Kotler, 1984: 23). A marketing manager's attention usually focuses on the four elements of the marketing mix (price, product, place and promotion) and how they may be manipulated to increase market share and revenue generation (Hall & McArthur, 1996: 26). Each may be used to stimulate visitation at a time when the life-cycle curve suggests the market is ready for a boost.

The price

One predictable manifestation of heritage sites being treated as products would be a new emphasis on price as a strategic component of the marketing mix. Some museums and other heritage attractions have attempted to cover their costs with increased admission charges or introduced them for the first time. Kirby (1988) provides an excellent résumé of the resulting controversy in the UK – attendances at the National Maritime Museum in London fell by 37% in the year charges were imposed. However, other museums reported initial problems followed by a gradual rise in numbers or an increase in visitation, such as that experienced by the Imperial War Museum in London (UK), when admission fees coincided with a major redevelopment programme (Lilley, 1990: 12). More recently, the sudden absence of admission charges at national (i.e. government-funded) museums in December 2001 resulted in the doubling of numbers at many (DCMS, 7 January 2002), stealing visitors from their competitors who have not benefited from the government's largesse. In this context, the decision to charge, and what to charge, has not been in line with sharp-nosed business practices. This is a marketplace where producers are not free to set competitive prices because the government is subsidising major players (HCCMSC, 2002: 88).

There is also some prejudice against charging premium prices at heritage sites because their mission is frequently seen as primarily educational and that therefore they should be accessible to all. For example, under the government legislation of 1983 that created English Heritage in the United Kingdom, it has a statutory duty to provide educational facilities, advice and information to the public (Prentice & Prentice, 1989: 155). One of its aims is the promotion of wider knowledge and enjoyment of England's heritage of ancient monuments and historic buildings (English Heritage Education Service, 1986). Meanwhile, Cadw (the government body responsible for Welsh historic monuments in the UK) 'seeks to broaden the awareness of all Welsh people wherever they may be, and the visitors to Wales, to help them learn, to understand, to enjoy the 6,000 years of history visible in the landscape' (Prentice & Prentice, 1989: 155–156). Many recently established heritage attractions incorporate educational aims in their mission statements (in the UK, the Ironbridge Gorge Museum, the York Archaeological Trust and Wigan Pier Heritage Centre are to a greater or lesser extent established as charitable educational organisations), although this does not stop them from charging higher prices than their publicly managed competitors.

In a study of factors affecting visitation in 1999, just 4% of historical, garden and museum attraction managers suggested that changes in admission charges were responsible for falling numbers, whereas 32% of them identified the weather as the cause (Hanna, 1994: A61). A study of pricing decisions at attractions in England concluded that the sector is cautious and conservative in its pricing decisions, with respondents stating that their admission fees were primarily linked to 'what the market will bear' (65%), costs (51%) or competitors' prices (23%) (Rogers, 1995). Rarely is price used to differentiate sites in the marketplace and the range of admission charges in the UK is very narrow – just 14% charge up to £1, while only 9% charge more than £5. The average price is £2.97 (Hanna, 1998: 29). Tourist attractions in general are thought to be overpriced by UK residents (MAI, 2000: 42). However, there is evidence that this is not true of heritage sites. A study of visitors at Warkworth Castle in 1994 suggested that they were (on average) prepared to pay 91 pence (29%) more than the adult admission price of £1.80 (Powe & Willis, 1996: 266). Studies of price elasticity in relation to increases at heritage sites have shown that it is generally low, particularly in the long term (Bouvaird *et al.*, 1984; Jones, 1984; Snaith, 1975).

There are few instances of cut-price admission fees offered in the last few days of an exhibition or lower prices for admission in the off-season. Still fewer heritage sites willingly banish charging altogether despite the clear relationship between free access and increased admission. When the National Museum and Galleries in Merseyside became free in December 2001, the number of visitors for the month rose by 56% on the previous December; and at the National Railway Museum in York there was an increase of 66% (DCMS, 7 January 2002). However, a MORI poll in September 2002 revealed that 41% of visitors to museums were not influenced by the abolition of entry fees and a further 40% were not aware that fees had been abolished (HCCMSC, 2002: 89).

Pricing policies may also be employed to preserve cultural assets intact both in terms of the visitor experience and the longevity of the resource. A £5 admission charge at Westminster Abbey was intended to reduce the impact on the building of nearly three million visitors a year and restore its atmosphere as a place of prayer (Fyall & Garrod, 1998: 226).

The UK lacks a tradition of philanthropy towards heritage resources in stark contrast to North America, where many museums and historic sites have enjoyed long associations with successive generations of a generous family (Alberge & Rumbelow, 2003: 3). In Europe too there are examples of art collections housed and presented at the expense of individual patrons such as the Museo Thyssen-Bornemisza in Madrid (Shnayerson, 2002: 74–83). Admission charges are therefore a fact of life for many heritage sites in the UK and yet there is little evidence that price is manipulated as a strategic component of their marketing mix.

The promotion

Heritage sites do not spend a great deal of money on promotion, whether it be through public relations or advertising campaigns. Alton Towers Pleasure Park spent £2.6 million on advertising in 1998 compared to Beaulieu's (a stately home with a Motor Museum) £175,000 and Historic Scotland's £153,000 (for 300 properties, 70 of which charge admission) in 1997 (Griffiths, 1998: 45). Hampton Court Palace struck a deal with media production company Bazal to develop a 'behind the scenes' television series to promote it around the world (Sturgis: 1998). Both Chatsworth and Woburn Abbey have offered similar televised peeps behind their green baize doors in the hope of boosting visitor numbers. However, promotional activity for most heritage sites is confined to a special events programme. These are often managed in-house, exploit local volunteer labour and use craftsworkers who sell their wares, amateur re-enactment societies or may rely on enthusiasts with visually impressive hobbies such as ballooning or vintage car restoration. Historically themed events are often designed to maximise attendance by taking a cavalier approach to the known history of the site. In order that special events are possible at Plimoth Plantation in Massachusetts (USA), 'historical events have to be glamourised a bit or historical dates shifted a little' (Snow, 1993: 88). A wedding of 1627 is knowingly recreated each year more lavishly than is 'probably proper' for the time and place. At other times of year, simple weddings are staged as a counterbalance to this festive special event (Snow, 1993: 88–89).

It is difficult to reconcile the promotional needs of a site with the reality of the place recorded in historical documents. Colonial Williamsburg in Virginia (USA) has wrestled with the evidence of 'unpleasant subjects, unappetising smells, and ugly sights' in 1770s Virginia, while offering 'itself as a holiday destination, a place for relaxing, entertaining, even romantic, vacation' (Leon & Piatt, 1989: 75). Themes are often reduced to simple dichotomies which are easy to transmit in advertising material and on-site information. Lévi-Strauss and other structuralists argued that humans establish oppositional sets in their minds (high/low, wet/dry, black/white) in order to process and store information (MacDonald & Alsford, 1989: 62). This tendency frequently reduces complex cultural phenomena to simplistic scenarios. The medieval tournament with its chivalric pomp and careful ceremony is often presented as the black knight (bad) losing to the white knight (good). A comprehensive survey of special events associated with historic houses in the USA found that a great many focus on 'mundane activities' such as household chores, often on seasonal themes, because 'they are fairly simple to stage' (Janiskee, 1996: 410). The special events are, for the most part, superficial representations of the history of the houses at which they are held (Janiskee, 1996: 407–409).

The chief executive of English Heritage has argued that special events are a 'taster', and that they invite people to investigate further these aspects of English history. Critics do not agree:

> These events are nothing but mere titillation, meaningless amateur dramatics promoting the postmodern simulacrum, a hazy image of a manipulated and trivialised past. The most ridiculous was the American Civil War garrison at Fort Brockhurst, Hampshire... History is decontextualised and mixed with non-history in a promotion of a pastiche. English Heritage has argued that because these so-called recreations are popular, that makes them acceptable. (Walsh, 1991: 102–103)

Promotion is not implemented with the rigour of commercial operations at most heritage sites. Low cost special events tend to be the mainstay of their promotional efforts and there is some evidence that their transience permits a lowering of curatorial standards (Sansom, 1996: 120).

The place

This element of the marketing mix has a radically different application to tourist attractions in that the customer travels to the product, rather than vice versa, and prepurchase is rare. It is theme parks which tend to use intermediaries to widen their point-of-sale via ticketing agencies as their prices offer a viable level of income as commission (Swarbrooke, 1995: 210–211). However, there are examples of heritage sites using intermediaries to sell advance tickets: for example, Buckingham Palace which also exploits the internet as a point-of-sale, levying a £1 booking fee on each transaction. Few tourist attraction websites allow online ticketing in this way, although they clearly fulfil a promotional role in offering up-to-date, comprehensive information about a site, its location and the visitor experience (Fenn, 2001: 53). There have been some questionable marriages between the commercial world and historic houses in attempts to widen the point-of-sale. In 2001, Historic Royal Palaces offered Sainsbury supermarket customers discounted admission tickets. However, heritage sites' use of this element of the marketing mix does not seem to have brought about a ruthless change in the way heritage sites sell themselves to potential visitors.

The product

Most commercial operations recognise the need to update and redesign their products for specific target markets. Critics (for example, Newby, 1994) suggest the consequence of this is that the presentation of heritage resources is primarily a marketing activity rather than marketing acting as a servant of the resource (Figure 10.4):

> This is a process involving both resource selection and packaging. It is not a marginal enhancement of a product but is, from the producer's viewpoint, the means by which the diverse elements are integrated... [it] involves a conscious series of choices about which history-derived products are to be produced, and conversely which are not. (Ashworth, 1994: 17)

It is arguable, however, that this selectivity has always been the case at museums, historic houses and other cultural resources. Usually owned and managed by the state or wealthy individuals, these places have rarely been hotbeds of subversive or radical re-presentations of the past. This view also suggests that visitors are passive receivers of heritage experiences, which is not borne out by studies into their methods of constructing meaning for themselves (Goulding, 2000: 849).

There are some aspects of heritage management activity that suggest that the visitor experience is being redesigned in subtle if not radical ways. Many subsidised historic sites are in the care of state or other public authorities and even here 'recent years have seen an increased

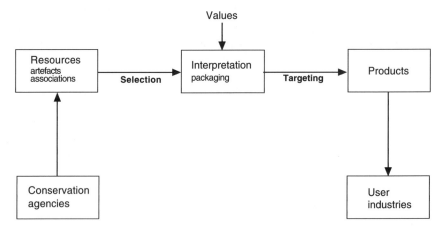

Figure 10.4 Components of the heritage industry (Ashworth, 1994: 17)

emphasis on customer care, corporate planning, greater management flexibility and performance measurement' (Davies, 1994: 25). The heritage sector of old tended to see the visitor as a disruptive force – an attitude long-held in service industries but undergoing a fundamental change (Bowen & Schneider, 1985: 132). Guidelines published by the then Museums and Galleries Commission urged museums to adopt ideas based on the 'National code of practice for visitor attractions' developed by the English Tourist Board (Hooper-Greenhill, 1994: 182).

If the theory of 'the augmented product' (Kotler, 1984: 463) was successfully applied to a package holiday (Callaghan *et al.*, 1994) and a theme park (Swarbrooke, 1995), why not a heritage site? For a product to be successful, all its constituent parts must be shaped to complement each other – from the core benefits, through its tangible features to the augmented elements (Figures 10.5 and 10.6). Catering, gift shops and membership schemes have been introduced or improved to make heritage sites more attractive to the visiting public (Crighton, 1992; Herbert, 1989; Palmer, 1994).

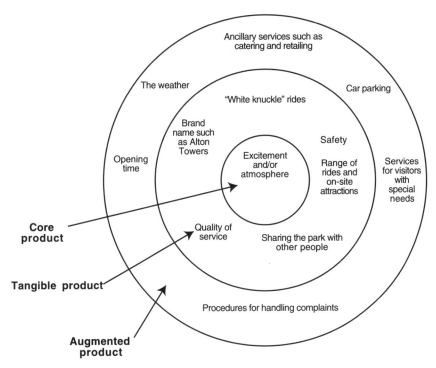

Figure 10.5 The three levels of product, the example of a theme park: After Kotler, 1994 (Swarbrooke, 1995: 40)

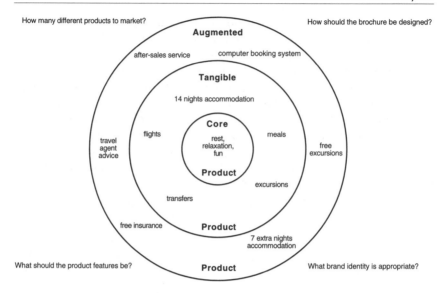

Figure 10.6 The elements of the travel and tourism products (Callaghan & Bottomley Renshaw, 1994: 213)

A great deal of effort has gone into the tangible and augmented levels of the heritage site product (mainly because these raise extra revenue) yet it seems unlikely that the visitor comes to a heritage attraction with expectations which may be marked off on a checklist: 'Tourists do not arrive in a destination simply in order to sleep, eat, drink, buy petrol and park their cars, and yet these amenities are said to produce the benefits of tourism' (Bull, 1985: 19). There is something beyond these facilities on offer, something beyond the physical properties of the place which satisfy other needs for the visitor. A product (or a heritage attraction) possesses two major characteristics: what it is and what it does (sometimes referred to as its extrinsic and intrinsic qualities). Its extrinsic features are what are usually described in brochures and in industry classifications. The intrinsic value of an attraction is the need it satisfies; its utility – what it does rather than what it looks like or how it is described (Bull, 1985: 24). While there is evidence that heritage site 'products' have been tinkered with at the edges, there is little to suggest that the core benefits have been challenged. Indeed, a typical example of an attempt to assess the quality of service at historic houses uses a checklist of 24 items. The items identify needs, such as the restaurant and directional signs (Frochot & Hughes, 2000: 161). None of them addresses the intangibles, the historic house's 'utility' for the visitor. If evaluations concentrate on the peripherals in this way, there is little likelihood that the heritage resource is seriously threatened by the results they provide.

Research has suggested that there are three main components to a heritage site's core product: atmosphere, learning and personal experience.

Atmosphere

Visitor surveys conducted by the United States National Trust for Historic Preservation and Colonial Williamsburg in Virginia have shown that people visiting historic sites were primarily attracted by the 'atmosphere' and ambience associated with them (Colonial Williamsburg, 1985; Mawson, 1984). 'A shock of confrontation with "the Other" is essential to a memorable museum experience' (Lowenthal, 1992: 26). Heritage tourism offers an encounter with nature or an opportunity to feel part of the history of the place (Hall & Zeppel, 1990: 87). 'Travel is no longer to see for the first time. It is to experience' (Collins, 1983: 59). It is the experiential nature of a visit to a heritage site which sets it apart from tangible products and other services too (Prentice, 1993: 202; Prentice *et al.*, 1993).

Heritage attractions put people in contact with the tangible remains of the past and this relationship is 'something we want to appreciate and experience to the fullest extent' (Masser *et al.*, 1994: 31). It is important, then, that each site offers visitors a unique and impressive atmospheric experience. Visitors to New Lanark in Scotland suggested that the lack of exhibits which offered immersion in the past (such as an underground mine trip or costumed demonstrators re-enacting what life would have been like) was a weakness in its provision compared to similar attractions (Beeho & Prentice, 1997: 84).

This emphasis on the visitors' opportunities for immersion rather than an attraction's physical features or facilities sits well with the 'gestalt' theory of museum experience (Falk & Dierking, 1992: 81). Gestalt is 'a structure or configuration of... phenomena, so integrated as to constitute a functional unit with properties not derivable from its parts in summation' (Webster's, 1983; Johns & Tyas, 1997: 475). All the parts must be considered within the context of the whole visitor experience (Johns, 1999: 127). That an experience cannot easily be broken down into its elements for analysis explains why well meaning research, which concentrates on facilities, reveals little about successful heritage site management.

Visitors have identified 'a sense of the past' as being an important component of the visitor experience (Malcolm-Davies, 2002: 577). This sense of the past may be connected with issues of perceived authenticity, which has been identified as 'the best predictor of visitor satisfaction' (see Figure 10.7) (Pearce, 1988: 77). Visitors may want an empirically 'real' experience of the past (an objective authenticity), their own idea of a 'real' experience (a constructivist authenticity), a 'real' fake experience

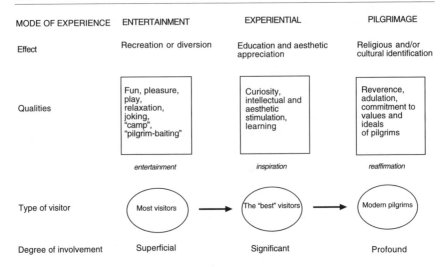

Figure 10.7 Three modes of tourist experience (Cohen, 1988) at Plimoth Plantation, Massachusetts, USA (Snow, 1993)

(a postmodern authenticity), a 'real' personal experience (existential authenticity) or a mix of these 'realities' (Wang, 1999).

Learning

Research into historic site visitors' priorities in four countries revealed that learning something is more important than atmosphere, although together they top the list of what people want from their visits (Malcolm-Davies, 2002: 469). Education was what most visitors to Burgos Cathedral (Spain), Nottingham Castle (UK) and Paleis Het Loo (Netherlands) identified as their motivation for visiting in a 1995 survey (Richards, 1996: 25). Visits to New Lanark in Scotland were perceived to have increased visitors' knowledge through a beneficial learning experience (Beeho & Prentice, 1997: 84). Another research project in Scotland suggests that a quest for active learning takes second place to enjoying oneself. A study of visitors to the ship Discovery in Dundee (UK) showed that 82% went to learn, compared with 63% who went to be entertained. However, these were secondary motivations indicated after 99.5% of visitors had already noted more pragmatic reasons for going, such as being on holiday and having a day out (Prentice *et al.*, 1998: 9). While 48% of visitors to an Australian ecomuseum said their principal reason for visiting was an interest in history or a desire to learn (Moscardo & Pearce, 1986: 473), only 2% of visitors identified 'self-education' as a reason for their last museum visit in another study (Merriman, 1991: 55).

Surveys of visitors to historic sites in Wales in the 1980s showed 62% of respondents wanting to be informed or educated (Light, 1995: 125).

A study at Cadw sites in Wales suggested that a small minority seek to be taught about a site in a formal sense but that a large group is interested in acquiring some knowledge (Herbert, 1989b: 198). The Commission on Museums for a New Century acknowledged this difference by committing itself to the concept of lifelong learning rather than formal education (CMNC, 1984: 59). The many and varied definitions of museums have adapted to these new expectations; the well founded 'functions' of a museum as defined by the American Association of Museums (collection, conservation, exhibition) are giving way to a more progressive idea of the 'purposes' of a museum (study, education, enjoyment) as defined by the International Council of Museums (MacDonald & Alsford, 1989: 37; Weil, 1986: 26–27).

Personal experience

The essential magic of a heritage attraction is that it provides a touchstone for the perceived benefits of the past. It is not necessary to feel dissatisfied with the modern world to appreciate these benefits, as critics of 'the heritage industry' have asserted (Hewison, 1987; Lowenthal, 1985; Samuel, 1994; Wright, 1985). A change of scene, an encounter with something other than the regular routine, was a feature of leisure activity long before it extended to the many rather than being limited to the few. Consumers are increasingly sophisticated and self-centred – because most people in industrialised societies are relatively comfortable, they seek experiences that offer more than sustenance, warmth and shelter (Maslow, 1954: 80–106). A new postmaterialist set of values has emerged, defined as needs for 'self-realisation, self-esteem, affection, a better quality of life and improved social relationships' (Walsh, 1991: 62).

Economic, social and technological changes have produced 'the thoughtful consumer', who puts more emphasis on the quality of life than material affluence (Martin & Mason, 1993: 37). Visitors seek quality of experience with opportunities for greater personal participation, whether they define quality by recreational values, intellectual stimulation or cultural meaningfulness (MacDonald & Alsford, 1989: 41). 'The emphasis is likely to be more on visiting with a purpose, going to an attraction because it offers something of particular interest or relevance to the visitor, rather than just because the destination exists and there is time to be occupied' (Martin & Mason, 1993: 39). Sociopsychological studies of leisure have revealed that such activities are goal driven and linked to the expected benefits or rewards gained. An individual will undertake those activities that produce a sense of competence, satisfaction and fulfilment (Light, 1995: 126). Facilities that help a visitor to develop a critical insight and appreciation of historic buildings provide a boost to self esteem (Herbert, 1989b: 197).

Arguably, visitors in the 21st century are more conscious of the way in which the world around them is constructed than visitors were in the 20th century. Gone, or going, is the classic realist text with its authoritative linear narrative and empirical truths (MacCabe, 1974: 8). *Tristram Shandy* (Sterne, 1760–1767), *Ulysses* (Joyce, 1914), *To the Lighthouse* (Woolf, 1927) and *The garden of forking paths* (Borges, 1941) paved the way in literature for fragmented narrative in film (for example, in *Natural Born Killers*, Oliver Stone, 1994) and (in the USA) television (for example, in Courthouse, Deborah Joy LeVine, 1995). All of these demonstrate the variety of ways a story can be told (Gibson, 1996). 'Most visitors today are oriented toward a multichannelled, cool-media approach to experience. They expect to be able to switch back and forth among channels easily, to experience a rapid transformation of frames' (Snow, 1993: 192).

The 'thoughtful' visitor is looking for something more nebulous – a 'real' experience (Martin & Mason, 1993: 39). They may enjoy it with their tongues firmly in their cheeks or see it as an opportunity to learn, depending on the authority with which it is delivered and the respect they accord it. The integrity and genuineness of what is offered will, in part, determine the lasting quality of the experience (Martin & Mason, 1993: 40). Whether the visitors actually learn anything is irrelevant; what is more important is that they think they have learnt something and learning can therefore be identified as a perceived benefit of their visit (Light, 1995: 134; Prentice, 1993).

Conclusions

If marketing theory were applied with rigour, product development techniques would be used to devise, pilot and refine visitor experiences at historic sites to provide learning, atmosphere and personal experience. Any assessment of a heritage attraction's strengths and weaknesses should attempt to gauge how effective it is in 'raising curiosity, appealing to fantasy, and in providing a challenge' (Schouten, 1995: 260).

One commentator notes 'the introduction of marketing as a concept has not always been easy in museums... None the less, suitable approaches have begun to emerge and there is now a growing body both of literature and good practice' (Hooper-Greenhill, 1994: 24). However, there is a paucity of radical examples of marketing theory applied to heritage sites. This may serve to demonstrate that lip-service only has been paid to the notion of market-led management. Promotion has been and remains heritage managers' priority to the exclusion of more developed marketing applications. Expansion has been based largely on opportunism, rather than on market research. Critics assert that many attractions have been product-led, promoting an otherwise redundant resource to a new market (Prentice, 1993: 223). Too many heritage sites continue to serve up the same old things or simply tart them up with quick fixes, which are assumed to bring the crowds. Costumed guides, for example, are often introduced in the belief that they act as a primary motivator when research has shown that this is true only for a minority of visitors (Malcolm-Davies, 2002: 477).

A truly market-led approach to heritage management would note the need for regular, expensive rejuvenation of the resource (such as the arrival of annual blockbuster exhibitions at national museums), widen the range of admission charges from bargain basement attractions to premium-priced exclusive visits (such as Dennis Severs' £12 visits to his tiny house in Spitalfields and evening tours at Buckingham Palace at £25), enhance the quality of the experience in line with what the traditional visitor segments like (as at Waddesdon Manor in Buckinghamshire), and pay attention to visitors' priorities as revealed by research. The introduction of the 'audience advocate', who researches the needs of visitors to aid exhibition design indicates museums may be leading the way in the proper application of marketing principles: 'Where in the past collections were researched, now audiences are also being researched' (Hooper-Greenhill, 1994: 1, 9). Croydon Clock Tower's museum galleries in Surrey were devised after an extensive public consultation process, which included questionnaires, interviews and focus groups (Susie Fisher Group, 1990). Academic research into visitors' responses to heritage sites has offered ideas for imaginative product development which have been translated into action at Blists Hill, Ironbridge (Goulding, 2000), the Black Country Museum in the West Midlands (Beeho & Prentice, 1996) and Castlefield in Manchester (Schofield, 2001).

It is not surprising, therefore, to discover that heritage attractions that are owned or operated by industrial production outlets or retailing groups (for example, Cadbury World in Birmingham) offer the clearest examples of marketing principles put into practice (Swarbrooke, 1995: 319, 322). Tetley Brewery Wharf was planned with a life cycle of three years while the brewery obtained planning permission for residential development of its site. Similarly, the Granada Studios Tour in Manchester closed after it had worked through a life cycle of eight years which began with 659,000 visitors per year, peaking at 750,000 and declining to 500,000 (Hanna, 1991, 1992, 1993, 1994, 1995, 1996, 1997, 1998). These, of course, are exceptions because they are not listed buildings, registered collections or symbolic ruins and battlefields. They are free to operate as commercial ventures. The difficulty for many historic properties competing in the marketplace is that they do not have the capacity to respond to the warning signs offered by the product life-cycle. Few can raise capital with ease and many lack the freedom to alter the layout of the building or dispose and collect in creative ways because of laudable legislation that preserves the remnants of the past from wilful destruction. Heritage attraction managers are fighting for market share with both hands tied behind their backs.

While curators cry over a revolution that has brought 'people who don't have a clue about heritage into the heritage sector' (Alberge, 2003: 3), the real tragedy is that proper application of marketing theories, including the product life-cycle, is long overdue in a sector that is fighting for its very existence. The traditional market for cultural resources is well heeled, well educated and in search of meaning in their lives – why aren't their millions subsidising the assets of the nation for those who have nothing?

Part 4
The TALC and Local Involvement

RICHARD W. BUTLER

One of the aspects of tourism destination growth that was not explicitly dealt with in the original article was the politics of development. It has become clear over the years that much more attention needs to be paid to the relationships between politics and development, both with respect to the impacts of politics at all levels on the nature and scale of development, and the impacts of such development on the political situation in destinations. The process of development discussed in the original model suggested that the stages of development would be affected by different levels of political (and economic) involvement. Keller (1987) argued that changes in the level of control and investment could be matched by periods of instability and turbulence (or chaos) in destination systems, but the general suggestion was that involvement would move consistently from local to regional to national and to international levels.

The first to challenge this view was Weaver (1990) and the first chapter in this section summarises and expands his arguments with respect to the different pattern of early development followed by destinations which had experienced a plantation type of initial economic development. He notes the different early patterns of development in such economies and the implications for the later stages. The chapter raises some interesting issues not explored fully here, relating to who might be termed a 'local' and who an outsider, and at what stage the latter may become the former. It also hints at some of the issues involved when the interests of various groups are not the same and thus the potential for conflict over the rate, scale and nature of development.

Johnston's discussion of the development process of Kona, on the Big Island, Hawaii, demonstrates the interplay between local residents and tourists. One of the themes which emerges is the growing power of local groups over tourism, as well the increasing role which they can play in shaping the direction of growth. The fairly long history of tourism on the Big Island reveals a variety of roles for local participants and the potential and actual conflicts that can emerge from increased visitation and development. Johnston's detailed review of this tropical island destination's relationship with tourism is marked by a more detailed identification of stages and phases of development, with marked changes in local involvement in development and limitations on development.

While Johnston's examination of development is more qualitative and descriptive, the chapter by Johnson and Snepenger takes a much more quantitative approach. Their study is the first detailed review of resident attitudes to tourism and tourism development in the early stages of the TALC. The location in which their study was undertaken is typical of many locations that in recent years have seen tourism replace other, more traditional resource-related activities when these resources have become uneconomic to continue to extract, or have been exhausted. They use four models to see if it is possible to predict residents' attitudes towards the overall impact of tourism in the early stages of the TALC in a specific community. They conclude that the stages of development are critical to understanding the perceived impacts of tourism in a community and that dispersing economic benefits across a community and encouraging positive interaction can aid the acceptance of tourism. Such longitudinal studies are clearly essential if a full understanding of the relationship between involvement and development through the TALC process are to be understood.

That theme is supported by Martin in her chapter, which examines the local politics in another North American location, Hilton Head in North Carolina. In her study she examines in detail local political attitudes and actions in a destination which has progressed a considerable way through its TALC. Confusion over the role tourism should play and the way that role could be controlled and directed had direct and unfortunate political results. There have been very few studies that have examined the transformation of attitudes of residents in a tourist destination into political action and the effect that these resulting political actions can have on subsequent tourism development and the direction of the TALC. The study makes it clear that there is often considerable apprehension about the process of the TALC and the nature of development in destinations, particularly those with a considerable proportion of the resident population not keen to see continued major change in the destination and not wanting to lose elements of local control over development.

The final chapter in this section by Marois and Hinch shifts location to South East Asia, and describes and analyses the process of tourism development in a Thai hill village. The community examined has proceeded through the TALC, with accompanying changes in emphasis on services provided and visitors received and local response and involvement have changed with the various stages of development. The level of control by locals has shifted and the roles they now undertake in tourism have changed considerably from the first period of contact with tourists. Efforts to ensure that the tourism industry on which the community has become partly dependent remains sustainable have not been entirely successful but the problems have been acknowledged. Even at the relatively small scale at which tourism occurs in this community, the problems of loss of control over development and subsequent changes in the tourist product which may threaten the viability and authenticity of the tourism experience are clear to the local population.

Chapter 11

The 'Plantation' Variant of the TALC in the Small-island Caribbean

D.B. WEAVER

Introduction

Harrison (1995) contends that the Butler sequence, as the most prominent TALC model, is most effectively regarded and utilised as an 'ideal type', or undistorted model of tourism development against which real life situations can be measured and compared. Once this has been achieved for a given destination, then the factors that account for the deviation (or the 'why') can be identified, with the aim of attaining a greater understanding of destination life cycle dynamics and diversity. Weaver and Oppermann (2000: 331), accordingly, argue that TALC researchers should focus on constructing around the ideal type a 'constellation of modified resort cycle models that take these real life circumstances into account'. Earlier research by Weaver (1988, 1990, 1993) has identified distinctive TALC processes in the British Caribbean islands that could contribute to the development of this constellation. Specifically, a 'plantation' model of tourism evolution is evident in Antigua (Weaver, 1988), while Grand Cayman Island displays significant deviations from the Butler sequence, especially in regard to the issue of empowerment (Weaver, 1990). An urban variant of the plantation model has also been proposed (Weaver, 1993). Each of these case studies, it is important to note, displays not just deviations but also a substantial level of conformity to Butler's ideal type. This chapter incorporates the above research into a broader investigation of small-island Caribbean TALC dynamics, toward the enunciation of one or more variant TALC ideal types. Modifications as well as conformities to the Butler model are accommodated in these models. The first section outlines the theoretical context that has influenced the study of the evolution of Caribbean tourism, with an emphasis on dependency theory. Subsequent sections examine this evolution in the sequence of stages and in reference to the characteristics provided by Butler (1980) in his original paper. Preliminary consideration is given in this context to the role of contemporary activities such as ecotourism and offshore finance.

185

Dependency Theory

Dependency theory, in its classical form, describes a group of neo-Marxist hypotheses which assert that low levels of development in the so-called 'third world' are primarily the consequence of the latter's chronic dependence (both economic and cultural) on the more advanced regions of the world, rather than of any innate shortcomings (Amin, 1976; Beckford, 1972; Frank, 1967; Rodney, 1972). This relationship is often described as a 'core–periphery' dichotomy in which the surplus produced in the periphery is commandeered by the core initially through the apparatus of formal colonialism (e.g. the British empire), and then (i.e. in the postcolonial era) through informal channels of transnational capitalism. The unequal and interdependent nature of this relationship is captured by Buchanan (1968: 83), who states that 'capitalist development simultaneously generated development and underdevelopment, not as separate processes but as related facets of one single process'. Accordingly, only by extricating itself from such a system can a country or society hope to achieve true development.

Modifications and reassessment

The harsh dichotomy of dependency theory has since been challenged by Wallerstein (1974, 1980, 1989), whose less ideologically charged world-system theory proposes the formation since 1492 of one global capitalist system with a single core, a single periphery and a transitional semi-periphery, the memberships of which are in a constant state of flux. Contemporary dynamics of globalisation, coupled with the collapse of the Soviet bloc (i.e. potentially the socialist alternative desired by the dependency theorists) and the rise of the East Asian economic bloc, appear to further elevate world-system theory at the expense of dependency theory. However, Surin (1998) argues that the fundamental elements (the phenomenon and persistence of uneven development that derive from the asymmetries of political and economic forces inherent to capitalism) of the latter remain valid. He consequently calls for a 'reanimation' of dependency theory based mainly on contentions that inter-regional (and internal) disparities have for the most part dramatically increased since the 1980s due to the very dynamics of globalisation, including the erosion of state control over economic policy and the substitution of highly mobile financial capital for productive capital. Yet, because these dynamics are significantly different from those that animated debate during the era of dependency theory, Surin admits that the called-for reanimation needs to be set in very different terms from the classic dependency theory prototype.

Relevance to the Caribbean and tourism

More than perhaps any other major world region, the Caribbean experience lends support to the basics of dependency theory. Five hundred years of interaction with the global core have witnessed the wholesale erasure of the indigenous Caribbean presence and its replacement by a 'plantation' system of production designed to create maximum wealth for the core with minimal consideration for the wellbeing of the periphery. The peripheralisation of the region within the global capitalist system was based initially on the production of agricultural goods, of which sugar was the mainstay and primary symbol (Mintz, 1971). For lack of viable alternatives, plantation-based agriculture dominated the Caribbean economy well into the 20th century despite chronic price instability, competition from European beet sugar and mainland producers (in the case of sugar), natural hazards, soil erosion and other problems. Tourism has existed in the Caribbean since the earliest days of the peripheralisation process, but it was not until after World War II that demand and supply factors combined to position tourism as a serious alternative (see below). Tourism eventually became dominant over agriculture in most Caribbean economies. However, this transformation from one sector to another was not accompanied by any systemic change in the essential core–periphery relationship. Tourism was introduced and evolved within a rigid and pervasive plantation system that maintained racially based social hierarchies (e.g. white hotel owners instead of white plantation owners), the diversion of profits to the core and other characteristics well familiar to the era of the sugar plantation (Beckford, 1972; Harrigan, 1974). It is because of this close association between tourism and the plantation system that Weaver (1988) refers to Antigua as an example of a 3S (sea, sand, sun)-based 'plantation' tourism landscape that fits well within Turner and Ash's (1975) concept of a global 'pleasure periphery'. The extent to which this has distorted Butler's TALC ideal type is discussed below. This discussion, moreover, also takes into account more recent tourism-related developments that appear to move beyond the 3S plantation model, such as the widespread adoption of ecotourism.

Exploration and Involvement

An interesting but rarely considered characteristic of the TALC is the absence of a commencement point. This appears to allow that some form of tourism, however negligible, may have occurred in any given area long before the arrival of individuals whose identity as tourists, at least in the contemporary sense, is indisputable. In the Caribbean, the existence of Carib, Arawak and other intraregional Amerindian 'tourists' prior to European settlement is an intriguing possibility that, accordingly, cannot be discounted. However, it also cannot be denied that the initial settlement process after 1492 dramatically altered the tourism situation by facilitating the arrival of visitors other than explorers, soldiers, missionaries and migrants. Hence, the plantation model per se begins with an *incorporation* phase during the exploration stage in which the indigenous population is subdued or at least held in check, formal claim is made over the land, and a rudimentary infrastructure of ports, fortresses and settlements is established to accommodate explorer-type tourism activity. In dependency theory terminology, incorporation is coexistent with the early *peripheralisation* process. In the case of Antigua and most eastern Caribbean islands, this occurred approximately from the 1620s to the 1640s.

Tourist motivations and markets

As per Butler, the tourists who visited the Caribbean from the mid-17th century to the mid-20th century were small in numbers, nonseasonal and motivated by a variety of factors related to the uniqueness of the area. These patterns are evident in the written accounts that were provided by these visitors, which include incidental descriptions of other visitors. Four primary motivations are evident in these written accounts. First, many tourists arrived in the West Indies for personal adventure, in keeping with the essence of the allocentric tourist who is purported to be prevalent during the early stages of the TALC. Examples include Brassey (1886), Paton (1887), Franck (1920) and Aspinall (1928). The travels described by these and other authors mostly consist of a multiple itinerary encompassing a sequence of islands, in keeping with the modern backpacker type of 'explorer' tourist. These adventurers, with their idiosyncratic and personal ruminations, are distinct in motivation from the tour guides, who intended their writings to provide factual guidance for other visitors. Examples of this typically more recent genre include Stark (1902), Ober (1908), Roberts (1948) and Clark (1952). A third motivation is health. This is cited as a personal factor by only a few of these authors (e.g. Baird, 1850), but is described by many others as a common motivation for visiting the Caribbean (e.g. Olley, 1937; Phillippo, 1843).

Significantly from a plantation model perspective, the fourth main motivation involves visitors, primarily members of Christian churches, who were interested in investigating the effects of Emancipation upon the black underclass (e.g. Bigelow, 1851; Gurney, 1840; Sturge & Harvey, 1838; Truman *et al.*, 1844). Like the other types of visitor, these 'social tourists' came mainly from the mother country of the UK, although some were also Americans monitoring the Caribbean experience as evidence for their opposition or support for slavery in the USA. This concentration of the market in just one or two source regions is contrary to Butler's proposal that such market concentration typically does not occur until the development stage, but it is entirely consistent with the nature of the plantation system wherein peripheralised islands are almost completely tied to their respective cores (e.g. Barbados and Antigua to Great Britain, Martinique and Guadeloupe to France, etc.), making visits from other core regions extremely difficult.

Accommodation

The pattern of accommodation revealed in the Caribbean during the exploration and involvement stages provides further support for a distinctive plantation variant of the TALC. A critical element here is the extent to which many visitors were literally accommodated within the plantation structure. For example, Baird (1850) stayed in the 'country homes' (i.e. plantations) of his Antiguan acquaintances, while Paton (1887) spent most of his time on that island residing with an 'estate owner'. Bigelow (1851) advises that visitors to Jamaica must look to the homes of planters for overnight accommodations when visiting any rural districts outside of Kingston. It is interesting to note that this use of active plantations for accommodation purposes persisted well into the 20th century. Cundall (1928: 127), writing about Jamaica in the 1920s, states for example that 'on enquiry may be found a few planters, pen keepers and others who are willing to take paying guests on suitable introduction'. This need for an advance 'introduction' is mentioned by other writers, and indicates that visitors so accommodated were members of the higher classes in the core region, that is, persons who had benefited directly or indirectly from the peripheralisation of their intended destination region.

Plantation owners who accommodated visitors were no doubt partly motivated by the desire for revenue as well as by a culture of hospitality projected toward individuals of similar class standing. However, there is ample evidence that planter openness to guests was more deeply motivated at least in some cases by the desire to attract white settlers, which would help to perpetuate the plantation system by reducing, however modestly, the huge disparity in population between whites and blacks. Phillippo (1843) explicitly states that planters were trying to attract visitors in the hope that they would settle permanently in Jamaica, where whites constituted just 3 or 4% of the population. More recently, Cundall's (1928) *Handbook of Jamaica* was targeted toward 'intending residents' as well as visitors, while the Tourist Trade Development Board (Olley 1937) was also mandated to provide advice for prospective settlers. Referring to one of the earliest hotels in Tobago, the Robinson Crusoe Hotel, Alford (1962: 27) describes its lounge in the following terms:

> this lounge is largely used as a meeting-place and sort of informal club by the local residents, so giving visitors a chance to meet the local planters, officials and British and American settlers and to enjoy their hospitality, of great assistance to those people who also might be thinking of settling in this beautiful island.

Taylor (1988: 214), moreover, suggests that the government-supported effort to develop good hotels in Jamaica during the 1890s 'would encourage visitors to come to Jamaica who, seeing at first hand the economic potential of the island, might decide to invest or even settle there'. The concept of 'involvement' in the plantation model, therefore, appears to extend well beyond the conventional and more superficial motivation of attracting temporary paying visitors, and thus is not of just 'relatively little significance' to the social life of the planters. Furthermore, this motivation is evident as early as the 1800s (and probably earlier), suggesting the onset at an earlier stage than anticipated in Butler's model. There is, however, little indication of the extent to which visitors were significantly motivated by the prospect of settlement or actually became settlers as a result of their tourism experience in the Caribbean. Certainly, this is not a motivation that is encountered in any of the travel accounts cited above.

Not all tourists were accommodated in plantation homes. Tobago, as well as most other British-controlled islands, also provided 'resthouses' in remote villages, which, while intended mainly for government officials while on duty, were also made available to tourists (Trinidad and Tobago 1912). More significantly, the plantation homes were paralleled on all islands by a network of guesthouses and similar accommodations located within prime urban areas such as Kingston (Jamaica), Saint Johns (Antigua), Bridgetown (Barbados), Basseterre (St. Kitts) and Port-of-Spain (Trinidad). Descriptions, locations and price structures of these facilities suggest that they catered to a middle class clientele, those with business in the urban area, and anyone newly arrived and unable to obtain immediate accommodation in a rural plantation. These guesthouses and small hotels are more indicative of the conventional involvement stage in that they catered specifically to tourists and other visitors.

More intriguing, however, is the ownership structure of these facilities as well as the plantations. Expatriates and the local elite controlled the plantations in roughly equal terms, with the boundary between the two being very fuzzy in many cases (e.g. a plantation owner who lives six months each year in England and six months in Antigua). This high level of non-local involvement contradicts a fundamental ascription of the early-stage TALC model regarding local ownership. Moreover, the resident planter class itself requires an important qualification because of its elitist character and very close ties to the mother country – characteristics that are not usually associated with the 'local community' described by Butler. But again, this anomalous profile of accommodation owners is entirely consistent with tourism's assimilation within a plantation system of production and social exchange. The above-mentioned guesthouses appear on perusal to be another matter entirely. Truman, Jackson and Longstreth (1844) stayed at urban guest-houses in Basseterre, Bridgetown and Port-of-Spain owned by 'coloured' women. Bigelow (1851) mentions that 'coloured people' kept all the boarding houses of Kingston, while Taylor (1988) cites a writer from the 1870s who bemoans the control held by 'lazy and independent negroes' over the small hotel sector in Jamaica. A more recent and detailed list of all such Kingston-based facilities provided by Olley (1937) confirms this remarkable pattern of female, non-white dominance, which is more in keeping with Butler's description of involvement-stage dynamics. Yet even this apparent anomaly can be explained in terms of the plantation system. Such owners are members of a small and mainly urban emergent class of free blacks, mainly mulatto, who occupy entrepreneurial and artisan positions that cannot be filled by the small white population and are considered inappropriate for slaves.

Development and Beyond

In most British Caribbean islands, the development stage (measured in terms of increases in visitation) commenced in the 1960s. The emergence of tourism as a viable alternative to agriculture during this time, as mentioned above, provided an incentive for suitably located plantation owners to pursue this sector more formally and vigorously. Often, this involved the physical conversion of their plantation homes and properties into resorts, expatriate housing estates and golf courses. Such conversions, an illustration of tourism-related functional adaptation in response to the demand for 3S tourism, were already evident during the involvement stage. The above-mentioned Robinson Crusoe Hotel in Tobago, for example, was originally a plantation home, as were two other coastally sited hotels established respectively in the 1930s and 1950s – the Bacolet and the Arnos Vale (both of which, interestingly, used the original estate name). In Antigua, the Antigua Beach Hotel opened in 1940 as a restored estate home (Weaver, 1988). The conversion process, however, accelerated during the development stage, which in Jamaica began in the 1950s. Chapman (1961) cites at least five plantation homes – Flamstead, Shaw Park, San San, Good Hope and the Manor House – that were converted into hotels during that time, although other Jamaican examples occurred as early as the 1920s (Taylor, 1973). In many of the smaller islands, similar transformations occurred in the 1960s. Even more common was the transformation of abandoned plantation properties into space-extensive tourism facilities such as golf courses. But as Harrigan (1974) reminds us, the occupational hierarchy of these hotels mirrored the plantation, with a typical structure of white and largely expatriate ownership, mulatto or 'coloured' middle management and Afro-Caribbean labourers.

Because the peripheralisation process encompasses small islands almost completely (excepting remote mountainous areas in some cases), the plantation TALC variant incorporates the indirect effect of tourism on noncoastal landscapes not directly impacted by this new sector. Weaver (1988) refers to this as 'tertiary' space that contrasts with 'primary' hotel strips along the beach and 'secondary' tourist housing estates adjacent to these hotels. Tertiary space, best exemplified by Antigua, consists of abandoned plantation lands whose condition is partly attributable to the transfer of investment to coastal tourism. This interior landscape also houses the Afro-Caribbean labourers who work in the coastal tourism industry. In conjunction with Butler's characterisation of the development stage, links between the remaining agricultural activity in this area and tourism are minimal, due to the maintenance of links with wholesale suppliers based in the core.

Other elements of the original TALC model are retained in the plantation variant, including the entry of new foreign hotel interests, increases in average hotel size, the use of imported labour and the dominance of a mid-centric tourist market. However, the pattern of locally owned urban guesthouses and small hotels persists (Weaver, 1993), perhaps reflecting a continuing lack of interest on the part of the core to become involved in this less lucrative aspect of the sector. With regard to market origins, the dependence on visitors from the mother country is replaced, contrary to Butler, by a pattern of greater market diversity, so that destinations such as Antigua and Barbados now count UK residents as a minority among a diverse clientele that also includes Americans, Canadians, mainland Europeans, other Caribbean islanders and South Americans. The 'monoculture' of 3S tourism also precludes the establishment of 'man-made imported facilities' such as theme parks and other contrivances. The peculiar, monocultural nature of the plantation system, furthermore, results in the pre-eminence of tourism within the island economy well before the consolidation stage (which is when Butler suggests that this pre-eminence will occur). Agriculture in Antigua still accounted for two-thirds of the island's GNP by 1950, but just 20 years later it was tourism that contributed a similar share (Weaver, 1988). This rapid transformation owes to the process through which opportunistic plantation owners took advantage of the 3S tourism market to abandon an agricultural sector that, as seen above, was plagued by chronic shortcomings.

Carrying capacity threshold range

Arguably the most significant characteristic of the original TALC model is the provision of the carrying capacity threshold range, the breeching of which eventuates in the decline of the tourism industry if no countermanding measures are adopted. This threshold implies a potential transition from a sustainable, functional state to one that is unsustainable and dysfunctional. The nature of the peripheralisation process, however, necessitates a rethinking of this concept. Beginning with the incorporation phase, indigenous societies in the Caribbean islands were brutally eradicated and supplanted by an imported population of African slaves. Emancipation in the 1830s did little to elevate the social or economic empowerment of this Afro-Caribbean underclass whose numbers were augmented on some islands by indentured labourers of Asian descent. Concurrently, natural environments were devastated as native habitat was converted into plantation land, which was in turn exhausted as a consequence of predatory farming practices. Again, Antigua provides the extreme example of this devastation. The implication for the TALC is that the environmental and social carrying capacities of these destinations were already exceeded during the exploration stage. However, because the breeching was the consequence of the overall early peripheralisation process rather than tourism itself, it is useful to refer to this breeching in terms of a *contextual carrying capacity*. Not surprisingly, the tourism that subsequently evolved in this unsustainable and dysfunctional setting was itself unsustainable and dysfunctional, relying for its existence on the apparatus of suppression instituted by the core and its local agents (e.g. local planters and police). Hence, early travellers refer to nervous planter-hosts keeping a close eye on their workers, and to blacks seen as sullen and silently hostile, or overly deferential. Of course, the writers in turn invariably perceive the black underclass in patronising or contemptible terms. Such dysfunctional relationships are evident in Trollope's visit to Jamaica during the 1860s, in which the author's constant frustration with the apparent impudence of the Afro-Caribbean hotel staff is interpreted by Taylor (1988: 212) as part of the latter's 'subtle struggle for dignity' and a 'manifestation(s) of passive resistance by the native hotel staff' (p. 213).

As the islands have progressed through the development stage, it is still relevant in the plantation model to retain the concept of the *tourism carrying capacity*, as by this time it is the growth of tourism per se that potentially induces a new round of environmental and social dysfunction. It would be greatly misleading to characterise this new round as an assault on a stable social and environmental setting, but new tourism-related problems are possible. For example, a devastated terrestrial environment (i.e. caused by three centuries of plantation agriculture) could now be accompanied by the destruction of coral reefs and offshore pollution. Similarly, an already dysfunctional social structure could be further skewed by the activities of 'beach boys' (i.e. male sex workers targeting mainly female tourists), the commodification of local culture and the need to compete with tourists for water and other vital services. Such tourism-related problems may indeed result in the predicted onset of 'consolidation', 'stagnation' and 'decline' dynamics, as demonstrated by the experience of New Providence Island (Bahamas) and parts of the US Virgin Islands. However, this is not inevitable. If the pre-existing conditions were already appalling, then local residents may perceive tourism, for all its faults and adherence to the plantation system, as a positive development. That is, employment as a low-paid bellhop in an air-conditioned Antiguan resort may be regarded as preferable to unemployment or backbreaking work as a labourer in the sugar cane fields. If such sentiments are widespread (and the critique of Harrigan (1974) and other dependency theorists is therefore just an elitist academic conceit), then the outbreak of widespread antagonism (as per Doxey's irridex) is unlikely. Indeed, tourism has not yet produced such an outcome on Antigua, Barbados or any of the other islands where the plantation model is evident. The plantation model, therefore, should be accompanied by the caveat that these tourism capacity thresholds may not have quite the import on plantation system islands as they do in other kinds of destinations.

Ecotourism and tax havens

A factor that complicates the discussion of the plantation model of tourism development is the recent emergence in the Caribbean of alternative 'postmodern' activities such as ecotourism and offshore finance that deviate from the 3S monoculture. Virtually every Caribbean island, including unlikely prospects such as Antigua and Barbados, now offers ecotourism as a component of their destination product mix. On first appearance, this sector offers an 'escape' from the plantation syndrome in so far as it purports to entail nature-based tourism experiences that are educational and contribute to the environmental, sociocultural and economic sustainability of the destination (Blamey, 1997). Ecotourism, however, can meet these criteria and still reinforce the plantation system by functioning as an auxiliary activity that diversifies and enhances the core beach-based 3S experience (Weaver, 2001). Ecotourism can also serve to incorporate remnant natural areas of the interior – that is, areas unsuitable for plantation agriculture or 3S tourism – into the economic orbit of the core, thereby extending the peripheralisation process. In this context, it is fitting that ecotourism, despite its alleged adherence to the principle of local community empowerment, is essentially an elitist Eurocentric concept with its own idealised perceptions of a (fictitious) pristine natural environment juxtaposed with traditional (primitive?) local communities. Ecotourism represents, by this logic, the most recent or 'post-modern' means by which the core imposes its demands on the small-island Caribbean periphery.

Some Caribbean destinations, the most notable example being the Cayman Islands, have opted to position themselves as offshore financial centres. In concert with the plantation model, early tourism initiatives on Grand Cayman Island were associated with expatriate interests (Weaver, 1990). However, the plantation system as such was never established in the Cayman Islands as an integral component of its peripheralisation, due to its low capacity for agriculture. This lack of a plantation system may have encouraged innovative responses to the lack of economic opportunity, including legislation in the 1960s establishing the colony as a tax haven. The subsequent accumulation of wealth enabled the resident population to invest in the rapidly growing tourism sector, thereby inverting the conventional TALC model wherein local ownership is superseded by non-local control. The Caymans example might be dismissed as a regional anomaly, except that many other Caribbean destinations (e.g. Dominica, St. Kitts, Antigua, Turks & Caicos Islands, Bahamas, Anguilla, Montserrat, Grenada, St. Lucia, St. Vincent) have since attempted to emulate its success as a centre for offshore finance. However, upon closer examination, it is clear that Grand Cayman Island is indeed an anomaly. The pursuit of offshore financial opportunities in virtually all other Caribbean destinations, while bound to be negatively affected by oversaturation, has been tainted by accusations of chronic impropriety, shady dealings and by the pursuit of related questionable (and desperate?) practices such as the sale of 'convenience' citizenships and the establishment of offshore medical schools and online gambling operations (Weaver, 2003). All of these other destinations, to a greater or lesser extent, are characterised by plantation systems, and therefore the question must be raised as to whether the unhappy story of these 'innovations' is yet another (nontourism) extension of the plantation model, wherein the prospect of increased local ownership of the tourism industry, unlike Grand Cayman Island, is remote. Certainly, this is compatible with Surin's (1998) contention (see above) that highly mobile financial capital has replaced productive capital as the main impetus underlying postmodern core–periphery relationships.

Conclusions

The following points reiterate and summarise the salient characteristics of the plantation variant of the TALC.

- The plantation model formally commences with an *incorporation*
  phase, which entails the beginnings of the peripheralisation process
  that opens the door to core-based tourists.
- Incorporation and its aftermath coincides with the breeching of
  the destination's contextual carrying capacity, that is, with the
  eradication of indigenous people and natural environments to
  accommodate, subsequently, a plantation system of agriculture.
- Early visitation patterns adhere strongly to the prevalent
  core–periphery relationship, so that the 'mother country' accounts
  for the overwhelmingly share of visitors.
- Early visitor motivations are focused on adventure, providing a
  guidebook for future visitors, health and 'social' considerations
  surrounding Emancipation. The latter is closely linked with the
  plantation system.
- Overnight accommodations outside of urban areas are mainly in
  plantation homes, indicating the degree to which early tourism is
  integrated into the plantation system.
- Host planters have, as at least one motive for their 'involvement',
  the desire to attract white settlers in order to help perpetuate the
  plantation system. Tourism is therefore of considerable significance
  to the white elite despite low levels of visitation.
- Expatriate interests rather than members of the local community
  own many if not most plantations.
- Local 'coloured' females control most urban guesthouses. This
  apparent conformity to Butler's statement about local ownership
  is actually consistent with the plantation model, as it indicates the
  existence of an intermediate class that occupies a niche unacceptable
  to whites and unattainable for the black underclass.
- Underclass Afro-Caribbean employees of the early hotels display
  passive forms of resistance toward tourism that are similar in
  essence to those adopted toward plantation owners.
- Tourism tends to supplant agriculture during the development
  stage, thereby indicating the opportunistic conversion of investment
  from a monoculture of the primary sector to a monoculture of the
  tertiary sector.
- The functional adaptation of some plantation homes into hotels is an
  important and widespread manifestation of this conversion.

- The development of the coast into a 3S tourism landscape is paralleled by the marginalisation of the interior, which serves mainly as a labour reservoir.
- Markets become more diverse as the strict core-to-periphery pattern of the past gives way to greater accessibility.
- Built attractions are conspicuous by their absence because of the monocultural nature of the 3S tourism product.
- This monocultural dimension also means that tourism becomes dominant within the destination economy long before the advent of the consolidation stage.
- The breeching of the *tourist carrying capacity* does not necessarily signal the demise of the destination, due to the distortions created when the contextual carrying capacity was breeched (see above). For example, passive resistance by Afro-Caribbean hotel employees toward tourists may actually diminish as markets diversify and working conditions improve.
- The introduction of ecotourism does not necessarily threaten, and may actually reinforce, the plantation system.

The above summary constitutes a preliminary profile of the plantation variant of the TALC, as a potential contribution to the constellation of variants proposed by Weaver and Oppermann (2000). Each characteristic, on its own, could be the topic of a full research project. Further study is also required to determine whether the model is a product of historically specific circumstances – that is, the peripheralisation process of the past 400 years, or whether more generic and timeless processes are at work. With regard to geographical coverage, it is likely that the plantation model in its essence captures the experience of many Pacific Ocean (e.g. Fiji, New Caledonia, Cook Islands) and Indian Ocean (e.g. Seychelles, Mauritius) island destinations, but may require revision in the case of island destinations that opt for a deliberately alternative tourism strategy focused on small-scale ecotourism, such as Dominica, St. Vincent, Montserrat and Samoa. In any case, this study has hopefully demonstrated the great utility of the original TALC model of Butler as an ideal type around which a more comprehensive understanding of destination dynamics can coalesce.

Chapter 12

Shoring the Foundations of the TALC in Tropical Island Destinations: Kona, Hawai'i

CHARLES S. JOHNSTON

This chapter is a case study of the TALC in Kona, Hawai'i Island (hereafter 'the Big Island', the name used throughout Hawai'i). The chapter attempts to integrate and apply the ontological and epistemological concepts that are discussed atomistically in the other volume. The purpose is to allow the research to function as a model for examining the TALC within the broader framework of 'place as process' (Pred, 1984).

The chapter is structured around two analyses, of unequal length. An initial boundary analysis focuses on establishing the spatial extent of the Kona destination region – the 'entity' being examined. The second, longer section of the paper is a 'sequence analysis' of the stages Kona has gone through as a tourist destination. This structure is similar to previous case studies in that a chronological discussion of stages is provided. It goes beyond the typical treatment through the use of two analyses that are embedded within the discussion of each stage. First, an identification of mechanisms introduces events that can be interpreted as defining changes in the stage or phase (substage) sequence. The importance of specifying mechanisms is to improve temporal bounding of stages by eliminating the arbitrary selection of cut-off dates. Mechanisms may be 'critical events' or 'blurry transitions'. The former affect the development of the institution of tourism in a profound way. Critical events may be different from 'critical junctures'. The latter focus on periods of crisis and/or issues of controversy but their resolution may not result in a stage or phase change. 'Blurry transitions' are more subtle; they are defined as the occurrence of a series of events subliminal to the scale of analysis. All events, critical or not, may be considered abstractly as 'additions', 'alterations', or 'cessations'.

Second, for each stage, after mechanisms have been identified, a 'pathway analysis' will look at epistemological features such as the 'internal characteristics' of the institution of tourism (including change in the resource attraction base and in resort morphology), the 'macrostructural' conditions (broad external factors), as well as the 'users' (tourists themselves). A pathway analysis focuses on the full development of the institution of tourism at the destination. Discussion in such a manner permits projection (though not prediction) of development patterns into the future.

For Kona, these analyses reveal that the destination has passed through a 'classical' stage sequence and is now in the stability phase of the maturity stage. The very success of the tourism industry, however, has led Kona into a broader urban era in its sequent occupance (Whittlesey, 1929). Tourism in the early 21st century is still important and still likely far away from the conclusion of its *longue durée* (Giddens, 1984), but it is no longer the driving institutional force in Kona.

Bounding the Destination Region

The word 'Kona' is typically translated as meaning 'leeward' in Hawaiian (Fornander, 1980; Pukui *et al.*, 1974). Figure 12.1 shows Kona to be roughly in the middle of the leeward (western) side of the Big Island, bounded by Kohala to the north and Ka'u to the south. The region is located on the steep slopes of two of the Big Island's five volcanoes, Mauna Loa and Hualalai. The recency of the island's creation means most of the Kona coastline is rugged lava bench, not white sand, a fact that has disturbed beach-seeking tourists for decades.

Kona's climate is somewhat atypical for Hawai'i. The great heights of Mauna Loa, Hualalai, and also Mauna Kea to the north prevent the trade winds from reaching the region. A localized diurnal land–sea breeze regime prevails instead (Juvik *et al.*, 1978). Precipitation is thus low *makai* (along the coast) but increases quickly *mauka* (upland) (Giambelluca *et al.*, 1986). Since Hawaiians first began to inhabit the region, most residents have lived in the wetter areas between Kailua and Kealakekua Bay. The different climatic conditions, hot and dry coastlines but cool mountain heights, have appealed to different visitors in different time periods. Charmian London (1917: 204), for example, noted that her husband, writer Jack, thought mauka Kona had a 'matchless equable climate'. This opinion has probably not been shared by most tourists since the 1950s, who have come for the makai sun and heat.

For purposes of analysis, the epistemological need to properly bound the area under study requires the selection of a destination that is appropriate in size and complexity of institutional tourist development. The Kona region, rather than the entire Big Island or the western half, was chosen as the most appropriate scale for analysis. The latter – 'West Hawai'i' – became quite important for planning by the State government beginning in the late 1960s. The town of Kailua (sometimes known as 'Kailua-Kona') was the site where tourism first became institutionalized. Since then, resort development has occurred in two

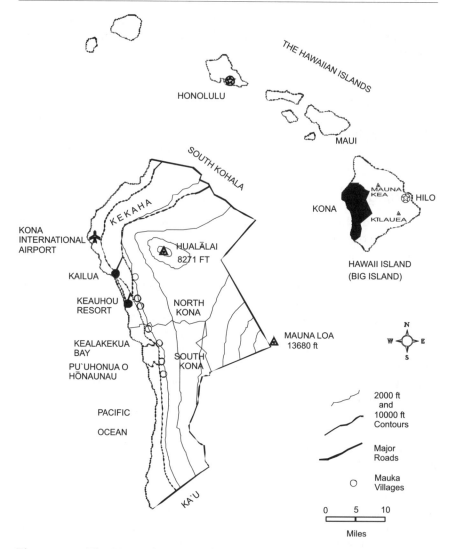

Figure 12.1 The Kona districts within the Hawaiian islands

other contiguous areas (Keauhou and Ali'i Drive) along the coastline, creating a 'linked' morphology, but the Kona district itself retains a distinctive identity that is meaningfully differentiated from the Kohala resort area to the north and Ka'u to the south. Kona was therefore chosen for study on the basis that it was of a spatial scale that destination life cycle theory could handle in its present state of development. Problems from multiple-site development were minimized, though not entirely eliminated.

Sequence Analysis of Life-cycle Stages

Table 12.1 shows the stages and phases of tourism development through which Kona has passed; it also shows the eras in the regional sequent occupance. To date, the Kona region's sequent occupance has consisted of four eras. Kona is also interpreted to have gone through a 'classical' set of stages. The Hawaiian royal capital and exploration stages (pretourism – see Young, 1983) have been followed by initiation, which led to a development-stage building boom that was in turn followed by maturity as growth slowed. All but the first of the stages are interpreted to have had two phases, as well. A variety of mechanisms – critical events and blurry transitions – have been listed in Table 12.1 to account for the changes.

Hawaiian Royal Capital stage

The first stage in the sequence has been named 'Hawaiian Royal Capital' on the basis that Kailua town was occupied by royalty – King Kamehameha and Governor Kuakini – much of the time between 1779 and 1844. During these 60+ years the presence and actions of royal rulers created a history for the region that was later used by tourists as an experiential (cultural) resource (see Table 12.2). The fact that Kona was the original seat of the Hawaiian kingdom established the region as the premier place for later visitors to see 'old Hawai'i'. This nostalgic longing for heritage experiences has been an institutional feature of tourist demand going well back into the 19th century.

Few people visited Kona during this time who could be called tourists. The arrival of the Wilkes (1970) expedition in 1840 was perhaps most typical: Kona was visited more by true explorers than explorer tourists. The years of the stage completed the 'Hawaiian' era of the sequent occupance, which had lasted several centuries (see Kirch, 1983). The stage and the era are interpreted to have ended on the basis of a cessation – Governor Kuakini's death in 1844.

Exploration stage

The second stage, exploration, is considered to be pretourism on the basis that although some tourists did come, there was little development of a tourism industry. The institution was thus incomplete. During these years ranching and coffee came to dominate the landscape and economic activity of residents (and thus the era in the sequent occupance has been termed 'agricultural hinterland'). Two phases of the exploration stage have occurred. The early phase is defined by the absence of Hawaiian royalty in Kona; the district became very isolated with the capital located in Honolulu. The late phase is interpreted to have begun in 1910, when

Table 12.1 Stages and phases of tourism development in Kona

Era in sequent occupance	Stage and phase in tourism life cycle	Date	Mechanism of change initiating stage/phase; critical event or blurry transition (addition, alteration, cessation), plus critical junctures
Hawaiian, prehistory to 1844	Hawaiian Royal Capital	1779–1844	Critical-addition: Cook reaches, and is killed at, Kealakekua Bay Critical-addition: Kamehameha sets up throne at Kailua, after establishing power over Hawai'i Nei Critical-cessation: Kuakini dies 1844
Agricultural hinterland	Exploration Early	1845–1928 1845–1910	Blurry-cessation: (above)
	Late	1910–27	Critical-addition: Circle-island auto road completed
1844 to 1953	Involvement Pioneer hotel	1928–63 1928–48	Critical-addition: Kona Inn opened Critical-addition: Old Kona Airport opened, facilitates local-scale recreational business district in Kailua
	Local morphology	1949–63	• Juncture: large accommodation projects inhibited • Juncture: regional development plans inhibited

Table 12.1 (*Continued*)

Era in sequent occupance	Stage and phase in tourism life cycle	Date	Mechanism of change initiating stage/phase; critical event or blurry transition (addition, alteration, cessation), plus critical junctures
Tourism 1954 to	Development Domestic morphology	1964–88 1964–75	Blurry-addition: Accommodation unit numbers break out above 400; rise continuously for a decade; multi-story hotels constructed • Juncture: Natural and cultural resource development projects inhibited • Juncture: Kailua pedestrian mall and high rises inhibited • Juncture: Keauhou Resort built nearby
1988	Linked morphology	1976–88	Critical-addition: Kailua Village Special District Commission created Blurry-addition: Heliotrophic development links Kailua and Keauhou; condominiums co-dominate with hotels
Urban 1989	Maturity Consolidation	1989–present 1989–93	Blurry-cessation: Accommodation unit growth peaks • Juncture: Kekaha subregion resort enclave projects inhibited
to present	Stability	1994–present	Critical-addition: Runway extension completed, renamed Kona International Airport; infilling of Kailua recreational business district facilitated

Table 12.2 Chronology of major historical events occurring in Kona during the Royal Hawaiian Capital stage

Year	Historical event
1779	Cook reaches Kealakekua Bay, Jan. 16, in the *Resolution* and *Endeavor*. He is worshipped as the god Lono the next day then is killed by Hawaiians on Feb. 14.
1792–93	Vancouver's expedition visits Kona.
1812	Having conquered the island-chain, by force or negotiation, Kamehameha returns to Kona to set up the seat of his kingdom from fortress 'Kamakahonu' on the north side of Kailua Bay. Several exploration expeditions (Arago 1971, Freycinet 1978, Von Chamisso 1986, von Kotzebue 1967) visit, spreading the fame of Kamehameha and Kona throughout the known world.
1819	May: Kamehameha dies; October: Liholiho (Kamehameha II) publicly eats with women, thus officially renouncing the *kapu* system, effectively overthrowing the traditional religion and the basis for priestly authority.
1820	January: Lihohiho wins the Battle of Kuamo'o at Keauhou Bay; advocates of *kapu* restoration are defeated. April: Missionaries arrive from North America. Step ashore onto 'Plymouth Rock' in Kailua. Liholiho moves royal court from Kailua to Honolulu. Kona is politically peripheralized.
1825	Kuakini, Governor of the Big Island, builds the first Christian church, Mokuaikaua, in Kailua. Made of wood, it burns in 1837.
1837	Kuakini builds Hulihe'i Palace as the governor's mansion, across from the church.
1838	Kuakini rebuilds Mokuaikaua Church, this time of stone.
1844	Kuakini dies.

a circle-island road for automobiles was completed. This addition enabled tourists to purchase circle-island trips in touring cars based in Hilo; they stayed at mauka hotels in Kona and took day trips to see important historical sites makai.

Early phase

In the early phase there were no major historical events to describe. A distinctive type of local did come into existence – the *paniolo* – a Hawaiian cowboy, who was to be a common sight on the Kona landscape well into the 20th century. The number of visitors was small. Travel, nearly always by ship, was difficult. Initially, interisland boat passage was on Hawaiian-owned 'poi clippers' (Day, 1955), referred to as 'the haole's [foreigner's] horror, the Hawaiians' pleasure' (Thomas, 1983: 31). By the 1870s, steamers built especially for Hawaii's rough interisland channels began to ply the waters regularly.

The major attraction of the Big Island was Kilauea Volcano. It was nearly continuously active during this time and the boiling cauldrons of the lava lake in central Halema'uma'u Crater drew tourists from around the world. Package tours from Honolulu were developed as early as the 1880s to facilitate access (Thrum, 1886). For these visitors, Kona was but a stopover on the return to Honolulu. From the decks tourists watched Hawaiians 'come galloping in' (Whitney, 1890: 29) from mauka villages, excited by 'steamer day' (Stevenson, 1973). Ships would stop at Kealakekua Bay, tourists would then go ashore to stand at the spot where Cook had been slain and re-live the scene. In the 1860s, after he recovered from seasickness traveling on a poi clipper, Twain (1966) visited the site and lampooned this behavior.

Along the coast, there was not much to do. In 1858, King Kamehameha IV visited the Hulihe'e Palace; his secretary later recorded him remarking that 'the place itself is so desolate that ennui was the order of the day' (Neilson, cited in Daughters of Hawai'i, 1979: 2). This opinion slowly began to alter in the 1890s, when tourists on steamers began to consider these sleepy coastal villages as 'romantic' (Burnett, 1892: 202).

Those tourists who did get off the boat in Kona generally went mauka, where they enjoyed themselves by riding through the forests (Chaney, 1879) to the summit of Hualalai. The truly adventurous, such as Isabella Bird (1966), went hunting for wild cattle with the Hawaiians. Robert Louis Stevenson (1973) was more sedate, limiting himself to a week's homestay with a Hawaiian judge who augmented his income through providing lodging and board to tourists.

Late phase

Change was slow to come to Kona, but around 1910 the district began to catch up with civilization as completion of the circle-island road, the Mamalahoa Highway, made auto travel possible. The circle-island tour was an attraction itself: it was conducted in large touring cars driven by Hawaiians, who made the long, dusty trip less arduous by entertaining the tourists with picnics and by singing and playing the ukulele (Morrill, 1919). Once in Kona, most visitors continued to stay mauka in small hotels, two of which are still popular with 'alternative tourists' today (Sodetani, 1985).

The historical features dating from the Hawaiian era, which had been slowly deteriorating in the sunny coastal landscape, were now legitimately old and represented the major attraction resources. Mokuaikaua Church and Hulihe'e Palace in Kailua, the twin landmarks left from Kuakini's rule, were particularly important. Several other historically and culturally important sites were improved, though not specifically for the purpose of attracting visitors. What MacCannell (1976) has referred to as 'sight sacralization' was beginning to occur. Kona's 'past glory' (*Paradise of the Pacific*, 1924) was more imaginable to the tourist. These makai sites were now visited during day trips by car. The long slow horse rides through the forest were ending. Cook's death site receded somewhat in importance for it was much less accessible (and remains so) by car than by steamer; reaching it required a long walk down and up the steep, hot and dusty Kealakekua fault line.

Other events occurred to increase the value of Kona as a destination. The first was an addition: the discovery around 1920 that billfish were abundant just offshore in the calm but deep leeward waters. Kona quickly attained a reputation as a 'rendezvous for game fishermen' (Sabin, 1921: 37) intent on catching marlin, swordfish and tuna. Second, an unusual cessation occurred that represented a change in the macrostructural tourist conditions. In 1924, the lava lake within Kilauea crater hardened over, and the living volcano became dormant. People came to Kilauea in ever-increasing numbers (Hawai'i Volcanoes National Park officials, October 1991, personal interview), but now the circle-island trip to see Hawaiian history had more appeal.

Kona was also one of the few places where it was still easy to meet and interact with 'native' Hawaiian people. Honolulu had become a modern city (a macrostructural alteration); the old ways of life were going fast. Photos taken well into the 1930s (e.g. *Paradise of the Pacific*, 1939) show Hawaiians smiling for the tourist cameras, or wearing only loincloths, frolicking with tourist ladies on the pocket beaches. Paniolos still walked the dusty streets of Kailua and the mauka villages.

By the mid-1920s, Kona had an identity as a tourist destination. The regional appeal was based on a diverse set of resources – environmental, cultural, and social. What Miossec (1977) has called the *perception globale* – tourists' ability to differentiate the destination as an attraction area from the neutral space surrounding it – had occurred. The only element missing from the picture was the true presence of the tourist industry itself.

Involvement stage, 1928–63

Butler (1980) defined an 'involvement' stage as when residents begin to provide facilities exclusively for tourists. The literature has described variations in how this happens; Din (1992) and Douglas (1997), in particular, have questioned whether 'residents' are not in fact immigrants. A variation along these lines also occurred in Kona, on the basis that outsiders from Honolulu were responsible for the event that initiated the stage. Two phases are interpreted to have occurred. A pioneer hotel phase first institutionalized Kailua as the nucleus for tourism. Later, the opening of the region's first airport helped bring in a local phase, when a local-scale resort morphology developed in the village.

Pioneer hotel phase 1928–48

The critical event that institutionalized tourism in Kona, and to the outside world, was the addition of a hotel in Kailua town, thus anchoring tourism on the coast rather than the uplands. The event occurred in 1928 when the Inter-Island Steamship Navigation Company (1930) opened the Kona Inn. The company had been actively trying to expand travel throughout the islands so that more tourists (especially residents of Honolulu – Hawai'i's 'domestic tourists') would book passage on its ships. The Kona Inn was a good example of a 'pioneer hotel'; it was built at higher-than-local standards and became an attraction in its own right. The hotel was an instant success and became 'the spot in all Hawai'i where you can utterly, completely relax in surroundings of modern comfort' (Thrum, 1940–41: 267).

Beyond the opening of the Kona Inn there were no other additions of significance in the tourism industry during this phase. Rather, the old Hawai'i ambience, which Kona contained in abundance, continued to age like good wine. A phrase – the 'Kona Way of Life' – made its way into the vocabulary to describe it. Tourists during the late 1920s and the 1930s went to Kona to steep themselves in the Kona Way of Life – a feeling that had faded in much of the rest of the Territory, particularly in Honolulu. The ambience took on an almost spiritual flavor; De Vis-Norton's (1925) comment that 'Kona is one of the most soul-satisfying districts on earth' is typical.

This phase carried on through World War II, when civilian interisland travel was completely halted. The war did not function as a macro-structural constraint; it seems to have been more of a hiatus to a region already known for slowness.

After the war, life for a few years returned to what it had been before. Locals were still living the Kona Way of Life; the Kona Inn was again open for business. At the mid-century point, Coll (1950: 17) would write that tourists were 'flocking' to Kona, on the basis that it was 'a place to get a quiet rest amid soothing tropic surroundings but if you feel a bit lively one can find plenty to do'. Yet even as he wrote, change had begun to occur. Progress was about to catch up to the sleepy little village, and it would come in the form of a developing tourism industry.

Local phase, 1949–63

The local phase began just before mid-century. The mechanism of change was an infrastructural addition, the opening of what is now called the 'Old Kona' airport on July 10, 1949 (HNCM, 1949). This was a critical event for within a year a local-scale resort morphology began to appear in Kailua village. Growth was not happening only in tourism, however. Agriculture still dominated the region as an economic activity and the ranching industry, in particular, also had infrastructural needs. The most important of these was for an up-to-date facility from which to transfer cattle onto boats going to Honolulu. For a century, cattle had been herded to the shore in Kailua Bay, and then paniolos on horseback swam with them out to the boat where they were lassoed and hoisted on board. This colorful procedure had been a tourist attraction of sorts for a long time but was not easy to accomplish. To improve the situation, a pier was built on the shore in the early 1950s. A resource conflict issue arose: whether to use the Bay for tourism or agriculture; but ultimately, tourist interests won, the shed was removed, and cattle were trucked to a different port. This conflict represents a critical juncture in the sequent occupance. Agricultural interests dominated less and less after this and Kona became perceived more as a tourist region than an agricultural one. The tourism era is interpreted to have begun at this time.

The construction of the Old Kona Airport in 1949 was brought about by the locals' need to be less isolated. Even before opening, it was considered responsible for inducing new business to Kailua (HNCM, 1949). Within a year, new hotels had opened, and houses were being converted into shops. A local-scale recreational business district had come into existence – 'the sleepy port of Kailua has become a bustling community' (HNCM, 1951). This growth was deemed good for the entire Territory, and the status quo understanding was that Kona was the rightful heir to becoming the no. 2 tourist destination in Hawai'i, after Waikiki (*Honolulu Advertiser* 1954, 1956, 1956b). Though people knew early on that this growth would affect the Kona Way of Life (Doyle, 1957; Stermer, 1954), the small scale of additions built throughout the phase did not impact it severely.

Two notable additions to the resource base occurred: the Pu'uhunua o Honaunau ('City of Refuge') was given US National Historical Site status in 1961 (Clark, 1985) and the annual Hawai'i International Billfish Tournament began in 1959 (Peter Fithian, tournament organizer, December 1991, personal communication). The latter event helped institutionalize Kona as a world-class destination for big game fishing. However, the 1950s penchant for the sun-sand-sea vacation was altering the use of the resource base in Kona. History and culture slowly ceased to be as important to visitors.

There were two developmental junctures in Kona during this phase, which are important to consider – even though they did not eventuate. They had a virtual quality that was real to residents at the time, even though tourists who passed through were probably unaware of the storms around them. The first juncture concerned accommodation. Throughout this phase only one domestic-scale facility was built, the

King Kamehameha Hotel, which opened in 1960 with 94 rooms. Several others, however, were announced in the newspapers. The aluminum magnate, Henry Kaiser, proposed constructing a megaresort consisting of four hotels with 800 rooms, a new beach, three yacht harbors, and hundreds of apartments and private homes on the site of the existing airport (*Honolulu Advertiser*, 1955). Bureaucratic inhibition constrained progress, and by 1957 Kaiser was to note that Kona 'wasn't ready for another big hotel' (*Honolulu Star Bulletin*, 1957). Nothing was ever built. Plans for at least three other domestic-scale hotel projects met the same fate during this substage, though none of them were as big as Kaiser's (*Honolulu Advertiser*, 1955b; *Honolulu Star Bulletin*, 1956).

The second juncture concerned planning. Territorial government development plans began to specify guidelines during this period. Height limits on buildings were set at two stories in central Kailua (Scott, 1957). Regional master plans were also done. The most ambitious, by the Territorial Planning Commission, was presented to the public in 1958 (Harland Bartholomew and Associates, 1960). This promoted tourism development but maintained the ambience of the region by specifying a set of seven 'resort centers' up and down the coastline. Residents' reaction to the plan was positive: 'They all like it, with few exceptions' (*Honolulu Star Bulletin*, 1958b). But, as with Kaiser's private sector project, nothing from the plan ever appeared on the landscape. Funding was dropped from the State budget in 1960, and jealousy from Hilo, the county capital, seems to have played a role in inhibiting any action to implement the plan (HNCM, 1960).

Throughout the 1950s and into the early 1960s, then, Kona's pathway was typified by a state of tension between what was perceived as the region's rightful position – the no. 2 destination in Hawai'i – and the slower of development that actually occurred. Facilitational forces made some small additions, but inhibitional forces had constrained all the 'big' projects that would have quickly shifted Kona into the development stage. Residents and members of the business community were left waiting, wondering when true development would come.

Development stage, 1964–88

One way to identify a 'development' stage is to look for a building boom, characterized by additions to the tourist landscape and particularly to the accommodation sector. Before 1960, statistics for numbers of accommodation units in Kona were nonexistent or approximate. After this, data on accommodation units outside of Waikiki began to be published for some resort areas, including Kona. It is possible to use these data as a means of interpreting stage and phase changes. On the basis of Figure 12.2, it can be interpreted that a 'breakout' occurred

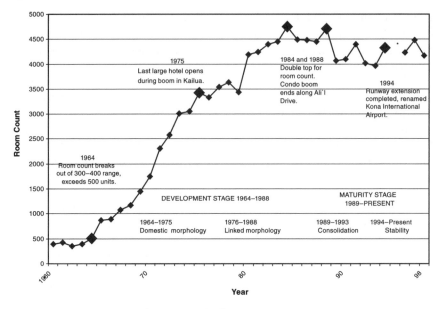

Figure 12.2 Accommodation totals for Kona
*1995: No survey was done by HVB
Source: Hawai'i Visitors' Bureau *Annual Research Reports* for years shown
and Thrum's *Annual* 1960–63

during 1964; the number of accommodation units rose above the 300–400
unit range and exceeded 500 units for the first time. A change of this
nature constitutes a blurry transition because no major event occurred.
Annual increases in accommodation would be the norm for the next two
decades. The development stage has been defined on the basis of this
graphical pattern.

Within the stage, two phases – domestic and linked – are interpreted
to have occurred, based on changes in the resort accommodation
morphology. Between 1964 and 1975, new hotels built in Kailua Village
were mainly of a domestic scale and attained several stories in height.
About five miles to the south, Keauhou resort was developed by a large
land-owning estate, and three enclave-scale hotel resorts were constructed within it by 1974. The final large hotel project built during the
phase – the King Kamehameha – was completed in Kailua in December,
1975. The domestic phase is interpreted to have ended with the opening
of this hotel and the corresponding cessation of construction in Kailua.
Room numbers had increased over seven-fold during this decade.

During the next phase, 1976–1988, increases in accommodation
facilities would mainly take the form of condominiums. The two separate
resort areas – Kailua and Keauhou – would become morphologically

and functionally 'linked' by condos built along the connecting coastline road – Ali'i Drive. Room totals were to reach a maximum of 4748 units in 1984 but would nearly reach this again in 1988. This 'double top' represents the end of the development stage. There has been a notable cessation of accommodation construction since, though one large enclave resort did open in the Kekaha subregion north of Kailua in the mid-1990s.

Domestic phase, 1964–75

The domestic phase of development for Kona was just over a decade long. Much was built, but much was prevented from being built. The conflict over the direction of growth was intense. It was notable that all contestants were seemingly protourism. It was particular visions of growth and Kailua's place-identity that were contested. Facilitational aspects will be discussed first, followed by inhibitional conflicts.

Hotel size in Kailua grew more or less organically. During the 1950s, the hotels that had been built in Kailua were nearly all small, averaging about 20 rooms. After 1964, however, facilities of three-to-four stories (height limits had been raised) with more than 100 rooms were the norm, over-topping the earlier generation. Just south of the existing village, on the south side of 'One'o Bay (Figure 12.3), Hilton opened a hotel in 1968, with over 300 rooms (Hawai'i *Tribune Herald*, 1968). This was Kona's first international-scale facility. Several other domestic-scale hotels were built nearby, either along the coast or just inland. These created a new southern anchor to the village, with empty land directly behind 'One'o Bay.

At about the same time, the Bishop Estate, Hawai'i's largest land owner, began work on a megaresort at Keauhou (West, 1967), about five miles south of Kailua, connected to the village by Ali'i Drive. Plans called for nine hotels, along with hundreds of condominium units, residential housing, shopping areas, coastal walkways, a golf course, and other recreational features. Keauhou was in fact to be a new city, larger than Kailua. Had development gone as planned, Kona might have ended up with two distinct destinations. However, private sector hotel developers did not come forward with the anticipated eagerness. Only three hotels had opened by 1974. These were international-scale enclave resorts, each containing several hundred rooms.

In addition to hotels, Kailua's recreational business district developed considerably. The shops of the 1950s were in turn replaced by small tourist-oriented malls in the 1960s and 1970s. By the late 1970s, when the trend had ceased, a travel writer was to note, 'The resort town of Kailua features ... more shopping malls per square mile than I have ever seen' (Riegert, 1979: 115). Together, the addition of these hotels and shops constituted the 'boom' typical of a development stage. Kailua had been

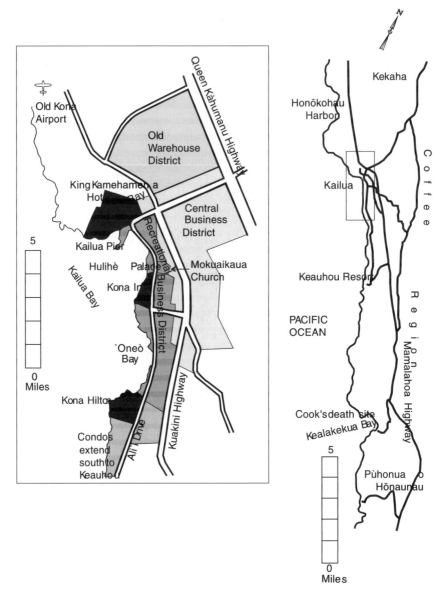

Figure 12.3 Major features of Kona's tourist landscape

attractive because of its ambience, its 'way of life'; this resource was severely degraded during the domestic phase. A series of newspaper articles complained about how noisy the village had become (Benham, 1970b; Hawai'i *Tribune Herald*, 1969, 1970). What were described as 'signs of growing pains' (Bryan, 1965) became more harshly phrased as a situation of 'Nightmare Not Over For Kailua' (Shapiro, 1974: A12). Shapiro went on to note that 'the tourist boom of the 1960s brought uncontrolled growth and tackiness, erasing much of Kailua's old charm.'

Another aspect of the building boom involved improving the regional infrastructure. In the late 1960s, Governor Burns had a dream of creating a 'Gold Coast' in West Hawai'i, running from the Kohala district north of Kona to the Pu'uhunua 'o Honauanu in South Kona (Hawai'i *Tribune Herald*, 1968b; *Honolulu Advertiser*, 1968). As governor, he directed millions of dollars into three particular projects so that private industry would find conditions feasible for investment in resorts. These projects were a new airport, a coastal highway connecting Kona with Kohala, and a new harbor blasted from the Kekaha lava shoreline. These three projects were of considerable importance in providing Kona with an adequate infrastructure. None, however, had the mechanistic impact of the original airport's opening. Rather, they fit in with other developments going on in the tourism industry itself during those years. Put abstractly, they could be considered to be 'tolerance' pathway factors; their construction in the 1970s would enable developers in the 1980s to propose large-scale resort projects.

Turning to inhibitional issues, several projects were highly contested, and discussion of these perhaps best brings out aspects of Kona's pathway. Two of these projects focused on developing natural and cultural attraction resources; they were proposed at almost the same time. The summit of Hualalai volcano had been a day-trip destination of 19th century tourists on horseback. Nearby, Hawai'i Volcanoes National Park included the summit of Mauna Loa. In the 1960s the National Park Service realized the landscape of the summit area of Hualalai was not of inferior quality and proposed expanding the park to include it (Hawai'i *Tribune Herald*, 1967b; Ketchum, 1969, 1969b). Road access from Kona would have made the national park much more accessible. Opposition developed from locals, however, who saw the expansion as a land grab by the federal government. The proposal collapsed, and the summit of Hualalai today remains off-limits to tourists.

The second project involved State plans for developing the land area around Kealakekua Bay. Nineteen seventy-nine was the bicentennial year of Cook's 'discovery' of Hawai'i and a decade earlier a plan had been made for upgrading the area (Creighton & Walters, 1969). The plan specified construction of educationally oriented facilities, focusing not only on Cook's death, but also on the archaeological ruins from nearby Hawaiian settlements. Again, conflict with residents inhibited the project. Probably the most offensive element in the plan was to turn the site of a small village on the south side of the Bay into a parking lot, displacing the residents (Benham, 1971; Hawai'i *Tribune Herald*, 1972).

The project did not receive approval, and the land surrounding Kealakekua Bay area remains 'unelevated' (after MacCannell, 1976) as a resource. The Bay area today is marketed more towards day-trip snorkelers than towards people curious about one of the major events in the history of Pacific exploration – the death of Cook.

These resource-related issues were of considerable importance, but inhibitional junctures within prodevelopment groups were even more so. Two burning issues arose during the phase – whether to turn Ali'i Drive into a pedestrian mall, and whether to allow high-rise buildings in the Kailua village center. In 1965, the owners of the Kona Inn had become concerned about the excessive traffic on Ali'i Drive and proposed turning the road into a pedestrian mall. They also proposed constructing a new road behind the growing recreational business district to eliminate this negative impact on the village ambience. An article written during that time stated bluntly that bus tours to the Kona Inn were responsible for most of the traffic 'chaos' (Hawai'i *Tribune Herald*, 1967). The business community reacted with extreme hostility towards the proposal, on the bases of prohibitive cost and that supplies could not be delivered to their small shops and hotels (Southward, 1966). Numerous plans regarding the mall were advanced (Southward, 1968), but all failed to satisfy the business community. The issue of the mall would wax and wane for a full decade. Some changes were made (e.g. Ali'i Drive was made into a one-way street), but there was no comprehensive solution.

The second issue was over high-rise buildings within Kailua Village. This erupted in 1968 when a developer proposed constructing a seven-story condominium adjacent to Mokuaikaua Church. The past few years had seen building heights gradually increase. For example, the King Kamehameha Hotel, built to four stories originally, had added two more. The Hilton, almost completed, was about to reach seven stories. There had been no major public opposition to the height of these structures. But such height next to one of the town's major landmarks was considered sacrilege by many, and the protest against the development was just as vehement as it had been against the pedestrian mall. At a 'Citizen's Conference' held in May 1968, residents debated the future identity of the village. There was a strong feeling that permitting high-rises would 'ruin' (Harada, 1968) Kailua by making it a 'poor cousin' (Southward, 1968b) of Waikiki. The twin landmarks of Hulihe'e Palace and Mokuai-kaua Church, now 130 years old, also perpetuated Kailua's 'old Hawai'i' ambience, in spite of the construction chaos. The argument that the project would destroy the ambience of the 'picturesque little village' (*Honolulu Advertiser*, 1969: B2) had some credibility (see Martin, this volume for a similar development, editor's note). The project was completely legal and within zoning allowances, but public opposition delayed groundbreaking ceremonies until 1972. By that time, the developer had conceded to community concerns. The site of the building was moved further away from the church and its height was limited to four stories (Tao, 1972).

The community impasse over these two issues did not mean there was a lack of vision about Kailua's future. There was nearly constant talk of creating a 'special and historic district' (*Honolulu Advertiser*, 1973). Yet by the early 1970s there was little left that was truly historic other than Kuakini's buildings. At one point a state legislator proposed the State buy the entire village (*Honolulu Advertiser*, 1970). The fighting finally ended in 1974, when money was released for a new urban plan (*Honolulu Star Bulletin*, 1974); by the end of the summer the central village area was given 'special district' status (Hawai'i *Tribune Herald*, 1974, 1974b, 1974c). The theme of the plan was that the appearance of central Kailua should be perpetuated as a small village. To oversee the implementation of the plan, the Kailua Village Special District Commission was created. From this time on the village has had an official body to mediate disputes. There have been no major variations permitted to builders for the past quarter-century. The 'tentacles of blight' (Southward, 1967) from the development boom were no longer present. Contemporary tourists strolling along Ali'i Drive continue to experience a pleasant ambience, though not one representing the 'Kona Way of Life'.

In December 1975, the second incarnation of the King Kamehameha Hotel opened to the public. With this event, the domestic phase came to a close for Kona. No major hotels have been constructed in Kailua since. Overall, the impact of inhibitional forces had dealt a severe blow to the organic development of tourism. Future development would be kept rigidly along community-approved lines. An international phase, identified by high-rise hotels, had been completely prevented. Kona thus did not fully complete the 'classical' development stage, as did Waikiki.

Linked phase, 1976–88

Figure 12.2 shows a continued rise in the number of accommodation units between 1975 and 1988. The linked phase has been interpreted on the basis of this pattern. Virtually all accommodation constructed was in the form of condominiums. The increase in numbers is significant; the 1984 peak (4748 rooms) is nearly 40% higher than the total for 1975 (3423 rooms). The initial condominium boom resulted from a spillover of demand for properties on Maui (Tune, 1980). Prices in Kona were considerably lower. The condos were mostly built during the good economic years; the second oil crisis in 1979 brought development to a halt for a while (*Sunday Star Bulletin and Advertiser*, 1984).

At the end of 1975, tourism development in Kona was still mainly centered in Kailua Village, with the Bishop Estate having partly developed Keauhou resort five miles away. Keauhou represented newness, high-quality facilities, and planning; Kailua was old and messy. One writer (Krauss, 1974b) noted that only 5–10% of visitors staying in Keauhou went into Kailua. Had the Bishop Estate's plans come to fruition, Kona would have become a binodal tourist destination. What resulted instead was that the Village and resort became spatially and functionally 'linked' through condominium construction along the coastal road, Ali'i Drive, which ran between them. For the next decade, development of condominiums gradually merged the two resort subregions. The district, as a destination, remained 'Kona' in identity.

Compared to the previous substage, the linked phase occurred in a straightforward manner. No major issues came to the fore. In terms of ambience, Kailua Village re-established something of its 'old Hawai'i' identity in the late 1970s, after the Planning Committee took control. The major event of the phase was the closing of the Kona Inn. The hotel was purchased by a local group, who closed it in 1978 and built a large shopping mall on the lawn (William Kimi, CEO, December 1991, personal communication). The change from a hotel to a shopping mall represented a major alteration for the Village. It was not a critical event in the life cycle, however, because a sufficient supply of room stock now existed elsewhere to meet demand.

One notable addition occurred during this phase, an annual special event. In the late 1970s, the original 'Ironman' triathlon had begun in Honolulu. The race was moved to Kona in the early 1980s (Hawai'i *Tribune Herald*, 1989). It has grown in popularity and, along with the Hawai'i International Billfish Tournament, has become what Getz (1991) referred to as an 'image-maker'. The Kona Way of Life was gone, but a new theme – sports – would begin to define the region.

Maturity stage, 1989–present

If the envisioning idea of development is growth, then maturity brings to mind the image of completed growth. Since 1989, the amount of accommodation available in Kona has remained fairly steady at just over 4000 units – defining the maturity stage. Not many events have occurred that produced visible changes on the resort landscape. The years between 1989 and 1993 have been interpreted as the consolidation phase on the basis of this lack of activity. In 1994, the runway at Ke'ahole Airport was extended, and it was renamed 'Kona International'. Long-distance jumbo jets could now land and take off. This alteration is considered to have initiated the present stability phase, on the basis that Kona is now directly connected to the rest of the world.

Consolidation phase, 1989–93

The consolidation phase will likely be remembered most for what did not happen – a failed third phase of development. To examine the situation properly it is necessary to return to the 1960s. In the middle years of the 1960s decade, two resorts opened north of Kailua Village. One was the Mauna Kea Beach Hotel complex, in South Kohala. The other was the Kona Village in Kekaha. Both catered to a luxury clientele and were quite successful. Governor Burns had understood the potential for luxury tourism when pushing through the infrastructure projects in the early 1970s. Had the private sector done its part, Kona and Kohala may have merged in identity as a tourist destination, as the Gold Coast. Two hotels did open in South Kohala in the early 1980s, both catering to a luxury segment. The fabulous Gold Coast, however, never really came into existence.

The land ownership pattern in Kekaha dated back to the 1850s. Extremely large ranches covered the lava desert. This pattern was suitable for megaresorts costing hundreds of millions of dollars. The necessary infrastructure (airport, highway, harbor) was in place. In the mid- to late 1980s, six projects were proposed. There was little difference in the plans; each specified large hotels, condominiums, and one or more golf courses set inland from one of the Kekaha's pocket beaches (County of Hawai'i, 1987). If completed as proposed, they would have added approximately 5000 hotel units and 6000 condo units (not all in the vacation rental market), more than doubling Kona's accommodation stock. Access to beaches by the public at this time was severely restricted. The public needed to cross private land to reach the beaches, but many were able to do so, and thus these were popular recreation sites, particularly on weekends.

The furor of the community over these projects was just as intense as it had been with previous issues. Unlike earlier fights in Kailua, the battles in the 1980s were between protourism developers (mainly outsiders) and anti-development residents. Two projects were proposed near a large pond that was a protected bird sanctuary. After initial permits were granted by the County, the State of Hawai'i itself came out in opposition to these (*Honolulu Star Bulletin*, 1988). Project-by-project, fights went on in public planning meetings throughout the late 1980s and into the early 1990s. One corporation did manage to get enough permits to begin construction (Hawai'i *Tribune Herald*, 1989) and eventually opened a large, luxurious resort enclave next to the Kona Village. By 2000, the remaining projects were still listed in the 'planned development' accommodation statistics collected on by the State of Hawai'i. Nothing about them has been mentioned for years however (Annie Earl, County of Hawai'i Planning Department, March 1999, personal communication).

One addition of note occurred during this phase, the elevation of coffee as a tourist resource. Kona had been a noted coffee district since at least the 1860s, when Twain (1966) made favorable comments about its quality. Tourists had often noted the presence of coffee growing in the mauka village areas, and aspects of its production had been an attractive feature for decades (Harlow, 1928; Musick, 1898). The development of tourism in the 1950s and 1960s had, however, hurt production; better paying jobs meant the crop was sometimes not picked (Smyser, 1972). The subdivisions that had followed tourism had also caused the price for land to explode during the 1980s. There was concern that the land would be rezoned for residences, though this did not eventuate (Harada-Stone, 1989). By the early 1990s, however, the coffee lifestyle of cities had diffused to the source region, and entrepreneurs in Kona were exploiting this resource by opening shops at which freshly roasted coffee could be consumed and purchased. The annual Kona Coffee Festival has also become elevated in importance and now represents a third 'image-maker' for the destination.

Stability phase, 1994–present

A stability phase suggests that little new is happening, but that existing businesses are doing well. This situation has existed in Kona for the past few years. Accommodation numbers have never reached the peaks of the 1980s but have remained at the levels of the early 1990s (Figure 12.2). The opening of the longer airport runway reduced dependence on Honolulu. Since then, more malls and restaurants have filled in the vacant lots inland from 'One'o Bay. This is now the new 'center' of nightlife. Kailua's recreational business district now is completely developed along the shores of Kailua and 'One'o Bays, but because planning guidelines remain effective, the recreational business district still looks and feels like a village (field inspection, April, 2000).

Though this took years to achieve, Kona presents itself as a contemporary tourist destination that has been able to reach a balance between facilitational and inhibitional forces. The growing pains of the development stage have ended. Attraction resources have changed and continue to do so. The Kona Way of Life ambience is gone but the region effuses an idyllic quality that is pleasant to experience. There is something of a new image that is distinctive in the State and not yet completely defined, based around sports-health and coffee. Kilauea Volcano, on the windward side of the Big Island, remains a day trip. The challenge for the community in the years to come will be to prevent the decline in quality of these attraction resources.

The Future of Kona's Tourist Life Cycle

Research on a destination life cycle that incorporates the concepts of mechanisms and pathways permits a limited projection into the future, on the basis that the past provides a certain understanding of what cannot likely happen again. Of course, there is no crystal ball, and so *ceteris paribus* is assumed. It is unlikely that Kona will undergo a further boom period, akin to what occurred during the development stage. There are three factors that suggest this. First, the entire length of coastline has by now either been developed for tourism or has had projects proposed then inhibited by community pressure. Further development faces tight planning guidelines, and the Kohala districts to the north are in the midst of their own destination life cycle and compete for tourists.

Second, by the early 1990s, the condominiums constructed during the development stage were being increasingly inhabited by their owners, not listed as available vacation rentals (field inspection, 1991–1992). Part-time residents do not behave exactly like tourists, hence the nature of the institution of tourism is slowly changing. Were tourist numbers to drop considerably and stay down for a period of time, Kona could likely be interpreted as being in the residential stage.

Third, Kona's success as a tourism destination has enabled it to grow into a multifunctional urban area. Prior to the 1950s, most inhabitants in Kona lived in mauka villages. Kailua's recreational business district then developed makai. However, there was no corresponding central business district; this was constructed behind the recreational business district along Kuakini Highway, beginning in the 1970s (Figure 12.3). Subdivisions for local residents were built back from the coast as well. In 1989, the Hawai'i County Planning Department released a *General Plan* that projected land use zonation into the future. The plan shows that most new development would be zoned residential, industrial, or urban, but not tourist or resort. When the planning maps are analyzed in relation to the nontourist types of additions that have already been constructed, it is feasible to interpret that Kona ended its tourism era in the sequent occupance around 1989, at the same time the maturity stage began. The plan thus represents a mechanism – the agency of County government – which had decided to concentrate on other forms of urban development. Though still a mainstay of the local economy, after a reign of roughly 35 years tourism gave way to urbanization at large, which is now in its own development stage. As an institution, tourism may remain stable for a long time; the life cycle cannot be expected to end soon. But a greatly expanded Kailua is fast becoming an important city in the State of Hawai'i, and tourism in the future can be projected to be just one of many institutionalized activities occurring there.

On the other hand, if *ceterius paribus* assumptions were removed, it is possible to conceive that Kona might yet have another developmental phase. It has been repeatedly noted that the base resources for tourists keep changing. Were tourists' tastes to return to those of a century or more ago, features of Kona that have been 'de-elevated' could again become resources for the industry. For example, if global warming worsens, appreciation of the cooler upland climates could cause a new 'boom' in the mauka areas to occur. Also, the continued appreciation of 'old Hawai'i', today redefined as heritage tourism, could result in the restoration of literally hundreds of important archaeological sites that have been left to weather in the tropical sun. The identifiable presence of additional, though currently undeveloped, attraction resources indicates that the future pathway of Kona as a tourist destination has not been completely predetermined by past events and accommodation trends and thus cannot be predicted.

Conclusion

This paper has presented a case study of the Kona region of the Big Island, Hawai'i. The structure and content have utilized an ontologically and epistemologically underpinned version of Butler's (1980) destination life cycle model. As a way of delimiting the scale of analysis Kona has, first of all, been spatially bounded. As a destination, Kona was shown to have had tourism development occur in three contiguous subregions, Kailua, Ali'i Drive, and Keauhou. Attempts to develop a fourth area, Kekaha, have mostly failed to date. Features of development in each of the three subregions were quite distinctive; yet the region as a whole retained an intact identity as a single destination. On this basis, Kona can be interpreted to be at the large end of the spatial scale appropriate for study in terms of presently developed theory.

Second, the paper analyzed the chronological stage sequence of development that has occurred, in terms of the mechanisms that have been interpreted to have caused stage and phase changes, and in terms of the pathway features that were most pertinent during each. This sequence analysis has shown that Kona has gone through a classical set of stages – none has been skipped or reached in an unusual order. All stages attained can be divided into phases, based on the occurrence of events functioning as mechanisms of change. In particular, analysis of change in accommodation units was useful in interpreting stage and phase change, particularly when the graph of room totals was discussed in terms of morphology – what types were built, where, and when.

Kona's pathway as a destination, however, has been much more complicated than a study of the mechanisms alone would indicate. Facilitational and inhibitional forces (with a bit of 'tolerance') collided for much of the second half of the 20th century. Developmental victories have produced the existing tourist landscape. Developmental failures, sometimes representing victories for anti-growth forces, meant a Waikiki-type environment (international-scale morphology) did not come into existence, and kept the Kekaha lava desert mostly free of large resort enclaves. The broader growth of Kona as an urban region, however, was not contained. Success at tourism has led to Kona becoming a sprawling urban area. Whether the region can maintain the idyllic quality for tourists, or whether it becomes a nice place to live, but not to visit, remains to be seen. The process of tourism development appears to be nearly completed, but the process of place-development at-large appears by no means finished.

Chapter 13

Residents' Perceptions of Tourism Development Over the Early Stages of the TALC

JERRY D. JOHNSON and DAVID J. SNEPENGER

Introduction

The Tourism Area Life Cycle (TALC) model is conceptually longitudinal; however, most studies applying the model are cross-sectional. There are many reasons why the literature is dominated by cross-sectional studies. First, it is pragmatically easier to acquire information at one point in time and then analyze the data across a sample of residents of the area. Secondly, the need for expedient publication motivates most researchers to publish cross-sectional studies. Third, there are few resources available to tourism researchers by way of grants or contracts to support impact studies over a decade or more.

Three notable longitudinal studies employing the life cycle model illustrate the research design complexity and the rich information available from these types of studies. The first study is 'Lifecycle models for Pacific Island destinations' (Choy, 1992). He employed visitation volumes over time for several popular and emergent island destinations in the Pacific. The most extensive set of data was for Hawaii and incorporated data from 1946 to 1988. Other island destinations utilized a smaller time frame for examining aggregate visitation patterns. Choy concluded that a general destination lifecycle model does not apply to most Pacific island destinations. A large variation in growth patterns was observed across the 13 destinations.

Another study by Johnson and Snepenger (1992) examined tourism development in Yellowstone National Park over two decades. 'Application of the tourism life cycle concept in the Greater Yellowstone Region' applied several elements to the TALC – the traditional tourism impact dimension, visitation trends, economic indicators, and biological indicators for the ecosystem. They concluded that tourism in the Greater Yellowstone is an intricate system where multifaceted parts can be in different stages of the TALC and that public land managers, private entrepreneurs and local government decision makers should coordinate development and maintenance of tourism assets.

The third paper, 'Tourism planning and destination life cycle', investigated Niagara Falls over the entire tourism destination life cycle (Getz, 1992). This comprehensive examination traces the chronological changes to Niagara Falls (New York, USA and Ontario, Canada) from the early inception of the attraction in the 1820s through to its consolidation in the 1990s and anticipated rejuvenation. Getz utilizes historical qualitative data, visitation and business data, and survey data from industry and municipal groups to conclude that stages within the TALC can be delineated and that it can be a useful construct if attention is also paid to monitoring and forecasting the complex market and product of the tourism attraction.

Measuring Tourism Impacts

Although others (Ap & Compton, 1998; Lankford & Howard, 1994) have designed alternative impact scales, conventional tourism impact studies use a generally accepted battery of 16 questions that investigate the economic, social, and environmental positive and negative consequences of hosting tourists (Lui & Var, 1986). The study of impacts from tourism on local communities takes in a range of literature that includes both the positive and negative effects of hosting tourists to a community.

Andereck and Vogt (2000) point out that residents of a tourist community differ with respect to the impacts resulting from tourism development. However, researchers agree that a necessary condition of successful tourism development strategy is the inclusion of residents of the entire community if tourism investment is to yield substantial returns (Allen *et al*., 1988, 1993; Jurowski & Uysal, 1997; Long *et al*., 1990; Snepenger & Johnson, 1991).

The existing tourism impact literature has for the most part relied on cross-sectional data (Allen *et al*., 1993; Andereck & Vogt, 2000; Ap, 1990; Jurowski & Uysal, 1997; Long *et al*., 1990; Snepenger & Johnson, 1991; Var & Kim, 1989). However, the TALC implicitly demands that any study of tourism dynamics view changes over time (Ap, 1990; Butler, 1980) and that the economic, social, and cultural impacts evident in any community are best viewed within a longitudinal context. One of the attractive features of repeated or longitudinal measures is that they allow for general statements of change over long periods of time. Knowledge of trends can lead to a better understanding of the community tourism system and may provide useful managerial information to community and tourism planners (Mueller *et al*., 1970; Snepenger & Ditton, 1985). Longitudinal analysis as utilized in this study is useful to indicate which, if any, demographic and tourism iteration variables explain how the community opinion toward tourism development changes over time. These trends may be important because as stated by many researchers, cohesive community feelings toward tourism aid in the development of sustainable tourism policy (Ap, 1992; Jones, 1993; Madrigal, 1994; Martin & Uysal, 1990; Teye *et al.*, 2002). In other words, unwilling hosts are not conducive to an effective tourism industry.

Longitudinal Investigation of Silver Valley, Idaho (USA)

The purpose of this chapter is to examine the early stages of the TALC in a regional economy previously based on natural resource extraction. The region is experiencing a transition from mining and timber production to one increasingly diversified to incorporate tourism attractions and services. The investigation utilized a longitudinal research design incorporating survey data from four different points in time.

The research setting for the study is Shoshone County, in the northern panhandle of Idaho, USA. The area is known as the Silver Valley, a narrow mountain river valley. Mineral deposits of silver, gold, zinc, and lead discovered in 1883 led to the development of underground mines throughout the 14-mile long valley. The Valley at one time produced over one-third of the world's supply of silver.

The valley is surrounded by National Forest lands that produce many of the local amenities residents find desirable and act as attractants for tourist visitors. Mountain biking, hiking, big game hunting, cross country and alpine skiing as well as water-based recreation opportunities such as fishing, river floating, and waterfowl hunting are available throughout the year. The small communities of the Silver Valley are developing into bedroom communities for nearby Coeur D'Alene, Idaho – a community of 35,000 people that is itself a popular tourist destination for year-round recreation only 56 km (35 miles) to the west via interstate highway. Lower housing prices in the Valley provide an incentive for people to drive the relatively short distance to employment in the larger urban center.

The local mining industry in the Valley collapsed in the early 1980s due to a multiplicity of issues and local residents were encouraged by community leaders to collectively rethink the basis of the local economy (Johnson *et al.*, 1994). The idea eventually presented to locals was to transform a 20-year-old local ski area into a four-season destination resort. The ensuing vision was a radically different way of thinking about the local economic base and centered on building a gondola to move skiers from a central location in the town of Kellogg, Idaho to the ski area over 5 km (3 miles) away and several thousand vertical meters above the community. Public meetings were held to educate residents and local business owners, politicians and community leaders to advance the idea of promoting tourism.

In 1986 political leaders initiated a market study to investigate the feasibility of a major year-round destination resort development for the Valley. The resort would be focused around a $20 million dollar project that at 3.1 miles in length would be the world's longest passenger-carrying gondola. It would serve the alpine ski area and eventually a year-round destination resort complex. Several setbacks occurred over the course of the development but by Fall 1990 the initial stages of the project, including the gondola, were completed and the new Silver Mountain Ski and Summer Resort, owned and operated by the City of Kellogg, Idaho began operations. The public ownership made the resort one of the few public sector owned ski resorts in the country.

However, confusing the economic and quality of life circumstances is the designation of the Valley as an Environmental Protection Agency (EPA) Superfund site. The designation constrains local business investment and pervades the local politics of the area. During the course of the ski area development, as part of the Superfund activity, all remnants of the mining operations that polluted the area were removed and the land mitigated. The Superfund designation has infused significant amounts of Federal spending into the Valley but uncertain liability concerns makes future business investment an unsure proposition (Fernandez, 1999). As a result, contrary to hopes and government efforts, very little non-mining and non-recreation investment has taken hold in the region.

The literature provides a few studies addressing the nature of transitional economies from resource dependency to one based on tourism, retirees, and attendant professional and consumer services. Historically, the economic base in most rural communities in the Rocky Mountain West was found in agriculture and natural resource extraction. Today, the contemporary economies of the West are more easily described as progressively more diversified. Timber harvest, mining, and agricultural production are still in evidence in much of the rural west but at diminished levels, but those employment opportunities are giving way to service-related employment including tourism, non-labor income, small business startups, light manufacturing, retail, and construction jobs. These nontraditional employment sectors dominate regional urban centers and adjacent rural communities (Beyers & Nelson, 2000).

An important component of the economic restructuring is tourism (Fly, 1986; Getz, 1986; Gunn, 1988; Liu & Var, 1986; Long *et al.*, 1990; Loyacono, 1991; Luloff & Steahr, 1985; Rafool & Loyacono, 1997). In the Rocky Mountains (USA) the travel industry provides over 381,300 jobs and accounts for approximately 6.5% of total state employment and in Idaho, the setting for this study, tourism generates almost 22,000 jobs or 4.8% of total employment in the state (Rafool & Loyacono, 1997). Future tourism-related job growth will continue to be an important component of the rural economies of the western USA (English *et al.*, 2000).

For natural resource dependent communities, tourism may be a last attempt at economic survival as the market for natural resources is increasingly global, regulated, or displaced with technological substitutes. Many rural locations, especially in the Western USA, enjoy close proximity to existing tourism resources such as national parks or scenic/historical resources (i.e. Yellowstone, Lewis and Clark route locations) and can take advantage of readily available nearby recreation on public lands (i.e. skiing, river recreation, mountain biking).

The issue of community acceptance of tourism or other form of economic diversification is important for communities where the economic shift away from commodity production is taking place. Power (1995) advises that there may be a considerable lag between recognition of economic myth about how the community formerly made a living and the acceptance of the new reality and eventual acceptance of the new set of economic conditions. This may be particularly acute in the case of tourism – an industry generally perceived to result in low quality jobs, part-time, or seasonal work, and low pay. Accordingly, Jurowyski and Uysal (1997) and Teye *et al*. (2002) suggest that given a lack of understanding or approval for an ongoing economic transition, tourism development efforts will suffer from a lack of local community support.

Three major communities comprise the Silver Valley: Pinehurst (pop. 1800), Kellogg (pop. 2591) – the location of the ski area base operation, and Wallace (pop. 1100). Total population for the region at the inception of the study was 5491 (US Census 2000). A random geographic cluster sampling design was utilized to acquire data from residents. A grid system was developed which partitioned each of the communities into several neighborhoods. Within each neighborhood a random sample of 30–35 households were surveyed. This was initiated by selecting a random starting point in each neighborhood and then randomly selecting dwellings within the neighborhood to contact. The self-administered questionnaires were given to one adult in each household and later retrieved at a predetermined time. Response rates and sample sizes for the four survey periods varied but were within acceptable limits for similar community surveys (Babbie, 2002: 256) and appear in Table 13.1.

Four household surveys monitored area residents' expectations of tourism development conducted in 1991, 1994, 1997, and 1999. The first survey was initiated at the end of the first season of operation. Because residents did not have enough experience with ski area resort destination tourism, the questions were reworded to query area residents' expectations and thereby their level of optimism, of tourism impacts as a result of development in the Silver Valley. These items asked respondents in 1991 to assess expected impacts and were reworded to assign values five years into the future. For example, where the original question was

Table 13.1 Response rates for survey periods 1991, 1994, 1997 in Silver Valley, Idaho

Year	Sample size	Response rate (%)
1991	385	349 (91)
1993	400	367 (91)
1997	300	221 (74)
1999	400	307 (76)

stated as 'One of the most important aspects of tourism is that it provides more jobs in the Silver Valley', the question was rephrased to read: 'One of the most important aspects of tourism is that it will provide more jobs in the next five years in the Silver Valley'. The questions for all surveys were developed using previously tested questions developed by Lui and Var (1986), Lui *et al.*, (1987), and Snepenger and Johnson (1991). The surveys were repeated during the same time of year in spring at the end of the winter ski season. These four data collection periods captured information during the exploration, involvement and early development stages of the TALC. Specifically two research questions were examined. The first was whether demographic variables, residents' contact with tourists, perceived economic consequences, and congestion scales predict residents' attitude about the overall impact of tourism across the early stages in the TALC.

This question examined the variables driving the residents' view of tourism development at each point in time. Furthermore, it analyzes the direction and magnitude of the demographic, contact, and impact variables on the dependent variable.

The second question compares results across the four models to assess the consistency or dissimilarity with respect to predictors and overall explanatory power across the early stages of the TALC. In other words, this question examines the stability of variables to predict and the level of prediction for tourism development across the early stages of the TALC.

In 1990 the resort was in the exploration stage of the TALC. As part of the economic redevelopment process the City of Kellogg adopted a mountain theme and sought to refurbish storefronts with alpine architecture. The nearby City of Wallace adopted an early mining theme. But most skier visits to the area were within a 100–150 mile radius – the locally defined skier market. Little additional tourism investment was taking place and the resort was not a major employer in the area.

By 1993 the town was experiencing some growth in the local business mix aimed at the tourism market and can be said to be in the involvement stage. A 61-room hotel was constructed at the ski area base and several eating establishments were built. In 1997, citing financial and management limitations, city officials sold the area to a tourism specialty firm based in Oregon. After some initial fear that the gondola complex would be moved to a ski area development in Oregon, the investors were able to assure residents that the ski area would remain in operation as they continued to invest in and expand the operation. At full operational levels the resort employed over 100 full- and part-time employees.

As early as 1999 the area can be said to be well within the development stage of the TALC. In 2000 the US Forest Service completed the conversion of a scenic section of abandoned rail-bed from the Milwaukee Road that has transformed the unused rail bed into a world-class bike and walking path. This adventurous 13-mile trail takes mountain bikers (and hikers) through nine tunnels and over seven high wooden rail trestles. The *Route of the Hiawatha* is already a regional attraction and expected to expand the visitor base to the region considerably. Also slated for completion in 2002 is a regional 75-mile long 'rails to trails' development, much of which will traverse the Valley. These developments will expand the tourist visitor base to include more seasons. In 2002 the present owners handed management of ski area services to a ski area specialty firm and planned for 2002–2003 is a new ski lift and condominium development at a second base location. The ski area has received some favorable national press coverage and continually expands skier visitor days.

The first set of questions asked respondents for demographic information including marital status, age, years of residency, political self-identification, education level, and household income. Two additional questions that inquired about respondent contact with tourists probed their frequency of contact with tourists and the sociability of contact. Quality of interaction was operationalized using the following question: 'When you talk with tourists around town, which one of the following best describes your contact with tourists?' The response format was five point scale ranging from: 'very negative' to 'very positive'. The frequency item was stated as follows: 'During an average week, how often do you talk with tourists around town?' The response format was: 'daily', 'almost every day', 'a couple times a week', 'once a week', and 'seldom or never'. 'Daily' was scored a five and 'seldom or never' was scored one.

The instrument contained five items for each of the three impact areas – economic, social, and environmental. These items were measured on a five-point Likert scale where $1 = $ strongly disagree and $5 = $ strongly agree. Two scales of three items each were developed to measure respondents' attitude about the economic aspects of tourism development and congestion resulting from tourism. The first scale was designed to quantify the potential consequences of tourism development on the local economy. The economic development scale consisted of the following three questions:

- Tourism provides more jobs in the Silver Valley.
- Tourism attracts more investment in the Silver Valley.
- Our standard of living has increased because of tourism.

In contrast, the other scale was developed to ascertain the perceived level of congestion resulting from the presence of tourists in the small communities. The congestion scale included the following items all reverse coded:

- Local residents suffer from living in a tourist destination area.
- Tourism results in overcrowded lakes, hiking trails, parks, and other outdoor places for locals.
- Tourists add greatly to traffic congestion, noise.

Presented in Table 13.2 is the reliability analysis for each of the two scales for each year of the study. The economic development scale and the congestion scale manifested acceptable internal consistency across all four time periods (Berman, 2002: 96). The higher the Cronbach alpha, the greater the internal consistency of the items in the scale. Scales with high internal consistency provide relevant measures of theoretical constructs (Babbie, 2001).

The dependent variable for the study was a single item statement that elicited information on the overall perceived benefits and costs that might be anticipated from tourism development: 'Overall, the benefits are greater than the costs of tourism to the people of the Silver Valley.' The item was scored 5 = strongly agree and 1 = strongly disagree.

Significant predictors of perceived overall tourism development were identified using stepwise multiple regression. Separate models were developed for demographics, the contact variables, the impact scales, and an overall model that utilized all predicators. Standardized betas are reported for each of the significant independent variables. Standardized betas allow direct comparisons for the importance of significant predictors which are measured on different units or scales. The larger the standardized beta, the greater the change in the dependent variable

Table 13.2 Reliability analysis of economic development and congestion scales using Cronbach's alpha

Scale	*1991*	*1993*	*1997*	*1999*
Economic development	0.7633	0.6628	0.7428	0.6836
Congestion	0.8561	0.7866	0.7992	0.8115

given a one unit change in the independent variable. An alpha level of 0.05 was utilized to trim the stepwise regression models.

Findings

In order to investigate whether demographic variables, residents' contact with tourists, perceived economic consequences, and congestion scales predict residents' attitudes about the overall impact of tourism across the early stages in the TALC, stepwise multiple regression analyses were performed for the three sets of independent variables.

Table 13.3 delineates the four separate models that were constructed at each point in time. The first model examined demographics, the second the influence of contact between residents and tourists, the third the significance of the impact scales, and the fourth was an overall model predicting the overall costs and benefits of tourism development. The demographic model in the exploration stage did not predict overall attitudes towards tourism development. The R^2 was 0.032 and the two significant predictors were political self-identity and years in residence.

The contact model, in contrast, did predict overall attitude towards tourism development. The quality and frequency of interactions with tourists were used as predictors. However, in 1991 only quality of interaction was significant and it explained almost 82% of the variance. The higher the quality of the interaction residents had with tourists, the more positive they were toward this form of economic development.

The third model employed the two impact scales: economic development and congestion. Only the economic development scale was significant with an R^2 of 0.867. The more positive residents viewed the economic impacts, the more favorable they were towards tourism development. Lastly, the overall model using all of the predictors identified the economic development scale and quality of interaction as significant predictors. The most important of these was economic development. The overall model had an R^2 of 0.879.

The next series of models explored predictors for the involvement stage. The early involvement stage used survey data from 1993, while the later involvement models used data collected in 1997. Several demographic variables were significant in 1993. Marital status was the most important followed by level of education, political self-identity, age, and lastly by income. For the contact model in 1993, only quality of interaction was significant with a beta of 0.940 and R^2 of 0.883. The impact scales model revealed that both scales were significant. The standardized beta for congestion was 0.320 and for economic development 0.655. The model had an R^2 of 0.924. Finally, the overall model for 1993 shows two significant variables as predictors – the economic

Table 13.3 Stepwise regression analysis for attitude towards overall benefits and costs of tourism to Silver Valley, Idaho using demographics, contact, and tourism impact scale variables as predictor variables*

Predictor variables	Stage in TALC			
	Exploration	*Involvement*		*Development*
	1991	*1993*	*1997*	*1999*
	$n = 294$	$n = 272$	$n = 173$	$n = 261$
Demographic model				
Age		0.168	0.304	0.205
Years in residence	0.116			
Income		0.132	0.208	
Marriage status		0.248		0.217
Education		0.235	0.342	0.317
Political self-identity	− 0.147	0.200	0.156	0.254
R^2	0.032	0.862	0.924	0.903
Contact model				
Quality of interaction with tourists	0.905	0.940	0.867	0.889
Frequency of interaction with tourists			0.103	0.087
R^2	0.819	0.883	0.915	0.927
Impact Scales Model				
Congestion		0.320	0.279	0.376
Economic development	0.931	0.655	0.704	0.610
R^2	0.867	0.924	0.939	0.946
Overall model				
Economic development	0.641	0.678	0.440	0.424
Quality	0.320		0.220	0.319
Education			0.134	
Age			0.133	
Congestion		0.300		0.247

Table 13.3 (Continued)				
Predictor variables	Stage in TALC			
	Exploration	Involvement		Development
	1991	1993	1997	1999
Frequency			0.079	
R^2	0.879	0.928	0.948	0.951

*Standardized betas reported, alpha = 0.05

development scale and the congestion scale. The overall model had an R^2 of 0.928.

The later involvement stage in 1997 was more complex. For the demographic model four variables – education, age, income, and political self-identity – were significant. Both interaction variables were significant as were both impact scales. In the overall model five variables were found to be significant with an overall R^2 of 0.948.

The final year of survey data describes the early development stage of the TALC in 1999. The demographic model explained 90% of the variance in the dependent variable and four variables were significant predictors: education, political self-identity, marital status, and years of residency. Both contact variables were significant and had an R^2 of 0.927. The impact scale items were also significant: R^2 was 0.946. The overall model contained three variables that were found to be significant: economic development, quality of contact with tourists, and the congestion scale item. Overall R^2 in 1999 was 0.951.

The ability of the models to demonstrate consistency or dissimilarity with respect to predictors and overall explanatory power across the early stages of the TALC was the next area of inquiry.

The level of prediction for tourism development across the early stages of the TALC improved over time. At the exploration stage respondents had a difficult time assessing tourism impacts. As the community tourism economy transitioned through the involvement and development stages, residents had a better sense of the benefits and costs of tourism development and the results for the statistical modeling became more convincing. Concurrently, those favoring and not favoring tourism development became easier to identify using demographic measures, contact, and impact variables. Over time, as evidenced by the increasing R^2 values, each of the four general models explained more of the variance in the independent variable.

Modeling perceived overall benefits and costs of tourism revealed that some variables were stable predictors over time. Across all four time periods the overall model demonstrated that economic development is the major driver in how residents view tourism. Those residents who believe tourism enhances the local economy tend to also have a positive overall view of tourism on their lives and the community while those who do not view tourism positively tend to believe that tourism will have negative effects.

The second most important variable across the stages of the TALC was the quality of interaction locals have with tourists. Those who enjoy favorable interaction tend to view tourism development positively. For those whose interaction with tourists is negative, their view of tourism is also negative.

The third variable that shows a systematic relationship over time is the congestion impact scale. Those who favor tourism tended to believe that congestion was not a problem with respect to overcrowded parks and other recreational facilities in the region. Those who perceive a crowding or congestion problem tend to hold a negative view of tourism development.

Finally, three demographic variables emerged as stable predictors in three of the four years. Education produced relatively high standardized betas and was the most important demographic predictor. The higher the educational attainment, the more predisposed toward tourism development they tended to be. Political self-identity was a weaker but consistent predictor. In the first year conservatives tended to favor tourism but the relationship shifted to reveal that the more liberal political stance favored tourism and a conservative political position held negative views toward tourism development. The last demographic variable that showed stability as a predictor over time was age; the relationship with the dependent variable was that older respondents supported tourism development while younger respondents were less supportive.

Discussion

Stages in the TALC are critical to understanding perceived overall impacts of tourism development (Johnson & Snepenger, 1992). In this study, different relationships between overall impacts, demographic measures, contact between locals and tourists, and tourism impacts emerged along the exploration, involvement, and development continuum. These changing relationships can be effectively modeled as noted by the increasingly high regression coefficients in the four models. A set of robust predictors were identified in this study as measures of economic development, quality of interaction, and congestion.

The economic development impacts of tourism are perhaps the most important to any community undergoing a planned economic transition. The economic development scale assesses (1) enhanced employment opportunity, (2) investments resulting from increased tourism activity, and (3) the possibility of enhanced standard of living for locals. Clearly, these were consistently the most important predictors of support for tourism. Local governments and tourism developers will find greater community support for tourism development if these economic criteria are explicitly addressed. For example, owners and promoters of emergent tourism enterprises can hire local labor and pay a living wage. Community economic development efforts can work to attract secondary businesses to a region that complements an attraction but can also help diversify the tourism economy by attracting other business not directly associated with tourism (Snepenger *et al.*, 1995). Local option tourist taxes can be utilized to make community and social investments to the region so that all residents share in the benefits of tourism development. Some tourist communities provide heavily subsidized public transportation or provide locals with inexpensive season ski passes. The fundamental lesson for tourism developers is that if residents believe that economic attributes for them are enhanced as a result of tourism development, they will tend to support it.

Related to increasingly positive economic activity is the quality of contact between tourists and locals. As long as that interaction is enjoyable and positive in nature, residents will tend to support tourism development. Public and private managers can encourage positive interactions by planning for community events that appeal to both locals and tourists – winter and summer festivals, farmers markets, and community free ski days are just a few examples. Locals can be encouraged to open their homes as B&Bs and can do so with planning and capital startup loans from various sources.

As previously noted, the TALC is both a cross-sectional and longitudinal construct, however there are very few longitudinal studies in the literature and further research is needed to explore the shifting long-term relationships between residents and tourism development. The tourism impact literature begs for additional longitudinal studies in other settings with other characteristics such as different economic transitions, ethnicity, level of tourism development, urbanization, and cultural settings, which could all provide valuable insight into the changing nature of tourism impacts and destination maturation processes.

In the Silver Valley, future research could include utilizing the scales discussed here as well as others by Ap and Crompton (1998), Lankford and Howard (1994), and Snepenger *et al.* (2001) to investigate both summer and winter tourism. The region will expand the visitor base and seasonality of visitation as mountain biking, bike touring, and water-based recreation continue to develop in future years. As the region moves through the TALC it will be critical to continue to monitor the impacts of the growing tourism segment of the economy – this is especially true as second home development grows in importance to the region (Johnson *et al.*, 2002; Snepenger *et al.*, 1995) and the traditional mining and timber economy recover from past decline.

Conclusion

Very few longitudinal empirical studies exist that help operationalize the TALC model. This study examines the early stages of the TALC from exploration through early development for a regional economy previously based on natural resource extraction and now increasingly diversified toward tourism and tourism services. The study examines the results of four surveys of residents in the region that monitor the perceived economic, social, and environmental tourism impacts over the 1990s.

The first research question examined which variables best explained residents' view of tourism development for each of the four time periods. The analysis included the direction and magnitude of demographic measures, residents' contact with tourists, and tourism impact variables. The results show that an economic development scale constructed from three of five standardized economic impact questions from the tourism literature was the most robust predictor of feelings toward tourism development for all four time periods.

The second research question compared results across time and TALC stages. This question examined the stability of variables to predict and the level of prediction for tourism development. The results again showed that the economic development scale was the most powerful predictor across the TALC continuum.

The findings present some opportunities for supporters of tourism development and it was suggested that policies that spread out the economic benefits of tourism development to include locals and at the same time enhance tourist/resident interactions can help ensure the community will be a willing host to tourists as visitation expands.

Continued monitoring of the expanding tourism base is suggested as a management tool to help foster a sustainable tourism economy in the region. This monitoring can prove useful to help foster lasting and expanding support for tourism development as the Silver Valley rebuilds its local economy and social infrastructure that were lost with the decline of the mining industry after 100 years of prosperity.

Finally, similar longitudinal studies may prove valuable across all stages in the TALC and could help manage existing tourism activity as it inevitably adjusts to emergent and shifting markets. As it does so, the impacts on residents of tourism-dependent communities will certainly change and it is possible that a different demographic, economic, and political cohort may be attracted (or repelled) to the community. These new residents may desire something different for their quality of life and their opinions may significantly impact the tourism economy. For example, as retirees who are uncoupled from the local economy are attracted to an area rich in recreational opportunities, they may wish for lower levels of tourism development in order to avoid perceived overcrowding (see Martin, this volume, editor's comment). In mature or declining tourism markets, residents may desire to radically retool the local economy as experienced in the Silver Valley. Other scenarios can be imagined. Local government decision makers and tourism entrepreneurs would be well advised to consider investing in continued and long-term monitoring of those who act as hosts for community tourism.

Chapter 14
The TALC Model and Politics

B. MARTIN

Introduction

'If you are leaving Hilton Head ... please take our mayor.' That bumper sticker seen on cars in Hilton Head, South Carolina in the mid-1990s signaled an increasing dissatisfaction with the mayor who had been elected a year and a half earlier. Hilton Head was in a political uproar, with the tourism industry at the center of the controversy. The mayor, a planner by profession, had been elected with strong support from the retirees on the island on what he construed as a 'no-more-tourism' platform. When he was elected, many had assumed that the incumbent would be re-elected and had complacently failed to vote. During his term, the mayor had created a furor because of his interpretation of his mandate. In interviews on national television and state papers he indicated that Hilton Head wanted less tourism. Many of the town's residents were quite disappointed with what they considered to be his irresponsible behavior (Hammond, 1993; Lofton, 1993). Even those who had voted for him believed that he had misinterpreted a controlled growth mandate as a 'no-more-tourism' mandate. For many, the bumper sticker quite clearly expressed their feelings.

The tourism industry on Hilton Head at that time enjoyed a visitation rate of 1.6 million people who spent $577 million on their visits (Lofton, 1993). There was no question that tourism was important to the economy of the town. Unlike many destinations, tourism in Hilton Head had been planned. According to the original major developer, Charles Fraser, Hilton Head had been planned to be both a resort and a retirement community. It had been highly successful in attracting both retirees and tourists, and therein lay the problem. Many residents, and especially retirees, were concerned that the number of tourists was growing and becoming a problem. A carrying capacity study conducted a few years previously had shown that transportation was the limiting factor for the island (Bell, 1994). Residents did not have to be convinced of that. There was only one major road through the island and only one bridge to be used for evacuation in the event of a hurricane. Traffic congestion was a serious problem and many on the island feared that Hilton Head was headed for other serious problems. This group was called the 'burn the bridgers', referring to their perceived desire to protect the community by burning the only bridge that gives access to Hilton Head. These were ostensibly the residents who had voted for the controversial mayor.

Both development and the control of development are based on political decision making. Governments are made up of politicians who are elected on specific platforms, supported by the public vote. It is quite common for that platform to be economic growth and development, which makes the situation in Hilton Head even more interesting, as the mayor's platform had appeared to be anti-growth. In addition, government agencies decide the rules of development through formulation of laws and regulations. Recognizing this is important to the study of the tourism life cycle. Government leaders, elected by interested citizens, who provide the framework for the development and growth of tourism. But are these government leaders always following the desires of their constituencies? Or are there other pressures put upon them that benefit a few but may not be in the best interest of the community. And what backlash can be expected when the public is discontented with government involvement?

Butler (1980) refers to some of these political pressures when discussing the involvement stage of the tourism life cycle. He states that in this early stage of tourism, development pressure will be put upon government and public agencies to provide or improve transportation and other facilities for visitors. Who is exerting this pressure and why? Is it simply those in the tourism industry that apply the pressure or might there be others within the community interested in growth from tourism? Although there has been some previous recognition of the involvement of government in the tourism development process (Elliot, 1997: 8; Getz, 1991: 134), not enough attention has been paid to the politics of tourism (Hall, 1994: 1; Hall & Jenkins, 1995: 97). This study of resident attitudes toward tourism in Hilton Head provides a unique view of some of the political ramifications of tourism development. Election of an anti-tourism mayor and his eventual political demise provide an interesting backdrop for enhancing understanding of the political aspects of the tourism life cycle. This chapter is a snapshot of Hilton Head in the mid-1990s that provides insight into the relationship between political processes and the tourism life cycle, from the perspective of the town's residents.

Historical Perspective of the Development of Hilton Head

Development of Hilton Head Island commenced in the late 1950s with the building of the James F. Byrnes Bridge to the mainland. In 1956 the Frasers acquired a totally uninhabited 5200-acre tract, which encompassed the entire southern end of the island, comprising approximately 20% of the total land area of the island. Charles Fraser proceeded to develop Sea Pines Plantation into a resort community designed to serve both retirees and vacationers. Fraser's development was based on a master plan that included the establishment of, and adherence to, three fundamental commitments: strict control of land use, the development of recreation land, and the preservation of two square miles of wildlife refuge. Fraser's goal was to maintain the natural beauty of the area by developing it in such a way that the island's natural attributes would be enhanced rather than destroyed. Careful planning and rigid standards were seen as the method for accomplishing this (Fraser, 1995). The early development of Sea Pines Plantation by Fraser implemented those standards. Homes blended in with the natural environment and wildlife roamed free. Fraser also had a great influence on other aspects of the island's development. Even today, Hilton Head is noted for its strict regulation of signage throughout the town.

Since the original development of Sea Pines, much development has occurred, not all of which adheres to the original goals. Charles Fraser never owned the entire island but the areas that he did own were well planned and protected. However, other developers during the 1980s were more interested in turning a profit than protecting the island. While a great deal of the island is comprised of gated communities in which care has been taken to provide only the best in amenities for the wealthy residents, several resort developments provide rental accommodations that barely meet city standards (Shields, 1987).

Most of the remaining undeveloped land in Hilton Head is owned by the African-American indigenous population. The town planner, as well as an African-American city councilman who is a native of the island, reported that some of these native islanders felt that their right to develop their land was being threatened by both current and proposed land use restrictions. According to one real estate agent (Kenney, 1994), some business people also felt that the island was not 'built out' and that there was room for continued growth. On the other hand, the election of the mayor gave evidence that many of the residents felt that restrictions on growth were very important.

Some residents believed the town administrators were attempting to control growth in what some considered a backdoor method; implementing regulations on new developments that would be restrictive enough to halt most development. For example, traffic impact statements were required for new developments. Developers had to show that their new facilities provided acceptable access to the only major road on the island and pay impact fees according to potential impact.

During this unsettled period in Hilton Head's history, the incumbent mayor was running for re-election. Ironically, his opponent was a local building contractor. Would the mayor be re-elected to continue his anti-tourism campaign? This was a vital question for the future of Hilton

Head. The mayor's political viewpoints had the potential to send Hilton Head into the decline stage of the tourism life cycle (Butler, 1980). A study that determined resident attitudes toward various aspects of tourism development could provide the answer to important questions. Were the residents of Hilton Head anti-tourism, anti-growth or neither? Were there differences in the opinions among residents about the future of Hilton Head, according to whether or not they were retirees, business leaders, or government administrators? Where did resident attitudes indicate that Hilton Head was on the life cycle continuum and what did residents want for their future? And what role did politics play in determining Hilton Head's progression through the tourism life cycle? Resident attitudes are an important determinant in assessing whether social carrying capacity is being exceeded in a manner that will affect the tourism life cycle stage of the community (Martin & Uysal, 1990)

A study of tourism in Hilton Head was conducted with the intent of discovering whether or not various groups of residents had consistent views of the future of tourism and whether there was indeed an indication of a political growth machine in Hilton Head that might be inclined to pressure the government into decisions that could result in the eventual demise of the tourism industry. Resident attitudes were the basis for this determination. The study was conducted using the Tourism Impact Attitude Scale to determine resident attitudes toward tourism and its continued growth on Hilton Head. Some of the results of that study have been reported previously (Martin, 1999; Martin *et al.*, 1998) and will be reviewed here. Not previously reported were the many long discussions held with the residents after they had completed the standardized questionnaire. The qualitative aspects of the research yielded valuable information for assessing the dynamics between politics and tourism growth that might propel a destination through the life cycle. Those conversations provide much of the basis for this chapter.

Growth Machine Theory and the Tourism Life Cycle

There are several theories of political influence on the development of communities (Harrigan, 1989). A year of background research on the situation in Hilton Head revealed that growth machine theory would be most useful in describing resident attitudes and the political atmosphere in Hilton Head (Canan & Hennessy, 1989; Danielson, 1995; Martin, 1998). Growth machine theory (Molotch, 1976) is based on the concept that community growth is frequently used as a platform for political gain, driven by influential members of the community, the 'elites'. Molotch contended that land-holding community leaders, and those in whose best interest community growth lies, dominate community policymaking. That faction makes up the growth machine. The main goal of the growth machine is to promote growth in order to maximize the economic return to land holders, as well as others in the community who benefit from growth. The growth machine is made up of landowners, financial institutions, lawyers, and local newspaper owners who are in a position to benefit from growth. This faction of the community dominates local government and seeks to influence local political leaders in order to bring them into the progrowth machine. Generally, city government plays a dichotomous role in dealing with the growth machine. First, it must support the growth machine's promotion of economic (i.e. tourism in the case of Hilton Head) growth on the grounds that growth increases job opportunities for residents and makes land more valuable. On the other hand, because it represents people in local neighborhoods, city government frequently finds itself playing an intermediary role in conflicts that arise when residents oppose particular development projects (Harrigan, 1989). According to Logan and Molotch (1987: 51), those who make up the progrowth machine 'use their growth consensus to eliminate any alternative vision of the purpose of local government or the meaning of community.'

Growth machine theory has important implications for discussions and assessments using the tourism life cycle model. The life cycle model is based on the concept that tourism destinations change over time (Butler, 1980). Those changes in the stage of tourism development generally are occurring based on various aspects of growth within the destination. Growth in tourist numbers and tourist facilities generates both potential benefits and costs to the community. These costs and benefits vary as the destination changes over time, *due to growth*. Resident attitudes may also change over time due to growth in the number of outsiders with whom they must share resources and space. Attitudes on the part of community residents are recognized as playing a vital role in the success of tourism for the community. Negative attitudes of residents are commonly acknowledged to result in reduced popularity of the destination for visitors (Doxey, 1975; Martin & Uysal, 1990). Resident attitudes toward tourism can also be manifested through the political processes that elect officials according to their plans for the community. Therefore, it would seem that more attention needs to be paid to the role of politics in the tourism life cycle process.

While it is often difficult to assess just how much growth is spurred by tourism and how much by other types of business in the community, in the case of Hilton Head it is far easier to see the effect of tourism. Tourism is the main economic engine on the island, with real estate running second in importance. However, real estate sales and tourism develop-ment are intricately connected to each other. As in many attractive resort areas, new residents are frequently prior tourists. Sometimes they purchase second homes during their working lives and then retire to live there permanently, and sometimes they move there for the first time when they retire. In either case, often their first attraction to the island is as a tourist. There is no doubt that Hilton Head has changed over time, with more and more residents living in more and more gated communities, as well as an increase in service industries to support the growing number of hotels and restaurants built for tourists. All of these changes could be expected to affect resident attitudes toward tourism. Did this growth result in negative attitudes of the residents toward current or future tourism development? What impact did resident attitudes have on the political processes that affect the tourism life cycle of resort communities?

Hilton Head Study

A survey of Hilton Head residents' attitudes was conducted during the summer of 1995. The data for this study were collected using a questionnaire based on the Tourism Impact Attitude Scale (TIAS) developed by Lankford (1994). The TIAS is a 29-item scale used to assess resident attitudes toward tourism development. It is a five-point Likert-type attitudinal scale, with possible responses ranging from strongly agree to strongly disagree. The questionnaire was slightly modified for relevance in Hilton Head. At the end of the questionnaire respondents were asked if there was anything else they wanted to discuss or clarify.

The sampling frame for the study was rather complex. A market research firm located in Hilton Head provided the list of businesses, as well as a list of permanent home owners. Business leaders were identified as owners or managers of all businesses on Hilton Head. Government administrators were identified by the Town Manager, using the criteria that those town employees who were in administrative positions which allow them to have input in the decision-making process would be surveyed. The six members of city council and the Mayor were also included in the sample of government administrators. Retirees were identified using a screening question for home owners. Those residents who were not retirees, business leaders or government administrators were identified as 'general residents'.

All respondents except government administrators were interviewed by telephone using the Dillman Total Design Method (1978) for telephone interviews. The Town Manager asked that government employees self-administer the questionnaire rather than participate in the telephone interviewing. A total of 287 respondents participated in the study, representing an 86% response rate. The breakdown of respondents by areas of interest showed that there were: 120 business leaders, 100 retirees, 28 government administrators, and 39 general residents.

Results

A sociodemographic profile of the respondents showed that 53.5% of the respondents were male and 46.5% female, 44.6% were over 55 years of age, and nearly 45% had incomes over $60,000. The vast majority of respondents reported that they were non-natives of Hilton Head. Although 81% reported being non-natives, this number was actually higher, as many who reported being natives also reported only living on Hilton Head for a fairly short period of time. The question was 'do you consider yourself to be a native of Hilton Head?' Perhaps due to the wording of the question, personal views of 'belonging' may have complicated the results.

An analysis of resident attitudes toward tourism revealed interesting results. Respondents were asked to rate their opinion of the statements on a scale from 1 to 5, with 1 being strongly disagree and 5 being strongly agree. Three statements stand out as having the highest means. One was that 'tourism is responsible for the traffic congestion in Hilton Head.' Another was 'long-term planning by city government can control the negative impacts of tourism on the environment.' The statement with the highest mean was 'the tourism industry will continue to play a major economic role in Hilton Head.'

A factor analysis was performed to examine underlying dimensions that would provide information for measuring attitudes toward the issue of growth from tourism development. A four-factor solution with high alpha reliabilities for each of the factors emerged. The four factors were: increased development, positive impacts, tourism support, and negative impacts.

The increased development factor contained items related to resident attitudes toward more development. These items included attitudes concerning more intensive development of facilities, becoming more of a tourist destination, attracting more visitors, development of more tourism facilities, and further tourism growth.

The second factor, positive impacts, included attitudes toward tourism's impact on recreational opportunities, the quality of public services, the standard of living, economic wellbeing, the job market, shopping opportunities, as well as generic benefits of tourism and the type of jobs provided by tourism.

The third factor was termed tourism support because all the items related to resident support for tourism in the community. The items in this factor included attitudes about government control of impacts, the value of tourists, government role in promoting tourism, support of tourism as vital to the community, support for tourism as the main industry, promotion of tourism, and support for tourism as a continuing economic force in the community.

The fourth factor, negative impacts, ascertained resident attitudes toward litter, crime, environmental impacts, and traffic congestion.

In order to test for differences among the four groups on the four factors, an analysis of variance (ANOVA) was performed. There was a statistically significant difference among the groups on each of the four factors at the 0.05 or better level. The first factor, Increased Development, was directly related to the issue of whether or not residents were interested in continued or increased growth as a result of tourism development. This factor explained 35.6% of the variance while all the other factors together explained 17.1%. According to Kachigan (1986), it is important to note the importance of the first factor when it explains an overwhelming percentage of the variance in comparison to other factors. As it was considered most important to assess attitudes toward growth, the Increased Development factor was considered an important indicator of those attitudes. Business leaders showed the strongest support for increased development, with general residents and government administrators showing more modest support and retirees being the mostly strongly opposed to further tourism development.

On the Positive Impacts factor, retirees and government administrators viewed tourism as having less positive impacts than did the general residents and business leaders. Business leaders were most aware of the positive impacts.

On the Tourism Support factor, retirees and government administrators showed significant differences from business leaders and general residents. There was more support for tourism from business leaders than from the retirees and government administrators.

On the Negative Impacts factor the only significant difference was shown between business leaders and all the other groups. Business leaders felt that there was less negative impact on the community from tourism development than did all the other groups.

Although significant differences were shown, it is important to understand that the differences were only in the *strength* of opinion or feelings on the issues. Differences did not indicate that different groups were pro or con on the issues. All residents' attitudes were on the same side of the spectrum. It was only the strength of their attitudes that was different. For example, all groups showed low support for the items in the factor Increased Development, ranging from 2.04 for retirees to 2.89 for business leaders. Although they were technically significantly different, it was not because any of the groups agreed with statements such as: 'Hilton Head should encourage more intensive development of tourist facilities'; 'Hilton Head should become more of a tourist destination'; and 'Overall, you are in favor of further growth from tourism development in Hilton Head'. The same was true of respondents for all of the factors. There were differences in the intensity of their agreement or disagreement with the statements but they were never polar opposites in their views.

Conversations with respondents

At the end of the questionnaire, respondents were asked if there was anything they would like to add to their responses on the questionnaire. Most residents were very willing to discuss issues not specifically addressed in the questionnaire or to explain their responses. Government leaders did not participate in this portion of the research because their questionnaires were not completed by phone. However, they did have a section at the end of the questionnaire for writing in comments.

Respondents were most anxious to express their dismay about the mayor's behavior. As for their attitudes toward the mayor and their intentions politically, respondents were overwhelmingly negative toward his bid for re-election. Retirees and business leaders alike felt that a new mayor was necessary. It was quite clear that the mayor was highly unlikely to be re-elected. Even those who had voted for him previously were against his re-election. They were pleased to be able to explain why they had voted for him originally and their comments gave a much richer understanding of the dynamics of politics, tourism, and growth on Hilton Head. Several respondents mentioned that the conversations were therapeutic, reflecting their emotions about the subject. Through these discussions, it became clear that these residents were indeed concerned about where the town was headed if growth of the tourism industry continued unabated. They were disappointed that the man elected to help solve the problems had created such negative, erroneous percep-tions of the Hilton Head tourism industry.

There were several other consistent themes running through the comments of the residents. Many residents reported that they felt that Hilton Head had 'reached saturation point'. They believed that Hilton Head was a thriving resort and retirement community but that it was essential that 'future growth be managed'. The term 'managed growth' was used many times in conversations with the residents in the study. They did not see themselves as anti-growth or anti-tourism. They believed that the best protection for Hilton Head would be in controlled and managed growth. Whether the respondents were business owners or retirees, their desires for controlling growth of the community were consistent.

Residents were quite fearful that Hilton Head would 'become another Myrtle Beach'. Myrtle Beach is also a coastal community in South Carolina, located approximately three hours north of Hilton Head. Myrtle Beach is highly developed, with many reasonably priced motels, restaurants, and a variety of amusement parks and country music entertainment. It is predominantly marketed to the middle class and has a very different image from that of Hilton Head. Myrtle Beach had gone through a rejuvenation stage during the late 1980s and early 1990s but was still not the type of high-class resort that Hilton Head had always been.

Many of the residents of Hilton Head were concerned about the ability of Hilton Head to maintain its upper-class image. They were hesitant in explaining their thoughts on this issue but nevertheless, many expressed concern that overbuilding and continued growth that was not consistent with this high-class image would result in the attraction of a type of tourist that would change the character of their community. The life cycle model predicts that the type of tourist will change over time and residents of Hilton Head were aware that they were in peril of watching this phenomenon become reality. There was a time in the 1980s when new construction in the upper end of the island was shoddy, resulting in what locals call 'stack a shacks'. These were poorly constructed condominiums that were much more affordable to the less affluent than the upper-class hotels such as the Westin and Hyatt. In addition, many new fast-food restaurants and low-cost motels had opened in the previous decade. Residents were concerned that this would lead to the end of the 'classiness' of their town. Business leaders and residents alike were concerned about the potential for negative change in the *type* of tourism Hilton Head had always enjoyed, as Butler predicts will happen without stringent controls.

Discussion

The consistency with which the residents were concerned about continued growth due to tourism was unexpected based on observation of the political dynamics of the town. It was expected that the residents would be divided along the lines suggested by growth machine theory; that business leaders would be much more supportive of growth of tourism than retirees and other residents. It seemed logical that business owners and managers would differ significantly from retirees and government officials in their opinions of the benefits and costs of tourism, as predicted by growth machine theory and by the mayor's election. Such was not the case. Despite the reported statistical differences, the residents were surprisingly on the same side in their views of the future of Hilton Head. Perhaps the fact that Hilton Head attracts so many highly educated, successful retirees who have themselves previously run large businesses, means that residents have more understanding of the importance of 'not killing the goose that lays the golden egg'. The business owners were quite savvy in understanding that principle and the retirees were quite aware of the importance of protecting the economy. After all, it is an economy that provides everyone with a number of amenities. Although many residents felt that a lot of the shopping opportunities are geared toward the tourists and frequently shop in upper-class shops in Savannah, the residents generally take advantage of the many other amenities such as the excellent restaurants and golf courses. Several of the retirees who were interviewed not only played on the golf courses but worked there part-time in what some might consider menial jobs but which they considered to be fun and interesting ways to keep busy.

What impact did the desire of Hilton Head residents to protect the image of the community have on the determination of life cycle stage? The fact that residents were concerned about the image of the town indicates that a change in image might have been occurring. The building of low-income tourist accommodations and fast-food restaurants certainly indicates that Hilton Head may be on the verge of a downturn in the ability to attract the high-income tourist. This would be one more indication that Hilton Head is moving towards a later stage of the life cycle and that it may need to take stringent measures to protect the resort from a potential decline stage. It is unlikely that Hilton Head will ever deteriorate to the point that tourists will not actually visit. However, there are several indications that the town is becoming less exclusive and becoming more attractive to the average-income tourist.

A confounding issue for keeping the image of Hilton Head intact is the inability of those who work in the tourism industry to actually live on Hilton Head. Most of the service workers are bused as much as an hour and half to work in tourism positions. Low-income housing is simply not available and therefore, the image of Hilton Head is, in an interesting manner, more easily protected. Molotch (1976) calls those who promote growth the 'elites'. Is the lack of affordable housing a case of the 'elites' of the growth machine protecting the image of the town in order to keep land values at a premium?

One important aspect of growth machine theory is the potential for an anti-growth coalition. Hilton Head did indeed appear to have a type of anti-growth coalition; one that wanted strictly controlled and managed growth. However, this is not to be mistaken for an anti-tourism coalition. Although it is difficult to distinguish between anti-growth and anti-tourism when it is generally tourism that is spurring the growth, residents made it clear that they were not anti-tourism. In the end, it seems that the residents were being proactive in demanding managed growth, rather than negative in being strongly anti-growth. Residents want the town to have the ability to maintain a viable and profitable tourism industry while residents enjoy a high quality of life. For them, being in favor of managed growth is the best possible method of protecting their quality of life and allowing for continued economic prosperity. Several residents commented that they believed that the physical limitation of the island would in itself be the final limitation to growth. As there are strict limitations on the height of buildings, which make it impossible for the town to grow *up*, there is some credibility to that idea.

Not taking any chances in protecting their island, the residents exercised their right to elect a true representative of their views in the Fall of 1995. A native of the local area who was an award-winning building contractor was elected as the new mayor. He then became the first mayor in the history of Hilton Head ever to be re-elected to a second term and recently won a third election. What makes this contractor-turned-politician so popular when a planner was so unpopular? His answers to questions posed by local media before his third election help explain (*Carolina Morning News*, 2001). He was asked what he saw as the top two issues facing the town and how he would address them. The first issue he stated was 'mainland growth', alluding to the impact that growth occurring just outside the town from a large retirement community is having on the town of Hilton Head. He stated that he would address the issue by working with the county 'to implement growth management techniques and ordinances that will allow growth to be implemented in a more orderly and less intense fashion'. The second issue was 'enhancing our sense of community'. When asked what experiences or qualities he had that would make him a good mayor for the next four years his answer was 'I am a consensus builder'. A consensus builder who understands the need for growth management and protection of their sense of community was exactly what the people of Hilton Head were seeking. His commitment to listening to the desires of the community in their vision of the future of the town has not only kept him in office but bodes well for keeping Hilton Head as a viable tourism destination.

Conclusion

The tourism life cycle as proposed by Butler (1980) has for many years provided a mechanism for studying the future of tourism destinations. However, little has been noted of the political aspect of the growth that occurs as tourism progresses through the different stages of the life cycle. The events in Hilton Head of the mid 1990s provide an interesting laboratory for assessing the relevance of the political aspects inherent in promoting growth. Growth machine theory postulates that avaricious residents will inordinately influence local politics in a manner that leads to excessive growth and the rise of an anti-growth coalition. On the surface, this did indeed appear to be the case in Hilton Head. However, the study of resident attitudes that specifically compared views of business leaders, government officials, and retirees did not find that in fact to be true. No group was found to want the growth of Hilton Head to occur at any cost. Instead, even retirees who would not monetarily benefit from allowing tourism to thrive were in favor of maintaining the current level of tourism. Business leaders with more to gain monetarily from tourism growth were prudent in acknowledging that too much growth could eventually destroy their profitable businesses. Government leaders were trying to provide the mechanism through regulation that would control growth.

Overall, all groups of residents made it clear that maintaining the quality of life and sense of community were what concerned them most. Business leaders were just as interested in maintaining a high quality of tourism business. It was evident that residents would take control of the political process in order to do so. The election of a mayor who became very unpopular was quite possibly the best thing ever to happen to Hilton Head. Although he did not turn out to be the right man for the job, never again could it be assumed that concerned citizens would not be heard on their views of the future of their community. The election that year and in subsequent years of a building contractor who understands the issues of growth was a direct result of the disastrous prior administration. It would seem that the best method of controlling an anti-tourism coalition that could result in descent into a decline stage is to elect a leader who cares about resident attitudes and takes action on their behalf.

As for the tourism life cycle, resident attitudes toward tourism provide evidence to support determination of the stage of the life cycle in which Hilton Head appeared to be at that particular time. Butler's consolidation stage seems to best represent Hilton Head's position on the life cycle. A major part of the island's economy is tied to tourism, major franchises and chains are well established, and efforts have certainly succeeded in extending the tourist season. Perhaps most importantly, the large numbers of visitors and facilities for tourists have aroused just enough opposition and discontent among residents to make them vigilant in protecting their quality of life.

From the first introductory stages of development in the late 1950s through the maturing of the town in the mid 1990s, Hilton Head has progressed from an inaccessible island to one of the world's greatest resorts. With savvy and concerned residents who are willing to use the political process to proactively protect the island's future, Hilton Head may never arrive at the decline stage of the life cycle.

Chapter 15

Seeking Sustainable Tourism in Northern Thailand: The Dynamics of the TALC

J. MAROIS and T. HINCH

Introduction

The concept of tourism area life cycles (TALC) is germane to this book. For the purposes of this chapter, however, it is also important to understand the concept of sustainable tourism development, as well as the general environment of TALC in Thailand. Sustainable tourism development is defined as:

> tourism which is developed and maintained in an area (community, environment) in such a manner and at such a scale that it remains viable over an indefinite period of time and does not degrade or alter the environment (human and physical) in which it exists to such a degree that it prohibits the successful development and well-being of other activities and processes. (Butler, 1993: 29)

Ideally, tourism developments should respect, and even improve, the viability of the natural environment and the social community.

Butler's (1980) conceptualisation of TALCs suggests that tourist destinations will not be sustainable indefinitely, at least in terms of tourism activity. The more pertinent question is, therefore, how to extend a constructive form of tourism in the destination rather than how to ensure the destination equivalent of immortality.

The essence of the tourist attraction in Ban Raummit, Thailand is the tribal culture of the Karen people. Tourists, particularly Westerners, travel to the hills of Northern Thailand in search of primitive 'others'. The distinct culture of the Karen has proven to be a powerful draw. Any discussion of the sustainability of tourism development in this village must, therefore, consider culture as a defining element of the community, as well as its manifestation in various tourism products. Although the TALC has already been used to examine sustainable tourism development in Northern Thailand (Cohen, 1979; Dearden, 1991; Dearden & Harron, 1994; Maneeorasert *et al.*, 1975), the dynamic inter-relationships between product and destination life cycles have not been emphasised. The purpose of this chapter is to consider the sustainability of hill tribe tourism in the Karen village of Ban Raummit, Thailand by examining these inter-relationships.

Previous studies indicate that commercial trekking began in this area around 1970 as small-scale operations in which a limited number of people, mostly scientists, travelled to learn about the hill tribes (Cohen, 1996). Guides were tribal people who knew how to access the villages. Dramatic growth over the next two and a half decades is reflected in the currently more than 200 trekking operators in Chiang Mai, the major starting point for treks into northern hill tribe villages by the mid-1990s (Cohen, 1996; Dearden, 1991). As the number of trekkers increased, Chiang Rai and Mae Hong Son have also grown as major departure points.

Two different types of tours emerged. The first was a *jungle trek* consisting of a guided trek into the forest to visit more remote and traditional hill tribe villages with few tourist facilities. These treks operate with an average of 10–12 participants and last three to ten days. The second type was a *tribal village or sightseeing tour* in which most of the transportation is by van, bus or boat. These tours travel through Northern Thailand, stopping at various villages for short 'picture opportunities'. Typically, sightseeing tours consist of relatively large groups of 20–40 people and last from one to three days. For both types of tours, the tour operator is responsible for the operational details including transportation, accommodation, food and luggage handling, thereby making these tours accessible to a wide range of visitors.

Dearden and Harron (1994) estimate that more than 100,000 people participated in jungle treks each year during the early 1990s. Given the high growth rates of this type of tourism and the rapid modernisation of hill tribe cultures, Dearden (1991) suggests that areas promoting jungle treks and sightseeing tours tend to move through their tourism life cycles relatively quickly. Other factors contributing to this rapid progression include increased accessibility to hill tribe villages by walking trail, road and waterways. The cycle formally begins for a village on the jungle trek when the trek operators make initial contact. These operators will continue to visit a village with their tours until their clients perceive it to be too developed or modern. As the number of visitors increase, the interactions between the visitors and the villagers become less intimate and more institutionalised. Villages originally featured as part of a jungle trek may be rejuvenated as destinations on the tribal village sightseeing tours as they become more accessible by land or waterway, but even these sightseeing stops may eventually be abandoned when visitors feel that they have become too modern.

Dearden and Harron (1994) argue that currently this cycle is not sustainable. Some operators have responded by adding more components to the treks such as commercial elephant and raft rides basing the tours more on adventure than culture. Although these changes make the industry more viable for the tourism operators, they tend to remove visitors from the villages, reducing opportunities for economic development. Nevertheless, Dearden (1991: 412) suggested 'trekking, appropriately managed and with input from the hill tribes, could become a key component in sustaining these communities in the future.' A greater understanding of the life cycles of these tourism products will provide a tool with which to better manage development within the villages.

The Tourism Area Life Cycle Revisited

Johnston (2001, other volume) suggests that, after 20 years, Butler's original TALC model needs some modification. In addition to the traditional graphic representation of TALC's general stages, he suggests three types of analysis are required. The first is a 'boundary analysis' in which the destination is defined to facilitate comparisons between like destinations. This analysis addresses two key questions. What is the region and what type of region is it?

The second type of analysis focuses on 'pathways'. It examines the internal characteristics, the users and the macrostructural conditions of the destination. A discussion of the scale of development and the ambience of a destination is required. Users are discussed in terms of quantity and type. This analysis also highlights macrostructural conditions including external elements that either constrain or enable the development of the destination. Once organised chronologically, these descriptions are used to identify the corresponding stages of the TALC.

Finally, an 'analysis of mechanisms' identifies the turning points that shift a destination from one stage to another. Three types of mechanisms are discussed: critical juncture, critical event and blurry transition.

Methods

An interpretive paradigm was used in this study. This approach 'seeks to describe and analyse the culture and behaviour of humans and their groups from the point of view of those being studied' (Bryman, 1988: 46). Because the reality experienced by the tribal group in Ban Raummit was different from that of other stakeholders, and because their culture was the tourist attraction, it was important to understand the tourism life cycles from their perspective.

Like many peripheral communities, a formal education system had only recently been introduced in Ban Raummit and the literacy rate among community members over the age of 20 was low. In addition, until recently few community members saw a need to record information about the number or type of visitor arrivals. Like many indigenous cultures, information had traditionally been communicated verbally rather than in written form. Detailed data related to visitor arrivals or visitor nights were, therefore, not available for TALC analysis. Instead, oral history as told by various community members served as the basis for the following analysis. The dates and numbers provided in this chapter are therefore approximations, but these oral histories have provided a rich description of development from the villager perspective.

The cross-cultural situation within which the research was conducted required the flexibility inherent in the emergent design of the case study approach. Data collection consisted of informal semi-structured interviews and participant observation conducted between September and December of 1997. Interviews were more structured than originally planned due to the challenges of working through an interpreter, but each new interview built on information gathered in the previous ones.

A combination of Butler's (1980) TALC, Dearden's (1991) study of hill tribe trekking and Johnston's (2001) reassessment of TALC is used as a framework for the analysis of the sustainability of cultural tourism in Ban Raummit. The balance of this chapter consists of a boundary analysis in which the village of Ban Raummit is described in terms of its tourism products and destination status. This description is followed by a chronological analysis based on Johnston's pathway analysis. Finally, analyses of three distinct tourism life cycles and the mechanisms of change within these cycles are provided. A tabular presentation of the mechanisms and stages is also presented in this section. This table draws from the chronological analysis to highlight the mechanisms of stage change. In doing so, it demonstrates the independent progression of the three inter-related life cycles of the trekking product, the tribal village or sightseeing product, and the destination in general.

Boundary analysis

The Karen is one of nine major ethnic tribal groups in this region of Northern Thailand. These ethnic groups have become known as the 'chao khao' or hill tribes. Less than one-third of all tribal people have Thai citizenship, and even fewer own land, reflecting their relatively low political status in Thailand. In 1959 the National Committee for Hill Tribes was created by the government of Thailand, and this group began to address what was known as the 'hill tribe problem' (TRI, 1995).

Hill tribes were initially considered a threat to national security as possible agents for the spread of Communism. The government also believed, and continues to believe, that the hill tribes have had a detrimental effect on the natural environment. Deforestation is seen as a major problem in Thailand with an estimated loss of about 75% of its natural forest cover between 1961 and 1994. Although the government has blamed hill tribe agricultural practices for much of this loss, others have suggested that non-hill tribe logging schemes are largely responsible (McCaskill, 1997). Another concern of the Thai government has been hill tribe involvement with the production of illegal narcotics. Reducing the amount of opium cultivation and use by tribal people in Thailand is a major objective of the government.

One development strategy that the Karen in Ban Raummit have pursued within this political and economic climate is to develop the regional tourism industry. The Karen culture is at the heart of this area's attraction. Tourists coming to this village hope to gain experiences with people significantly different than themselves. For example, one particularly popular manifestation of the Karen culture in Ban Raummit is the domestication of elephants. Traditionally, the Karen used elephants to work in the forests and as a means of transportation. Their self-identity is tied to this practice as suggested by an elephant controller's observation that 'after WWII, the government told the Karen people to take food to Japan with their elephants ... because only Karen people can control elephants' (elephant controller).

The spatial scale of this destination is that of a village with a population of approximately 600 residents. Ban Raummit is located along the Mae Kok River in Chiang Rai province in Northern Thailand. Access to Ban Raummit is dominated by boat and motor vehicle. The road to Chiang Rai is partially paved and a one-way trip takes 40 minutes.

A tourist district has developed within the community along the river where most tourists arrive and is extended along a few main roads in town. While most tourists remain in this area, tourism activity is dispersed beyond this service district into the surrounding bamboo forests where visitors hike or ride elephants. A small number of the more intrepid visitors also venture into the nearby rice fields to watch and photograph farming activities.

Chronological analysis

Ban Raummit provides a unique opportunity to follow the evolution of a village from the time of its conception to the present due to its relatively recent creation. Tourism product life cycles (trekking and sightseeing), as well as the overall destination life cycle clearly emerged over this period.

1962–1974

This village was created about 35 years ago [∼ 1962]. Mr. Oo gave the name to this village. He was the first man to build here. The groups of people that lived here came from Mae Tro in Chiang Mai province. It was near Doi Inthanon. There were four families that left this place [Mae Tro] because of opium. They did not want to smoke it so they left. (Karen elder)

While the village was originally named for the first man who lived in the area, the name was recently changed to Ban Raummit. 'Raummit' is a Thai word meaning a mixture, and 'ban' means town. The name change occurred to reflect the changing nature of the village given the multiple ethnic groups now living in the community.

This particular site was chosen because 'this land is good to make agriculture. Have good farm. It is near the river' (Karen resident). Its location made it a favoured spot because of the accessible water source and plentiful fish supply. In addition, the forests were rich and the land was fertile. These traits were well suited to the subsistence lifestyle of the Karen.

About 10 years after the creation of the village (~ 1972), the area was placed under the control of Thailand's Royal Forestry Department (RFD) as a forest conservation area. Village boundaries were defined and the RFD implemented strict land use controls including the restrictive distribution of land titles (Sumrauy Nhusaeng, personal communication, November 15, 1997). Technically, people were not allowed to purchase the land in the conservation forest, but the Karen feel that exceptions have been made in the case of well financed buyers.

The villagers want to have the documents for the land, but when they ask the RFD they cannot. They will not sign because this is a conservation forest. But, if the person has money, they will get the documents. (Karen resident)

For the first 15 years, the village grew at a moderate rate. People who moved to this village were mostly relatives of the first families. The headman gave each family a parcel of land to farm. An older villager described the process by stating that:

. . .after one year he said that he want everyone in this place to go and choose the land where they want to live and farm. The headman will share it with the others so they will have one rai [land area measurement] for each family. (Karen elder)

1975–1979

Tourism began in this village during this period. It was introduced by a missionary who had spent some time in Japan where he learned about trekking. Upon his return to Thailand, he came to Ban Raummit and suggested that they begin to offer elephant treks. At that time, the village had three elephants that they used to work in the forest.

In the past, the elephants were used for labour in the forest. They had only three elephants to start with. There were no roads, so they used the elephants for transportation to the fields. The fields were far from home. ... After that, villagers used them for trekking. They took the trekkers to the Lahu and Yao villages. When they did this there were only 5-6 people at a time (not Thai people just foreigners). They used to spend the night. (elephant controller)

The total number of visitors to Ban Raummit averaged about 20 people per month. During this early stage, there were no specific tourist facilities or infrastructure. Most trekkers stayed and ate in the villagers' homes, particularly the home of the headman. Their visits were irregular so none of the elephants were solely dedicated to transporting tourists. Because the trekking groups were small and these groups stayed in the homes of the tribal people, interactions between these visitors and the Karen were fairly intimate.

Before we only had older tourist about 40– 50 years old. They liked to experience the culture. Some were even 60– 70 years old and very fat. They could only put one on each elephant. When they stayed over night the Karen did show performances at night. Tourists could talk to the Karen and eat their food. (village headman)

During this period, the tourists were as interesting and different to the Karen as the Karen were to the tourists. The Karen people considered these visitors to be their distant brothers and sisters, therefore making this stage of tourism development quite enjoyable for them. They appreciated the opportunity to demonstrate parts of their culture to others. Tourism was also a relatively minor activity in the community. Only 'seven to eight of the villagers were involved with the trekkers' (elephant controller), so the impacts of trekking were not widespread.

Basic services were also introduced around 1975 with the construction of the first school in the community. Volunteers from Julalongkan University in Bangkok came to teach in the village. Today, this school is run by the national government and it services the surrounding villages as well. Another structure included 'the first church built 1 kilometre from here. The Karen would walk to that church. Then it changed to be built in this village about 20 years ago (1977). It was built by missionaries from the United States' (Karen resident). These missionaries still come to this village on a regular basis to distribute shirts, blankets, mosquito nets and similar goods.

1980– 1991

A significant amount of tourist development occurred during this period. One operator noted, 'I was one of the first tour companies here – more than 12 years. When I first came, there was no guesthouse, there were no toilets... Well there were toilets, but not up to European standards' (Thai tourism operator). This early tourist development was led by Thai people who moved to the village rather than by the original Karen residents. For example, a Thai-owned tourist restaurant opened along the river. The next tourist operation, a Thai-owned souvenir shop, opened shortly afterwards. Two more Thai-owned restaurants were in operation by 1988.

A permanent tourist police station was built in 1983. The police presence was needed partly in response to some problems with robberies and shootings of trekkers near the Burmese border. Trekking guides and their tourists were required to register here prior to entering more remote areas.

1992–1995

> The big companies came about five years ago [1992]. Big groups are sightseeing not trekking. They started to come because Chiang Mai, these places not have many elephants and big groups needed lots of elephants. (Karen resident)

Several developments occurred between 1992 and 1997 led by an increase in the number of elephants used in the tourism industry. By 1994, there were over 40 elephants in the village that were actively used for tourism. Because of the limited disposable income of most Karen persons, one elephant was often owned by a group of local investors who pooled their resources to purchase the animal. 'Elephants cost about 150,000 Baht. This is very expensive here. That means that many people put their money together to buy the elephants. Ten people may save to buy one elephant' (elephant controller). Each elephant has its own 'mahout' or elephant controller. The construction of an elephant loading area was also completed during this period to make elephant rides accessible to a broader range of clients including less mobile village tour participants.

By 1993, ten tourist shops and three local shops were operating in the village. At this point, only one of the shops was Karen operated. For many years, the village authorities had not allowed other tribal groups to open tourist shops, but the Karen were apparently not interested in, or possibly not able to, pursue these opportunities themselves. Thai people led this type of development. As visitation continued to grow, the pressure for further development increased. Finally, however, the village authorities agreed to let other tribal groups open shops. By 1996 there were over 40 shops in Ban Raummit operated by a broad range of ethnic groups.

Most tourist shops sold crafts, souvenirs and postcards. Few of these crafts were made in this village, or by the tribal person selling them. One Karen vendor noted, 'My crafts come from Mae Sai or Lamphun. I do not go there because I have no transportation. People [wholesalers] come here to sell the stuff. Sometimes they may come two–three times each month, other times only once' (Karen villager). There were a few exceptions to this practice of importing goods. The Karen weavers who worked by the river making belts, bracelets and bags sometimes sold their wares in the local shops. Most shops were located along the roads frequented by tourists including the main one connecting Ban Raummit to Chiang Rai, and the two smaller connector roadways leading to the boat docks.

Allowing other tribal groups to own and operate shops has influenced immigration to the community. Karen villagers differentiate people moving into Ban Raummit in terms of their ethnicity and livelihoods.

> People that move here have two styles. From Mae Tro, they come because they have family here and they give them the land to come here. Another group that want to sell. They are not Karen. They buy the land to do the shops for sell from the Karen people, but not buy the land to do the farm. (elephant controller)

As the number of other tribal people moving to Ban Raummit has increased, conflicts have begun to emerge.

> First time have one or two families. I never mind cause there was little. They have shop so nothing. Now there are many, many. The Lisu and Hmong, they cut the trees everywhere. When I tell them 'don't do,' they don't listen. Some people who buy land to stay here are good. But, those who rent the land are not so good. (Karen elder)

Most of these people do not plan to stay in the village indefinitely. They follow the tourists, and as a result, their investment in village development was lower than the Karen's. The newcomers appear to be gaining significant benefits from the visitors while the Karen people are forced to deal with many of the costs.

Vehicle access was greatly improved around 1993, when a portion of the road from Chiang Rai to Ban Raummit was paved. Although the pavement did not reach all the way to the village, even the unpaved section was widened to improve access. A portion of these road improvements was financed by revenues earned through elephant treks. Prior to these improvements, the trail to Chiang Rai was only passable by foot or motorcycle. With the completion of the roadwork, a one-way trip by car between Chiang Rai and Ban Raummit was only 40 minutes.

1996–1997

Electricity was introduced to the village after a visit from Thailand's royal family in 1996. This development seemed to change the attitude of the Karen people towards their involvement in tourism. Prior to this point, they perceived little need for additional cash income and were content with a subsistence lifestyle based on agriculture. However, the introduction of electrical power created new demands for rice cookers, refrigerators, stereos and an assortment of other appliances. Karen involvement in tourism increased as one way to earn the disposable income necessary to make these purchases.

By this point, the villagers had reduced the number of elephants that they owned and managed to 32. In addition, Karen shop ownership had increased to 14 of the 51 shops in operation (Table 15.1).

Because there were no controls over entrance to this village, the exact number of visitors was impossible to determine, but information from the records of the Tourist Police and the elephant operators provide an indication of the magnitude of the tourism in the community. During November 1997, an estimated 2500 people visited Ban Raummit. Of this total, about 1800 people rode the elephants. November was considered an average month for tourism visitation as a villager explained that, 'July and August are the busiest. March, April, May and September are the slowest.'

Although Ban Raummit was no longer considered one of the better villages in which to observe traditional Karen culture, trekking tours continued to visit. The village's location made it a convenient staging point for their journey into the hills to visit more remote and primitive villages. Many trekking groups hired the elephants in Ban Raummit for the next portion of their journey. These trekkers often bought food and drink in the village to prepare for their expeditions, but they purchased few souvenirs. Local villagers made a clear distinction between trekkers and sightseers.

> If the people have backpacks they are trekkers. But if they have only a camera and a small purse they are sightseers. There are more of these tourist. They don't want to take the elephant rides. (elephant controller)

Table 15.1 Shop ownership and target markets

Target market	Operator ethnicity							Total
	Karen	*Thai*	*Hmong*	*Akha*	*Lisu*	*Yao*	*Swiss*	
Tourist	11	4	17	10	2	1	1	46
Local	3	2	0	0	0	0	0	5

Relatively easy access by road or waterway, good linkages to other destinations, along with improved tourist services and infrastructure, made Ban Raummit an increasingly popular stop on tribal village sightseeing tours. A typical itinerary for a sightseeing tour was described as:

> [After leaving Chiang Mai and travelling to Thaton], they go on to Chiang Rai by boat. Along the river they see the hill tribes; about 20 in total. May stop at four to five villages along the way. After Chiang Rai, they go on to the Golden Triangle and Mae Sai. Stop at interesting villages – not the small ones. They may have four to five families. Hill tribes stay by the water so it is easy to see them. (International sightseeing operator)

The sightseers accounted for the majority of the visitors to Ban Raummit during this period. Most of these visitors arrived in groups of 20–30 people while other visitors came in groups as small as two to four people.

Those sightseers with limited interest in the Karen culture typically stayed in one of the restaurants by the river enjoying the scenery and a soda. Others ventured into the village to shop or take pictures of the various tribal shopkeepers or Karen villagers. Still others rode the elephants. These rides tended to be shorter village tours of 20–30 minutes rather than the longer forest treks. Some sightseeing tour groups with their own guides took time to find a Karen person with whom they could talk. One Karen elder in particular enjoyed the opportunities to share his stories with these visitors. 'Tourists have tour guide to talk with me. Tour guide knows me and bring tourists to tell stories. I enjoy it very much to tell them my stories' (Karen elder).

As the number and type of tourists have changed, villagers directly involved in the provision of tourism services increasingly received formal training in customer service. Sightseers tend to have higher service expectations than trekkers. At the same time, villagers have developed a deeper appreciation of the important role that tourism plays in generating income for the village. The villagers therefore decided to address these expectations as 'everybody wants to have tourists because they can make money' (elephant controller). Formal customer service training seminars were offered to the mahouts, shop keepers and boat drivers by the Tourism Authority of Thailand (TAT) at the Mae Kok Farm across the river from this village.

While the growth in tourism was significant, it was still not the most prominent industry in the village. Agriculture had continued to dominate. Few of the Karen villagers who generated income through participation in the tourism industry considered it their main source for survival as reflected in the following statements.

- Mostly I make rice on the farm.
- Now only this, but before corn too. I make corn at the same time as rice, but corn is finished. I grow it to eat and sell: rice and corn... Farm about the same with or without tourism.
- I built the store with my husband. Now he still works in the field as a farmer. (Karen villagers)

Even the mahouts, who have invested significant amounts of time into tourism, acknowledged that tourism would not be the main source of income throughout their lifetimes.

> Old people cannot control elephants. If they control one day, they are sore with back aches the next few. Usually they stop controlling around 36 years old... Then he will go work on the farm. All the controllers have farm land. (elephant controller)

Plans emerged in 1997 to create a formal 'cultural village' attraction. The village authorities anticipated that this addition would serve multiple purposes. It was seen as an enjoyable activity and source of information for sightseers, thereby encouraging increased spending in the village. To the trekkers heading to more primitive villages, it would provide vital information to prepare them for more intimate interactions. Finally, and potentially more importantly, it would be an instrument through which elements of tribal cultures could be maintained, taught and enjoyed.

> We are working on a project now to build a place in this village to show people about the Karen lifestyle. They will be able to go to the farm and show about agriculture. This will be not only for Karen though. They want to show all tribes. The more they conserve, the more tourists. (village headman)

Mechanisms and Stages

The preceding chronological analysis has outlined the history of Ban Raummit in relation to tourism development. Table 15.2 draws from this analysis to highlight the existence of three separate tourism life cycles and the turning points within each of these. These turning points are labelled as critical junctures, critical events or blurry transitions. A critical juncture is an issue that once resolved moves the destination to a new stage. Critical events are particular actions that trigger the progression from one stage to the next. Finally, blurry transitions are turning points that occur as the result of a number of smaller events that combine to bring about a shift to the next stage. Typically any of these mechanisms can manifest itself as an addition, alteration or cessation in terms of the product or destination life cycles.

A critical event began the life cycle of the trekking product in 1975 with the introduction of elephant treks (Table 15.2). Initial interactions between the Karen villagers and trekkers were based on mutual interest. The blurry transition to the development stage occurred around 1980 when outside influences such as the introduction of the Thai police and entrepreneurs institutionalised the trekking product. Another blurry transition led to the consolidation stage around 1992. More tourist infrastructure was added and the village modernised. Other tribal groups opened shops along the main streets creating a tourist space that limited interactions between the Karen hosts and the trekkers. Much of the primitive nature of the village disappeared, however, many trekking groups continued to use the village as a staging point to get supplies and purchase elephant rides to more remote villages. In 1996 a critical event, the introduction of electricity, spurred an increase in Karen involvement, and began trekking's reorientation stage. This event increased the Karen's demand for consumer items, and tourism was identified as a viable cash income generator. The Karen recognised that the village was no longer as attractive to those trekkers seeking contact with primitive others but was well positioned to serve as a staging point. Village authorities determined that the addition of a cultural village could fulfil an educational function to prepare these trekking groups for more intimate interactions in remote villages.

The exploration stage for the sightseeing product began around 1980. Simple tourist services had been added to the village and a few Thai operators brought small groups of sightseeing tourists. A number of additions led to the blurry transition initiating the development stage around 1992. Larger groups started to arrive, precipitating the purchase of more elephants. In addition, the type of visitors arriving required additional services such as a loading dock for elephant rides and more shops. To facilitate this growth, the village authorities allowed other tribal groups to open shops. Development continued into the late 1990s as Karen interest in tourism increased, leading to more Karen shop ownership. In addition, the village committee decided to build a cultural village to showcase tribal cultures and gain additional income from the sightseers.

The third life cycle concerns the village of Ban Raummit as a tourist destination. It is shaped by the life cycles of each individual product along with an assortment of other trends. Like the trekking product, the arrival of the first trekkers initiated the exploration stage, and the process of commercialising the Karen culture for visitors. A blurry transition moved the destination to the development stage. This transition resulted from the institutionalisation of tourism and the beginning of outside involvement. The Thai police station was built to minimise danger to international tourists because of incursions around the Burmese border.

Table 15.2 Mechanisms of change for three tourism-related life cycles in Ban Raummit

Chronological era	Trekking product		Sightseeing product		Destination	
	Mechanism	Stage	Mechanism	Stage	Mechanism	Stage
1962–1974	N/A	Pretourism	N/A	Pretourism	N/A	Pretourism
1975–1979	Critical event additions • Missionary recommends offering elephant treks • First trekkers arrive • Natural interactions between hosts and guests begin	Exploration	N/A	Pretourism product	Critical event additions • First trekkers arrive • Initial stage of the commercialisation of culture	Exploration
1980–1991	Blurry transition Addition • Tourist police station is built Alterations • 3 Thai-owned restaurants open	Development	Blurry transition Additions • 3 Thai-owned restaurants open • 1 Thai-owned shop opens	Exploration	Blurry transition Additions • State involvement in village tourism begins • Involvement of international	Exploration

Table 15.2 (*Continued*)

Chronological era	Trekking product		Sightseeing product		Destination	
	Mechanism	Stage	Mechanism	Stage	Mechanism	Stage
	• 1 Thai-owned shop opens • More trekkers stay in village		• 1 Thai-owned shop opens • Sightseeing operators begin to visit with small groups		tour companies and Thai entrepreneurs begins • Trekkers outnumber sightseers • Initial tourist services and infrastructure develop	Development
1992– 1995	Blurry transition Alteration • Other tribal shops open (~40) Cessations • Interactions between hosts and guests are institutionalised	Consolida-tion	Blurry transition Additions • More elephants are bought • Elephant loading dock is built • Road access improves • Large sightseeing groups arrive	Development	Critical juncture Additions • Policy change occurs • Other tribal groups become active in tourism • Front stage develops	Development

Table 15.2 (*Continued*)

Chronological era	Trekking product		Sightseeing product		Destination	
	Mechanism	Stage	Mechanism	Stage	Mechanism	Stage
	• Fewer overnight stays occur • Karen identity of village decreases Additions • Becomes a staging point for treks rather than a stop on route		• Customer service training begins Alterations • Policy change facilitates arrival of other tribal vendors • Commodification of culture increases		Alterations • Tourist infrastructure increases • Road access improves • Population increases • Village modernises • Sightseers outnumber trekkers Cessation • Fewer natural interactions between hosts and guests occur	

Table 15.2 (*Continued*)

Chronological era	Trekking product		Sightseeing product		Destination	
	Mechanism	*Stage*	*Mechanism*	*Stage*	*Mechanism*	*Stage*
1996–1997	Critical event Additions • Electricity is introduced • Village authority proposes plans for cultural village Cessation • Loss of primitive image in village	Reorientation	No stage change Addition • Village authority proposes plans for cultural village Alterations • Infrastructure upgrades continue • Increases in Karen involvement in shop ownership continues	Late development	No stage change Addition • Electricity is introduced Alterations • Village infrastructure improves: roads, sewage • Increases in Karen interest and involvement in directing future growth • Conflict between Karen and other tribal groups emerges	Mid-development

Thai entrepreneurs opened businesses to earn tourism income. The number of visitors continued to increase, encouraging the further development of tourist services. A policy change allowing other tribal vendors led to a critical juncture in the early 1990s. The arrival of these vendors altered the appearance of the village through the development of a front stage that further formalised host–guest interactions. As this process continued into the late 1990s, conflict between the Karen and other tribal vendors emerged. Although 1997 marked a stage change for the two product life cycles, it was not a turning point for the overall destination. The cumulative effects of the changes were becoming evident, but neither the villagers nor their village committee had begun to address them in a dramatic way.

By examining the three life cycles separately and identifying the stages and mechanisms in each, Table 15.2 clarifies some seemingly contradictory occurrences. Turning points classified as additions to one product represent cessations for other products. This is not surprising considering the base of Ban Raummit's attraction is culture, and culture is dynamic. Tourism products cannot remain static while their base moves forward. The relatively rapid progression of the trekking product through its life cycle stages is indicative of the rapid pace of change faced by tribal cultures here and elsewhere (Butler & Hinch, 1996).

Conclusion

Ban Raummit has been a dynamic tourism destination over its relatively short existence. The hill tribe trekking product has progressed rapidly through its life cycle with a shift from the village being a featured stop on the early trekking tours to it being an important staging point for treks to more isolated villages. As the village was losing its appeal as a 'primitive' stop for trekking tours, it was gaining popularity as a major stop on sightseeing tours. Indicators suggest this sightseeing product is currently in a mid to advanced development stage. Visitor demands are being met through increased tourism services and infrastructure. Yet, these vestiges of modernity have reduced its 'charm' as a relatively traditional village. Manifestations of modern life are undercutting Ban Raummit's appeal as a stop on sightseeing tours and accelerating its trajectory through the TALC. The proposal to commodify the Karen culture through the development of a 'cultural village' represents a new type of cultural product, which by its institutionalised nature may provide greater control over this life cycle. Finally, the destination itself has undergone a cycle of development that is a complex amalgam of individual tourism product cycles and a multitude of external cycles and trends. The fact that the economy of Ban Raummit remains based in agriculture serves as a buffer to the volatility of tourism. It is clear, however, that tourism has become an important contributor to economic development in the community. Tourism has enabled the Karen to continue residing in a rural area by integrating them into the global cash economy. In the process, they have retained more control over their culture than have other hill tribe peoples that have been forced to move to large urban areas in order to survive. It is clear, however, that Ban Raummit's residents must actively manage tourism if it is to serve them well in the future.

Beyond the direct insights that this chapter has provided about tourism in Ban Raummit, it has also provided insight into the TALC. Two of the most important contributions concern the confirmation of multiple life cycles and the merit of using qualitative data to examine tourism-related life cycles. In the first instance, it has been demonstrated that there are multiple life cycles that have a direct bearing on tourism destinations. Even in the case of destinations that are based on sensitive cultural attractions, a variety of tourism products may emerge and interact with each other and the life cycle of the community as a whole. Researchers need to appreciate this complexity if these analyses are to be beneficial. Secondly, tourism destinations populated by indigenous people living traditional lifestyles are not likely to be characterised by data bases neatly organised into time series formats that can accurately quantify the number of visitors for TALC analysis. Qualitative data can, however, be used to provide a useful approximation of TALC patterns in terms of boundaries, chronological progression and the mechanisms of change. In fact, qualitative data can be used to interpret quantitative data, thereby providing a much richer understanding of tourism area cycles.

Finally, the relationship between cultural attractions, the TALC and sustainability bears additional consideration. This chapter has demonstrated that cultural tourism products like hill tribe treks are dynamic. Tourism is one of many agents for change in these communities and ultimately serves as a factor in changing the culture of the hosts or the 'others' in this case. This change in culture is one of the factors that moves tourism products through their life cycles. Yet in the case of tourism in Ban Raummit, the culturally based tourism product of hill tribe trekking appears to be being replaced by other forms of cultural tourism like sightseeing tours. The proposed cultural village represents yet another generation of cultural tourism products in this village. Ban Raummit has retained its vibrancy throughout these various product life cycles. The perplexing question of when life starts or finishes must be asked in the case of TALCs just as it is asked in the case of human life cycles. The TALC offers a useful tool to track development, make decisions about the pace and nature of change in the present and to predict change in the future. It does not, however, allow for definitive statements on sustainability.

Part 5
The TALC and Rejuvenation

RICHARD W. BUTLER

The conclusion of the TALC model in its original form was that without appropriate intervention a destination would eventually enter into decline. Two possibilities were proposed as being capable of altering this result. One was suggested to be a continuation of operation at a level that remained within the capacities of the destination, so that its attractivity remained at a sufficiently high level to continue to attract investment and visitation to remain viable, in other words, to achieve sustainability (although the term had not been used then in its now current context). The other was for the destination to be rejuvenated in a variety of ways, including changing to a new focus, finding an additional focus and repositioning the destination with respect to markets. It is this stage of the TALC that is examined in the three chapters in this last section, which provide specific examples of the way destinations have redeveloped themselves. A more conceptual discussion of the rejuvenation and exit processes is dealt with in the other volume by Agarwal, Cooper and Baum.

In her chapter, Corak discusses the case of the Opatija Riviera on the Adriatic Coast of Croatia, a destination that has experienced a wide range of circumstances and influences. She argues that there have really been four cycles which this destination has gone through and is experiencing. The intervention of three wars has served to move the destination back, if not to the beginning of a new cycle, at least some way in reverse, and forced it to reposition itself several times. The changes in accessibility, in markets, in political and other exogenous forces have meant that the destination has suffered from instability and enforced change, and thus had to attempt to rejuvenate itself three times at least. She posits a somewhat different development curve in this case because of the unique forces to which this area has been exposed.

The example of Atlantic City described by Stansfield represents what is, perhaps, the most classic of all attempts at rejuvenation by a mature tourist destination. Atlantic City, like the 19th century resorts of Northern Europe, had had a full cycle of development through to decline by the last quarter of the 20th century. Without rejuvenation it was dying a slow but inevitable death as far as tourism was concerned. The identification of legalised gambling as a tool of rejuvenation was the first step in a relatively rapid process that has seen Atlantic City experience massive reinvestment and redevelopment on a scale not anticipated initially. How long the new cycle will last is unknown. The explosion of legalised gambling across the USA and Canada has undoubtedly deprived Atlantic City, earlier than it would have wished, of its unique comparative advantage on the East coast of the USA, similar to that held by Nevada in the West. It still remains, however, probably the best example anywhere of successful large-scale rejuvenation of a resort that had almost completed its TALC.

The Gold Coast of Queensland, Australia, has had a much more rapid process of development and potential decline than the New Jersey shore, but gambling and private investment on a large scale have also been witnessed there. Faulkner and Tideswell describe and interpret in considerable detail the process of rejuvenating this area. Sadly, this chapter marks one of the last pieces of research and writing undertaken by Bill Faulkner before his tragically early death in 2002. He completed the first draft less than two months before his death. The chapter reveals the full and complex process that he and colleagues had organised to identify, evaluate and decide on specific directions for the future development of the region. One of the great successes of the CRC programme in Sustainable Tourism has been achieved by involving the private sector with the academic sector in identifying best practice and development options. The model developed and discussed in this chapter represents a successful approach to the complicated and often undesired process of repositioning a mature destination. The initial reluctance of the private sector to accept the idea of a 'revisioning' exercise and the final acceptance of a 'visioning' exercise (because the latter did not imply the change of direction and hence implication of earlier mistakes or a current need for a change in direction) is indicative of the reluctance of those in destinations to admit that all may not be well in tourism and that rejuvenation is needed.

Chapter 16

The Modification of the Tourism Area Life Cycle Model for (Re)inventing a Destination: The Case of the Opatija Riviera, Croatia

SANDA CORAK

Introduction

In the rich tourism literature on TALC, many studies have demonstrated the general validity of observing tourism development within an evolutionary framework. In this study, the life cycle model is used to determine the stages and to analyse the market position of the Opatija Riviera, a destination that has been developing tourism for more than 150 years. The TALC is applied to identify four distinct stages and it is argued that those stages could also be analysed as separate life cycles. The chapter also discusses how the strategic options proposed by the original model could help destination managers and planners to 'reinvent' this heritage resort on the Adriatic coast.

Croatia is a Mediterranean tourism destination and a country with a long tourism tradition. Although the most intensive tourism development in Croatia started after World War II, its tourism history began at the end of the last century when Opatija, located on the Northern Adriatic coast, emerged as the first tourism destination in this country. The long and rich tourism history of the Opatija Riviera is the focus of this chapter.

Tourism in the Opatija Riviera (stretch of 15 km, Figure 16.1) is traced back to 1844, when Higinio Scarpa, a wealthy wheat and timber merchant from the nearby industrial and port town of Rijeka, built his villa 'Angiolina', where he hosted guests such as Josip Jelacic, Croatian governor of the time, Maria Anna, the Queen of Austria, Romanian King Karol and the likes. In particular, a visit of the Empress of the Austrian–Hungarian Empire sparked much interest for this completely unknown place. A further impetus for the popularity of Opatija came when a group of eminent professors from the Vienna University opened a health retreat there (at the time a so-called 'sanatorium'), taking advantage of the

271

Figure 16.1 The Opatija Riviera

healing properties of the Riviera's mild climate and Adriatic Sea. Subsequently, in 1889, Opatija was given official *'kurort'* or health retreat status. The accelerated development of health retreat facilities and hotels was accompanied by diversification of additional services and facilities. A public library and tennis courts were opened, while there were music events staged in the central park as well as regular morning and evening music concerts. The flow of visitors was increasing steadily and their numbers were statistically recorded from 1883.

From that time until today the Riviera has travelled a long and often rough road of tourism development. Three key phases can be identified. It was initially a health retreat and winter tourism destination for wealthy aristocracy. In the second phase of its development the Opatija Riviera became a summer holiday destination for mass tourism. Currently, attempts are being made to rejuvenate Opatija's tourism through the introduction of new products that would make Opatija one of the most important conference centres in Croatia. Proximity to major urban centres together with increasing road accessibility make it viable for day-trippers and short-break tourists drawn to the Opatija Riviera by a variety of revived traditional events and festivals. Such a long and rich history of tourism lends itself to analysis based on the tourism area life cycle (TALC) model. Through such analysis it is possible to identify the turning points in the Opatija Riviera's history and also to discuss the current tourism development policy of what is still one of the most developed destinations in Croatia.

Many well known tourism destinations started to develop touristically only after World War II and their tourism products are currently in the growth or maturity phase. Application of the TALC model, in general, faces certain difficulties. Wall (1982) and Haywood (1986) discussed difficulties of gathering sufficiently suitable data to test models, and the operational problems involved in defining and distinguishing the individual phases. The problems most frequently encountered are those of comparability of spatial units and of interpreting transition points on the curve where the end of one phase and the beginning of another must be identified. The utility and applicability of the TALC model to destinations with a centennial tourism history has been tested in several cases (e.g. Cooper & Jackson, 1989; Getz, 1992; Russell & Faulkner, 1999). From the existing literature it can be concluded that such analysis enables a more holistic approach to the planning of a destination's future development options. Given that Opatija's tourism industry is currently undergoing restructuring (especially of its accommodation sector) accompanied by the reconstruction of many attractions, a decision was made that a strategic marketing plan ought also to be developed. For the purpose of that plan, the TALC model was used to evaluate tourism development to date and to assess the strategic steps that need to be taken to (re)invent Opatija's attractive, but at the moment neglected and insufficiently utilised, resources. These resources, due to the long and interesting history of the area, make it not only an attractive seaside destination, but, providing the heritage buildings are restored to their original glory, it could also become one of the leading heritage tourism destinations in the Adriatic region.

In this chapter, the analysis is conducted using Butler's model (1980) combined with a historical analysis approach in order to investigate the trends in tourism development on the Opatija Riviera and provide insights into issues affecting the rejuvenation of this area as a tourism destination. Stages in the life cycle of the Riviera are identified, graphically presented and described. It is argued that, because the area's tourism development was halted four times due to the wars that have affected this region, each of the four periods should also be examined as a separate life cycle.

The Life Cycle Model and the Opatija Riviera

For the purpose of this research, historical records were collected from official statistical data, historical monographs, brochures, tourist guides, articles in newspapers and magazines. Most time studies have suffered problems in the operationalisation of the concept (Foster & Murphy, 1991), in the search for appropriate indicators of development and concrete historic data to define the various phases. However, in contrast, as already noted, statistical data on tourist numbers were officially collected in Opatija from 1883.

Data for the Opatija Riviera indicate that the area has, through its centennial history, witnessed all phases of the life cycle (Figure 16.2). Throughout, the same area is analysed – the coastal region, hinterland and several microlocations as illustrated in Figure 16.1. Detailed analysis of the data for the number of arrivals in this area indicates that the entire life cycle could be divided not only into separate phases of development, but also some phases could be analysed in terms of separate life cycles. The sharp declines in visitor numbers were not caused by strategic development measures, but by the same exogenous factor – the wars that routinely halt tourism activity in affected areas. These were World War I, World War II and the most recent War of Independence from 1991

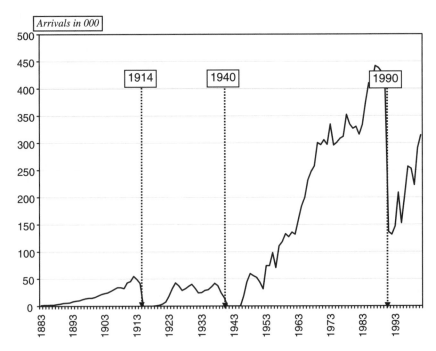

Figure 16.2 TALC for the Opatija Riviera (1883–2001)

to 1995. Thus, in this area tourism has developed from almost zero activity four times and, not surprisingly, each phase is characterised by a different nature of tourism development. The turning points of particular significance are: (a) the transition from an exclusive, winter resort to the summer holiday destination which occurred between 1915 and 1940; (b) development of a mass holiday destination after World War II and, finally, (c) the attempt to manage the maturity and differentiate the destination through the introduction of new products. The tourism history of the Opatija Riviera provides also an impetus and a source of inspiration for crafting its future tourism development. At the same time its history acts as a constraint, given that the history does not necessarily provide all the solutions to the dilemmas faced when planning future tourism development.

Tourism development and growth (1883–1914)

The first phase of tourism development on the Opatija Riviera was marked by a slow but steady growth of visitor arrivals. Construction of the road connecting the main port town in Croatia (Rijeka) with the seaside resort (Lovran) facilitated better communication between these two localities, influencing Mr. Scarpa's decision to build his villa 'Angiolina', named after his wife. The attractiveness of the villa was further enriched by the lush landscape dotted with exotic plants that thrived in the mild climate of Opatija, the centre of the Riviera. As mentioned earlier, Opatija became the favourite excursion spot for the wealthy citizens of Rijeka, while Scarpa himself hosted an array of friends, among whom were some of the leading figures of the public life of the time. The arrival of the Empress, Maria Anna, the wife of the Austrian Emperor, Ferdinand I, in this area in the 1860s marked another turning point when Opatija started to be considered a health retreat. The Empress stayed there on the recommendation of her doctors and this 'royal confirmation' generated much interest for visiting this place within the boundaries of her monarchy. This was followed by the construction of the first sanatorium and the important transport connection of the railway line between Vienna and Rijeka, built by the South Railway Company.

Tourism development of Opatija accelerated when the area was officially declared a health winter resort (on the basis of climate and spa) and the first hotel, a pavilion with a warm seawater pool, a beach pavilion and a coastal walking path were constructed in 1883. From the very beginning of Opatija's development great attention was given to the construction of buildings, their design and the equipment of the sanatoria. Newly built hotels offered additional services and accommodation, in particular massage and warm sea baths. Finally, when hotels were electrified in 1896 and running water installed, conditions for even more accelerated growth were provided. The growth in popularity of the resort was further fuelled by the official meeting there between the Emperor, Franjo Josip I, and the German Emperor, Vilim I. This event ensured Opatija the status of a first-class elite health retreat and fashionable gathering spot. The fact that Opatija was the first resort to host an international conference on thalassotherapy in 1908 testified to its reputation as a health resort. After the meeting of the emperors, Opatija was visited by the heads of many European monarchies and the Austria-Hungarian aristocracy, to industrial elite and many writers of repute. In the records of the time it could be found that the Romanian royal couple donated a significant sum of money for construction of walkways, a forest path and a viewing platform, which still carry the king's name – Karol I – today.

At that time the health tourism product dominated. The main season had different characteristics from the main summer season, as we know it today in Opatija. The largest number of guests was in the wintertime, as visitors were drawn to the mild climate in their desire to avoid the severity of the winters in the North. Historical records indicate that, at the beginning of the 20th century, Opatija Riviera had 10 large hotels, 44 pensions, 83 villas and five baths. Given the steady increase in popularity and accommodation capacity, the number of tourists grew continuously (Figure 16.3).

The best results were recorded in 1912 when there were almost 55,000 overnight guests. The jobs generated by such demand could not be met by the local population, therefore many Austrians with experience in hospitality and trade were attracted to Opatija to take advantage of the growing opportunities that tourism development offered. At that time a

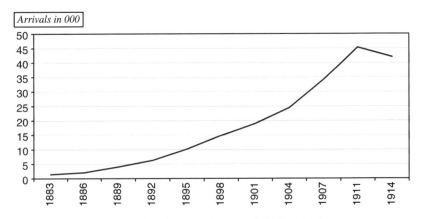

Figure 16.3 Arrivals to the Opatija Riviera (1883–1914)

regional tourism association with its headquarters in Opatija was established, while a weekly tourist newspaper was published to update visitors on events and attractions. Transport connections were also improved by regular bus line between Trieste and Opatija, while an electric tram operated along the Riviera.

Opatija in that era was a lively and vibrant destination with continuous special events. Apart from the beautiful villas built mostly in secession style, the Austrian Tourist Club 'Abbazia' started construction of the 12-km long coastal walkway, called *lungomare*, which is still one of the Riviera landmarks today. Its numerous meticulously maintained parks further enhanced the exclusive atmosphere of the place. Historical documents include some information on the construction of the park around the villa 'Angiolina' between 1845 and 1860, where exotic plants from Japan, China, South America, Australia and other parts of the world were planted. Among them is the *Camellia japonica* that has also become the flower symbol of Opatija. In this period the vision of a few enthusiastic individuals that pictured Opatija as an exclusive health resort was fully achieved. It could be assumed that tourism would continue to grow, but it was halted abruptly with World War I in 1914, an event that stopped all tourists flows for several years.

The changing tourist product (1919–1940)

The next phase in the tourism development of the Opatija Riviera was characterised by the weakening of the quality of the entire tourism product. The absence of a tourism development vision had an adverse effect on tourism activity in the period between the two world wars and as a consequence, great fluctuations in tourism demand were recorded. In this period the area was under Italian rule and with the introduction of the Italian government the number of visitors declined significantly. While the former Austria-Hungarian rulers had stimulated development of tourism in the Opatija Riviera, seeing it as part of their own territory, the newly established Italian government did not have the same attitude. For them the region was simply an occupied territory to be exploited (Miskulin, 1994). With such an attitude, they perceived Opatija as a strong competitor to their own resorts and therefore introduced measures degrading Opatija from an official health resort to firstly, a health and bathing place (*stazione climatica e balneare*), and then further degrading it in 1933 to simply a tourism destination (*luogo di soggiorno*).

By losing the status of health centre, converting sanatoria into hotels, letting the existing hotels go into decay and not investing in new facilities, the Opatija Riviera quickly lost its noted reputation. Consequently, this led to changes in market demand turning to less demanding clientele. From being initially a winter destination, Opatija became a summer holiday resort. The tourist season was shortened and hotels

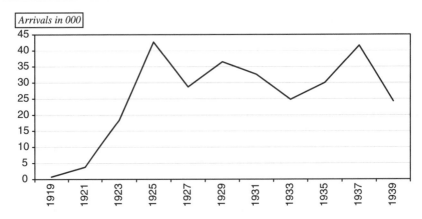

Figure 16.4 Arrivals to the Opatija Riviera (1919–1939)

operated for only three summer months. The largest number of arrivals during the period of Italian rule, of about 43,000, was recorded in 1925, but soon the economic depression that hit Europe between 1929 and 1933 adversely affected tourism flows again (Figure 16.4).

The change in tourism orientation that was most noticeable in the change of the main tourist product and the nature of visitors attracted to this area led to the decrease in the visitor numbers, so that the peak performance from 1912, when almost 55,000 arrivals were recorded, was never repeated between the two world wars. A particularly vivid illustration of the drop in tourism numbers could be found in the daily papers of the time and various chronicles. There, for example, one could read an article from 1930 which noted that Opatija had only 45 taxis and four horse carriages, in comparison to hundreds of these that were cruising the town at the beginning of the century (Blazevic, 1994). In this phase, political decisions adversely affected tourism development, leading to a lowering of the product quality and an unsuccessful reorientation to a different tourist product. Thus, in the period between the two world wars tourism development in Opatija stagnated. This phase, just like the earlier one, finished with the beginning of another world war.

Transition to mass tourism (1946–1990)

For the third time, the Opatija Riviera was back on the tourist map and with the available resources attempted to create an interesting tourism product. Tourism started to grow more intensely after 1948 when numbers of 50,000 bed-nights were reached again. The 1950s continued to witness a sharp increase in visitations levels, when the travel agency 'Kvarner Express' opened and particularly in the late 1950s with the opening of the Institute for Thalasso-Therapy, specialising in curing respiratory and heart diseases. At the same time the College for Tourism Studies was established, and was later upgraded to University level.

This was the era of mass tourism with the 'sun and sea' product prevailing internationally. This product was developed largely unplanned and lacked development controls along the entire Croatian Adriatic coast (Weber, 1998), and the Opatija Riviera was not spared. Tourism development in Croatia was affected by two factors: the demand of the citizens of Western and Northern Europe for a holiday in the sun and a warm, clean sea, and the country's proximity to the main generating markets. The practically continuous growth in tourism demand over a period of 30 years (1957–1987) illustrates the attractiveness of the Opatija Riviera as a summer holiday destination (Figure 16.5).

Its tourism product has occupied a relatively stable market position, mainly relying on exploitation of the natural and ecological components of supply that consumers of that era preferred. Following growth that only occasionally fluctuated during the 1980s (1982), there were no noticeable trends of the stagnation that characterised tourism demand in other Adriatic destinations.

Throughout the 1960s and 1970s several large up-market hotels with congress facilities were constructed in an attempt to introduce new products and diversify demand. However, these were only sporadic efforts, which did not demonstrate expected financial returns although the number of visitors and bed-nights were still on the increase. In that period the quality of the entire tourism industry of the area was well below the quality of the destination itself. A more detailed examination into the tourism supply indicated a decline in quality of service and a loss of identity of accommodation facilities, as architecturally the new

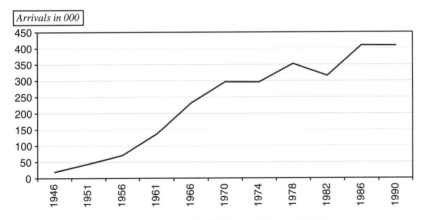

Figure 16.5 Arrivals to the Opatija Riviera (1946–1990)

hotels were not in harmony with their surroundings. There was also a lack of inventiveness in creating the various activities and services. This 'mediocracy' of supply and standardisation of individual elements of supply lead, for example, to identical forms of entertainment and menus in restaurants. This resulted in a decline in tourism numbers, an increased discrepancy between declared and achieved average prices, large price reductions outside the main season and loss of any real relationship between price and quality of supply. Destination marketing did not exist as a business philosophy. Suppliers relied mainly on infrequent and uncoordinated promotional efforts and there was a complete lack of a consistent and innovative product policy.

This was the period when Croatia was part of the former socialist Republic of Yugoslavia when the entire tourism development was characterised by unplanned activities, and when the success of the tourism sector was measured only superficially in terms of tourist flows and not the income generated from tourism. Nevertheless, there were attempts over that period to diversify the product and extend the summer season from three months. Thus, in addition to the classical 'sun and sea' product, congress tourism was stimulated (10% of all over-nights). Likewise, the hotels introduced new health services in an attempt to revive Opatija's century-old reputation as a health retreat destination. The entire product was enriched by the construction of a marina, which is still one of the best in Croatia. However, the quality of product offered was still well below the product that was offered in the previous eras. For the third time the growth phase was abruptly interrupted by external factors.

Differentiating the tourist product (1991–...)

Although the War of Independence did not directly affect the area, it did nevertheless result in a drastic reduction of tourism activity for several years (see Figure 16.6). Tourism in the area has been rejuvenated again, although affected by both positive and negative consequences of the rich tourism history. Although the Riviera has an indisputably valuable architectural and urban heritage, long tourism tradition, favourable geographical location and good accessibility, it has to face numerous problems associated with a mature tourism product. Although this area is already recognisable as the 'Riviera' product, the old-fashioned concept of accommodation facilities and entire tourism infrastructure necessitated relatively unfavourable market positioning, despite the fact that growth of visitors was still recorded (Figure 16.6). While the Opatija Riviera can match competitors in Italy and France in terms of physical attractiveness, it falls behind in many other aspects, such as restaurants, shopping, entertainment and recreation and even

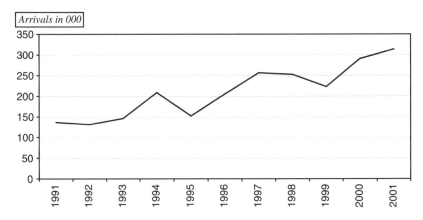

Figure 16.6 Arrivals to the Opatija Riviera (1991–2001)

hotels. To a large extent these are problems inherited from the past as over the long period there was little investment in maintaining and upgrading existing hotels, and these were further degraded when refugees were housed in them for four years of war. The last 10 years have witnessed also significant residential development that, coupled with the poor standard of the wastewater treatment, has resulted in marine pollution. A permanent problem also has been the lack of parking spaces in the town centre, while beaches and public spaces have not been maintained at the appropriate standard.

In this period the Riviera, in addition to maintaining the classic summer tourism, has continually strived to develop congress tourism. Attempts have also been made to upgrade and innovate the traditional health product to modern standards. To this end a few hotels are developing 'wellness' centres with a variety of services – fitness, massage, baths, beauty treatments and a variety of specialised health products, ranging from thalassotherapy to aromatherapy. It is still customary that most hotels sell half and full-board packages instead of offering the variety of services and experiences necessary to suit current demand. The Opatija Riviera is currently positioning itself as a non-stop event destination, packed with festivals and carnivals that are slowly becoming a symbol of Opatija. These events also provide an impetus for maintaining and reviving historical traditions and are, as such, important for the local community. There are also two casinos in the area and attempts are currently being made to improve the range of entertainment opportunities.

Overall, the marketing efforts of the Opatija Riviera could be assessed as insufficient and poorly targeted. However, in the current circumstances intensive tourism development and improvement in accommodation facilities are obstructed by the lack of development capital and a slow privatisation of hotels. It is encouraging though that the development plan for the Riviera, which defines development vision, market positioning and mix strategies is near to completion. The future of tourism development now depends mostly on the extent to which the main stakeholders of the area – the tourism industry, local government and the local community – will endorse this plan.

Applicability and Modification of the TALC Model

The aim of this chapter is to evaluate the manner in which the TALC model could be used in the case of the life cycle of the Opatija Riviera – an area with specific features of tourism development. The long tourism life of this destination was abruptly halted three times by wars so that the destination has not followed the classic development curve of the original TALC model. The main departure from the original model has been that in each era several life-cycle stages could be identified, as illustrated by Table 16.1.

Period I: 'Exploration and involvement'

Applying Butler's life-cycle stages, it is clear that the first period of tourism development on the Riviera could be identified as going through the exploration and involvement stages if the entire period is analysed as part of the development cycle. In this first era the destination partly

Table 16.1 Phases of destination development: The experience of the Opatija Riviera

Phase	Period I (1883–1914)	Period II (1919–1940)	Period III (1946–1990)	Period IV (1991–)
Exploration	Completely	Partly	Partly	Partly
Involvement	Completely	Partly	Partly	Partly
Development	Partly	Skipped	Almost completely	Completely
Consolidation	Skipped	Skipped	Partly	Partly
Stagnation	Skipped	No	No	Partly
Decline	Complete	Several times	Completely	No (can be expected)
Rejuvenation	No	No	No	No (can be expected)

experienced a development phase, although it is, because of the time and data available, difficult to assess with a degree of certainty. Consolidation and stagnation were not experienced as tourism development was halted under the influence of external factors. This first period of the tourism history was also marked by a clear vision of its development driven by several actors who, sensing the area's attractiveness and its potential including its favourable geographical location, developed the infrastructure and built capacity necessary for tourism development. As health tourism dominated in this period it could be said that the destination product was homogeneous and thus it is relatively easy to apply the TALC model. Recommended strategies for this stage of tourism development were selling new products/services to new markets (Ansoff, 1965) and building market share (Heath & Wall, 1992). According to the data available it could be safely concluded that the area successfully applied the latter strategy. Key development directions of this period were quality of services, hotel accommodation, care for the environment, and product exclusivity that enabled it to attract tourists with a high spending power and to develop unique product features.

Period II: 'Involvement and decline'

The second period was characterised by the development of new products and thus health tourism ceased to dominate. The development features lead to a conclusion that the destination was at this time in the involvement phase with some characteristics of the decline stage. The destination product was no longer homogeneous; the destination used the risky strategy of new product development, including orientation to new markets and new market segments. However, this reorientation was mostly driven politically, rather than by the stakeholders involved in tourism development. The consequence of such repositioning was a fluctuation in tourist numbers while the product itself suffered degradation in quality. The growth of demand in certain years could be attributed mostly to the area's inherent attractiveness and uniqueness.

Period III: 'Development'

Following several years of war, when all tourism activity ceased, the Opatija Riviera again experienced initial stages of tourism development – exploration and involvement, but this time it relatively quickly entered the development phase. However, that time was marked by the nonexistence of a tourism development plan. The principles of the market economy were applied only partially and, therefore, tourism development was not a subject of strategic decisions. There was some evidence that the overall cost leadership strategy was applied rather intuitively. Such a strategy, in general, can return a profit even from consumers at the lower end of the market who are those mostly attracted to a destination. That was not achieved at the Opatija Riviera for several reasons, primarily because of insufficient marketing, unsophisticated promotional efforts and at best a confused development vision. In this phase, congress tourism was developed as a new product and slowly introduced to the market. However, this product was still not accompanied by the necessary investments in infrastructure, research, customer service and marketing. In this period an opportunity to better utilise the area's attractiveness and to build on the experiences gained from past successes was lost.

Period IV: 'Development and consolidation'

In this period, after the War of Independence, the area was again on the tourist market but this time really carrying the burden of the inherited problems. It went through initial and development phases. It can be argued that the Opatija Riviera also entered a phase of consolidation and partly stagnation according to some parameters such as slowing growth rate, low occupancy rate, heavy reliance on repeat trade and reaching the limits of carrying capacity. Along with the dominant holiday tourism product, congress and health tourism were in a growth phase. Although tourism continued to grow, because of several problems with infrastructure and an aging product, the decline stage began to emerge slowly. Thus if the area fails to increase investments and does not apply appropriate strategic measures that would enable it to enter the rejuvenation phase, decline is inevitable. Some commentators, such as Gilbert (1990), suggest that one of the recommended strategies in this case would be to move from a position of 'commodity area' to a position of 'status area' by differentiating its products from competitors. Extending existing products/services for sale to new markets as suggested by Ansoff (1965) would also help the Opatija Riviera to enhance its attractiveness and competitiveness.

Conclusions

Assuming that the Opatija Riviera opts for a successful expanded tourism future, development should not be left to uncontrolled, sporadic activities, as has been the case in the past. A planned approach to tourism, which identifies and evaluates the optimal development options, should be applied.

The most important benefits derived from the application of the TALC model are:

- Identification of the phases in the life cycle of a destination indicate different characteristics of tourism development, of which the most important in this case is the reorientation from a winter health tourism to a mass summer holiday destination. That, in turn, led to an overall decrease in destination attractiveness and associated unsatisfactory financial returns.

- Tourism development was successful in the periods when a clear vision existed (mostly in the first phase), when the product responded to market demand and when the entire destination's development was in harmony with the specific products that were dominant at the time.
- Identification of the positive and negative effects of tourism, as it is worth remembering that the 'exclusivity and quality' achieved in the first phase positioned the Riviera on the tourist map of Europe, while this reputation was quickly lost in the period between the two world wars due to the absence of a planned approach.
- Although most of the turning points to date depended on the external factors and not on destination planning and management, further growth of tourism, in the face of strong market competition, will depend on the ability of the Opatija Riviera to reposition itself and reinvent its products. This could be achieved only if development is planned and the appropriate destination management tools applied. The planning options are partly determined by the specificities of the development to date (i.e. several introduction phases, simultaneous existence of two phases), where the measures characteristic of the rejuvenation phase should be applied, such as combined efforts from government and private bodies or the construction of artificial attractions such as theme parks.

The case study of tourism development on the Opatija Riviera illustrates how extrinsic factors can influence the evolution of a destination and make it unique. It can be concluded that several phases existed simultaneously and this was a result of tourism activities being halted several times due to the armed conflicts, creating a necessity to start tourism development from scratch each time. The TALC model is fully applicable in the situation where a single tourism product dominates a destination. In the case of the Opatija Riviera, where the latest phase of development is characterised by several products, the model should be applied to each product separately. Development of a tourism destination database and continuous market research into tourist motives will make it possible to test the applicability of the TALC model at this destination in the future.

Although in the tourism literature there are many case studies demonstrating the conformity/validity of Butler's model (e.g. Cooper & Jackson, 1989; Hovinen, 1982; Meyer-Arendt, 1985; Strapp, 1988), there are also cases demonstrating deviation from the model (Agarwal, 1997;

Choy, 1992; Getz, 1992). Regardless of the outcome, all derive conclusions and evaluate past and expected developments of a destination under study. The applicability of the TALC model in the case of the Opatija Riviera lies in its ability to identify development phases according to the stipulated characteristics and recommended strategies and not solely in their succession according to the classical model. A relatively simple model such as the TALC also assists a combination with other methods such as market share analysis, portfolio management model and various planning indices to determine what could be a direction for future research.

Chapter 17

The Rejuvenation of Atlantic City: The Resort Cycle Recycles

CHARLES STANSFIELD

Introduction

Geographers and other scholars long have been intrigued that it might be possible to better comprehend the apparent waxing and waning of a region's economic or political fortunes as evidence of a predictable sequence or cycle. Economists study, interpret and try to predict a variety of business activity cycles. Climatologists seek to understand possible climate cycles. Noted political geographer Samuel Van Valkenburg compared the state's 'life cycle' to a human life cycle, noting that the organism of the state could repeat, or recycle, this sequence.

Stansfield appears to have been the first to use and exemplify the term 'resort cycle' in a publication in 1978 (Stansfield, 1978). Butler was the first to define, structure, and generalize the specific stages of this cycle (Butler, 1980). Can the resort cycle 'recycle' or repeat, as in the manner of Van Valkenburg's age cycle of states? Atlantic City's 'rebirth' as a world-class, successful resort seems to be evidence that it can.

Why Atlantic City?

An important question about Atlantic City's spectacular renaissance through the agency of legalized gambling is, why Atlantic City? Why was Atlantic City the first jurisdiction in the USA to break Nevada's long monopoly on legalized gambling? The answer lies in the resort cycle as exemplified by Atlantic City's history, its sad decline, and in political solutions to economic problems. Politics – lots of politics – are involved.

The old Atlantic City, 'B.C.' (Before Casinos) suffered from a combination of economic and social problems. Chief among them were seasonality, obsolescence of tourism infrastructure and changing life-styles and vacation habits. To be sure, this list applies to all aging resorts; in Atlantic City's case, though, it was the scale and intensity of those problems that contributed to a bold move to use legalized gambling as a tool of urban renewal.

Gambling on Renewal: Background to the Legalization of Gambling

By the 1970s, Atlantic City was in deepening trouble. Approximately 120 years after Atlantic City was founded on a then desolate offshore sandbar, the city's economy, social health and reputation all were in desperate condition. The once glamorous, fabled 'Queen of the Jersey Shore' had sagged into a frayed and peeling version of its glory days. Atlantic City's appeal, its crowd-attracting formula combining natural and created attractions, no longer encapsulated the extravagant and fantastic illusion on which great resorts flourished. In his landmark study of Atlantic City, Charles Funnell concluded

> ultimately, changing modes of transportation practically destroyed the resort's ability to attract patronage across class lines, threatened the physical appearance of the city, and sapped the illusion – creating potential the town once so vigorously exploited. Atlantic City did not 'fall' – it was abandoned. It persevered in formulas which had been highly successful, but though a large part of its patronage continued to respond eagerly to what it offered, an important minority left it behind, to return no more. (Funnell, 1975: 154)

Atlantic City's plight by the 1970s explains much of its determination to seek revitalization through legalized gambling. Some of Atlantic City's problems can be viewed as yet another instance of the urban cancer affecting virtually all aging cities in America. Other aspects of the resort's decline are related to causes unique to resorts. Atlantic City's sad decay is illustrated by data from the 1970 census. The city's census tract (neighborhood) with the lowest mean income had less than half the county mean, while only two tracts of 21 in Atlantic City exceeded the county mean. The percentage of families below the official poverty level, slightly under 10% for the entire county, varied within Atlantic City from 3.5% to 46% in the north end urban renewal area. Some neighborhoods reported as much as 80% of the population over 65, and old age and lower incomes often go together. Two-thirds of the housing occupied year-round had been built before 1940, and looked it. This was a city that had 40 pawnshops, but not a single supermarket or movie theater (if we don't count porno).

Basically, the people of New Jersey felt sorry for Atlantic City and its citizens. It had been such a great place in memory; now it needed help. If Atlantic City couldn't help itself – and evidently it couldn't – how could the state help the old resort to once again rise to success? What to do?

The road to renewal first needed an answer to the question, what went wrong? For one thing, owners and operators of hotels, restaurants, and entertainment businesses had failed to keep up with changing tastes. Aging buildings weren't kept fresh and up-to-date, typical of the decline stage in the resort cycle. New facilities just were not being built. The places that attracted, accommodated, and entertained visitors had become shabby and old-fashioned. Profits were being drained away without making necessary reinvestments in modernization or replacement.

Early success: The period of rapid expansion

Obviously, all the facilities in Atlantic City's early days were new, and new commonly equals desirable for American tourists. The early success of Atlantic City is illustrated by the size and plush nature of its hotels. For example, the United States Hotel, which occupied an entire city block, was described in a contemporary account as having rooms for 600 guests which were

> large, airy, comfortable, carpeted and furnished in walnut, with gas in every room and in every respect will compare with a first class city hotel. There are also attractive billiard rooms, ten pin alleys and shooting galleries and daily morning, afternoon and evening open air concerts are given by a celebrated orchestra. (Rose, 1878: 42)

Host to President Grant in 1874, the hotel was one of the most successful ventures of the railroad company which had literally created the resort. By 1894 it had been torn down, an example of the energetic drive to 'keep up to date'. New resorts as summarized and generalized in Butler's landmark study on resort cycles (Butler, 1980) are characterized by intensive real estate speculation, and rapid construction of new, plush accommodations, restaurants, and transport facilities of the latest design. The reputation of the resort, carefully nourished by enthusiastic public relations efforts, is at its height. It is an 'in' place with a magnetic appeal to the trend-followers.

As leisure time and disposable income were democratized, successively lower income groups arrived to sample Atlantic City's well publicized delights. This trend toward a broadening of the social strata patronizing the resort is closely related to the progressive lowering of the time and money cost of travel to the resort.

At the apex: Triumph and decline

By World War I, Atlantic City had reached a plateau. It appeared that all was well, that the tried and true formulas still worked, but by that time, most of the resplendent and extravagant seafront hotels had been built; few more on the truly grandiose scale would be added. The railroad was still fulfilling its dominant role although motorists were beginning to clog the highways in summer. The costs of reaching Atlantic City were decreasing. The railroad, whose speed made day-trips feasible, was carrying progressively lower income groups to Atlantic City. The entertainment complex increasingly reflected their tastes and disposable incomes. This shift in emphasis towards working class tastes was both a cause of and a consequence of the upper middle class's declining allegiance to Atlantic City. As observed of Coney Island at the same period, 'The working classes, those most effected by the increasing pace and increasing mechanization of life, accepted mechanized Coney most readily... they did not see close contact with nature as a "spiritual necessity"... mechanized, time structured leisure may simply reflect mechanized, time structured lives.' (Snow & Wright, 1976: 960–975).

The mechanical amusements, cheap vaudeville theaters and garish entertainments which so thrilled the working classes helped to drive away the upper middle class from the ornate hotels and high-class restaurants. The 'takeover' of a resort by a lower-income group than had originally dominated it may be partially explained, however, by the upper-income group's desire for new recreation environments. Tourism is an industry in which fashion and the search for the new and different play important roles.

The physical complex of hotels, restaurants, and the more expensive, higher-class entertainments was allowed to slowly deteriorate. No new investment was attracted due to diminishing patronage, at least of the higher-priced facilities. Unfortunately, the fact that Atlantic City's fortunes were tied to trains was both good and bad news. Trains had created, and built, Atlantic City. The last excursion trains were phased out after World War II, leaving Atlantic City with only minimal, commuter-oriented train service. The two replacements for trains in vacation travel, limited-access, high-speed highways and jet airplanes, both favored other resorts over Atlantic City. Atlantic City was the loser under these new rules. Although Atlantic City's Bader Field, the first municipal airport in the nation, is convenient to downtown and nearby Atlantic City, Pomona can accommodate large jets, the air age has not greatly benefited Atlantic City. Other than convention trade, few visitors arrived by air until after the casinos were built. The time in the air from most of the neighboring cities of the northeast Megalopolis to other resorts such as those of southern Florida is not all that much greater than that to Atlantic City. Also, economical operation of fast jets on a regularly scheduled basis requires termini in busy markets. A short-haul service to Atlantic City from Philadelphia has continued, and a longer-distance jet service has a bright future.

Obsolescence of infrastructure

The individual mobility of automobile vacations led to a quite different style of vacation from that of the old railroad resorts. The railroad had provided only point-to-point mobility for its users. Whether for a day or a month, the Victorian vacationer was tied to that one city, perhaps even to the vicinity of a particular hotel. The vacationer's dollars were spent mostly within the confines of that resort. Private automobiles had two major impacts upon recreation patterns, neither of which really benefited Atlantic City. Vacationers arriving in cars wanted to be able to park their cars conveniently and, preferably, free of charge. Crowded, densely built-up Atlantic City was friendly to pedestrians but not to cars. By the auto age, most of the city's buildable land was occupied by multi-story structures packed tightly together. The narrow streets of an earlier era could not accommodate both heavier traffic and curb parking on both sides. Relatively few new, large motels were constructed in a city where many hotel rooms were empty even in peak season. Cost-conscious vacationers could stay at cut-price motels constructed along the high-ways and drive daily to the beaches, crowding Atlantic City's beaches and streets, but leaving little money behind. The much sought-after middle class 'family trade' increasingly preferred the smaller, less crowded, less expensive, less noisy towns along the coast. The new highways that brought vacationers to Atlantic City also facilitated their going to other resorts, or their commuting into Atlantic City from less expensive locations. Highway improvements ever increased the distance that day-trippers could travel from home to resort to home in one day.

Proof of Atlantic City's decline and obsolescence was the loss of about 3500 hotel rooms (to demolition, mostly) between 1964 and 1969, accompanied by a loss of 2500 'guest house' rooms. While motels did add approximately 1000 rooms during this period, the net decrease in transient rooms available was nearly 20% of the total in just five years. In this last stage of the resort cycle, the natural amenities that led to the founding of the resort were of deteriorated quality, with environmental pollution a serious and intensifying problem. Commonly, declining resorts attempt to modify and rejuvenate their appeal to vacationers. Due in some measure to uncontrollable or unforeseeable changes in leisure patterns, transport technology, and fashion, and through environmental pollution and plant obsolescence, the resort can no longer rely on its original set of attractions. The resort may choose to emphasize its historical and cultural uniqueness rather than its deteriorated, less-attractive physical site amenities. In other words, superior climates, lower costs, relatively comparable degrees of accessibility resulting from changing transport technology, more modern and glamorous facilities, less crowded beaches – all of these assets may characterize other and newer resorts. Some unique quality of the artificial or human-created environment can, conceivably, be emphasized to lure tourists, for example, the huge stock of accommodations and entertainment facilities which are available at lower rates in attracting conventions.

A notable example of capitalizing upon the historic cultural landscape is nearby Cape May's largely successful preservation of its Victorian townscape. Cape May's stock of 1850s through 1890s architecture helps draw visitors to an otherwise out of the way site with relatively narrow beaches. By the 1970s, Atlantic City's architecture, while flamboyant and varied in the remaining great hotels of the turn-of-the-century through 1920s period, was not quite old enough to yet draw the full interest of the preservationists and nostalgia buffs who had made a pet of Cape May. At that time, great gaps in Atlantic City's oceanfront skyline, the product of demolition of antiquated hotels, resembled broken or missing teeth in a smile – a reminder of old age and neglect. While small town Victoriana at Cape May is charming, Atlantic City's seafront, what there was left of it, seemed more isolated in a sea of slums and consequently dreary. Atlantic City simply could not become another, larger Cape May.

Atlantic City was beginning to show its age. No major new hotels had been built for decades. The all-too-short 'season' left many locals on the unemployment rolls for about eight months a year. For the first time, local business and political leaders publicly discussed the possibility of legalized gambling as an economic stimulus. Major hotel owners were split on the controversial proposal. The owners of the Chalfonte-Haddon Hall Hotel, for example, who were Quakers, strongly opposed legalizing casinos. The year? 1956. Twenty years later, a referendum question approving casinos in Atlantic City was successful. The first casino to open, in 1978, was Resorts International, the new owner of the Chalfonte-Haddon Hall property.

The Beginning of a New Beginning: Recycling the Resort Cycle

The problems of Atlantic City spurred a variety of governmental efforts to revitalize the city by the 1960s. A new high-speed toll highway, the Atlantic City Expressway, was built to the aging resort. A new state college was built on the mainland nearby. There was talk of extending a suburban high-speed commuter railway from Philadelphia all the way to Atlantic City. The most intriguing (and, initially, controversial) suggestion was to legalize gambling. Legalization was at first opposed on the grounds that it might attract organized crime. A referendum on gambling casinos, which appeared on the November 1974 ballot, was resoundingly defeated, three to two. The defeat was achieved by well organized opposition ('no dice on casino gambling'), particularly from church groups. The 1974 proposal, however, while supposedly designed to help Atlantic City, would have made casinos a matter of local option anywhere in the state. Clearly, the possibility of a casino in everyone's hometown was unpopular. The 1976 ballot proposal was restricted to legalized casinos in Atlantic City only. This time, state revenues from casinos were to be devoted to property tax and utility bill relief for the elderly poor – a maneuver which attracted many votes. The sugar coating of charitable impulse helped ease the pill of legalization of casino gambling down the throats of the voters. Popular ambivalence toward casino gambling has characterized Americans long before the 1976 referendum, and it continues. The campaign of the 'Committee to Rebuild Atlantic City' succeeded.

But, would casinos thrive by the sea? Would the new industry bring prosperity to the old resort? New Jersey's governor helped open the first casino, Resorts International, on the Memorial Day weekend of 1978. It was a winner – an instant hit. Local legend has it that this pioneer casino took in so much money in those first days that the 'counting room' couldn't handle the volume of cash. It is said that supermarket bags full of bills accumulated on the floor until the accounting staff caught up. Resorts' seven-month-long first year of operations earned a gross income of $156 million, representing a 200% return on equity (Hawkins, 1982: 120–128).

Here is a snapshot of the casino industry 19 years after Resorts International first opened its doors to the crowds lined up on the boardwalk. This is Atlantic City about midway from the first legalized gambling to the present:

> On an average day in Atlantic City, nineteen years into the casino era, 110,000 visitors and non-resident workers joined the city's 37,000 residents. Over 82,000 people visited the city's twelve casinos and gross winnings in casinos amounted to about 6.5 million dollars. At the same time, 1,452 charter buses arrived in town. Gamblers dropped over 46 million quarters in slot machines. (Russell, 1987: np)

By the dawn of the new century, Atlantic City had become America's most popular resort destination, with over 37 million visitor-days per year. In comparison, Walt Disney World hosts about 18 million visitor-days per year. Hotel/casino industry wages topped $700 million a year, employing over 46,000 people directly in an industry that did not exist until 1978. Between 1976, the year in which the casino referendum was approved by New Jersey voters, and 1984, per capita income in the US doubled. In the same period, New Jersey's per capita income increased faster, 109%, while Atlantic City's grew by 134%. In 1976, Atlantic City had one-tenth as many visitors as it had by 1987. The state's 8% tax on gross revenues of casinos already had transferred over $1 billion to the state treasury. Indirect taxes – sales taxes and the city's luxury tax paid by casino patrons – generated another $20 million per year.

Early impacts of casinos

The visible impacts of the casino industry on Atlantic City can be compared to a growing snowball, or maybe it was more like an avalanche filmed in slow motion. At first, little seemed to be happening, at least for the better. In her book about Resorts International, owners of the first casino to open in Atlantic City in May 1978, author Gigi Mahon described the scene in the summer of 1977 – a year after the voter approval of legalized gaming in Atlantic City, but a year before opening day.

> Up at the Chalfonte-Haddon Hall, a handful of construction men labored through the heat, a renovation under way. But for that, the facades of the old hotels remained as they had for years, sagging, gray, like the faces of the people who sat on the Boardwalk day after day. It was the same Atlantic City, long ago duchess of resorts, now an arthritic and dowdy dowager trying desperately to cling to her past. A bag of worn-out bricks on splintered pilings. (Mahon, 1980: prologue)

Did legalization of gambling work?

In a word, yes. Look at the skyline of Atlantic City, then consider this: $60 billion dollars. That is the total brought to the State of New Jersey's treasury by casino revenues from 1978 to the present. That is enough money that the state could have written a check for over $7200 to every one of the state's estimated 8,359,000 citizens and it is 60 billion dollars worth of state services that New Jersey taxpayers didn't have to pay for directly.

The legalization of casinos in Atlantic City has created almost 50,000 jobs directly in the casino industry, and an estimated additional 50,000 jobs in industries within New Jersey that supply and service the casinos. This creation of approximately 100,000 jobs in the state did not cost the state, or any of its municipalities, anything directly.

In contrast, other states and local governments have not hesitated to spend millions in efforts to attract new jobs into their economies. Pennsylvania spent a quarter of a billion dollars to secure a Volkswagen assembly plant near New Stanton, PA. Tennessee paid for $15 million worth of site improvements and issued $450 million in bonds to build a facility in order to lure a Nissan assembly plant; Nissan also was given a substantial tax exemption, all to add 6000 jobs to the state's economy (Sternlieb & Hughes, 1983: 3).

Gambling on the future, gambling in the future

Atlantic City's present and future depends on Americans' attitudes toward gambling. The industry itself prefers the term 'gaming' – it sounds classier and less controversial than 'gambling.' Americans have changed their attitudes several times about permitting, encouraging, or criminalizing gambling, er, gaming. Colonial America openly tolerated lotteries. Such upright citizens as Benjamin Franklin printed lottery tickets, which were sold to support good causes, much as 'chances' today are sold on new cars to raise money for volunteer fire departments. Many a colonial college and church were built with lottery proceeds. Then, in the mid-19th century, Americans evidently decided that gambling was undesirable and should be officially frowned upon. By the 1890s, though, state lotteries again were common and gaming was widely tolerated. The notoriously crooked Louisiana State Lottery, however, caused a national scandal and by the early 20th century, public opinion had once again swung in favor of criminalizing gambling.

Using legalized gaming as a tool for urban renewal in Atlantic City was not the first time that gambling was used to revitalize a depressed economy. In the Great Depression of the 1930s, Nevada was particularly hard hit. Mining and ranching jobs were declining. With the important exception of the Sierras along the California border (such as at Lake Tahoe), Nevada had no natural landscapes of special appeal to tourists. Plenty of people crossed Nevada, to or from San Francisco and the rest of the country, but few planned to stay. Nevadans decided to legalize all forms of gambling anywhere in the state, and the modern gaming industry was born. Until 1978, when New Jersey's first casino opened, Nevada enjoyed a national monopoly on legal gaming.

If gaming could rescue a whole state's economy, maybe it could also rescue Atlantic City.

Gambling industry expert Jerome Skolnik (1978: 8) has observed,

Vice is a fascinating social phenomenon. Leading dictionaries define it as immoral or evil conduct. But the dictionary definition is incomplete. The term vice suggests pleasure – and popularity – as well as immorality. Murder, robbery, and theft are generally regarded as immoral, but not much fun. In contrast, gambling, illicit sex and drug use are vices because they combine pleasure with 'evil.' The whole point about the phenomenon of vice is its duality: it is conduct that can be enjoyed and deplored at the same time, sometimes by the same people.

It is this duality that, combined with the charitable destination of a portion of the revenues, helps explain the geographic pattern of casino gambling in the USA.

Easy money: Gambling as voluntary taxation

By 1984, 17 states and the District of Columbia had legal, government-run lotteries; these lotteries had total sales approaching $7 billion. Typically, states keep about 30–40% of ticket sales, after paying out prize money and administrative costs. As with legalized casinos in Atlantic City, some portion of revenues is allocated to projects that appeal to social consciousness – to a conservation trust fund in Colorado, aid to the elderly in Pennsylvania, and funds for the arts in Massachusetts. State lotteries tend to spread geographically as the government and citizens of a state without a lottery, but adjacent to one with one, see their own residents buying lottery tickets from their neighbor. Now 48 states have some form of state-sponsored gaming – lotteries, off-track betting, casinos, or a combination of these. Utah and Hawaii are the only exceptions to this relatively recent trend.

Lotteries, and now casinos, are seen as a painless form of voluntary taxation. Legalized casino gambling is most attractive to states when most of the gamblers are from out-of-state. In this way, most of the gambling losses are 'exported.' After all, revenues from gambling are based entirely on net losses by gamblers. This 'export' of gambling losses is the factor that makes Nevada's legalized gambling so lucrative to that state. State lotteries, while serving as tax collectors from volunteer taxpayers, are non-basic economic activities; they do not expand the state's economic base to any significant degree. As long as legal casinos serve largely out-of-state gamblers, they contribute to basic economic growth within that state.

Nevada's nationwide monopoly on legalized gaming ruled until Atlantic City became a competitor. Still, at least the Western half of the country was closer to Nevada than Atlantic City. But, Atlantic City had not only become a competitor to Nevada. Its success served as a role model for depressed regions elsewhere. Gambling came to many reservations as Native Americans (the poorest of the Census-tabulated minorities) sought economic growth. Riverboat gaming came to many of the Midwest's depressed old industrial cities, and to Mississippi, America's poorest state.

Expansion of the casino industry

Expectations for legalized gaming in Atlantic City ran from strongly negative to equally strongly positive. Just exactly why did the 1974 public question on the ballot (legalizing casinos anywhere in the state) lose but the 1976 question, legalizing casinos only in Atlantic City, win? Richard Lehne pointed out that public opinion polls showed little change in attitude from 1974 to 1976 (Lehne, 1986) (see Table 17.1).

Table 17.1 Opinion poll results

Month, Year	Yes on casinos (%)	No on casinos (%)	No opinions (%)
1, 74	59	34	7
9, 74	56	38	6
9, 76	59	36	5

Source: Lehne, 1986

Voter turnout in 1974 was less than 2 million. But in 1976, a presidential year, voter turnout was over 2.7 million. It seems that the legalization of casinos was a 'hot button issue', highly motivating those opposed, but when more voters showed up, the 'yes' votes prevailed. An analysis of who voted how summarized the yes vote as favored by males, inner city residents, and Catholics. Those opposing tended to be females, Protestants, and suburban residents.

Expansion of the casino industry in Atlantic City has not been one of continuous growth at a steady pace. Instead, as shown in Table 17.2, the early success of Resorts International produced a boom between 1978 and 1981, in which the number of casinos jumped from one to nine. In those first three years, casino square footage multiplied almost eight times, casino employees increased from 3226 to almost 28,000, and hotel rooms in casino hotels went from 724 to 4781. The legalization authorizing casinos in Atlantic City stipulated that casino hotels must have a minimum of 500 rooms. To guarantee more construction jobs, each hotel room had to be of sufficient square footage that old hotels, with their characteristically smaller rooms, would have to be substantially renovated. The annual increase in casino gross revenue or 'winnings' remained in the double digits until 1985. Between 1981 and 2002, only three more (net) casinos opened, and growth rates slowed noticeably. The increase rate of the gross 'win' stayed below 10% per year after 1984. During the 1990s decade, the number of casino employees fluctuated between about 44,000 and 49,000.

However, both casino floor areas and number of hotel rooms were higher by 2001 than they had been in 1991. Casino floor area, which since 1993 has included simulcast horseracing rooms, has gone from 773,000 square feet in 1991 to 1,230,000 square feet by 2001, a percentage increase of just under 60%. What is even more impressive is the growth in casino hotel rooms, from 9419 in 1991 to 11,466 by 2001, a somewhat surprising and healthy 22%.

The increase in the number of hotel rooms is significant because it points to a new trend that few had predicted. Atlantic City clearly is moving from a largely 'daytrip' resort towards a destination resort, in

Table 17.2 Expansion of casino gaming in Atlantic City

Year	No. of casinos	Casino floor sq. footage (000s)	Casino employees	Gross revenues (000s)	% Increase in win	No. of hotel rooms
1978*	1	52	3226	134,073	–	724
1979	3	160	11,301	325,480	42.7	1572
1980	6	281	21,351	642,693	97.4	3257
1981	9	412	27,842	1,099,799	71.1	4781
1982	9	425	28,093	1,493,164	35.7	4770
1983	9	422	30,958	1,770,941	18.6	4779
1984	10	510	35,356	1,951,766	10.2	5503
1985	11	577	38,686	2,138,651	9.5	6342
1986	11	593	37,251	2,281,206	6.6	6351
1987	12	664	39,336	2,495,728	9.4	6835
1988	12	696	41,205	2,734,775	9.5	7314
1989	12**	648	39,603	2,806,990	2.6	7584
1990	12**	770	43,399	2,952,582	5.1	8828
1991	12	773	41,473	2,991,562	1.3	9419
1992	12	777	44,240	3,215,968	7.5	8961
1993	12	854***	44,111	3,301,366	2.6	8946

Table 17.2 (Continued)

Year	No. of casinos	Casino floor sq. footage (000s)	Casino employees	Gross revenues (000s)	% Increase in win	No. of hotel rooms
1994	12	928	43,900	3,422,614	3.7	9227
1995	12	959	46,513	3,748,158	9.5	9404
1996	12	1081	48,956	3,813,598	1.7	10,533
1997	12	1173	49,123	3,879,651	1.7	11,891
1998	12	1211	48,542	3,991,612	2.8	11,880
1999	12	1170	47,366	4,119,507	3.2	11,361
2000	12	1198	47,426	4,275,783	3.8	11,361
2001	12	1230	45,592	4,279,034	0.07	11,466

Source: Compiled from the annual reports of the New Jersey Casino Control Commission, 1978– 2001
*220 days
**Eleven casinos from 22 May 1989 to 4 April 1990
***From 1993 forward, figure includes simulcast-racing room

which vacationers stay longer and to which they travel increasing distances. In 1979, Economic Research Associates made the following predictions, based on an analysis of trends in the overall economy, legalized gaming in general, and Atlantic City's casino industry in particular. By 1990 there would be: 26 casinos (compared to 1979's three); a permanent population of 75,000 (there were 41,322 in 1979); 24 million visitors a year (7,500,000 in 1979), and 55,000 hotel rooms by 1990 (as against 1572 in 1979).

So much for scientific predictions, especially those made during a period of rapid expansion with the assumption that expansion will continue at a frantic pace. However, the 22% increase in hotel rooms, 1991 to 2001, is a respectable achievement, and one trend that will continue. 'By the summer of 2004, Atlantic City should have an additional 3,200 hotel rooms – an increase of approximately 33 percent over what currently exists.' (Casino Control Commission, 2001: 4).

Since the 2001 figure of 11,466 rooms was reported, Harrah's has built another 452-room addition; Resorts is adding another 459-room tower; Tropicana is adding 502 rooms; and Showboat is adding 544 rooms. The Borgata, opening in 2003, will contribute another 2010 rooms. The Sheraton Atlantic, a new, non-casino hotel next to the $268 million Convention Center, has 502 rooms. A Boardwalk non-casino hotel, Atlantic Palace, has 302 units, many of them two-bedroom suites.

Atlantic City seems poised for another period of fast growth despite the miniscule increase in win reported for 2001 – a year of deepening recession, falling stock markets, and, of course, the tragedy of September 11, which considerably slowed the entire tourism and travel industry. Indeed, the disasters of September 11, which had a strongly negative impact on air travel, may have actually helped Atlantic City in the long run by increasing tourism at resorts that can be reached by road and rail rather than by air. Atlantic City's casino industry enjoyed a remarkable fourth quarter, with gross operating profits up almost 25% over the October–December period of 2000 (Casino Control Commission, 2001: 4).

The casinos

Before the first casino opened in Atlantic City, the size of the legalized gambling market was unknown. The 'convincer' that a huge, formerly unserved market existed in the Northeast was the success of Atlantic City's first casino, Resorts International. Resort's seven-month long first year generated a gross income of $156 million, which was a 200% return on equity. In its first full month of operation, Resorts' 'win' was $16 million.

When Resorts had the only game in town during the summer of 1978, the only 'marketing' problem was one of security and crowd control.

Lines of people four or five abreast waited on the Boardwalk for hours before being admitted, and once a patron got inside his most lucky break of the day might be finding a spot of play! But as each new casino opened, patrons began to choose their casino, and the market was shared even though it continued to grow. (Smith, 1982: 116)

'Casino fever,' a belief that there would be no end to the boom, prevailed among otherwise sane people.

As more and more casinos opened, they began to develop marketing strategies to differentiate themselves and establish unique identities. James Smith (1982) pointed out that Nevada's casinos generally fell into one of two categories: 'premium' or 'grind joints'. Premium casinos strove for an upscale image. Lavishly decorated, they emphasized table games with fairly high minimum wagers. Premium casinos rely heavily on 'high rollers' who may stay several days and gamble large sums. For their select clientele, premium casinos are happy to 'comp' them with complimentary luxury suites, preferred seating at shows featuring big-name entertainment, and any other services that will keep the high rollers coming back. These wealthy players routinely risk many thousands of dollars. Typically, they stay for days, not hours, and expect elegant and impeccable service. They play table games in which experience and familiarity with the rules count in their favor, they hope. Premium houses' showrooms feature top name entertainment (it is said that the late Frank Sinatra was the champion 'draw' for high-rollers) (Smith, 1982).

In contrast, 'grind' houses (also known as 'sawdust joints' in contrast to 'carpet' or premium casinos) prospered on a high volume of gamblers who bet less individually, a lot less, than the high rollers. Grind houses typically featured many slot machines, with relatively fewer table games. Grind houses thus rely on large numbers of low-rollers who, individually, wager modestly but who as a group, are highly profitable. Senior citizens arriving by chartered bus, prepared to lose little more than the $10 roll of quarters that is part of their daytrip package, are the main patrons of the grind houses. Food is often buffet-style, most patrons do not stay overnight, and the showrooms feature revues rather than renowned stars. While premium houses offer tickets to boxing matches and other special events to their high-rolling clientele, grind houses offer meal coupons, chances to win cars and discounted revue tickets to their clients. Many patrons of grind houses have too little experience to confidently play table games where skill counts; instead they prefer the no-skill slot machines.

Historically, Nevada's casinos were mostly grind houses. Ben 'Bugsy' Siegel's ground breaking 'Flamingo', opened at Las Vegas in 1946, not only pioneered the Vegas Strip (as opposed to downtown's Fremont Street) but was a true premium house. High rollers arrived by chartered planes; dealers wore tuxedoes.

Smith (1982) illustrated the premium–grind contrast by comparing the MGM Grand in Las Vegas with Atlantic City's Resorts International. The MGM Grand was the largest hotel in the state when it opened (1973) and boasted the largest casino. In addition to 2100 rooms, it featured a shopping arcade, two large showrooms and a jai alai fronton. Resorts, Atlantic City's first casino, and its largest in 1981, had little more than a third of MGM's hotel rooms, and a very different mix of games.

MGM versus Resorts offered a strong and obvious contrast (see Table 17.3). However, contrasts among Atlantic City's casinos in 2001 are much less obvious or consistent. Table 17.4 lists number of slot machines, number of (all) table games, the ratio of gaming tables to slots, and the percentage of slot machines that are nickel slots. Premium houses would be expected to have lower ratios of slots to tables, and lower proportions of nickel slots. The table also shows that Showboat, at 56 slots per gaming table, has a much higher ratio of slots to tables than Tropicana, with a 1 to 24 ratio, or Trump Taj Mahal (1 to 23). Harrah's, another high slots to gaming tables operation, suggesting a possible 'grind' classification along with Showboat, has less emphasis on nickel slots (which are surely an indicator of 'grind' appeal) than five other casinos, including the more prestigious Hilton and Bally's. All of Atlantic City's casinos seem to be aiming at as broad a market segment as possible. Economic survival requires satisfying all varieties of gamblers. Atlantic City operations may emphasize their appeals to premium or grind clienteles, but they are determined to discourage no one.

Atlantic City seems to have pioneered a hybrid premium–grind operation. These premium–grind operations seek distinctive identities

Table 17.3 Contrasts between casino characteristics

	MGM (1973 data)	*Resorts (1981 data)*
Hotel rooms	2100	723
Slots	930	1698
Blackjack tables	61	82
Crap tables	10	20
Roulette wheels	6	14
Big 6 wheels	3	4
Baccarat tables	3	3

Table 17.4 'Premium–grind' characteristics of Atlantic City casinos

	No. slots	No. table games	Ratio of table/slots	Nickel slots as % slots
Atlantic City Hilton	2024	84	1/24	24
Bally's Park Place*	4316	155	1/28	24
Caesar's	3856	123	1/31	19
Claridge	1777	63	1/28	20
Harrah's	3171	69	1/49	20
Resorts	2583	74	1/35	18
Sands	2060	79	1/26	19
Showboat	3390	61	1/56	22
Tropicana	4114	171	1/24	21
Trump Marina	2528	78	1/32	22
Trump Taj Mahal	4825	207	1/23	17
Industry	37,483	1247	1/30	20

*Includes Bally's Wild, Wild West
All data calculated from New Jersey Casino Control Commission Annual Report, 2001

through 'themes', which are shaped and expressed by architecture, interior decoration, costumes of dealers, bartenders, waitresses, etc., and even names of lounges, showrooms, and restaurants. The most obvious example of theme operations include Showboat's 'New Orleans Mardi Gras,' Taj Mahal's Oriental–Arabian nights fantasy and Caesar's Imperial Roman orgy.

Atlantic City's 13th casino, the Borgata, at the time of writing is under construction in the Marina District. The $1-billion, 480-foot high casino will open in the summer of 2003. The Borgata will add 135,000 square feet to Atlantic City's casino floor space, will house 11 restaurants, and will employ 4700. Plans are firming for a $1.5 billion MGM Mirage to be located next to the Borgata on what was, until recently, the city dump. A recent expansion of Harrah's Atlantic City will (temporarily) make it the state's largest hotel at 1626 rooms. Gaming industry insiders predict that Atlantic City will be home to 17 casinos within five years. Atlantic City will continue to reign as the Queen of the Jersey Shore as it moves to more closely resemble its original model, Las Vegas.

The revitalized resort draws more visitors than any other single locale in the USA, more than 37 million visitor-days per year. About 7 million were overnight guests. At 94% occupancy year-round, Atlantic City has a much higher occupancy rate for hotels than the US average. The casinos are a big draw, but not the only attraction.

Atlantic City's casinos pay 70% of all property taxes collected by the city. There are now over 1 million square feet of casino 'floors' (including simulcast rooms), over 10,000 rooms in casino hotels, and nearly 50,000 casino employees (compared to Atlantic City's resident population of some 38,000).

Conclusions: The Coming Megaresorts

The casino industry has big plans for Atlantic City. Huge new 'megaresorts' are planned for vacant land on the bayside. These future mammoth hotels will out-glitz the city's existing casinos – no small challenge there. They will feature 'total resort environments', more family-oriented, with amusement rides, video games, shopping areas, lavish showrooms, continuous entertainment and, of course, a slot machine or two. Sound familiar? As in the 'New' Las Vegas? Atlantic City has consciously imitated Las Vegas since New Jerseyans authorized casinos at the beach in 1976. Las Vegas' fantastic success made it Atlantic City's role model.

The success formula for Las Vegas' incredible expansion (the city grew by 86%, 1990–2000) has been Bigger! Better! More extravagant! More fantastic buildings! Set new standards of size, design, and flamboyance and blow away the competition! And when the competition begins to catch up, raise the stakes again.

Las Vegas, which has featured gambling joints since the 1930s, has witnessed several escalations in investment and the scale and lavishness of casinos. When gangster Bugsy Siegel built the 'Flamingo' in 1946, its glitz set new standards. When Caesar's Palace opened in 1966, its fabulous blend of fantasy theme park and casino was hugely popular; there was a new game in town, again. Then came the first mega resort, the $630-million Mirage in 1989. Again, the challenge to the competition was clear: match it or fold.

Atlantic City certainly will soon enter the era of megaresorts. Increasing competition from riverboats and Amerindian reservation gambling leaves little choice. Besides, when did Atlantic City shrink from a little more glitz and hype? Clearly, the resort cycle is well into its second sequence; the cycle recycles.

Note

Some of this material has been adapted from Charles A. Stansfield, Jr., 'Atlantic City and the Resort Cycle', published in *Annals of Tourism Research* 5 (1978), 238–251. Reprinted by permission, Pergamon Press. Discussion of more recent developments in Atlantic City is adapted from Charles A. Stansfield, Jr. (1998) 'From East Coast Monopoly to Destination Resort: The Geographic Content of Atlantic City's Transformation' in K. Meyer-Arendt and R. Hartmann (eds) *Casino Gambling in America: Origins, Trends, and Impacts*. Elmsford, NY: Cognizant Communications. Reprinted by permission.

Chapter 18

Rejuvenating a Maturing Tourist Destination: The Case of the Gold Coast, Australia

BILL FAULKNER and CARMEN TIDESWELL

Introduction

In an increasingly competitive global environment, strategic planning has become a fundamental element of business survival. The lead times involved in effectively responding to market trends mean that an on-going environmental scanning and strategic assessment process is necessary. This is no less so in the tourism industry than in any other area of economic activity. As Ritchie and Crouch (2000) have observed, while tourism has been growing over the last 50 years, it has been relatively easy for most tourist destinations to maintain a healthy rate of growth despite declining market shares. They add, however, that this is changing as growth in the total market size is slowing down and more destinations are emerging to compete within this market. Competitiveness in this setting requires the establishment of a more strategic focus at both the individual enterprise level and for the destination as a whole. Indeed, planning at these two levels needs to be an integrated process. The tourism product in any setting is a composite of services and goods, and the quality of the visitor's experience depends, to some degree, upon the extent to which the range of providers involved coordinate their efforts and have a common sense of purpose. A 'whole of destination' approach is therefore required in the development of the strategic focus and it has been the recognition of this imperative that has underpinned the creation of tourist destination marketing organisations.

In assessing the competitive position of a tourist destination and extrapolating this assessment to the consideration of future directions of development and the strategic measures necessary to ensure competitiveness within the emerging environment, consideration needs to be given to how the destination has evolved. An understanding of the sequence of events or phases that have marked the history of the destination can assist in bringing its inherent potential and the impediments to achieving this into sharper focus. Also, it enables comparisons with general patterns of destination development as an aid to understanding the dynamics of destination development and predicting what might happen in the future. In this latter regard, in particular, Butler's (1980) Tourist Area Life Cycle (TALC) has proven to be a useful organising framework for interpreting the stage of development of a destination and canvassing scenarios regarding its potential future.

This paper looks at the specific case of Australia's Gold Coast as an example of a maturing and potentially stagnating destination to illustrate the methods being developed in that context to avert stagnation. These methods are discussed in the context of the Gold Coast Visioning (GCV) project, the overall aim of which was to construct a vision for the future of Gold Coast tourism. More specifically, the objectives of this project were:

- To provide a systematic and comprehensive overview of the current status of Gold Coast tourism, covering such considerations as market position, competitiveness and a variety of tourism impacts.
- To develop scenarios for future global, national and local socio-economic, technological and environmental conditions and assess the implications of these trends at the Gold Coast destination level.
- To combine insights from the above with the principles of sustainable tourism development to produce a shared vision for the Gold Coast's tourism future.
- To utilise the shared vision as a framework for generating a set of issues, core values and principles for evaluating future development options.
- To arrive at a consensus on preferred tourism development options consistent with the vision and the actions/approaches necessary for this to become a reality.

Given that the GCV project was essentially concerned with establishing directions for tourism development in the longer term, the principles of sustainable tourism development were adopted as a fundamental philosophical foundation for the planning process. That is, only those options for the Gold Coast's tourism future that satisfy the needs of residents and visitors alike, preserve the cultural and natural assets of the region, and are economically viable were considered (Bramwell & Lane, 1993; Twining-Ward, 1999). There are two basic implications of this caveat, which are reflected in the approach described below. Firstly, the achievement of sustainable tourism objectives hinged on the adoption of a participatory model (Murphy, 1985), involving the meaningful engagement of the community, along with industry stakeholders and relevant government agencies. Secondly, the 'whole of destination' approach referred to earlier was necessary, encompassing the integration of tourism with other sectors of the economy along with an understanding of the inter-relationships and synergies between sociocultural and environmental dimensions. A shift from a 'destination marketing' to a 'destination management' approach was therefore advocated (see Cooper, other volume, editor's comment).

The paper begins with an overview of the status of the Gold Coast as a tourist destination, with particular reference to the indicators of impending stagnation. Background on the methodological foundations of the GCV project is then provided, with specific attention being given. Finally, the translation of these principles into the approach to rejuvenating the Gold Coast is described.

The Gold Coast at a Turning Point

The Gold Coast has long been acknowledged as one of Australia's premier tourist destinations (Gold Coast City Council, 2000). In 1999 it was the third most popular tourism region visited by Australia's international visitors, behind the key arrival ports of Sydney and Melbourne (Bureau of Tourism Research, 2000). This position has been established because of a fortunate combination of natural assets and a sequence of visionary entrepreneurs whose initiatives ensured that this destination was always at the cutting edge of many innovations in Australian tourism development (Russell & Faulkner, 1999). This history is reflected in the destination's international market performance in particular, as indicated in Figure 18.1, which reveals strong growth in the number of international visitors to the Gold Coast from the mid-1980s, when Australia's appeal as an international destination first began to gain momentum (Faulkner, 1990), through to the late 1990s. The profile also reveals a strong resemblance to Butler's scenario, to the extent that the rate of growth is declining in later years and, indeed, suggests that the Gold Coast had already entered the stagnation stage. The dramatic

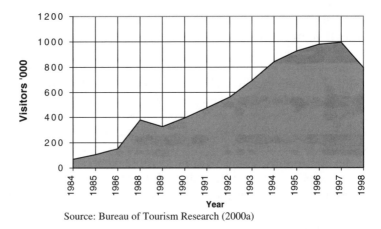

Source: Bureau of Tourism Research (2000a)

Figure 18.1 Trends in international visitor numbers to the Gold Coast

decline in international visitors in the late 1990s, however, is a reflection of the impact of the Asian financial shock, rather than a long-term trend that might suggest the destination is already in decline. While this market has recovered more recently, the dramatic impact of this event highlights the destination's vulnerability arising from its heavy dependence on a narrow band of the market. As illustrated in Figure 18.2, the Gold Coast's performance in the domestic market had been somewhat erratic and less conclusive in terms of any interpretations regarding the Butler model.

While trends in visitor numbers have been the most commonly used indicator of the stage reached in a destination's evolution, a number of authors have identified a more comprehensive range of indicators of stagnation (Butler, 1980; Cooper, 1990; Haywood, 1986; Morgan, 1991). These are outlined in Table 18.1. Preliminary analysis of the Gold Coast's position with respect to some of the indicators contained in Table 18.1 is useful for the purposes of highlighting the rationale underpinning the objectives of the GCV Project.

An examination of data from the Australian International Visitors' Survey (IVS) and the Domestic Tourism Monitor (DTM) reveals a consistent downward trend in the duration of stay of both international and domestic visitors to the Gold Coast over the last decade – from 7 to 4.5 days in the former and from 5.5 to 4.5 in the latter (Bureau of Tourism Research, 2000a,b). The IVS also reveals an increased emphasis on 'organised mass tourism' within the international market, with the proportion of visitors on package, all-inclusive tours increasing from 48 to 75% over the last decade. The plateauing of the international visitor

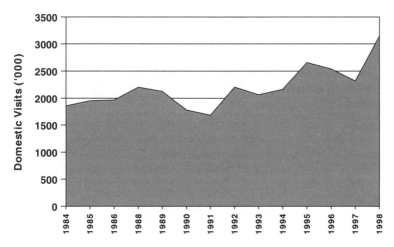

Figure 18.2 Trends in domestic visitor numbers to the Gold Coast. *Source*: Bureau of Tourism Research (2000b)

Table 18.1 Indicators of stagnation and their potential relevance to the Gold Coast

Area of destination performance	Indicators
1. Changing markets	• Growth in low-status, low-spend visitors and day visitors. • Overdependence on long-haul market, and lack of penetration of short-stay market. • **Emphasis on high-volume, low-yield inclusive tour market.** • **A decline in visitors length of stay.** • **Type of tourists increasingly organised mass tourists.** • A declining proportion of first-time visitors, as opposed to repeat visitors. • **Limited or declining appeal to overseas visitors.** • Highly seasonal.
2. Emerging newer destinations	• Competition from emerging newer destinations. • The destination is well known, but no longer fashionable.
3. Infrastructure	• Outdated, poorly maintained accommodation and amenities. • Older properties are changing hands and newer properties, if they are being built are on the periphery of the original tourist areas. • **Market perceptions of the destination becoming overcommercialised, crowded and 'tacky'.** • **Tourism industry over capacity.** • **Diversification into conventions and conferences to maintain numbers.** • **Large number of man-made attractions, which start to outnumber the more natural attractions that made the place popular in the first place.**
4. Business performance	• **Declining profits of major tourism businesses.** • Lack of confidence in the tourism business community. • A decline in the elasticity of advertising (lower return in terms of increased visitors per advertising dollar investment) and an increase in process elasticity. • Lack of professional, experienced staff.

Table 18.1 (*Continued*)	
Area of destination performance	*Indicators*
5. Social and environmental carrying capacities	• Visitor levels approaching or exceeding social and environmental carrying capacities. • Local opposition to tourism as the resort's residential role increases;
6. Institutional environment	• Local government reorganisation (amalgamation) diluting the political power of resorts in larger authorities. • Demands for increased operational efficiency and entrepreneurial activity in local government. • Short-term planning horizons in local government owing to financial restrictions and a low priority given to strategic thinking. • Shortage of research data.

Indicators in bold apply to the Gold Coast on the basis of existing data (based on Butler, 1980; Cooper, 1990; Haywood, 1986; Morgan, 1991; Russell & Faulkner, 1999)

numbers shown in Figure 18.1 suggests that the destination was losing some of its appeal in the international market, while the shift-share analysis contained in the Vision Project's Market Analysis Report (Faulkner & Tideswell, 2002) indicated that newer destinations, such as Tropical North Queensland, had eroded the Gold Coast's market share in both the international and domestic markets. It appeared possible that the destination had become 'well known, but no longer fashionable'. Furthermore, even though there had been no marked or consistent decline in hotel occupancy rates, it is arguable that this is only so because of aggressive price cutting in room rates, which has produced a persistent profitless volume problem. The high volume/low yield syndrome is also a reflection of the heavy reliance on the inclusive tour market and the tight margins associated with this market. Finally, while it cannot be claimed that the Gold Coast's tourism infrastructure is aging and in need of refurbishment generally, the Visioning Project's Infrastructure Audit study indicated there were pockets of decay that presented a real prospect of an 'infrastructure time-bomb' (Moore, 2002). The symptoms of stagnation that appear to apply to the Gold Coast have been highlighted in bold in Table 18.1.

The destination's heavy reliance on built attractions (theme parks) and the increasing emphasis on the convention sector that will follow the completion of the convention centre which was under construction in 2002/03 could be cited as symptoms of stagnation according to the literature. However, it might be equally argued that such developments are manifestations of rejuvenation strategies.

On the basis of this overview of the current status of the destination, it is reasonable to conclude at least that the Gold Coast is a mature destination showing some early signs of stagnation. Given this, it is clear that a fundamental shift in the approach to destination planning and management is necessary if the region is to rejuvenate and remain competitive in the longer term. In short, a reorientation from destination marketing to a more encompassing destination management approach was necessary. One of the Gold Coast's major competitors (at least, in the Japanese market) had recognised this and adjusted its approach to tourism development and marketing accordingly, as the following excerpt from an Hawaii Tourism Authority (1999: 9) report reveals.

> Destination tourism management is increasingly becoming more sophisticated worldwide. The success of many tourism destinations has been driven by an integrated tourism management structure, including effective integration of tourism policy, long-term planning, product development and marketing. This successful tourism management approach has also led to strong and mutually supportive private/public sector partnerships that have been driven by a common tourism strategy and policy.

Apart from the tourism development and marketing considerations emphasised above, it is also arguable that the challenge confronting the region was heightened by the need to reconcile the demands of tourism with those of urban growth currently being experienced and likely to continue in the future. With a population of over 400,000 residents, the Gold Coast has been one of the fastest growing urban areas in Australia over the last 10 years. The same assets of the area that make it as a pleasant place to visit also make it an attractive lifestyle choice for new residents and the quality of life of these residents in the future will depend to a large extent on how effectively the potentially competing demands of tourism and urban growth are managed.

Steps Towards a Rejuvenation Strategy: Methodological Issues

Any meaningful strategic assessment of a destination's tourism development future must involve at least the basic ingredients of the traditional strategic planning approach recognised in the literature (Getz, 1986; Gunn, 1988; Heath & Wall, 1992; Inskeep, 1991). It is envisaged that refinements of the strategic planning model are applicable to maturing destinations in general. Each of the key refinements considered in the

GCV Program are now discussed in turn and elaborated on in relation to the TALC Model.

The sustainable tourism development framework

Since sustainable tourism development principles were formally recognised as a goal for modern tourism development, initially in the Manila Declaration (WTO, 1980) and later in the Hague Declaration (WTO, 1989), this set of guidelines has become, in principle at least, the universally accepted basis for destination management and planning.

The emerging sustainable tourism development philosophy of the 1990s can be viewed as an extension of a broader realisation that a preoccupation with economic growth without due regard to its social and environmental consequences is self-defeating in the longer term. Within this perspective, tourism can be construed as essentially a resource-based industry, where the integrity and continuity of the tourism product in a region is inextricably linked with the preservation of its natural, social and cultural assets (Murphy, 1985).

The impediments to the implementation of sustainable tourism development principles go beyond simply a question of awareness levels and intentions among decision makers at the destination level. Noting the tendency for socioculturally and environmentally pristine locations to be degraded once they become too popular as mature tourist destinations, Twining-Ward (1999: 187) asks 'why is it that despite knowledge of the risks, as well as increased understanding of conservation issues, destinations continue to make the same mistakes?' She offered three basic reasons:

- Ecologically and culturally sensitive areas that are most vulnerable to deterioration are also the most attractive to tourists.
- Many of the resources that are so important for the tourism product are 'common pool' resources which the private sector taps free of charge and over which no single company or authority has responsibility for management. They therefore suffer from the 'tragedy of the commons' syndrome, with over-use and a lack of investment in management ultimately degrading the resource (Healy, 1994).
- A reluctance on the part of government to regulate economic activity and thus control levels of activity within sustainable limits.

Earlier interpretations of sustainable tourism development have been criticised on the basis of their focus on ecological sustainability, at the expense of sociocultural and economic, and for the fixation of alternative tourism as the route to sustainability (Farrell, 1999; Twining-Ward, 1999). Farrell (1999) has noted how the sustainable development agenda was captured by the environmental movement and how this has distorted policy and planning practice in a manner that tends to overlook the social and economic dimensions of the 'three dimensional sustainability trinity'. He referred to this trend as a form of 'environmental funda-mentalism', which produced a tendency for those responsible for this agenda to resist change of all kinds irrespective of the bigger picture issues re longer-term sustainability. This agenda also encouraged a belief that only alternative forms of tourism (Krippendorf, 1987) (i.e. alter-natives to organised mass tourism) were consistent with sustainable tourism objectives. This assumption has since been challenged by many authors, who have pointed out that alternative forms of tourism can have an equally devastating effect, especially where this involves the disper-sion of tourists to environmentally or culturally fragile areas (Butler, 1990, 1992; Cater, 1993; Javiluoma, 1992; Wheeller, 1993; Zurick, 1992). Alternatively, if managed properly, mass tourism can be instrumental in controlling tourist movements more effectively, thus enabling them to be contained within 'site hardened' areas where their impacts can be managed.

Farrell (1999: 91) advocated an interdisciplinary and more encom-passing approach to sustainable tourism development, involving 'a commitment to provide healthy long-term tourism thoroughly integrated with other elements of the economy, and with the environment and society in such a manner that a policy change in one does not unduly interfere with the optimal functioning of any of the others.' Drawing on this and other insights referred to above for the purposes of the Gold Coast strategy, the objectives of sustainable tourism development are summarised in Table 18.2.

There are several general implications raised by Ritchie (1999) that had a particular bearing on the proposed approach to the GCV Program. Firstly, the need for 'long term planning horizons' and an 'integrated

Table 18.2 Sustainable tourism objectives for the Gold Coast

• To enhance visitor satisfaction and the competitiveness of the destination within the tourist market;
• To improved profitability and the return on investment of the industry;
• To maximise economic benefits to the region;
• To protect and enhance natural environmental assets;
• To provide a foundation for enhancing the host community's quality of life and life opportunities;
• To ensure that development is consistent with the local community's sociocultural values.

Source: Faulkner, 2002

cumulative perspective' highlight the need for a shift from the destination marketing orientation. Secondly, Ritchie (1999) refers to the need for the meaningful involvement of the community, with industry stakeholders, in the development of a consensus on the directions of future development and the actions necessary for the preferred outcomes to be realised. This consensus might be expressed through 'the sharing of a common destination vision'.

Shifting from a destination marketing to a destination management perspective

As emphasised by Ritchie's (1999) initial two points, one of the more obvious implications of the sustainable tourism development agenda is the need for a more comprehensive, integrated and holistic approach that goes beyond the traditional focus on destination marketing to take into account a broader range of environmental, social and economic issues. The fact that the necessity of such an approach is beginning to be recognised by major tourism destinations has been referred to earlier in the reference to the Hawaii Tourism Authority's (1999) latest tourism plan.

The failure of more traditional tourism development plans, with their 'top-down', market-oriented approach, has been observed in several settings (e.g. Alipour, 1996; Choy, 1991; King et al., 2000). Choy (1991: 329) has suggested that, given that 'tourism plans have little probability of influencing market forces to achieve economic success, government planning efforts might be better spent on resolving issues involving...market failure, leaving the private sector to assume the planning and financial risk of tourism projects.' Areas of market failure he referred to include: public interest in products and services which are consumed collectively (parks, beaches, historic sites); external effects (positive and negative) that affect people not directly involved in tourism activity (e.g. construction of a resort may restrict locals' access to the beach); and costs and benefits not reflected in market prices (value of open space, costs of social impacts, benefits from environmental preservation). However, while there are obvious differences in the focus of public and private sector interest, the demarcation of their involvement in this way loses sight of the inter-relationships and synergies that need to be developed. A demarcated, as opposed to a truly integrated, approach will produce the sort of 'dysfunctionality' in tourism plans observed by Butler (1991). Thus, for instance, it might produce a conflict between policy mechanisms aimed at limiting environmental impacts by minimising tourist numbers, at one level, and elements of policy at a higher level that encourage increases in visitor numbers in order to improve economic benefits.

An approach that gives due consideration to the various dimensions of the sustainability agenda, while at the same time avoiding the dysfunctionality trap, hinges on a process involving participation by a broad range of stakeholders within a framework that fosters the development of a consensus on preferred directions of future development and the building of collaborative relationships. The key issue related to the desire to rejuvenate a destination following maturity is that continuing growth should not be attempted by merely chasing larger numbers of tourists through increased marketing initiatives, but rather it should be pursued through better management of the industry as a whole.

Community participation and the building of collaborative relationships

One of the seminal works on community participation in tourism development planning is Murphy's (1985) book, *Tourism: A Community Approach*. Murphy proposed an ecological/systems-based model for community involvement in tourism planning and in the process anticipated many of the elements of sustainable tourism development principles described above. In particular, he argued that:

> Residents must put up with the physical development, but have little say so in the decision-making process that will inevitably affect their community and way of life. Development and planning in isolation from the community at large cannot continue if the industry is to develop in harmony with the capacity and aspirations of destination areas. To become self renewable resource industry and agent of hospitality will require more citizen participation in the development, or non-development, of a destination. (Murphy, 1985: 163)

The above rationale for community involvement is largely based on ethical considerations, in the sense that it emphasises the resident's stake in the process in terms of the potential impacts of tourism on their way of life. Emphasis is therefore placed on the need to ensure that changes associated with tourism are both within the bounds of their adaptive capabilities and consistent with the retention or enhancement of their quality of life. There is, however, another perspective, which has a more pragmatic orientation. Kotler and Armstrong's (1984) societal marketing concept has been invoked to highlight that members of the host population are simultaneously consumers of product and beneficiaries or victims of the effects of production (King *et al.*, 2000; Mill, 1996). Thus, if the industry can be construed as using the community itself as part of the product it sells to the market, then a planning and management regime that becomes insensitive to community interests will undermine the quality of the product, to the extent that this will precipitate a community backlash. From the perspective of the TALC model, a destination which has reached maturity and may be experiencing some of the traditional tensions between local residents and supporters of further tourism development cannot hope to resolve these issues and move forward towards rejuvenation without the support and involvement of community members.

While the rationale for a community-based approach to tourism planning is compelling, how extensively and effectively this approach has been adopted is another question. As Joppe (1996) has observed, despite the rhetoric about community participation in tourism planning, most instances of this are driven by government (and business) agendas, rather than community interests. Part of the problem arises from the difficulty of defining the community and assumptions made about the homogeneity of interests within it. While to some the notion of community implies a coherent entity with a shared identity and common sense of purpose, in reality communities generally consist of an agglomeration of special interest groups who are often antagonistic towards each other and competing for scarce resources or power (Manning, 1999). Thus, for example, it is not uncommon for residents to favour options that will benefit them personally in some manner (e.g. product based on parks, outdoor recreation, restaurants) regardless of market conditions or the potential of the area (Andereck & Vogt, 2000). In such circumstances, the task of building a consensus or shared vision on the future of tourism in the destination is a major challenge that is compounded by the need to reconcile a diversity of views and interests.

The need for such an approach is illustrated by Backman *et al.*'s (2001) reference to how planning in the ecotourism context involves overlapping agendas of various stakeholders. The distinction between public and private sector involvement has therefore become blurred and, as observed by Backman *et al.* (2001: 454), this provides the opportunity for previously unrecognised synergies to be developed:

> Whether the motivation is economic or stewardship, organisational missions and strategies are beginning to coalesce around the idea of ecotourism, capitalising on public interest in the environment. Therefore the need for collaboration, cooperation and synergy among this multitude is as obvious as it will be challenging. In the past, economics have often run counter to protection and preservation interests. But ecotourism, perhaps for the first time, provides a feasible mechanism to align economic incentives with stewardship of the environment.

The specifics of the above argument apply to the Gold Coast situation to the extent that the natural environment is an integral part of this destination's tourism product. There are a range of potential synergies between the tourism sector and various avenues of economic development recognised in the Gold Coast's economic development strategy. Significantly, many of these synergies hinge on the potential of tourism development to enhance the lifestyle of residents.

Building a shared vision

The articulation of a shared vision among stakeholders was envisaged as being the initial and most critical step in the consultative process that would lead to the development of the Gold Coast's tourism strategy. In its simplest terms, a vision can be construed as a shared view on a preferred future. Alternatively, as described by Senge *et al.* (1994: 302), a vision can be construed as '...sense of shared purpose and destiny...', '...a picture of the future we want to create...that gives shape and direction to the organisation's future'.

The visioning exercise was critical in two respects. Firstly, a well designed visioning exercise had the potential to provide a 'circuit-breaker' and a 'call to action', to the extent that it was instrumental in galvanizing opinion on the need for a fundamentally different approach from that which had prevailed in the past to allow rejuvenation to occur.

Secondly, a well articulated vision that has been constructed in a manner that ensures it represents a consensus among primary stake-holders provides a focus for the strategic planning process and a vehicle for mobilising cooperative action. Here, the word 'cooperative' is used very deliberately as an alternative to 'coordinated' action. The former implies a group of equal stakeholders working together towards the same end, while the latter implies one party exerting control over others to ensure that all their activities contribute to a mutually agreed outcome. The distinction is subtle and, in reality, one cannot be achieved without the other. However, the emphasis on the equality of stakeholders in the achievement of mutually agreed outcome and the reciprocity implied by the word 'cooperation' makes this a more meaningful concept in this context. The nexus between the visioning process and action is fundamental, as implied in the following popular quote from Joel Barker (1992).

> A vision without action is merely dream. Action without vision just passes the time. Vision with action can change the world.

A vision provides a framework for choosing appropriate responses and for cooperative action. External events (including changes in government policy agendas at all levels, international developments and random disasters) have the potential to profoundly affect the competitiveness of the Gold Coast as a tourism destination, and thus the direction of tourism development. While we have little control over these events, a long-term shared perspective (a vision) is necessary for not only determining how we respond, but also for ensuring that we respond in a coordinated and effective way. Without a vision, we will become locked into the past. That is, an incremental approach, where the focus is on responding to immediate contingencies in a piecemeal fashion, leads us to a position where the options available for us to cope with longer-term eventualities are progressively reduced.

Like most elements of strategic analysis and planning, it might be said that the route taken in constructing a vision is as important as the destination. The meaningful engagement of the community, with industry stakeholders and relevant public sector agencies, in the development of a consensus on the directions of future development and the actions necessary for the preferred outcomes to be realised is an essential ingredient in the visioning process. Such engagement of stakeholders is essential if the vision that eventuates is to provide an accurate reflection of a truly shared position of all concerned and if it is to provide a relatively stable reference point for future action. The importance of this has been emphasised by Senge *et al.* (1994: 313):

> A vision is not really shared unless it has staying power and evolving life force that lasts for years, propelling people through a continuous cycle of action, learning and reflection.

The following comment by Mintzberg (2000: 209–210) provides a useful summary of the main point regarding the role of a vision and, in particular, it alludes to linkages with the learning organisation concept, which is explored further below:

> The visionary approach is a more flexible way to deal with an uncertain world. Vision sets the broad outlines of a strategy, while leaving the specific details to be worked out. In other words, the broad perspective may be deliberate but the specific position can emerge. So when the unexpected happens, assuming the vision is sufficiently robust, the organization can adapt – it learns. Certain change is thus easily accommodated. Of course, when even vision cannot cope, then the organization may have to revert to a pure learning approach – to experiment in the hope of capturing some basic message and converging behaviors on them.

Learning organisations and organisational change

The notion of learning organisations has been developed as a tool for assisting commercial organisations to adjust to change primarily in the North American context (Senge *et al.*, 1994). In one sense, a tourist destination represents a more complex situation, at least to the degree that it involves an amalgam of separate public and private sector organisations, along with a loose array of community-based interests and alliances, all pursuing separate agendas that both overlap and conflict with each other to varying degrees. However, as Senge *et al.* observe, these characteristics are not uncommon within large corporations and the art of developing a learning organisation approach involves reconciling the tensions, finding common ground for collective action and channelling rivalries into creative energy that benefits the organisation as a whole. It follows that elements of the learning organisation philosophy may be applicable to the development of a strategic approach to destination management.

As defined by Senge *et al.* (1994: 4), a learning organisation is one that is '...able to deal with the problems and opportunities of today, and invest in its capacity to embrace tomorrow, because its members are continually focused on enhancing and expanding their collective awareness and capabilities.' It would become integral to the planning and management process, rather than, as is too often the case, a marginal activity restricted to a few specialist researchers.

The introduction of the learning organisation approach to the Gold Coast setting required a fundamental shift in mindsets and organisational approaches in that setting. The Gold Coast had grown and flourished in a relatively benign regulatory regime, which had fostered a combative private enterprise mentality driven by market forces and a fiercely competitive business culture. Public sector engagement in aspects of tourism development had been minimal and regarded with suspicion by the business community. One of the consequences of this had been a policy and planning void, whereby the lack of a tourism agenda within the state and local government bureaucratic structures had meant that the tourism implications of various policy and infrastructure initiatives have not been adequately addressed. Despite this, the laissez-faire environment provided a fertile setting for a range of flamboyant entrepreneurs to introduce innovations that have rejuvenated the destination at various points in its history (Russell & Faulkner, 1999). However, the scale and complexity of tourism development in the region had reached a point where it was increasingly difficult for the actions of individual entrepreneurs to initiate major shifts in the fortunes of the destination as a whole. A more collaborative and cooperative approach, involving the private, public sector agencies and other stakeholder groups within the community, was necessary if the challenges of the future were to be effectively addressed. This implies that the Gold Coast's problem was essentially one of organisational change.

Like organisations in general, the Gold Coast can be envisaged as having evolved towards a point where internal rigidities associated with hierarchical structures, specialisations and demarcations have impeded internal communication, and the inertia of established values and approaches threaten to constrain responsiveness to changing conditions (Hurst, 1995). This makes the destination both less adaptive and more prone to disaster. In an observation that perhaps encapsulates the 'catch-22' predicament of many maturing destinations, Hurst (1995: 139) suggested that many organisations were caught by the 'renewal process paradox', whereby 'the change process cannot begin until the failure of the old order is manifest, but the process is likely to be more successful if it gets underway before too much damage is done.' Given the symptoms of stagnation evident in the Gold Coast case, as demonstrated in the analysis in earlier sections of this paper, it could be argued that 'the failure of the older order' was clearly manifest. While it may be overstating the case to suggest that too much damage has already been done to make the situation retrievable, it was certainly evident that any delay in the reassessment of future directions and approaches, such as that proposed in the GCV process, would make the eventual demise of the destination inevitable.

Scenarios and the art of strategic conversion

Visions can be construed as 'complexity reducers', which provide a common frame of reference for organising information. They provide the signpost for signals for navigating against a noisy background. Scenarios, on the other hand, are 'shared and agreed upon mental models of the external world...created as internally consistent and challenging descriptions of possible futures...' (van der Heijden, 1997: 5). They complement the visioning process through their value as a basis for exploring possible futures and the opportunity they provide for stakeholders to see the world through different lenses. Scenario-generating exercises help participants to see things they may not have otherwise been disposed to look for, thus dislodging them from established mindsets.

Scenario planning is distinct from the more traditional approaches to strategic planning by virtue of its more specific focus on ambiguity and uncertainty in the strategic issues being examined. The affinities of this approach to the learning organisation perspective are explicit in the following observation:

> The most fundamental aspect of introducing uncertainty into the strategic equation is that it turns planning for the future from a once-off episodic activity into an ongoing learning proposition. In a situation of uncertainty planning becomes learning and never stops. (van der Heijden, 1997: 7)

Recognising that we operate within a turbulent environment which makes our efforts to predict the future with any degree of certainty a futile endeavour, scenario planning instead aims to identify and consider multiple, equally plausible futures. Scenarios are helpful in assisting organisations to cope with future events in three ways. Firstly, they help organisations to understand the environment, and allow many decisions to be put into perspective through them being seen not so much as isolated events, but as part of a process of 'swings and roundabouts'. Secondly, they highlight the inherent uncertainty of the environment and, in the process, foster an appreciation of exposure to 'accidents' and undue risk. Finally, they help organisations 'to become more adaptable by expanding their mental models and thereby enhancing the perceptual capabilities needed to recognize unexpected events' (van der Heijden, 1997: 86).

To add one final clarification of the nature of scenarios, it is useful to consider the distinctions between scenarios and forecasting. Forecasting assumes that the future can be accurately predicted and is usually carried out be 'experts' who are detached from decision makers, whereas scenario planning is process oriented and accepts that uncertainties invariably restrict the extent to which the future can be predicted. But by involving decision-makers in the process, rather than the latter abdicating responsibility to detached experts, the planning process is more attuned to the risks and variety of possibilities involved. In short, scenario planning is more consistent with the type of informed decision-making identified with learning organisations.

The use of scenarios was incorporated into the GCV project to provide a set of 'what if' situations for stakeholder groups to consider in relation to their potential impact on the future movement of the region along the destination life cycle mode.

The Gold Coast Visioning (GCV) Project Approach

In order to ensure that the stagnation stage of the TALC did not become engrained in the Gold Coast region, the approach adopted in the GCV project involved a combination of the methods employed in traditional strategic planning with refinements involving the concepts of visioning, organisational learning and scenario-based strategic conversion. The approach adopted included the following components.

- An 'audit' process involving an integrated series of research projects aimed at overviewing the current status of Gold Coast tourism in terms of social, economic (including tourism marketing) and environmental considerations has been carried out as 'front-end' inputs to the process.

- A survey of tourism industry stakeholders (Tourism Industry Barometer) was conducted to provide an indication of industry perceptions on the status of tourism development on the Gold Coast, individual visions of the future and preferred options for tourism development.
- A one-day futures workshop, involving representatives of key stakeholder groups, was planned with the aim of producing a consensus on likely future scenarios affecting the Gold Coast.
- A two-day workshop aimed at constructing the vision and strategy for the Gold Coast's tourism future was to be convened.

The above activities were carried out in five stages as identified in Figure 18.3. As the figure suggests, the approach involved a systematic examination of the Gold Coast situation at the time (Destination Audit); an analysis of the implications of this audit and the future prospects for tourism on the Gold Coast (Destination Barometer and Megatrends Analysis) and, finally, it culminated in the development of a shared vision for the future via the 'Visioning Workshop'. The last four of these steps are described in more detail in Table 18.3.

Outcomes

The Visioning Program produced a number of significant outcomes, known as the 'Visioning Statement' that linked the past, present and future position of the Gold Coast tourism industry. The generic outcomes of the process are highlighted in Table 18.4. Beginning with a historical overview of what had occurred within the region's tourism environment to date, the process was concluded with the formulation of an ultimate 'vision' of how the industry should progress in the future in order to ensure not only that rejuvenation of the destination continues, but also that the needs of both residents and tourists alike are managed in an optimal manner.

In terms of specific outcomes of the GCV Project, a series of reports were produced and disseminated to key stakeholders involved in the industry for consideration. A summary of the key issues raised in these documents is contained in Table 18.5.

Related Initiatives

The outcomes of two other initiatives that had a bearing on the examination of strategic directions for the Gold Coast tourism industry were also taken into account in the approach outlined above. These initiatives included the 1999 Edward de Bono Workshop organised by the Property Council of Australia's Gold Coast Chapter (PCAGC) and

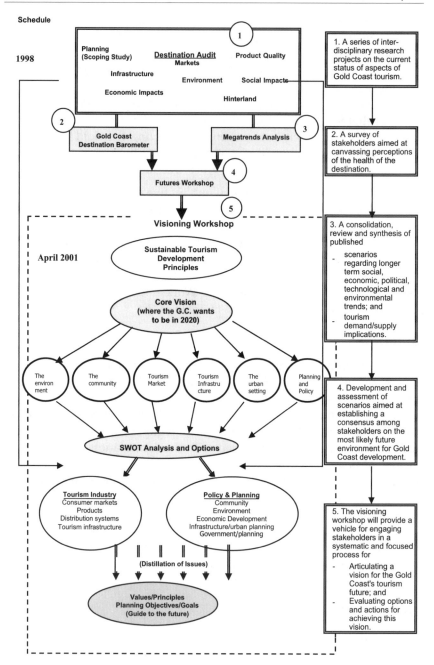

Figure 18.3 The Gold Coast Visioning approach
Source: Faulkner, 2002

Table 18.3 Method of the GCV Process

Phase	Method	Objectives/desired outcomes
1. Gold Coast Destination Barometer	Survey of key stakeholders aimed at gauging perceptions of the health of the destination in terms of: • Image and positioning. • Competitiveness. • Market trends. • Yields and profitability. • Aging and condition of infrastructure. • Community reactions.	• To encourage participants to reflect on the health of the destination and begin focusing on the issues that were eventually addressed in the workshops. • To highlight indicators of the Gold Coast's stagnation and thus reinforce the need for challenges confronting the destination to be addressed.
2. Mega-trends Analysis	Consolidation, review and synthesis of: • Scenarios regarding longer-term social, economic, political, technological and environmental trends; and • tourism demand and supply-side implications of these trends.	• To ensure that the development of scenarios and consideration of their tourism implications in the futures workshop were informed by analyses carried out elsewhere.
3. Futures Workshop	A one- or two-day workshop involving panel discussions on long-term trends in each dimension followed by break out groups aimed at constructing most likely scenarios and considering their tourism demand and supply side implications. Key issues covered include: a. Panel discussion on socioeconomic and political/policy (global and domestic) scenarios. b. Panel discussion on technological,	• Long-term scenarios regarding social, economic, political, technological and environmental trends at the macro level; • The general tourism implications of these trends. • A consensus on the most likely general, global and domestic scenarios on socioeconomic, technological, environmental and political/policy trends in 2020 and their tourism implications.

Table 18.3 (*Continued*)		
Phase	*Method*	*Objectives/desired outcomes*
	environmental and urban/regional planning scenarios, followed by break-out groups and plenary session.	
4. Visioning Workshop	A two-day workshop aimed at construction of a vision for Gold Coast tourism in 2020. Key components of the workshop included: • A reiteration of the need for, and objectives of, the visioning process, with reference to the linkages between this and the previous workshop. • A guide to sustainable tourism development principles in the future; • Where do we want to be in 2020? • Future Scenarios Revisited. A briefing on the outcomes of the Futures Workshop. • Issues and actions. Key planning, policy and management issues emerging were addressed.	• A shared view among stakeholders on a preferred future for Gold coast tourism. • An appreciation of the importance of the project and an understanding of the approach among participants. • A draft core vision comprising a brief statement encapsulating the essential ingredients of the desired tourism future of the region. • To refocus participants' minds on the likely emerging environment in which the preferred future identified in the vision statement was to be achieved. • A synthesis of threats, challenges and opportunities affecting the achievement of the vision was produced. • A consensus view on key planning, policy and management issues associated with the vision and the actions required to achieve the vision.

Source: Faulkner, 2002

Table 18.4 Indicative format of the GCV Statement

Component	Description
Executive summary	A one-page outline indicating the purpose of the visioning process and summarising key outcomes produced by the process.
Introduction	A concise statement addressing the following points: • The history of the Gold Coast as a growing urban conurbation and tourist destination. • The current status of the Gold Coast as a tourist destination and place to live. • The challenges confronting the destination in terms of the achievement of sustainable tourism development objectives. • Why a vision is necessary. • The nature of, and approach to, constructing a vision. • A 'mud map' indicating the format and contents of the document.
The core vision and elements of the vision	A brief statement encapsulating the essential ingredients of the desired future of the region. This was supplemented by a series of more detailed statements, articulating principles and benchmarks for preferred outcomes in specific dimensions of tourism development: • The environment (ecological impacts). • The community (social impacts). • Tourism markets and visitor experiences (tourism demand). • The tourism sector (supply side development). • The urban environment (infrastructure and urban planning). • Governance and urban planning/policy frameworks.
Future scenarios and their implications for the Gold Coast	A summary of outcomes of the futures and SWOT analysis, structured in terms of the dimensions identified above: • Future scenarios. • SWOT analysis. • Core issues vis-à-vis the dimensions of the vision.

Table 18.4 (*Continued*)	
Component	*Description*
Conclusion	The visioning exercise, and the documents that record its outcomes, aims to provide a framework for developing a tourism strategy for the region, rather than being a strategic plan in its own right. This document will therefore fall short of providing explicit guidelines for implementation. Within the conclusion, however, recommendations will be provided on how the visioning process might be carried forward to the development of the strategy.

Source: Faulkner, 2002

the Gold Coast City Council's (GCCC) Draft Economic Development Strategy (2000).

The de Bono Workshop

A workshop organised by the PCAGC in October 1999 engaged Edward de Bono to assist business leaders and other stakeholders to focus on issues associated with setting some strategic directions for the refurbishment and rejuvenation of the Gold Coast. Initially concerned primarily with the Surfers Paradise precinct of the Gold Coast, it was recognised that issues affecting the rejuvenation of Surfers Paradise could not be examined in isolation from the rest of the Gold Coast. A 'whole of Gold Coast' approach was therefore advocated, and it was also realised that this implied that a diverse range of stakeholders needed to be engaged in the process (The Property Council of Australia Gold Coast Chapter, 2000).

What was of particular interest to the process of averting the onset of the stagnation stage of the TALC model was the realisation of the need to counteract negative perceptions of the Surfers Paradise precinct through cooperation and education. Here it was recognised that the business community could play a lead role in this by 'adopting a broader all-encompassing view' and not allowing personal agendas to distract them from an approach that leads to benefits for the whole community. The remainder of the recommendations focused on the measures necessary to reinvigorate Surfers Paradise specifically and these generally amounted to the presentation of a case for additional local government support to strengthen the role of the public sector subsidised Surfers Paradise central management association.

Table 18.5 Core issues generated by GCV research projects

Research project	Issues
Issues, policy and Planning Audit (Scoping Study)	• A tourism policy and planning void exists on the Gold Coast (GC): the actions of the various (state and local) government and quasi-government (GC Tourism Bureau) agencies who have a role to play in tourism development are not well coordinated, and the tourism implications of their policy and planning agendas are not taken into account. • The ad hoc, incremental approach to tourism development of the past will not work in the future: the scale and complexity of tourism development in the region means that a more holistic, strategic approach is necessary in the future. • The region suffers from a major image and positioning problem in the domestic market in particular: this problem is compounded by the dominance of Surfers Paradise as a visual icon, and the perception of this precinct as 'glitzy' and deteriorating. • The lack of tourism industry involvement in environmental planning needs to be remedied: the natural assets of the region, encompassing the beaches, waterways and hinterland areas, remain as fundamental ingredients of the area's attractiveness. • A purpose-built convention centre is essential if the GC is to build on it natural advantages as a MICE destination and retain its pre-eminent position.
Market Audit	• While the GC has consistently exceeded national average growth rates in inbound tourist numbers over the last 15–20 years, its performance in the domestic market has been patchy: there have been periods where GC domestic tourism growth has both exceeded and lagged behind national levels. • The strength of the GC in the inbound market has been particularly attributable to its performance in Asian markets: with two-thirds of all international visitors coming from Asian countries, however, the vulnerability of the Gold Coast to potentially crippling impacts of external shocks was highlighted during the Asian financial crisis. • Far North Queensland (FNQ) and Sydney are the main competitors in the inbound market, while Victoria, FNQ and, to a lesser extent, the ACT, have been the main competitors in the domestic market.

Table 18.5 (*Continued*)	
Research project	*Issues*
	• The core attractions of the GC revolve around four elements: beaches/relaxation; theme parks/excitement; nightlife/action; and nature and wildlife. The main market segments associated with these attractions are families, midlife and older couples and younger singles/couples. • The GC has consistently performed well in the young families and younger solos markets, but its younger and older couples markets have stagnated.
Infrastructure Audit	• There is an 'infrastructure time-bomb' on the GC, with there being a number of potential black spots arising from concentrations of high-rise accommodation of similar age: refurbishment or replacement of buildings in these areas will be inhibited by mixed ownership and associated unrealistic expectations regarding capital appreciation. • There is a substantial high-volume, low-yield ('profit-less volume') problem in GC accommodation infrastructure: this has emerged as a consequence of the over-reliance upon inclusive tour markets and the erosion of margins associated with this. • An unresolved question concerns the extent to which a large holiday flat/unit rental sector exacerbates or ameliorates this problem.
Product Quality Audit	• Satisfaction levels among visitors regarding the quality of services and experiences associated with the GC's accommodation, theme parks, restaurants and beaches are generally high. • The main negative perception among visitors concerns value for money from theme parks. • The major danger for the GC regarding service quality is the prospect of high satisfaction levels encouraging complacency: regular monitoring of satisfaction levels is essential so that lapses in the quality of services can be promptly detected and remedied, while the competitiveness of the environment necessitates a more systematic approach to the continuous improvement of services in all areas.

Table 18.5 *(Continued)*	
Research project	*Issues*
Social Impacts Audit (preliminary)	• GC residents are generally positively disposed towards tourism and its impact on the community: tourism is seen to have a positive effect on the economy, job opportunities lifestyle and aspects of amenity, although costs associated with noise and congestion are also recognised. • At the aggregate level, perceptions about the impacts of tourism do not appear to vary among major demographic groups: older residents appear to be no more or less vulnerable to negative impacts of tourism and, indeed, appear to benefit from the same features of the GC that make it an appealing destination for visitors. • Supplementary work needs to be carried out to canvas resident reactions to alternative approaches to tourism development in the future and the impacts of tourism in specific situations, such as in areas where permanent resident and visitor accommodation are integrated.

Source: Faulkner, 2002

Draft Gold Coast 2010: Economic Development Strategy

This document also reinforced the theme that the Gold Coast was at 'the cross-roads', with the vulnerability of the region associated with its dependence on the narrow economic base provided by tourism and construction being emphasised (Gold Coast City Council, 2000).

The strategy document acknowledged the inescapable – that is, whether we like it or not, tourism would have a continuing and significant role in the economy. However, the report appeared to imply this was a liability, rather than a potential strength. That is, the dominance of tourism (and the associated sunbelt migration phenomenon) may provide some resistance to the diversification agenda to the extent, for instance, that this produces employment and demographic patterns that are not consistent with the development of 'clever', 'new-age' industries. Reference was made to the Gold Coast as a city of 'experiences', but it did not give sufficient emphasis to this theme. It is a distinctive feature of the Gold Coast that separates it from a myriad of other regions that are probably putting together similar arguments for the development of a knowledge-based focus for regional development at this time, and would, therefore, serve as a useful platform from which to launch the destination into the rejuvenation phase of the TALC model.

Table 18.6 Tourism synergies associated with key industry strategies identified in the draft economic strategy

Key industry strategy	Tourism synergies
Communication and information	• Lifestyle implications of tourism's enhancement of leisure opportunities have the potential to play a role in locational decisions of IT firms/ entrepreneurs.
Education and training	• Educational tourism: educational services attract international students who, with visiting family members, also become tourists. • Lifestyle factors in student choice: the attractiveness of the Gold Coast as a tourist destination also makes this region an attractive place to live while studying. • Alumni networks: former international students become ambassadors for Gold Coast tourism and the Gold Coast generally upon their return home. • Tourism management and planning research capabilities of the CRC and Griffith University are elements of the 'knowledge industry' development
Environmental	• Adoption of 'Green Globe' as a framework for benchmarking tourism-related environmental management on the Gold Coast, along with the identification of this concept with the CRC for Sustainable Tourism, provides an opportunity for the Gold Coast to promote both its environmental management technical capabilities abroad and its environmental tourism destination assets. • A stringent environmental management regime is essential for protecting environmental assets that are central to the region's sustainability as a tourist destination.
Film and interactive media	• Film and interactive media applications to entertainment technology underpin the continual renewal of theme parks such as Movieworld. • Reinforcement of the leisure theme, which is central to the Gold coast's image as a tourist destination.
Food, beverage and aquaculture	• Restaurants and fine food are essential elements of the range of services that make the Gold Coast an attractive destination. • There are potential synergies between the marketing of the Gold Coast as a tourist destination and the marketing of its food products.

Table 18.6 (*Continued*)

Key industry strategy	Tourism synergies
Health and medical	• There are tourism sector spin-offs from the provision of medical services to international markets (families accompanying patients and patients themselves during recuperation may engage in tourist activities). • For the reasons alluded to in the previous point the Gold Coast's attractiveness as a tourist destination can give its medical providers a competitive edge in international markets.
Marine	• The marine environment constitutes a major tourism asset in the area and potential synergies exist between the marketing of pleasure craft manufactured in the area and the recreational boating opportunities available to tourists. • The proposed cruise shipping terminal would provide access to an additional tourism market.
Urban development	• Urban development capabilities will support the enhancement of existing tourism infrastructure and the construction of new quality infrastructure, such as resorts, marinas, etc.

Source: Faulkner, 2002

There are many synergies between tourism and the key industry strategies identified in the report. Some examples are provided in Table 18.6, which are also useful in analysing the prospect of rejuvenation and growth of the tourism industry in the region.

Conclusion

As with any industry, a tourism destination must keep pace with the growing pressures of increasing competition for the tourists' attention and, as a result, must continually reassess its position and ensure that sufficient change and improvement takes place to maintain its attraction to key markets. It must also maintain a quality of life for its local resident population which is not hindered by further tourism growth. The ultimate challenge, faced by a mature destination such as the Gold Coast, is to avoid becoming too locked into strategies used in the past to develop tourism within the region. Change and new directions are often required to ensure that stagnation does not occur and that the area follows the rejuvenation path of the TALC model.

In the Gold Coast setting, the need for a more focused strategic approach to destination management and planning is accentuated by a history that has been distinctively ad hoc and piecemeal. At the outset of the GCV Program, many of the key indicators suggested the destination may have already entered the stagnation phase. This chapter has provided an example, based on the GCV Program, of how an agreement on a shared vision among stakeholders represents the first step towards developing a strategy for rejuvenating the destination. In this context, the relevant stakeholders were broadly defined to include tourism and other businesses, industry organisations, public sector agencies at the local and state government levels, and representatives of the resident community. Such a broad spectrum of involvement reflects the necessity of a holistic approach, which recognises that social and environmental considerations warrant equal consideration with the economic dimension in the mapping of a course toward a sustainable tourism future.

The difficulties apparent in rejuvenating a mature tourist destination such as the Gold Coast were highlighted through the GCV Project. Growth and continual change to ensure the destination meets the ever-changing needs of both visitors and residents cannot be achieved merely by adding new attractions or increasing marketing exposure for the destination. The GCV Project was founded on the acknowledgement that a shared vision had to be achieved by industry stakeholders including tourism developers, industry managers, government departments involved in the region and local residents of the region. The process of developing the vision was instrumental in developing an informed and considered dialogue among stakeholders, to such an extent that the destination will represent not only a consensus among this group, but also it will reflect a thorough and rigorous analysis of the issues. Such

Table 18.7 Why a vision and a plan are so necessary for Gold Coast tourism

• By creating a more structured, strategically focused and shared framework for individual enterprises and organisations to operate within, we can ensure that decision makers at all levels take longer-term considerations into account in their day-by-day decisions.
• A modest up-front investment in planning avoids the need to think through every crisis situation from scratch. It creates a readiness for the unexpected.
• Appropriate planning facilitates the transition from individual insights to collective/institutional action.
• Well developed planning systems create an institutional learning and memory system.
• Reduce the prospects of repeating past mistakes and/or reinventing the wheel.

Based on van der Heijden, 1997

support and involvement of a wide range of stakeholders is essential to ensuring the path taken to rejuvenation of the destination is not only agreed upon, but is the ultimate vision towards which those involved in the community will work towards achieving.

The Visioning exercise itself was used as a catalyst for bringing about the permanent changes in the structure of the destination planning and management process that were necessary for the Gold Coast to become a 'learning organisation' at the destination level. That is, the visioning project was instrumental in establishing a systematic planning regime that was supported by a strong research base and a rigorous evaluation system. Such a regime will underpin the institutional learning process and memory that is so essential for creative adaptation to the challenges of the future and reducing the prospect of repeating past mistakes or reinventing the wheel (van der Heijden, 1997).

Strategies for rejuvenation of tourism in the Gold Coast region were developed in a strategic and comprehensive manner through the GCV Project. The integration of sustainable tourism principles into the shared vision for the future direction of the industry was the lynchpin to the future success of the region's tourism potential. Rejuvenation of the destination life cycle was the ultimate goal, and, as summarised in Table 18.7, the creation of a suitable industry 'vision' was the key to developing a platform from which this objective can be pursued.

Part 6
Conclusion

RICHARD W. BUTLER

One of the common problems with edited books is that there is often no final chapter that provides a conclusion to the often widely differing contributions from the set of authors. It had been my intention to write such a chapter for this volume to avoid that problem. It is not an easy task, as, having written the links to the sections, it would have been redundant to make similar summarising comments in the conclusions. Given that the focus of this volume is on the application and modification of the TALC as demonstrated in the previous chapters, it would not have been appropriate either to write a general conclusion to the TALC and therein discuss some of its relevance for the future in terms of conceptual development. That is dealt with in the final chapter to the other volume that deals with theories and concepts relating to the TALC, particularly with respect to the nature of future development in tourism and its implications for destinations.

The preceding chapters have provided some excellent examples of the settings in which the TALC has been applied, and some of the ways in which it has been modified to better fit specific destinations and their unique situations. Clearly no destination is exactly the same as another, despite the best efforts of many tour companies, their marketing agencies and developers. Each one represents a unique mix of geography, politics, economics and ethnography at least, along with elements such as individual behaviour and chance. To model the infinite variety of pathways that development can take is unrealistic except at a general level, and that is what the TALC attempted to do. It would be amazing, indeed impossible, to produce a 'one size fits all' practical model, but it may be possible to produce such a conceptual model. Whether the TALC really fits each and every destination to a reasonable and acceptable degree is yet to be determined, and probably never will be. It does remain intuitively appropriate and after the large number of applications discussed earlier in this book in the specific chapters, it still appears to be generally accurate. Refinements which make the fit better in one location may make it worse in another, and whenever trying to fit a line to data, compromise has to be made to obtain the best overall fit. It is clear that more than one cycle may be in operation at any one time in many destinations, as most locations cater to more than one market segment. The TALC is an attempt to model the overall pattern and process of

337

development for destinations and the existence of multiple cycles does not invalidate that. In the future, further application and subsequent modification of the TALC may result in a more accurate and more widely applicable curve, a more precisely defined set of stages and a better explained process of development for destinations. At the end however, they are still products and will have a pattern of development and ultimately decline. The most we can do is intervene and manage appropriately in order to maximise the successful period of operation for residents and visitors.

In looking for a chapter, therefore, to close this volume, the solution emerged fortuitously. Those who have read his works, and particularly those who have heard Brian Wheeller present his views on tourism development and on rock and roll in person, will realise that it is next to impossible to follow him at a podium or in a volume (and to follow Elvis Presley is something which no-one has dared try to do since 1954). In his chapter Wheeller takes the unlikely pairing of Elvis Presley and sustainable tourism and manages to make sense of their seemingly impossible relationship in the context of the TALC. He argues effectively that what may seem like deterioration and reduced appeal to one 'market' is not always that to all markets. Perhaps more importantly, he links spatial location and stage of development in the context of ecolodges that are likened to the King of Rock and Roll. He also focuses, unlike most of the other authors, on the analogy of the TALC to the population life cycle of wildlife, again, with comparisons to Presley. Apart from containing many images that are poignant and relevant to those of us who grew up with real rock and roll, it is both a perceptive and thought-provoking chapter with which to end this volume.

Chapter 19

The King is Dead. Long Live the Product: Elvis, Authenticity, Sustainability and the Product Life Cycle

BRIAN WHEELLER

Introduction

In the welter of references to, and articles on, Butler's Tourist Area Life Cycle model (TALC) there has, to my knowledge at least, been no mention of Elvis Presley. So far.

Clearly, there are a number of ways Elvis, and the Elvis phenomenon, can be seen as a part of tourism and the tourist industry – manifesting, most obviously, as a generator of tourism trips. Evidenced in the pilgrimages to Graceland, to locations featured in his dubious backlog of films, even to Prestwick Airport in West Scotland, site of Elvis's only – recent sightings apart – visit to the UK, there can be no doubt that Elvis is big tourism business. Appearing regularly in the travel pages of contemporary newspapers and magazines, he remains a huge attraction – Graceland is second only to the White House for tourist visits to US Historic Places (Davis, 1997).

But there are other, somewhat more tenuous, links between Elvis and tourism. It is these that are, perhaps ambitiously, suggested and explored in this chapter. Just how he fits in with the TALC model might at first sight seem tangential – and with ecolodges, obtuse. And yet 'sustainable' tourism developments in the Amazon jungle seem to me an admittedly quirky, yet appropriate, environment in which to locate Elvis. The parallels drawn in this chapter then, call for considerable flexibility and (vivid?) imagination on the part of the reader. What is more, although traditionally set in a linear/temporal, evolutionary framework, the intention here is to tentatively explore a spatial dimension to the life cycle concept. It is recognised that adopting a two-tier analytical framework on which to hang unconventional empiricism, further complicates the picture. Hopefully, however, it is considered neither irreverent nor irrelevant, but simply seen as an attempt at an unorthodox take on the TALC.

Of the two fundamental supports underpinning Butler's model, the concept of the life cycle of animal species in the wild appears to be relatively unexplored (although discussed earlier in this volume, and by Coles, and Ravenscroft & Hjihambi, other volume; editor's comment). Relative that is, to the considerable attention afforded the other pillar – namely the concept of the life cycle of the product. If the sheer volume of subsequent written material on the subject reflects the relative importance of the two founding concepts, one is left with the suggestion of somewhat uneven foundations and (possibly) an unbalanced structure. However, I suspect, it could simply be the result of unbalanced critique rather than lop-sided edifice.

Going some way to addressing this imbalance, initial attention is focused here on the animal/nature perspective – though clearly the notion of 'the product' remains crucial to any discussion or, indeed, analysis. Elvis, it could be argued, bridges these two concepts. He was the wild animal that became the managed, domesticated, cultivated product. He metamorphosed from a feral, wild cat – a hip, hep, hell cat – to the big, flabby, neutered pet pussy cat of his later years. His rise, decline – from erotic to neurotic, demise and then subsequent rejuvenation (resurrection might be more apposite here) mirrors, and serves as metaphor for, the well researched phases of the resort life cycle.

Ecolodges and The Jungle Cycle

Given some poetic licence, Butler's reference to 'the life cycle of animal species in the wild' (Butler, 2000: 288) could be interpreted loosely and widely (though not necessarily wisely) to embrace all species including man in the wild. Now, it would seem, modern man trapped in the 'urban jungle' yearns, ostensibly at least, to escape from civilisation by going back to nature and experiencing the wild.

Where better to engage with nature at its most sublime, and encounter wild animals, than the jungle? And where more evocative than the mythical Amazon jungle? Fabled for its golden roofed opera house, Manaus, the city in the jungle, is the tourist gateway into the Amazon. Once there, tourists partake to varying degrees in the jungle experience. In the mid 1990s I was afforded the wonderful opportunity and experience of several field study visits to the Amazon to explore the developing eco-lodge phenomenon. Somewhat surprisingly it was there, during those forays into the jungle, that the relationships and parallels between Elvis, ecotourism, sustainability and the life cycle first struck me – as did the relevance of incorporating a linked spatial/temporal perspective to the analysis.

To establish a sequential profile of change, the tendency is to view the resort development through a linear time frame. To actually achieve this we mentally, and instantaneously, leap back – usually to the time when the resort was created/born – and begin our analysis there and then. Tracing, as we do, the resort's progress from its inception, we move to the present day and on to predictions of future options. When we 'read' the resultant graph, our eyes glide from left to right, taking in and absorbing chronologically the life cycle from birth – youth – maturity – old age; from $A \rightarrow B \rightarrow C$ etc. Although how we leave the present and arrive mentally at the birth of the resort is ignored and may be of more significance than we think, once there at the origin, the process, and our analysis, appears to flow naturally and chronologically.

While travelling, against the current, back in time up the Amazon (more precisely, the tributary River Negro), I experienced this process in reverse. The 40-hour boat trip (in effect the often overlooked, neglected and, for me up until then, instantaneous, 'leap back' stage of the TALC) furnished me with time for literal – and littoral – reflection. Time to reflect on the passing of time, of, for example, the realisation of distant childhood dreams of the jungle. But only now venturing there (both childhood and jungle) from the vantage – or disadvantage – of middle age. And time to realise that the subjectivity inherent in where one is in terms of one's own personal life cycle must surely have some relevance to any analysis one attempts.

It was this journey up the river from Manaus that made me aware of going back in time. This spatial/temporal dimension was later reinforced when reading Winchester's *The River at the Centre of the World. A Journey up the Yangtze, and Back in Chinese Time*. 'The Yangtze flows for 4,000 miles from the pristine glaciers of the pre-industrial Tibetan plateau to the polluted, extended mouth in Shanghai. As it flows it traces China's history' (Winchester, 1997: 17). A graphic account of journeying up the Yangtze (a slow boat in China?), as the title suggests travelling upstream from Shanghai was to Winchester, searching for China's heart and soul, like retreating from civilisation – like going back in time. Similarly in the Amazon, the further the distance up river by boat from Manaus then, generally speaking, the wilder, the more primeval the environment/ ambience. This, in turn, is reflected in the 'nature' of the ecolodge situated on the banks. The further up river they are then, as a rough indicator, the more 'primitive' the ecolodge, and concomitantly the more natural, the more supposedly authentic the visitor experience. Conversely, those lodges in close proximity to Manaus offer the tourist a safer, sanitised environmental bubble. Generally speaking then, the distance from the tourist gateway influences/determines at what stage each ecolodge is at in terms of the overall life cycle of the generic Eco-Lodge.

To me, each successive individual ecolodge I encountered on my journey up river epitomised a different stage in the life cycle of the still growing and evolving generic Eco-Lodge. Logistically the picture unfurled in reverse. The isolation of the ecolodges in the Amazon makes it possible to establish their respective characteristics in a cross-sectional analysis and to locate their comparative position in the overall life cycle of the Eco-Lodge – as opposed to a conventional time-series analysis of an individual resort. Different stages of the product life cycle can, in these circumstances, be determined therefore not by tracing the life cycle of one single 'resort'/product over time but rather by identifying at what stage of the generic life cycle model the particular lodge is at. Here space/distance represent time. Consequently we can view each individual ecolodge as a manifestation of a different life cycle phase, in this case chronicling the process in reverse sequence from the luxurious to the primitive.

For this purpose, the Ariau Tower, situated approximately three hours by boat from Manaus, serves as an example of the lodge where ecotourists are pampered, in a protected environment offering the relative luxuries of air-conditioning, swimming pool and, perhaps the ultimate convenience, flush toilets. At the other end of the spectrum, for those prepared to penetrate further in their quest for the authentic, is the small Xixuau Nature Reserve. This basic ecolodge, bereft of creature comforts, is some 40 hours by boat from Manaus. Put rather simplistically, the sizeable Ariau Tower was catering for the mass ecotourist, the Xixuau for the would-be intrepid traveller.

The Life Cycle from Memphis to Las Vegas

Now superimpose on this profile Elvis's earthly life cycle, from youth to premature death at 42. The Xixuau reserve then equates to the raw teen idol Elvis circa 1956 and the Ariau tower to the commodified, bloated, idle Elvis of later years.

Distanced from civilisation, the wildness of the Xixuau lodge – its primitive, unpretentious, no frills, natural authenticity – represents the unconstructed Elvis from his early days. Aptly monikered 'King of the Cats', he was then both the Lion and Loin King. Roar/raw sex. Via the racially slurred, nastily labelled 'jungle music' of rock'n'roll (itself jazz terminology for sex) he brought black music to a white audience – the dark, the dangerous and the forbidden. Effortlessly mimicking the 'primitive', King not by birthright but by revolution, he brought rebellion. And he was sex, animal sex. The impact was cataclysmic. 'Elvis was electric, when he sang "Turn me Loose" that was the feeling. And he spat out his songs and shook and murmured with the bottled up emotion we felt. When he moved we knew it was sex. Rock'n'roll was a euphemism for sex, but not the girl next door. We wanted to fuck the world' (Gosling, 1980: 39) This Elvis was not for the fainthearted.

But already there were problems. How to maintain, and sustain, the momentum of success? 'By 1958, Elvis had ruled for two years solid ... He had racked up twenty world-wide million sellers. Still, he had some long term problems. He was already twenty three, he could not go on being a teen idol for ever. The difficulty was how to turn him from an adolescent rebel into a respectable established figure ...' (Cohn, 1973: 26).

His manager, the enigmatic impresario, Colonel Parker, had the answer 'The King of the Cats' was to be emasculated, tamed and domesticated: turned from beast to cuddly toy. Initially, Elvis seemingly acquiesced in this transition. 'Put a chain around my neck and lead me anywhere' (Mann & Lowe, 1956) proved painfully prophetic. 'I don't want to be your tiger, cos tigers play too rough. I don't want to be your lion, cos lions aren't the sort your lovin' of – I just want to be your teddy bear.' (Mann & Lowe, 1956). The lyrics say it all.

Already the wheels had been set in motion. Elvis had moved from Sun Records to RCA, from specialist to mainstream; from small to mass market, from local to national to international. Moulded to take full advantage of market opportunities, Elvis was stage managed.

Some might see Elvis's commodification and concomitant democratisation as a positive, not negative evolution/development – simultaneously becoming more acceptable and accessible to a far wider audience. To others though, the taming of the wild, dangerous Elvis, his sanitisation and commodification marked the beginning of the end. Are there specific pivotal moments to which decline can be attributed? Or, being evolutionary, is the process slow and defining moment indecipherable? For John Lennon it was Elvis joining the army, and the haircut; for Gambacini it was the contrived television appearance where Elvis, in tuxedo, sang 'Hound Dog' to a lugubrious Basset hound (Gambacini, 2002). To them the 'true', 'authentic' Elvis has been irretrievably lost. This is assuming that there was such a thing in the first place. But what was the 'real' Elvis, and the 'authentic' Elvis experience? At his wildest while performing, apparently off stage he was just a Bible reading country boy from the backwoods who loved his mother. Frontstage–backstage authenticity epitomised? (A perfect paradigm for a cross-sectional analysis.) So was the 'real' Elvis the one performing on stage or was it the shy, polite Elvis backstage?

To find out, Dunk (2002: 63), in his newspaper article 'Discovering the real Elvis in folksy Tupelo' suggests distancing yourself from the gaudy Graceland and commercialisation of the big city, and going (backwards?) to the backwoods to discover the home-spun country boy – his private persona.

Even on stage though, things were not necessarily all they seemed. Decoding early Elvis appearances, Cohn believes '... it was sex in a vacuum. He looked dangerous but ultimately he was safe and clean. That is what young girls have always wanted from their idols, an illusion of danger, and Elvis brought a new thrill of semi-reality to the game' (Cohn, 1973: 26). The girls in the audience were uninhibited, shouting, screaming, fainting, whatever, while Elvis was performing on stage because that precisely was where he was – on stage. There was always a safety belt because he was unreachable, unreal and nothing could actually happen.

From Natural to Comfortable

The audience desires excitement and danger, but only from afar. Like viewing caged creatures in the zoo, or perhaps a tamed circus act. Or, from the safely strapped sanctuary of a Land Rover, the 'wild', exotic animals at a safari park. While fostering our delusion of wanting the authentic, in reality we much prefer a sanitised, safe and commodified version of nature – the staging of the wild.

So too with tourism. According to Dunn (1998: 38), 'MacCannell (1976) draws on Goffman's (1959) recognition of the division between public and private to suggest that tourists seek out the authentic in the private back regions in places which they visit' (Shades of the 'real' jungle adventure of the Xixuau compared with the staged Ariau Tower experience). He continues 'Much of MacCannell's *The Tourist* is concerned with deliberate staging of authenticity and whether tourists are in a position to differentiate between staged and actual' (Dunn, 1998: 38).

With the ecolodge, the jungle adventure is experienced from the safety of the environmental bubble. Even at the edge, as tourist/travellers in the most 'authentic' ecolodge we, of course, don't experience the 'true' experience of the wild. We are protected, cocooned. We have the safety (and mosquito) net of Mosiguard and malaria tablets, our purified water tablets. We have our tampons and suntan lotion. And our indefatigable illusion/delusion of being at one with nature.

Further down river, in close proximity to the tourist gateway, we have the 'staged authenticity', the sham experience of the Ariau tower, the commodified ecolodge 'hotel', representing the kitsch, Graceland Elvis of the mid 1970s. Pseudo-ecotourists cosseted in the comfort zone of the Ariau tower lounge; Elvis, corseted, lounge lizarding in the jungle room at Graceland.

Certainly, the décor of this jungle room is more pseudo experience than real. Graceland is, in effect, the mummification of 1970s garish Elvis (should that be mummyfication? He did, after all, originally purchase Graceland partly for his adored, and adoring mother, Gladys). Equally, it could be argued, by that time Elvis had himself become a pseudo-experience. A far cry from his own younger self, he was reliant on artificial stimulants and drugs to generate the energy and vitality that in his youth had come naturally to him – a contrived effort to maintain his younger unspoiled, uncultivated persona, to prolong his success and avert decline. When exactly did Elvis become the first Elvis impersonator? And which of them was 'real'?

Not easy. As Harry Chapin says, 'Reality is only just a word' (Chapin, 1976). Adopting a time series rather than cross-sectional perspective, should we be looking at a youthful Elvis or the Elvis approaching middle age? Both were 'real' and both had their own frontstage/backstage personas. Latter day impersonators of Elvis usually opt for mimicking his rhinestoned, jump suited days/daze. Yet the purists unequivocally see the early Elvis, before he was corrupted by commodification, as being the 'real', 'authentic' Elvis. Ironically though, it was this early Elvis that was seen by many as a, if not the, corrupting influence – more the devil incarnate than in disguise. In much the same way, to aficionados of travel, the traveller and the travel experience are held in high esteem, above reproach, whereas the tourist and mass tourism are worthy of only ridicule and scorn. But isn't the very same traveller the vanguard of the tourist, the harbinger of change/decline? Isn't there a familiar inevitable process – that inextricably links conspicuous consumption (Veblen, 1970), successive class intrusion (Pearce, 1982) and the pleasure periphery (Turner & Ash, 1975)? And, at the macrolevel, isn't tourism surely beyond coordinated management (Wheeller, 1991)?

However, it would appear that (at the microlevel?) Butler is more positive – if only in the sense that he believes management can avert the otherwise inevitable decline. To Butler, the process of development, unless managed appropriately, is invariably linked with decline. In order to stave off deterioration he calls for 'responsibility and control over development' (Butler, 2000: 294) and consequently views management as the means of sustaining the product and ensuring its long-term survival. This seems optimistic. To me, too optimistic. It calls, on the part of management, for the replacement of short-term profit maximisation blinkers by unimpeded vision, imagination, integrity and compassion. (However, one might argue that the Rolling Stones have survived four decades as the greatest rock and roll group in the world through 'sustainable change' and still sound as good on stage as in the 1960s, so perhaps I am not being too optimistic, editor's comment).

Certainly with Elvis, the role of management seemed somewhat dubious, less altruistic. Parker had control, but whether he matched this with responsibility is another matter. Lacking in integrity, his prime agenda appears to have been procurement of maximum cash flow. Short-term this managerial approach had paid dividends. Mid-term, fuelled by industrial quantities of drugs, gluttony and indolence, Elvis's decline was exacerbated further by those perhaps initially responsible. First by rapacious management,

If he had held control of his own life, he might have chosen to lock himself away in Graceland and never come out again. That wasn't an option. Tom Parker was a compulsive gambler and needed Elvis to keep working. So the King was dispatched to Vegas again, and then on tour, zig-zag-ing across America, with ever decreasing breaks, until he finally imploded. (Cohn, 2002: 23)

And then secondly by leeching friends. Desperate to sustain their milch cow, his immediate 'friends' – whose sobriquet the 'Memphis Mafia' seems so apposite – fed him a potent cocktail of drugs. Rejuvenation/regeneration at all costs. Rather than taking care of Elvis, their motto 'Taking care of Business', attested to their priorities and true loyalties.

This potent cocktail progressively took its toll. Elvis the Pelvis became Elvis the Product. The cost? Elvis the Person. Local boy made god, his fall from grace was one of tragic proportions. 'It is a sad and salutary tale: the beautiful prince, kissed by Fate, who turned into a toad' (Melly, 2002: 15). But as in all true tragedies it was one of overwhelming irony. Because of course, long term for the Elvis phenomenon death proved the ultimate career move. Elvis the idle idol becomes Elvis the icon.

Conclusion

Does it matter if the product 'deteriorates' and is 'ruined' in the process? If the prince turns into a toad? If the proverbial goose is cooked? As sustenance to the masses, maybe it is easier to digest that way. The venerated golden goose may, after all, be a dispensable luxury. While the product undergoes physical decline and decay, the assumption that the utility derived simultaneously declines seems a little doubtful. Individual utility might, or might not, decline. But given the increased accessibility to, and acceptance of, the product by a wider (less discerning?) market, then even though the product deteriorates, the aggregate pleasure/utility may very well increase.

Simple common sense – surely? But maybe, in a sense, simply because it is 'common' it is conveniently ignored, indeed eschewed, by the 'sophisticated'. We need only look at the huge tourist numbers to Las Vegas, Niagara or the Blackpools of the world to realise this. Comparing these figures with visitor numbers to the niche, ecodestinations of say, Costa Rica and Belize, confirms the fact that despite its prominence in tourism academic research, and gushing rhetoric from politicians and the tourism industry, eco/sustainable tourism is still only a small, very minor segment of the overall tourism market. Like it or not, mass tourism demand reigns supreme. When it suits, the 'informed', the 'educated', the 'sophisticated' again choose to ignore this too.

And so with Elvis. Because of, rather than despite, commodification and 'inauthenticity', the number seeing the King – live or on film – in the

1960s and 1970s far exceeded the rock'n'roll aficionados of his mid-1950s, early 'authentic' years. What to some constituted Elvis's decline to others was, perversely, the very reason for his continued success. His transition from rebel outsider to mainstream good guy and the subsequent pathos of the ultimately sad, suffering tragic hero ensured his enduring popularity – albeit with an (arguably) less discerning market. Beauty is in the eye of the beholder – what to some is ugly and degenerate to others appeals. Content with kitsch, for many this is beauty.

Pilgrims to Graceland:

> are not the cool or the hip. Like Elvis himself, they come from the great amorphous white millions, who scuffle to get by, who blunder through lives filled with mess and waste and odd moments of joy, untouched by changing fashion. Small wonder Elvis is their once and future king. They love him, not in spite of his excesses and his grotesque end, but in large part because of them. He suffered so much. He is their martyr. (Cohn, 2002: 23)

And this is the conundrum possibly at the heart of the life cycle/ sustainability model – Is (perceived) deterioration in quality necessarily synonymous with decline?

To some – often the pretentious and condescending – be they academic experts, pseudo-travellers or music connoisseurs, the answer invariable is 'yes'. But the majority – the mass market – maybe see things from a different, less privileged, more prosaic angle. To them, the supposed decline may appear merely as a shift in focus, a change that brings the product within their economic and cultural compass. Happily wrapped in their safety blanket, it is suggested here that many don't feel the need or even want to see beneath the surface, beyond the immediate – particularly if that necessitates any potential discomfort or danger. They prefer the staged to the actual, the superficial to the real.

Similarly, with the ecolodges. While changes to facilities may make the product more attractive to the wider market, do they enhance the jungle experience? The introduction of air-conditioning dilutes the experience of the wild but simultaneously makes it more bearable and, therefore, acceptable to more tourists – who without the decadence of incongruous luxury would not be prepared to experience the jungle at all. And, of course, because it maintains cash flow, the modification is, in a sense, 'sustainable' (Wheeller, 1994). So changes determined by market forces/ entrepreneurial intervention do not necessarily enhance the soul of the product – indeed they may remove the essence, the very heart. But does it really matter as long as it keeps the customer satisfied? The supposedly progressively less discerning customer, that is.

The King is Dead. Long Live the Product.

References

Abernatthy, W. and Utterback, J. (1978) Patterns of industrial innovation. *Technology Review* 80, 41–47.

Agarwal, S. (1994) The resort cycle revisited: Implications for resorts. In C.P. Cooper and A. Lockwood (eds) *Progress in Tourism, Recreation and Hospitality Management* (Vol.5, pp. 194–208). Chichester: Wiley.

Agarwal, S. (1997) The resort cycle and seaside tourism: An assessment of its applicability and validity. *Tourism Management* 18 (3), 65–73.

Agarwal, S. (1998) Reply – What is new with the resort cycle? *Tourism Management* 19 (2), 181–182.

Agarwal, S. (1999) Restructuring and local economic development: Implications for seaside resort regeneration in South West Britain. *Tourism Management* 20 (5), 511–522.

Agarwal, S. (2002) Restructuring seaside tourism. The resort life-cycle. *Annals of Tourism Research* 29 (1), 25–55.

Aglietta, M. (1979) *A Theory of Capitalist Regulation*. London: New Left Books.

Aiken, K.G. (1994) Not long ago a smoking chimney was a sign of prosperity: Corporate and community response to pollution at the Bunker Hill Smelter in Kellogg, Idaho. *Environmental Values* Summer, 67–86.

Alford, C. (1962) *The Island of Tobago* (Vol. 7). London: The Ranelagh Press.

Alipour, H. (1996) Tourism development within planning paradigms: The case of Turkey. *Tourism Management* 17 (5), 367–377.

Allen, L., Long, P.T., Perdue, R.R. and Kieselbach, S. (1988) The impact of tourism development on residents' perceptions of community life. *Journal of Travel Research* Summer, 16–21.

Allen, L.R., Hafer, H.R., Long, P.T. and Perdue, R.R. (1993) Rural residents' attitudes toward recreation and tourism development. *Journal of Travel Research* Spring, 27–33.

AMBIO (1877) The Mediterranean, Special issue. Stockholm: Royal Swedish Academy of Science.

AMBIO (1981) The Caribbean, Special Issue. Stockholm: Royal Swedish Academy of Science.

Amin, A. and Thrift, N. (1994) *Globalisation, Institutions and Regional Development in Europe*. Oxford: Oxford University Press.

Amir, S. (1976) *Unequal Development: An Essay on the Social Formations of Peripheral Capitalism*. New York: Monthly Review Press.

Andereck, K.L. and Vogt, C.A. (2000) The relationship between residents' attitudes towards tourism and tourism development options. *Journal of Travel Research* 39 (1), 27–36.

Anonymous (no date) *Renewal Scheme for Traditional Seaside Resorts*. On WWW at http://www.mayo-ireland.ie/Mayo/CoDev/RenSeaRs.htm. Accessed 23.2.2001.

Ansoff, H. (1965) *Corporate Strategy*. Harmondsworth: Penguin.

Ap, J. (1990) Residents' perceptions: Research on the social impacts of tourism. *Annals of Tourism Research* 17 (4), 610–615.

349

Ap, J. and Crompton, J. (1998) Developing a tourism impact scale. *Journal of Travel Research* 37 (2), 120.

Apo, P. (2000) Waikiki: At heart a Hawaiian destination. *Waikiki News* July. On WWW at http://www.waikikinews.com/0700/0700apo.html. Accessed 22.3.2001.

A.R. (1883) The preservation of Mt. Desert. *The Nation* August 9, 116–117.

Arthur, B. (1994) *Increasing Returns and Path Dependence in the Economy*. Ann Arbor: The University of Michigan Press.

Arthur, W.B. (1990) Positive feedbacks in the economy. *Scientific American* 262 (2), 92–99.

Aspinall, A. (1928) *A Wayfarer in the West Indies*. London: Methuen.

L'Association des Vingerons du Quebec (1995) Prenez le chemin des vignobles du Quebec. Pamphlet et communications orales.

Ateljevic, I. and Doorne, S. (2000) Staying within the fence: Lifestyle entrepreneurship in tourism. *Journal of Sustainable Tourism* 8 (5), 378–392.

Atkinson, J. (1984) Manpower strategies for flexible organisations. *Personnel Management* 16 (8), 28–31.

Atkinson, J. (1986) *Changing Work Patterns: How Companies Achieve Flexibility to Meet New Needs*. London: National Economic Development Office.

Aunger, R. (2001) Review of technological innovation as an evolutionary process (Zimon, J., ed). *Journal of Artificial Societies and Social Simulation* 4 (4). On WWW at http://jasss.soc.surrey.ac.uk/4/4/reviews/ziman.html.

Australian Bureau of Statistics (1999) *Consumer Price Index: Table 1B. All Groups Index Numbers – Quarterly (Base Year 1989–90 = 100)*. Product number 6401.0. Canberra: Australian Government.

Avlonitis, G.J. (1990) Project dropstart: Product elimination and the product life cycle concept. *European Journal of Marketing* 24 (9), 55–67.

Babbie, E. (2000) *Practicing Social Research*. Belmont, CA: Wadsworth Publishing.

Backman, S., Patrick, J. and Wright, B.A. (2001) Management tools and techniques: An integrated approach to planning. In D.B. Weaver (ed.) *The Encyclopedia of Ecotourism* (pp. 451–462). Wallingford, UK: CABI Publishing.

Bacon, W. (1998) Economic systems and their impact on tourist resort development: The case of the spa in Europe. *Tourism Economics* 4 (1), 21–32.

Bagguley, P. (1987) *Flexibility, Restructuring and Gender: Changing Employment in Britain's Hotels*. Lancaster Regionalism Working Group Working Paper No. 24, University of Lancaster, Lancaster Regionalism Group.

Bagguley, P., Mark-Lawson, J., Shapiro, D., Urry, J., Walby, S. and Warde, A. (1990) *Restructuring Place, Class and Gender*. London: Sage.

Bagus Oka, I. (1992) Traditional tourist resorts; problems and solutions: The case of Bali. International Forum on Tourism to the Year 2000: Prospects and Challenges, Acapulco, Mexico.

Baird, R. (1850) *Impressions and Experiences of the West Indies and North America in 1849*. Philadelphia, PA: Lea & Blanchard.

Baker, M. (1991) One more time – what is marketing? In M. Baker (ed.) *The Marketing Book* (Vol.2, pp. 3–9). Oxford: Butterworth-Heinemann.

Bao, J. (1994) Big theme park distribution research. *Research of Georgraphy* 13 (3), 83–89.

Bao, J. (1998) Tourism planning and tourist area lifecycle model. *Architect* 12, 170–178.

Bao, J. and Peng, H. (1995) Tourist area expanding research: Case study of Danxia Mountain. *Science of Geography* 15 (1), 63–70.

Bao, J., Chu, Y. and Peng, H. (1993) *Tourism Geography* (p. 134). Beijing: Higher Education Press.

Bao, J. (1994) Tourism development of karst cave. *Geographic Sinica* 50 (4), 353–359.

Barker, J.A. (1992) *Discovering the Future: The Power of Vision*. Florida: Infinity Limited.

Barr, T. (1990) From quirky islanders to entrepreneurial magnates: The transition of the Whitsundays. *Journal of Tourism Studies* 1 (2), 26–32.

Barrett, J. (1958) The seaside resort towns of England and Wales. Unpublished PhD thesis. London: University of London.

Barrot, T-A. (1978) *Unless Haste is Made: A French Skeptic's Account of the Hawaiian Islands in 1836*. Kailua, HI: Press Pacifica.

Basalla, G. (1988) *The Evolution of Technology*. Cambridge: Cambridge University Press.

Baum, T. (1998a) Taking the exit route: Extending the tourism area life cycle model. *Current Issues in Tourism* 1 (2), 167–175.

Baum, T. (1998b) Tourism marketing and the small island environment. Cases from the periphery. In E. Laws *et al*. (eds) *Embracing and Managing Change in Tourism*. London: Routledge.

Baum, J.A. and Singh, J.V. (1994) *Evolutionary Dynamics of Organisations*. New York: Oxford University Press.

Beckford, G. (1972) *Persistent Poverty: Underdevelopment in Plantation Economies of the Third World*. New York: Oxford University Press.

Bell, M. (1994) Personal interview, Hilton Head Island Planning Office, Hilton Head, SC.

Benham, B. (1970) Kealakekua Bay remains 'unlisted'. Hawaii *Tribune Herald* 9 August, 2.

Bennett, R.C. and Cooper, R.G. (1984) The product life cycle trap. *Business Horizons* 27 (Sept–Oct), 7–16.

Benson, J. and Shaw, G. (eds) (1999) *The Retailing Industry. Volume I: Perspectives and the Early Modern Period*. London: I.B. Tauris.

Berman, E.M. (2002) *Essential Statistics for Public Managers and Policy Analysts*. Washington, DC: CQ Press.

Berry, E.N. (2001) An Application of Butler's (1980) Tourist Area Life Cycle Theory to the Cairns Region, Australia, 1876–1998. PhD Thesis, Tropical Environment and Geography, James Cook University, Cairns Campus. On WWW at www.geocities.com/tedberry_aus/tourismarealifecycle.html.

Beverland, M.B., Hoffman, D. and Rasmussen, M. (2001) The evolution of events in the Australasian wine sector. *Tourism Recreation Research* 26 (2), 35–44.

Beyers, W.B. and Nelson, P.B. (2000) Contemporary development forces in the nonmetropolitan West: New insights from rapidly growing communities. *Journal of Rural Studies* 16, 459–474.

Bianchi, R. (1994) Tourism development and resort dynamics: An alternative approach. In C. Cooper and A. Lockwood (eds) *Progress in Tourism, Recreation and Hospitality Management* (Vol.5, pp. 183–193). New York: John Wiley & Sons.

Bieger, T. (2000) *Management von Destinationen und Tourismusorganisationen*. München, Wien: Oldenbourg.

Bigelow, J. (1851) *Jamaica in 1850. Or, the Effects of Sixteen Years of Freedom on a Slave Colony*. New York: George P. Putnam.

Bird, I.L. (1966) *Six Months in the Sandwich Islands*. Honolulu: University of Hawaii Press.

Bird, J. (1963) *The Major Seaports of the United Kingdom*. Hutchinson of London.

Blamey, R. (1997) Ecotourism: The search for an operational definition. *Journal of Sustainable Tourism* 5, 109–130.

Blanchard, O.J. and Fischer, S. (1989) *Lectures on Macroeconomics*. Cambridge, MA: MIT Press.

Blazevic, I. (1994) Opatija Chronicle. In Proceedings, *150th Anniversary of Tourism in Opatija* (pp. 15–24). University of Rijeka, Faculty of Hotel Management, Opatija.

Boniface, B. and Cooper, C. (1987) *The Geography of Travel and Tourism*. Oxford: Butterworth Heinemann.

Booth, J.D. (1982) *Railways of Southern Quebec* (Vol.I, 1982; Vol.II, 1985). Toronto: Railfare Enterprises Ltd.

Bordieu, P. (1977) *Outline of a Theory of Practice*. Cambridge: Cambridge University Press.

Bordieu, P. (1984) *Distinction: A Social Critique of the Judgement of Taste*. Andover: Routledge and Kegan Paul.

Borenstein, S. (1992) The evolution of U.S. airline competition. *Journal of Economic Perspectives* 6 (2), 45–73.

Bosselman, F.P., Peterson, C.A. and McCarthy, C. (1999) *Managing Tourism Growth: Issues and Applications*. Washington, D.C.: Island Press.

Bouchikhi, H. (1993) A constructivist framework for understanding entrepreneurship performance. *Organization Studies* 14 (4), 549–570.

Bournemouth Borough Council (2002) *Tourism Facts*. Bournemouth: Bournemouth Borough Council.

Boyd, S.W. (1995) Sustainability and Canada's national parks: Suitability for policy, planning and management. Unpublished PhD thesis: Department of Geography, University of Western Ontario, London, Canada.

Boyd, S.W. (2000) Tourism, national parks and sustainability. In R.W. Butler and S.W. Boyd (eds) *Tourism and National Parks: Issues and Implications* (pp. 161–186). Chichester: Wiley.

Boyd, S.W. (2003) Marketing challenges and opportunities for heritage tourism. In A. Fyall, B. Garrod and A. Leask (eds) *Managing Visitor Attractions: New Directions* (pp. 189–202). Oxford: Butterworth-Heinemann.

Boyd, S.W. and Butler, R.W. (2000) Tourism and national parks: The origin of the concept. In R.W. Butler and S.W. Boyd (eds) *Tourism and National Parks: Issues and Implications* (pp. 13–27). Chichester: Wiley.

Boyer, R. (1986) *La Theorie de la Regulation: Une Analyse Critique*. Paris: Editions La Decouverte.

Bramwell, B. and Lane, B. (1993) Sustainable tourism: An evolving global approach. *Journal of Sustainable Tourism* 1 (1), 1–5.

Bramwell, B. and Lane, B. (2000) (eds) *Tourism Collaboration and Partnerships: Politics, Practice and Sustainability*. Clevedon: Channel View Publications.

Brassey, S. (1886) *In the Trades, the Tropics, & the Roaring Forties*. London: Longmans, Green, & Co.

Braunlich, C.G. (1996) Lessons From the Atlantic City casino experiment. *Journal of Travel Research* 34 (3), 46–62.

Briere, R. (1966) Le Tourisme au Quebec. Unpublished PhD dissertation, Geography Department, Universite de Montreal.

Briere, R. (1967) Les grands Traits de l' Evolution du Tourisme au Quebec, *Bulletin de l'Association des Geographes de l'Amerique Francaise* No. 11, Quebec.

Briggs, J. and Peat, F.D. (1999) *Seven Life Lessons of Chaos*. St. Leonards, NSW: Allen & Unwin.

Britton, S. (1991) Tourism, capital and place: Towards a critical geography. *Environment and Planning D: Society and Space* 9, 451–478.

Brookes, R. (1989) *Managing the Enabling Authority*. Harlow: Longman.

Brougham, J.E. and Butler, R.W. (1972) The applicability of the asymptotic curve to the forecasting of tourism development. Paper presented to the Research Workshop, Travel Research Association 4th Annual Conference, Quebec, July 1972.

Brown, B.J.H. (1985) Personal perception and community speculation: A British resort in the 19th century. *Annals of Tourism Research* 12 (3), 355–369.

Brown, S. (1987) Institutional change in retailing: A geographical interpretation. *Progress in Human Geography* 11 (2), 181–206.

Brown, S. (1988) The wheel of the Wheel of Retailing. *International Journal of Retailing* 3 (1), 16–37.

Brown, C. (1995) *Chaos and Catastrophe Theories*. Thousand Oaks, CA: Sage Publications.

Brown, K. (2002) Innovations for conservation and development. *The Geographical Journal* 168 (1), 6–17.

Bryan, J. (1965) 3 new Kona resort areas planned. Honolulu *Star Bulletin* 24 March, A2.

Bryman, A. (1988) *Quantity and Quality in Social Research*. London: Routledge.

Buhalis, D. (2000) Marketing the competitive destination of the future. *Tourism Management* 21 (1), 97–116.

Bullock, W.B. (1926) *Beautiful Waters Devoted to the Memphremagog Region*. Vermont: Memphremagog Press.

Bunge, W. (1966) *Theoretical Geography*. Lund: C.W.K. Gleerup Publishers.

Bureau of Tourism Research (2000a) *International Visitor Survey*. Canberra: BTR.

Bureau of Tourism Research (2000b) *Domestic Tourism Monitor*. Canberra: BTR.

Burnett, C.C. (1892) *The Land of the O-o*. Cleveland, OH: The Cleveland Printing and Publishing Co.

Burns, D. and Murphy, L. (1998) An analysis of the promotion of marine tourism in Queensland, Australia. In E. Laws, B. Faulkner and G. Moscardo (eds) *Embracing and Managing Change in Tourism: International Case Studies* (pp. 415–430). London: Routledge.

Busenitz, L.W., Gomez, C. and Spencer, J.W. (2000) Country institutional profiles: Unlocking entrepreneurial phenomena. *Academy of Management Journal* 43 (5), 994–1003.

Butler, R.W. (1973) The tourist industry in the Highlands and Islands. Unpublished PhD thesis, Glasgow: University of Glasgow.

Butler, R.W. (1980) The concept of a tourist area cycle of evolution: Implications for management of resources. *The Canadian Geographer* 24 (1), 5–12.

Butler, R.W. (1990a) The resort cycle revisited – a decade of discussion. Paper presented to Association of American Geographers Conference, Toronto, April 1990.

Butler, R.W. (1990b) Alternative tourism: Pious hope or trojan horse. *Journal of Travel Research* 28 (3), 40–44.

Butler, R.W. (1991) Tourism, environment and sustainable development. *Environmental Conservation* 18 (3), 201–209.

Butler, R. (1993) *Pre- and Post-Impact Assessment of Tourism Development. Tourism Research: Critiques and Challenges*. New York: Routledge.

Butler, R.W. (1997) The destination life cycle: Implications for heritage site management and attractivity. In W. Nuryanti (ed.) *Tourism and Heritage Management* (pp. 44–53). Yogyakarta: Gadjah Mada University Press.

Butler, R.W. (1998a) Still peddling along. The resort cycle two decades on. Paper to *Progress in Tourism and Hospitality Research*. CAUTHE Conference, Gold Coast.

Butler, R. (1998b) Sustainable tourism – looking backwards in order to progress? In C.M. Hall and A. Lew (eds) *Sustainable Tourism: A Geographical Perspective* (pp. 25–34). New York: Addison Wesley Longman.

Butler, R.W. (2000) The resort cycle two decades on. In B. Faulkner, G. Moscardo and E. Laws (eds) *Tourism in the 21st Century: Reflections on Experience* (pp. 284–299). London, New York: Continuum.

Butler, R.W. and Boyd, S.W. (2000) Tourism and parks – a long but uneasy relationship. In R.W. Butler and S.W. Boyd (eds) *Tourism and National Parks. Issues and Implications* (pp. 3–11). Chichester: Wiley.

Bywater, M. (1992) *The European Tour Operator Industry.* Special Report No. 2141. London: Economic Intelligence Unit.

C.P. (1883) The boarder and the cottager. *The Nation* August 2, (944) NP Cairns Post. 1976–1998.

Canan, P. and Hennessy, M. (1989) The growth machine, tourism, and the selling of culture. *Sociological Perspectives* 32, 227–243.

Canestrelli, E. and Costa, P. (1991) Tourist carrying capacity: A fuzzy approach. *Annals of Tourism Research* 18 (2), 295–311.

Capra, F. (1982) *The Turning Point.* London: Flamingo.

Casagrandi, R. and Rinaldi, S. (2002) A theoretical approach to tourism sustainability. *Conservation Ecology* 6 (1), 13–35.

Caserta, S. and Russo, A.P. (2002) More means worse. Asymmetric information, spatial displacement and sustainable heritage tourism. *Journal of Cultural Economics* 26 (4).

Casino Control Commission Annual Report (2001) p. 4.

Cater, E. (1993) Ecotourism in the third world: Problems for sustainable tourism development. *Tourism Management* 14 (2), 85–90.

Catry, B. and Chevalier, M. (1974) Market share strategy and the product life cycle. *Journal of Marketing* 38, 29–34.

Cauthorn, R. (1989) *Contributions to a Theory of Entrepreneurship.* New York: Garland Publishing Inc.

Cazes, G. and Potier, F. (1996) *Le Tourisme Urbain.* Paris: Presses Universitaires de France.

Centre for Tourism Policy Studies, School of Travel Industry Management, University of Hawaii (1998) *Repositioning Hawaii's Visitor Industry Products: Development Strategies for the New Tourism Environment.* On WWW at http://www.state.hi.us/tourism/reposit.pdf. Accessed 14.2.2001.

Centre for Travel and Tourism, New College, Durham in association with Business Education Publishers Limited.

Chaney, G.L. (1879) *Aho-ha! A Hawaiian Salutation.* Boston: Roberts Brothers.

Chapin, H. (1976) Corey's Coming. From *On the Road to Kingdom Come.* Electra Records.

Chapman, E. (1961) *Pleasure Island: The Book of Jamaica* (Vol. 5). Kingston: Arawak Press.

Chemin des Vignobles du Quebec (2001) Pamphlet. Associaton des Vignerons du Quebec.

Chen, J. (2001) Disscusion on "the lifecycle of the tourist products". *Journal of Guilin Technical College* 3, 18–20.

Cheshire, P. and Gordon, I. (1996) Territorial competition and the predictability of collective (in)action. *International Journal of Urban and Regional Research* 20 (3), 383–399.

Chorley, R. and Haggett, P. (eds) (1967) *Models in Geography*. London: Methuen.

Choy, D.J.L. (1991) Tourism planning: The case for market failure. *Tourism Management* 12 (4), 313–330.

Choy, D. (1992) Life cycle models for Pacific island destinations. *Journal of Travel Research* 30 (3), 6–31.

Christaller, W. (1933) *Die Zentrale Orte in Süddeutschland* [*The Central Places in South Germany*]. Jena: Gustav Fischer Verlag.

Christaller, W. (1955) Beiträge zu einer Geographie der Fremdenverkehr. Erdkunde, Band IX, Heft 1, February 1955, 1–19.

Christaller, W. (1963) Some considerations of tourism location in Europe: The peripheral regions – underdeveloped countries – recreation areas. *Regional Science Association Papers* XII, Lund Congress, 95–105.

Chunxiao (1997) Thoughts on "tourist products lifecycle". *Tourism Tribune* 12 (5), 44–47.

Circuit des Arts (2002) pamphlet.

Clark, J.R.K. (1985) *Beaches of the Big Island*. Honolulu: University of Hawaii Press.

Clark, S. (1952) *All the Best in the Caribbean*. New York: Dodd, Mead & Co.

Clawson, M. and Knetch, J.L. (1963) *Economics of Outdoor Recreation, Resources of the Future Inc*. Baltimore: Johns Hopkins University Press.

Clegg, A. and Essex, S. (2000) Restructuring in tourism: The accommodation sector in a major British coastal resort. *International Journal of Tourism Research* 2 (2), 77–96.

CLICOR (1971) Canada Land Inventory Land Capability for (Outdoor) Recreation, Montreal H31 map sheet. Ottawa: Department of Energy, Mines and Resources.

Cloke, P., Philo, C. and Sadler, D. (1991) *Approaching Human Geography. An Introduction to Contemporary Theoretical Debates*. London: PCP.

COAST (1993) *COAST*. Brussels: European Commission.

Cohen, E. (1972) Toward a sociology of international tourism. *Social Research* 39 (1), 164–182.

Cohen, E. (1979a) Rethinking the sociology of tourism. *Annals of Tourism Research* 6 (1), 18–35.

Cohen, E. (1979b) The impact of tourism on the hill tribes of Northern Thailand. *International Asienforum* 10 (1/2), 5–38.

Cohen, E. (1996a) A phenomenology of tourist experiences. In Y. Apostolopoulos, S. Leivadi and A. Yiannakis (eds) *The Sociology of Tourism: Theoretical and Empirical Investigations* (pp. 90–114). London: Routledge.

Cohen, E. (1996b) *Thai Tourism, Hilltribes, Islands and Open-Ended Prostitution*. Bangkok: White Lotus and Co., Ltd.

Cohn, N. (1973) *AWopBop aLooBop ALopBamBoom*. St Alban: Paladin.

Cohn, N. (2002) The king is dead. *Observer Magazine* 11 September, 17–23.

Coles, T.E. (1999a) Competition, contested retail space and the rise of the German department store, c.1870–1914. *International Review of Retail Distribution and Consumer Research* 9 (3), 275–290.

Coles, T.E. (1999b) Department stores as innovations in retail marketing in Germany: Some observations on marketing practice and perception in the Wilhelmine Period. *Journal of Macromarketing* 19 (1), 34–47.

Coles, T.E. (2004) Tourism, shopping and retailing: An axiomatic relationship? In C.M. Hall, A. Lew and A.M. Williams (eds) *A Companion to Tourism* (pp. 360–373). Oxford: Blackwell.

Coll Jr., R. (1950) Visitors flocking to Kona. Honolulu *Advertiser* 17 January, 17.

Connely, W. (1955) *Beau Nash Monarch of Bath and Tunbridge Wells*. London: Werner Laurie Ltd.

Constant, E. (2000) Recursive practice and the evolution of technical knowledge. In J. Zimon (ed.) *Technological Innovation as an Evolutionary Process* (pp. 219–233). Cambridge: Cambridge University Press.

Convention Concerning the Protection of the World Cultural and Natural Heritage (16 November 1972) On WWW at www.unesco.org/whc. Accessed 12.2002.

Convention on Wetlands of International Importance (2 February 1971) On WWW at www.ramsar.org/. Accessed 12.2002.

Cooke, P. (1987) The changing urban and regional systems in the UK. *Regional Studies* 20 (3), 243–251.

Cooke, P. (1989) *Localities*. London: Unwin Hyman.

Cooper, C. (1990a) Resorts in decline – the management response. *Tourism Management* 11 (1), 63–67.

Cooper, C. (1990b) The life cycle concept and tourism. Unpublished Conference Paper, *Tourism Research into the 1990s*. University of Durham (cited in Shaw & Williams, 2002).

Cooper, C.P. (1992) The life cycle concept and strategic planning for coastal resorts. *Built Environment* 18 (1), 57–66.

Cooper, C.P. (1994) The destination life cycle: An update. In A.V. Seaton, C.L. Jenkins, R.C. Wood, Dieke, P.U.C., M.M. Bennett, L.R. MacLellan and R. Smith (eds) *Tourism: The State of the Art* (pp. 340–346). Brisbane: Wiley.

Cooper, C.P. (1995) Strategic planning for sustainable tourism: The case of the offshore islands in the UK. *Journal of Sustainable Tourism* 3 (4), 191–209.

Cooper, C.P. (1997a) *Inaugural Lecture*. University of Bournemouth.

Cooper, C.P. (1997b) The environmental consequences of declining destinations. *Progress in Tourism and Hospitality Research* 2 (3), 337–345.

Cooper, C.P. (1997c) Parameters and indicators of the decline of the British seaside resort. In G. Shaw and A. Williams (eds) *The Rise and Fall of British Coastal Resorts* (pp. 79–101). London: Cassell.

Cooper, C. and Jackson, S. (1989) Destination life cycle: The Isle of Man case study. *Annals of Tourism Research* 16 (3), 377–398.

Cooper, C.P. and Lockwood, A. (1993) *Progress in Tourism, Recreation and Hospitality Management* (Vol.5, pp. 181–193). Chichester: Wiley.

Cooper, R.G. and Kleinschmidt, E.J. (1993) Screening new products for potential winners. *Long Range Planning* 6 (6), 74–81.

Cooper, C., Fletcher, J., Noble, A. and Westlake, J. (1996) Changing tourism demand in Central Europe: The case of Romanian tourist spas. *Journal of Tourism Studies* 6 (2), 30–44.

Cooper, C., Fletcher, J., Gilbert, D. and Wanhill, S. (1998) In R. Shepherd (ed.) *Tourism: Principles and Practice* (2nd edn). Harlow: Longman.

CORD (Canadian Outdoor Recreation Demand) Surveys (1969–72) Ottawa: Parks Canada.

Coriat, B. (1979) *L'Atelier et al Chronometer*. Paris: Bourgois.

Costa, P. and Manente, M. (1995) Venice and its visitors: A survey and a model of qualitative choice. *Journal of Travel and Tourism Marketing* 4 (3), 45–69.

Costa, P. and van der Borg, J. (1988) Un modello lineare per la programmazione del turismo. *COSES Informazioni* 32/33, 21–26.

County of Hawaii: Office of the Mayor (1987) *A Summary of Planned Developments in West Hawaii, County of Hawaii*. Hawaii: Hilo.

Crawford, C.M. (1984) Business took the wrong cycle from biology. *Journal of Consumer Marketing* 1 (Summer), 5–11.

Creighton, T.H. and Walters, G.S. (1969) *The South Kona Coast Historic and Recreation Area, Island of Hawaii*. Honolulu: Hawaii Department of Land and Natural Resources.

Cundall, F. (1928) *Jamaica in 1928: A Handbook of Information for Visitors and Intending Residents with some Account of the Colony's History*. London: The Institute of Jamaica.

Curtis, S. (1997) Seaside resort: Spanish progress and British malaise. In *Insights* (C9–18). London: British Tourist Authority/English Tourist Board.

Cypriot Tourism Organisation (2002) Strategic tourism plan, 2010. Nicosia: Government of Cyprus.

da Conceição Gonçalves, V.F. and Roque Águas, P.M. (1997) The concept of the life cycle: An application to the tourist product. *Journal of Travel Research* 36 (2), 12–22.

Danielson, M. (1995) *Profits and Politics in Paradise: The Development of Hilton Head Island*. Columbia, SC: The University of South Carolina Press.

Darling, F.F. (1936) *A Herd of Red Deer*. Oxford: Oxford University Press.

Darling, F.F. (1941) *Island Years*. London: G. Bell and Sons Ltd.

Darling, F.F. (1943) *Island Farm*. London: G. Bell and Sons Ltd.

Darnell, A.C. and Johnson, P.S. (2001) Repeat visits to attractions: A preliminary economic analysis. *Tourism Management* 22, 119–126.

Daru, R., Vreedenburgh, E. and Scha, R. (2000) Architectural innovation as an evolutionary process. Abstract of paper presented at the Generative Art Conference, Politecnico di Milano, Italy, 14–16 Dec 2000. On WWW at www.generativeart.com/abst2000/abst77.htm.

Darwin, C. (1859) *The Origin of the Species*. New York: P.F. Collier & Son.

Daughters of Hawaii (1979) *Treasures. . .Hulihee*. Honolulu.

Davidson, W.R., Bates, A.D. and Bass, S.J. (1976) The retail life cycle. *Harvard Business Review* 54 (November–December), 89–96.

Davies, P. (1992) Wish you here? *Landscape Design* (December), 21–24.

Davis, C. (1997) Bloated victim of a fallen world. *Sunday Times* 13 July.

Dawkins, R. (1986) *The Blind Watchmaker*. London: Penguin Books.

Day, A.G. (1955) *Hawaii and Its People*. New York: Dull, Sloan and Pearce.

Day, G.S. (1981) The product life cycle: Analysis and applications issues. *Journal of Marketing* 45 (Fall), 60–67.

de Albuquerque, K. and McElroy, J.L. (1992) Caribbean small-island tourism styles and sustainable strategies. *Environmental Management* 16 (5), 619–632.

Dean, J. (1950) Pricing policies for new products. *Harvard Business Review* November–December, 45–53.

Dearden, P. (1991) Tourism and sustainable development in Northern Thailand. *Geographic Review* 81, 400–413.

Dearden, P. and Harron, S. (1994) Alternative tourism and adaptive change. *Annals of Tourism Research* 21, 81–102.

Debbage, K. (1990) Oligopoly and the resort cycle in the Bahamas. *Annals of Tourism Research* 17, 513–527.

Debbage, K. (1992) Tourism oligopoly is at work. *Annals of Tourism Research* 19 (2), 355–359.

Decker, R.W., Wright, T.L. and Stauffer, P.H. (eds) *Volcanism in Hawaii* (pp. 149–189). US Geological Survey Professional Paper.

de Kadt, E. (1979) *Tourism: Passport to Development*. Oxford: Oxford University Press.

Del Viscio, J. (no date) Atlantic City: A Renaissance Resort. On WWW at http://www.travelbase.com/auto/localview-new.cgi?article = 142. Accessed 30.3.2001.

Department for Culture, Media and Sport (2000a) Seaside 2000 Consultation. London, DCMS.

Department for Culture, Media and Sport (2000b) Government Report to the Tourism Summit: Tomorrow's Tourism.

Department of Culture, Arts and Leisure (2001) *Guidance to District Councils on the Development of Local Cultural Strategies*. London: Department of Culture, Arts and Leisure. On WWW at http://www.culture.gov.uk/tourism/govt_report.html. Accessed 16.2.2001.

De Vis-Norton, L. (1925) The island of Hawaii, a paradise for tourists. *Paradise of the Pacific* 38, 13–15.

Dewailly, J-M. (1999) Sustainable tourist space: From reality to virtual reality? *Tourism Geographies* 1 (1), 41–55.

Dhalla, N.K. and Yuspeh, S. (1976) Forget the product life cycle concept. *Harvard Business Review* 54 (January/February), 102–112.

Diamond, N.P. (1988) A Strategy for Cold Water Resorts into the Year 2000. Unpublished MSc Thesis, University of Surrey, UK.

di Benedetto, A.C. and Bojanic, D. (1993) Tourism area life-cycles. *Annals of Tourism Research* 20 (3), 557–570.

Dicken, P. (1998) *Global Shift: The Internationalisation of Economic Activity* (3rd edn). London: Chapman.

Digance, J. (1997) Life cycle model. *Annals of Tourism Research* 24 (2), 452–455.

Dillman, D.A. (1978) *Mail and Telephone Surveys*. New York: John Wiley & Sons.

Din, K.H. (1992) The "involvement stage" in the evolution of a tourist destination. *Tourism Recreation Research* 17 (1), 10–20.

Din, J. and Bao, J. (2000) A study on the life cycle of special karst cave with a case of Jinashui Swallow Cave in Yunnan Provice. *Carsologica Sinica* 19 (3), 284–289.

Douglas, N. (1997) Applying the life cycle model to Melanesia. *Annals of Tourism Research* 24 (1), 1–22.

Doxey, G.V. (1975) A causation theory of visitor–resident irritants: Methodology and research inferences. *Proceedings of the Travel Research Association 6th Annual Conference* (pp. 195–198). San Diego: Travel Research Association.

Doyle, G. (1957) The magic of Kona coast. *Paradise of the Pacific* 69 (11), 22–41.

Drucker, P.F. (1973) *Management*. New York: Harper and Row.

Drucker, P.F. (1985) *Innovation and Entrepreneurship: Practices and Principles*. New York: Harper & Row.

Duncan, S. and Savage, M. (1989) Space, scale and locality. *Antipode* 21 (3), 179–206.

Duncan, S. and Savage, M. (1991) New perspectives on the locality debate. *Environment and Planning A* 23 (2), 155–164.

Dunk, M. (2000) All shook up by the King's birthplace. *Daily Express* 6 May.

Dunn, D. (1998) Home Truths from Abroad. PhD Thesis, University of Birmingham.

Dziembowska-Kowalska, J. and Funck, R.H. (2000) Cultural activities as a location factor in European competition between regions: Concepts and some evidence. *Annals of Regional Science* 34, 1–12.

Eadington, W. (1982) The Gambling Papers: Proceedings of the Fifth National Conference on Gambling and Risk Taking. Vols 8&9: Issues in Casino Gambling: Nevada and Atlantic City. Reno, NV: University of Nevada.

Eastern Townships regional Tourist Guidebooks (2000) Association Touristique des Cantons de l'Est, Tourisme Quebec.

Eidsvik, H.K. (1983) Parks Canada, conservation and tourism: A review of the seventies – a preview of the eighties. In P.E. Murphy (ed.) *Tourism in Canada: Selected Issues and Options*. Western Geographical Series, 21 (pp. 241–269). Victoria: University of Victoria.

English, D.B., Marcouiller, D.W. and Cordell, K.H. (2000) Tourism dependence in rural America: Estimates and effects. *Society and Natural Resources* 13, 185–202.

English Tourist Board (1991) *The Future of England's Smaller Seaside Resorts*. London: English Tourist Board.

EUROPARC and IUCN (2000) *Guidelines for Protected Area Management Categories*. Grafenau: EUROPARC and WCPA.

Evans, R. and Harding, A. (1997) Regionalisation, regional institutions and economic development. *Policy and Politics* 25, 19–30.

Evans, K., Barnes, J. and Schlacter, J. (1993) A general systems approach to retail evolution: An existing institutional perspective. *International Review of Retail, Distribution and Consumer Research* 3 (1), 79–100.

Farrell, B. (1992) Tourism as an element in sustainable development: Hana Maui. In V.L. Smith and W.R. Eadington (eds) *Tourism Alternatives* (pp. 115–132). Philadelphia: University of Pennsylvania Press.

Farrell, B.H. (1999) Conventional or sustainable tourism? No room for choice. *Tourism Management* 20 (2), 189–191.

Faulkner, B. (1999) Qualitative Research Methods (unpublished chapter).

Faulkner, B. (2002) *Our Gold Coast: The Preferred Future*. Gold Coast: Cooperative Research Centre for Sustainable Tourism.

Faulkner, B. (2003) Rejuvenating a maturing tourist destination: The case of the Gold Coast. In E. Fredline, L. Jago and C. Cooper (eds) *Progressing Tourism Research*. Clevedon: Channel View Publications.

Faulkner, H.W. (1990) Swings and roundabouts in Australian tourism. *Tourism Management* 11 (1), 29–37.

Faulkner, B. and Russell, R. (1997) Chaos and complexity in tourism: In search of a new perspective. *Pacific Tourism Review* 1 (2), 93–102.

Faulkner, B. and Russell, R. (2001) Turbulence, chaos and complexity in tourism systems: A research direction for the new millennium. In B. Faulkner, G. Moscardo and E. Laws (eds) *Tourism in the 21st Century*. London: Continuum.

Fayos Sola, E. (1992) A strategic outlook for regional tourism policy: The white paper on Valencian tourism. *Tourism Management* 13 (1), 45–49.

Fernandez (1999) *Shoshone News Press*. (personal communication).

Finch, J. and Groves, D. (1983) *Labour of Love: Women, Work and Caring*. London: Routledge and Kegan Paul.

Fly, J.M. (1986) Tourism and nature: The basis for growth in Northern Lower Michigan. Unpublished paper.

Foglesong, R. (1999) Walt Disney World and Orlando: Deregulation as a strategy for tourism. In D. Judd and S. Fainstein (eds) *The Tourist City* (pp. 89–106). Newhaven: Yale University Press.

Formica, S. and Uysal, M. (1996) The revitalisation of Italy as a tourist destination. *Tourism Management* 17 (5), 323–331.

Fornander, A. (1980) *An Account of the Polynesian Race: Its Origins and Migrations*. Rutland, VT: Chas. E. Tuttle Company.

Foster, D.M. and Murphy, P. (1991) Resort cycle revisited – The retirement connection. *Annals of Tourism Research* 18, 553–567.

Foster, C. (2000) A new look for Waikiki. *Travel Agent* May 1. On WWW at http://www.findarticles.com/cf_0/m0VOU/18_299/63298501/print.jhtml. Accessed 5.3.2001.

France, L. (1991) An application of the tourism destination area life cycle to Barbados. *Revue de Tourisme* 46 (3), 25–30.

France, L. and Barke, M. (1991) The development of Torremolinos as an international resort: Past, present and future. Occasional paper produced for the Centre for Travel and Toruism, New College, Durham, in association with Business Education Publishers Limited.

Franck, H. (1920) *Roaming through the West Indies*. New York: Blue Ribbon Books.

Frank, A. (1967) *Capitalism and Underdevelopment in Latin America*. New York: Monthly Review Press.

Franklin, A. and Crang, M. (2001) The trouble with tourism and travel theory? *Tourist Studies* 1 (1), 5–22.

Freidmann, J. and Alonso, W. (eds) (1974) *Regional Development and Planning: A Reader*. Cambridge, MA: MIT Press.

Fritz-Nemeth, P. and Lundgren, J.O. (1996) Tourist attractions – from natural to industrial. *TEOROS* 15 (2), 23–30, Montreal: UQAM.

Funnell, C. (1975) *By the Beautiful Sea: The Rise and High Times of That Great American Resort, Atlantic City* (p. 154). New York: Alfred A. Knopf.

Gambicini, P. (2002) *Elvis*. BBC Radio 2.

Gardner, D.M. (1987) The product life cycle: A critical look at the literature. *Review of Marketing* 162–194.

Garmise, S. and Rees, G. (1997) The role of institutional networks in local economic development. A new model of governance? *Local Economy* 12 (2), 104–118.

Garrod, B. (2003) Managing visitor impacts. In A. Fyall, B. Garrod and A. Leask (eds) *Managing Visitor Attractions: New Directions* (pp. 124–139). Oxford: Butterworth-Heinemann.

Garrod, B. and Fyall, A. (2000) Managing heritage tourism. *Annals of Tourism Research* 27 (3), 682–706.

Gartner, W.C. (2002) Cultural tourism trends and implications for tourism development. Paper Presented at the International Conference on: The Tourist-Historic City: Sharing Culture for the future, 17–20 March 2002, Bruges.

Gershuny, J. and Miles, I. (1983) *The New Services Economy: The Transformation of Employment in Industrial Societies*. London: Frances Pinter.

Getz, D. (1983) Capacity to absorb tourism concepts and implications for strategic planning. *Annals of Tourism Research* 10 (1), 245–257.

Getz, D. (1986) Models of tourism planning. Towards integration of theory and practice. *Tourism Management* 7 (1), 21–32.

Getz, D. (1991) *Festivals, Special Events, and Tourism*. New York: Van Nostrand Reinhold.

Getz, D. (1992) Tourism planning and destination lifecycle. *Annals of Tourism Research* 19 (4), 752–770.

Getz, D. (2000) Festivals and special events: Life cycle and saturation issues. In W.C. Gartner and D.W. Lime (eds) *Trends in Outdoor Recreation, Leisure and Saturation Issues* (pp. 175–185). Wallingford: CABI.

Giambelluca, T.W., Nullet, M.A. and Schroeder, T.A. (1986) *Rainfall Atlas of Hawaii*. Honolulu: State of Hawaii. DLNR.

Giddens, A. (1984) *The Constitution of Society*. Berkeley: University of California Press.

Gilbert, D. (1990) Strategic marketing planning for national tourism. *Tourist Review* 45 (1), 18–27.

Gilbert, E.W. (1939) The growth of inland and seaside health resorts in England. *Scottish Geographical Magazine* 55, 16–35.

Gilbert, E.W. (1954) *Brighton – Old Ocean's Bauble*. London: Methuen.

Gist, R.R. (1968) *Retailing. Concepts and Decisions*. New York: Wiley and Sons.

Glaser, B. (1978) *Theoretical Sensitivity*. Mill Valley, CA: The Sociology Press.

Glaser, B. and Strauss, A. (1967) *The Discovery of Grounded Theory: Strategies for Qualitative Research*. New York: Aldine De Gruyter.

Gleick, J. (1987) *Chaos: Making a New Science*. London: Heinemann.

Goad, P. and Crispin, S.W. (1999) Tourism: Wish you were here. *Far Eastern Economic Review*. On WWW at http://www.feer.com/9909_30/p60tourism.html. Accessed 21.2.2001.

Godkin, E.L. (1883) Evolution of the summer resort. *The Nation* July 19, 47–48.

Goffman, E. (1959) *Presentation of Self in Everyday Life*. New York: Doubleday.

Gold Coast City Council (2000) Draft Gold Coast 2010: Economic Development Strategy. GCCC.

Gordon, I. and Goodall, B. (1992) Resort cycles and development processes. *Built Environment* 18 (4), 41–56.

Gordon, I. and Goodall, B. (2000) Localities and tourism. *Tourism Geographies* 2 (3), 290–311.

Gormsen, E. (1981) The spatio-temporal development of international tourism, attempt at a centre–periphery model. In *La Consommation d'Espace par le Tourisme et sa Preservation*. Aix-en-Provence: Centre d'etudes touristiques.

Gosling, R. (1980) *Personal Copy. A Memoir of the Sixties*. London: Faber and Faber.

Gössling, S. (2000) Tourism development in Sri Lanka: The case of Ethukala and Unawatuna. *Tourism Recreation Research* 25 (3), 103–114.

Gould, S.J. (1980) *The Panda's Thumb*. New York: W.W. Norton & Co.

Graham, B. (1998) Liberalization, regional economic development and the geography of demand for air transport in the European Union. *Journal of Transport Geography* 6 (2), 87–104.

Green Globe News (2000) Country Focus: Spain. On WWW at http://www.greenglobe21.com/pdf_files/june2000.pdf. Accessed 13.2.2001.

Gregory, D.J. (1994) 'Logical positivism', 'model', 'structurialism' entries. In R.J. Johnston, D. Gregory and D.M. Smith (eds) *The Dictionary of Human Geography* (3rd edn, pp. 350–351, 385–386, 599–600). Oxford: Blackwell.

Gunn, C.A. (1988) *Tourism Planning*. New York: Taylor and Francis.

Gunn, C.A. (1993) *Tourism Planning: Basics, Concepts, Cases* (3rd edn). Washington, D.C.: Taylor & Francis.

Gurney, J. (1840) *A Winter in the West Indies, Described in Familiar Letters to Henry Clay, of Kentucky*. London: John Murray.

Hall, C.M. (1996) Personal communication on the relevance of lines in sand pits to resort life cycles. April, London, Ontario.

Hall, C.M. (2000) *Tourism Planning – Policies, Processes and Relationships*. Harlow: Prentice Hall.

Hall, C.M. and McArthur, S. (1998) *Integrated Heritage Management*. London: The Stationery Office.

Hall, C.M. and Page, S.J. (1999) *The Geography of Tourism and Recreation: Environment, Place and Space*. London: Routledge.

Hall, C.M. and Page, S.J. (2005) *The Geography of Tourism and Recreation: Environment, Place and Space* (3rd edn). London: Routledge.

Hall, C.M., Williams, A.M. and Lew, A. (2004) Tourism: Conceptualisations, institutions and issues. In A. Lew, C.M. Hall and A. Williams (eds) *Companion to Tourism* (pp. 3–21). Oxford: Blackwells.

Hammond, J.T. (1993) Hilton Head Island's growing pains centered on mayor-elect. *The News* 29 November.

Handy, C. (1994) *The Age of Paradox*. Boston: Harvard Business School Press.

Harada, W. (1968) Kona group seeks 3-story limitation. Honolulu *Advertiser* 29 May [Hawaii Newspaper Clippings Morgue, Hamilton Library, University of Hawaii-file Kona Building Heights]

Harada-Stone, D. (1989) Kealakekua ranch's plans worry neighbours. Hawaii *Tribune Herald* 10 January, 1.

Harland Bartholomew and Associates (1960) *A Plan for Kona*. Honolulu: Prepared for the Hawaii State Planning Office.

Harlow, G.S. (1928) *Hawaii: By a Tourist*. Los Angeles, CA: West Coast Publishing.

Harmon, M. (1999) Long Beach, Successful Meetings, June. http://global.umi.com/pqdweb?ts = 98. . .&Sid = 7&Idx = 10&Deli = 1&RQT = 309&Dtp = 1. Accessed 9.3.2001.

Harnischfeger, U. (2000) Preussag focuses on leisure. *Financial Times* 5th October.

Harrigan, J.J. (1989) *Political Change in the Metropolis*. Illinois: Scott, Foresman and Company.

Harrigan, N. (1974) The legacy of Caribbean history and tourism. *Annals of Tourism Research* 2 (1), 13–25.

Harris, C. (1954) The market as a factor in the localization of industry in the United States. *Annals of the Association of American Geographers* 64, 315–348.

Harrison, D. (1995) Development of tourism in Swaziland. *Annals of Tourism Research* 22 (1), 135–156.

Hart, C. (1999) The retail accordion and assortment strategies: An exploratory study. *International Review of Retail, Distribution and Consumer Research* 8 (2), 165–182.

Hart, C.W., Casserley, G. and Lawless, M.J. (1984) The product life cycle: How useful? *The Cornell Quarterly* 25, 54–63.

Hartwell, M. and Lane, J. (1991) *Champions of Enterprise*. Double Bay, NSW: Focus Books Pty Ltd.

Harvey, D. (1969) *Explanation in Geography*. London: Edward Arnold.

Harvey, D. (1989) *The Condition of Post-Modernity*. Oxford: Blackwell.

Hawaii County Planning Department (HCPD) (1999) On WWW at http://www.hawaii-county.com/text.version/annual96_97/r&d01.htm. Accessed 21.1.2000.

Hawaii Newspaper Clippings Morgue (HNCM), Hamilton Library, University of Hawaii [original newspaper unknown, subject heading shown in brackets below]

_____ (1949) Kona airport induces new business. 9 Sept. [Kona Airport 1929/1953]

_____ (1951) Kona's airport: An asset for Hawaii. [Kona Airport 1929/1953]

_____ (1953) 'Cow pen' battle continues at Kona. 30 Apr. [Kona Cattle Pen Controversy at Kailua Wharf]

_____ (1957) 'Natural' look to prevail by Kona landscaping project. 5 June [Kona Sea Wall]

_____ (1959) Kona water supply called adequate for now. 17 Nov. [Kona Water 1957/1958]

_____ (1960) Sen. Lymanm Moves to drop $1.7M Kona area projects [Kona Master Plan]

Hawaii Tourism Authority (HTA) (1999) *Competitive strategic assessment of Hawaii tourism* (Executive Summary). Hawaiian Tourism Authority.

Hawaii Tribune Herald (HTH) (1967a) Planners recommend Kona maps. 21 February, 1.

Hawaii Tribune Herald (1967b) New golf course proposed by County for South Kona. 25 October, 8.

Hawaii Tribune Herald (1968a) Kona Hilton opening brings room level to over 2,100. 25 February, 3.

Hawaii Tribune Herald (1968b) Editorial. Emphasis on 'Gold Coast'. 5 February, 4.

Hawaii Tribune Herald (1969) Nearly 3,500 new rooms planned for Kona. 26 January, 3.

Hawaii Tribune Herald (1970) Girders, construction worker's pounding reshape Kailua and ... New Kona of modern buildings rises along isle's 'sun coast'. 26 July, 2–3.

Hawaii Tribune Herald (1972) Proposed development, scenic route are termed 'monstrosity'. 18 January, 1.

Hawaii Tribune Herald (1974a) Kailua Village development bill gets county support. 31 July, 1.

Hawaii Tribune Herald (1974b) Council oks bill for Kailua-Kona. 22 August, 10.

Hawaii Tribune Herald (1974c) Kona chamber applauds district approval. 18 September, 16.

Hawaii Tribune Herald (1989) Ground blessing held or Ka'upulehu Four Seasons. 2 May, 1.

Hawken, P., Lovins, A. and Lovins, L.H. (1999) *Natural Capitalism: Creating the Next Industrial Revolution*. Boston, MA: Little, Brown and Company.

Hawkins, M. (1982) The Atlantic City Experience: Casino Gambling as an Economic Recovery Program.

Haywood, K.M. (1986) Can the tourist area life-cycle be made operational? *Tourism Management* 7 (3), 154–167.

Haywood, K.M. (1988) Responsible and responsive tourism planning in the community. *Tourism Management* June.

Haywood, K.M. (1992) Revisiting resort cycle. *Annals of Tourism Research* 19 (2), 351–354.

Haywood, K.M. (1998) Economic business cycles and the tourism life-cycle concept. In D. Ioniddes and K. Debbage (eds) *The Economic Geography of the Tourist Industry* (pp. 273–284). London: Routledge.

Heath, E. and Wall, G. (1992) *Marketing Tourism Destination: A Strategic Planning Approach*. New York: Wiley.

Hiss, T. (1990) *The Experience of Place*. New York: Alfred A. Knopf.

Hobbs, C. (1913) The ruin or the redemption of Lake Quinsigamond. *The Worcester Magazine* February, 35–38.

Hodgson, G.M. (2002) Darwinism in economics: From analogy to ontology. *Journal of Evolutionary Economics* 12 (3), 259–281.

Hofer, C.W. (1975) Toward a contingency theory of business strategy. *Academy of Management Journal* 18 (December), 784–809.

Holder, J.S. (1991) Pattern and impact of tourism on the environment of the Caribbeans. In S. Medlik (ed.) *Managing Tourism*. Oxford: Butterworth-Heinemann.

Hollander, S.C. (1960) The wheel of retailing. *Journal of Marketing* 25 (July), 37–42.

Hollander, S.C. (1980) Oddities, nostalgia, wheels and other patterns in retail evolution. In R.W. Stampfl and E.C. Hirschmann (eds) *Competitive Structure in Retail Markets: The Department Store Perspective* (pp. 84–94). Chicago: American Marketing Association.

Holloway, J.C. (1994) *The Business of Tourism* (Vol. 4). London: Pitman.

Holloway, J.C. (1998) *The Business of Tourism* (Vol. 5). Harlow: Longman.

Honolulu Advertiser (HA) (1954) Long range thinking urged in Kona area. 13 January, 1.

Honolulu Advertiser (1955a) Chamber unit ok's Kaiser Kona tourist project. 11 January, A1.

Honolulu Advertiser (1955b) Local corporation plans $1 million Kona resort. 5 August, A3.

Honolulu Advertiser (1956a) Time grows short. 3 August, A3.

Honolulu Advertiser (1956b) Kona backs four-point development. 17 September, B1.

Honolulu Advertiser (1968) Kimurao opposes Kona high-rises. 18 May, A10.

Honolulu Advertiser (1969) Editorial. Saving Kona's assets. 5 February, B2.

Honolulu Advertiser (1970) Bill proposes State buy Kailua-Kona village. 7 March, A6.

Honolulu Advertiser (1973) Historic district proposed for Kona resort area. 7 February, B6.

Honolulu Star Bulletin (HSB) (1956) Plans for Two $1 Million Hotels in Kona Announced. 10 July, 1B.

Honolulu Star Bulletin (1957) Kaiser pegs plans to tourist growth. 14 February, 1B.

Honolulu Star Bulletin (1958a) Navy barge reaches Kona with 9-to-10 day water supply. [HNCM Kona Drought]

Honolulu Star Bulletin (1958b) Big Isle reaction to Kona plan stresses water, airport need. 2 Dec. [HNCM Kona Master Plan]

Honolulu Star Bulletin (1970) Kona's time to plan. 1 July, A14.

Honolulu Star Bulletin (1974) On the Big Island. 31 Mar. [HNCM Kailua-Kona 1962/1975]

Honolulu Star Bulletin (1988) State opposes resort near wildlife area. 13 July, A4.

Hough, M. (1990) *Out of Place: Restoring Identity to the Regional Landscape*. New Haven, CT: Yale University Press.

Hourglass Foundation (2001) *Where Are We Headed?* Lancaster, PA: Hourglass Foundation.

House, J. (1954) Geographical aspects of coastal holiday resorts. Unpublished PhD thesis, Durham: Kings College.

Hovinen, G.R. (1981) A tourist cycle in Lancaster County, Pennsylvania. *The Canadian Geographer* 25 (3), 283–286.

Hovinen, G.R. (1982) Visitor cycles: Outlook for tourism in Lancaster County. *Annals of Tourism Research* 9, 565–583.

Hovinen, G.R. (1995) Heritage issues in urban tourism: An assessment of new trends in Lancaster County. *Tourism Management* 16 (5), 381–388.

Hovinen, G. (1997) Lancaster County, Pennsylvania's heritage tourism initiative: A preliminary assessment. *Small Town* 27, 4– 11.

Hovinen, G.R. (2002) Revisiting the destination lifecycle model. *Annals of Tourism Research* 29 (1), 209– 230.

Hudson, R. (1992) Industrial restructuring and spatial change: Myths and realities in the changing geography of production in the 1980s. *Scottish Geographical Magazine* 108 (2), 74– 81.

Hunziker, W. (1942) *The Tourist Doctrine*. Switzerland: St. Gallen.

Hurst, D.K. (1995) *Crisis and Renewal: Meeting the Challenge of Organizational Change*. Boston, MA: Harvard Business School Press.

ICARE – International Center for Art Economics (1997) *Applicazione della Telematica alla Gestione dei Flussi di Visitatori*. Research Center Telecom Italia S. Salvador, mimeo.

Idzes, I. (1988) *Corporate Lifecycles: How and Why Corporations Grow and Die and What To Do About It*. Englewood Cliffs, NJ: Prentice Hall.

Inskeep, E. (1991) *Tourism Planning: An Integrated and Sustainable Development Approach*. New York: Van Nostrand Reinhold.

Inskeep, E. (1994) *National and Regional Tourism Planning: Methodologies and Case Studies*, edited by the World Tourism Organization. UK: Routledge.

Inter-Island Steam Navigation Company, Ltd. (1917– 44) *President's Report for the Year*. Honolulu: Advertiser Publishing Co.

Ioannides, D. (1992) Tourism development agents: The Cypriot resort cycle. *Annals of Tourism Research* 19 (4), 711– 731.

Ioannides, D. and Debbage, K. (1998) *The Economic Geography of the Tourist Industry: A Supply-side Analysis*. London: Routledge.

Irish Tourist Board (2001) On WWW at
http://www.ireland.travel.ie/aboutus/tourismfacts.asp;
http://www.irlgov.ie/finance/budget/budget01/budmeasu.htm#PARTIII;
http://www.irlgov.ie/finance/budget/budget01/speech01.htm.
Accessed 6.3.2001.

Ishii, K. and Stevels, A. (2000) *Environmental Value Chain Analysis: A Tool for Product Definition in Eco Design*. San Francisco, CA: IEEE ISEE.

Isle of Man Department of Tourism and Leisure (1996) *Marketing Plan 1996*. Douglas: Government of the Isle of Man.

IUCN (1994) *Richtlinien für Management-Kategorien von Schutzgebieten*. Gland, Cambridge, Grafenau: IUCN, WCMC and FÖNAD.

IUCN (1998) *1997 United Nations List of Protected Areas*. Gland and Cambridge: WCMC and WCPA.

IUCN, UNEP and WWF (1980) World Conservation Strategy. Living Resource Conservation for Sustainable Development. Gland: IUCN.

Jablonka, E. (2000) Lamarckian inheritance systems in biology: A source of metaphors and models in technological evolution. In J. Zimon (ed.) *Technological Innovation as an Evolutionary Process* (pp. 27– 40). Cambridge: Cambridge University Press.

Jain, S.C. (1985) *Market Planning and Strategy*. Cincinnati, OH: South Western.

Jansen-Verbeke, M. (1986) Inner-city tourism: Resources, tourists and promoters. *Annals of Tourism Research* 13 (1), 79– 100.

Javiluoma, J. (1992) Alternative tourism and the evolution of tourist areas, *Tourism Management*, 13 (1), 118– 120.

Jawahar, I.M. and McLaughlin, G.L. (2001) Toward a descriptive stakeholder theory: An organisational life cycle approach. *Academy of Management Review* 26 (3), 397– 414.

Job, H. and Weizenegger, S. (1999) Anspruch und Realität einer integrierten Naturschutz- und Entwicklungspolitik in den Großschutzgebieten Schwarza-frikas. In G. Meyer and A. Thimm (eds) *Naturräume in der Dritten Welt. Ausbeutung, nachhaltige Nutzung oder Schutz?* (pp. 37–64). Mainz: Interdisziplinärer Arbeitskreis Dritte Welt, Veröffentlichungen 12.

Johnson, J.D. and Rasker, R. (1995) The role of economic and quality of life values in rural business location. *Journal of Rural Studies* 11 (4), 323–332.

Johnson, J. and Snepenger, D. (1993) Application of the tourism life cycle concept in the Greater Yellowstone Region. *Society and Natural Resources* 6, 127–148.

Johnson, J.D. and Snepenger, D.J. (in progress) Community solidarity regarding tourism development in a transitional rural economy.

Johnson, J.D., Snepenger, D.J. and Akis, S. (1994) Host resident perceptions of tourism in a transitional rural economy. *Annals of Tourism Research* 21 (3).

Johnson, J.D., Maxwell, B.M. and Aspinall, R. (2003) Moving nearer to heaven: Growth and change in the Greater Yellowstone Region. In R. Buckley, C. Pickering and D. Weaver (eds) *Nature Tourism and Environment*. Wallingford: CAB International.

Johnston, C. (1995) Enduring idylls? A geographical study of tourism in Kona, Hawaii Island. University of Hawaii: Unpublished PhD dissertation.

Johnston, C.S. (2001) Shoring the foundations of the destination life cycle model. Part 1: Ontological and epistemological considerations. *Tourism Geographies* 3 (1), 2–28.

Johnston, R.J. (1991) *Geography and Geographers. Anglo-American Human Geography since 1945* (Vol. 4). London: Arnold.

Johnston, R.J., Gregory, D. and Smith, D. (1986) *The Dictionary of Human Geography* (2nd edn). Oxford: Blackwell.

Jones, P. and Pizam, A. (1993) *The International Hospitality Industry – Organizational and Operational Issues*. London: Pitman.

Joppe, M. (1996) Sustainable community tourism development revisited. *Tourism Management* 17 (7), 475–479.

Jordon, P. (2000) Restructuring Croatia's coastal resorts: Change, sustainable development and the incorporation of rural hinterlands. *Journal of Sustainable Tourism* 8 (6), 525–539.

Juelg, F. (1993) Tourism product life cycles in the Central Eastern Alps: A case study of Heiligenblut on the Grossglockner. *Tourism Recreation Research* 18 (1), 20–26.

Jurowski, C., Uysal, M. and Williams, D.R. (1997) A theoretical analysis of host community resident reactions to tourism. *Journal of Travel Research* 36 (2), 3–9.

Juvik, J.O., Singleton, D.C. and Clarke, G.G. (1978) Climate and Water Balance on the Island of Hawaii. *Mauna Loa Observatory, a 20th Anniversary Report* (pp. 129–139). National Oceanic and Atmospheric Administration.

Kachigan, S.K. (1986) *Statistical Analysis*. New York: Radius Press.

Kaplan, R.S. and Norton, D.P. (1990) *The Balanced Scorecard: Translating Strategy into Action*. Boston, MA: Harvard Business School Press.

Kaplan, R.S. and Norton, D.P. (2001) *The Strategy Focused Organisation: How Balanced Scorecard Companies Thrive in the New Business Environment*. Boston, MA: Harvard Business School Press.

Katsanis, L.P. and Pitta, D.A. (1995) Punctuated equilibrium and the evolution of the product manager. *Journal of Product and Brand Management* 4 (3), 49–60.

Keane, M.J. (1997) Quality and pricing in tourism destinations. *Annals of Tourism Research* 24 (1), 117–130.

Keller, C.P. (1987) Stages of peripheral tourism development – Canada's Northwest Territories. *Tourism Management* 8, 2–32.

Kenney, J. (1995) Personal interview. Hilton Head, SC.

Kermath, B.M. and Thomas, R.N. (1992) Spatial dynamics of resorts: Sousa, Dominican Republic. *Annals of Tourism Research* 19, 173–190.

Ketchum, L. (1969a) Denial recommended for rezoning 146-Acre Kona parcel for homes. Hawai'i *Tribune Herald* 20 April, 1.

Ketchum, L. (1969b) A look at Hualālai – proposed addition to Volcanoes Park. Hawaii *Tribune Herald* 10 July, 16.

Keys, N.H.E. (1985) Tourism evolution in Queensland. Unpublished MA Thesis. Nathan, Queensland: Griffith University.

King, R.D. (1935) Districts in the Hawaiian Islands. In *A Gazetteer of the Territory of Hawaii*. Compiled by Hohn Wesley Coulter (pp. 214–225). Honolulu: University of Hawaii Research Publication #11.

Kirch, P.V. (1983) Introduction. In *Archaeological Investigations of the Mudlane-Waimea-Kawaihae Road Corridor, Island of Hawaii* (pp. 3–24). An Interdisciplinary Study of an Environmental Transect.

Klepper, S. (1996) Entry, exit, growth, and innovation over the product life cycle. *The American Economic Review* 86 (3), 562–583.

Knowles, T. and Curtis, S. (1999) The market viability of European mass tourist destinations: A post-stagnation lifecycle analysis. *International Journal of Tourism Research* 1, 87–96.

Kokkranikal, J. and Morrison, A. (2002) Entrepreneurship and sustainable tourism: The houseboats of Kerala. *Tourism and Hospitality Research* 4 (1), 7–20.

Kotler, P. (1976) *Marketing Management* (Vol. 3). London: Prentice Hall.

Kotler, P. (1997) *Marketing Management, Analysis, Planning and Control* (9th edn). New Jersey: Prentice Hall.

Kotler, P. and Armstrong, G. (1984) *Principles of Marketing* (4th edn). Englewood Cliffs, NJ: Prentice-Hall.

Kotler, P. and Turner, R.E. (1993) *Marketing Management* (Canadian 7th edn). Prentice-Hall, Canada Inc. See pp. 3271–3397 re: 'product life cycles'.

Krauss, B. (1974a) Opening up north Kona coast. Honolulu *Advertiser* 13 April, A3.

Krauss, B. (1974b) Tale of two tourist towns. Honolulu *Advertiser*, 15 March, A3.

Kraybill, D.B. and Nolt, S.M. (1995) *Amish Enterprise: From Plows to Profits*. Baltimore, MD: The Johns Hopkins University Press.

Krippendorff, J. (1975) *Die Landschaftsfressser-Turismus- und der Erholungslandschaft-verderben oder segen*. Bern und Stuttgart: Hallvall Verlag.

Krippendorf, J. (1987) *The Holiday Makers*. London: Heinemann.

Krueger, N.F. and Brazeal, D.V. (1994) Entrepreneurial potential and potential entrepreneurs. *Entrepreneurship Theory and Practice* 18 (3), 91–104.

Krugman, P. (1995) *Development, Geography and Economic Theory*. Cambridge, MA: MIT Press.

Kuratko, D. and Hodgetts, R. (1998) *Entrepreneurship: A Contemporary Approach*. Fort Worth, TX: The Dryden Press.

Lake Memphremagog, topographic map sheets 31 H/1, 1917–2000, 1:50,000. Ottawa: Department of Energy, Mines and Resources.

Lamarck, J.B. (1809) *Philosophie zoologique*. [Translated 1963 as *Zoological Philosophy: an exposition with regard to the natural history of animals*]. New York: Harner Publishing Co.

Lancaster County Planning Commission (1998) *Heritage Tourism Plan*. Lancaster, PA: Lancaster County Planning Commission.

Lander, H. (1937) *Cairns Timetable and General Information*. Cairns: Lander, H.

Langston, P., Clarke, G.P. and Clarke, D.B. (1997) Retail saturation, retail location and retail competition: An analysis of British grocery retailing. *Environment and Planning A* 29, 77–104.

Langston, P., Clarke, G.P. and Clarke, D.B. (1998) Retail saturation: The debate in the mid-1990s. *Environment and Planning A* 30, 49–66.

Lankford, S.V. and Howard, D.R. (1994) Developing a tourism impact attitude scale. *Annals of Tourism Research* 21, 121–139.

Lash, S. and Urry, J. (1987) *The End of Organised Capitalism*. Madison: University of Wisconsin Press.

Laws, E. (1995) *Tourist Destination Management: Issues, Analysis and Policies*. London: Routledge.

Laws, E., Faulkner, B. and Moscardo, G. (1998) *Embracing and Managing Change in Tourism: International Case Studies* (pp. 95–115). London: Routledge.

Lehne, R. (1986) *Casino Policy*. New Brunswick, NJ: Rutgers University Press.

Lenoir, T. and Ross, C. (1996) The naturalized history museum. In P. Galison and D. Stump (eds) *The Disunity of Science: Boundaries, Contexts and Power* (pp. 370–397). Stanford, CA: Stanford University Press.

Le Pelley, B. and Laws, E. (1998) A stakeholder benefits approach to tourism management in a historic city centre. In E. Laws, B. Faulkner and G. Moscardo (eds) *Embracing and Managing Change in Tourism: International Case Studies* (pp. 70–94). London: Routledge.

Lerner, M. and Haber, S. (2000) Performance factors of small tourism ventures: The interface of tourism, entrepreneurship and the environment. *Journal of Business Venturing* 16, 77–100.

Levasseur, H. (2002). Freligsburgh, telephone interview.

Levitt, T. (1960) Marketing myopia. *Harvard Business Review* July–August, 45–56.

Levitt, T. (1976) Management and "post-industrial" society. *The Public Interest* 44, 69–73.

Lewis, R. and Green, S. (1998) Planning for stability and managing chaos: The case of Alpine ski resorts. In E. Laws, B. Faulkner and G. Moscardo (eds) *Embracing and Managing Change in Tourism: International Case Studies* (pp. 138–160). London: Routledge.

Lipietz, A. (1986) New tendencies in the international division of labour: Regimes of accumulation and modes of regulation. In A. Scott and M. Storper (eds) *Production, Work, Territory* (pp. 16–29). Boston, MA: Allen and Unwin.

Liu, J.L. and Var, T. (1986) Resident attitudes to tourism impacts in Hawaii. *Annals of Tourism Research* 13 (2), 193–214.

Liu, J.L., Sheldon, P.J. and Var, T. (1987) Resident perception of the environmental impacts of tourism. *Annals of Tourism Research* 14 (1), 17–37.

Lloret Turisme (2002) *Looking Towards Lloret of the Future*. Lloret de Mar: Lloret Turisme.

Lofton, D. (1993) Island may shut door to growth. *The State* November 5.

Logan, J.R. and Molotch, H.L. (1987) *Urban Fortunes: The Political Economy of Place*. Berkeley, CA: University of California Press.

London, C. (1917) *Our Hawaii*. New York: The Macmillan Company.

Long, P.T., Perdue, R.R. and Allen, L. (1990) Rural resident tourism perceptions and attitudes by community level of tourism. *Journal of Travel Research* Winter, 39.

Lorenz, E.N. (1963) Deterministic non-periodic flow. *Journal of the Atmospheric Sciences* 20 (2), 130–141.

Lösch, A. (1940) *Die Raumliche Ordnung der Wirtschaft* [*The Spatial Order of the Economy*]. Jena: Gustav Fischer Verlag.

Loyacono, L.L. (1991) *Travel and Tourism: A Legislator's Guide*. Washington, D.C.: National Conference of State Legislatures.

Lu, L. (1997) A study on the life cycle of mountain resorts: A case study of Huangshan Mountain and Jiuhanshan Mountain. *Scintia Geographic Sinica* 17 (1), 63–69.

Luloff, A.E. and Steahr, T.E. (1985) The structure and impact of population redistribution: Summary and conclusions. In T.E. Steahr and A.E. Luloff (eds) *The Structure and Impact of Population Redistribution in New England*. University Park, PN: Northeast Regional Center for Rural Development, Pennsylvania State University.

Lundgren, J.O. (1984) Geographic concepts and the development of tourism research in Canada. *Geojournal* 9, 17–25.

Lundgren, J.O. (1988) Tourist destination development and problems of management – Case Lake Memphremagog. *TEOROS* 7 (2), 10–16, Montreal: UQAM.

Lundgren, J. (1996) The tourism development process in the Eastern Townships – the changing tourist product composition. *Journal of Eastern Townships Studies* No.8, Spring, 5–24, Lennoxville, Que., Canada: Bishop's University.

Lundtorp, S. and Wanhill, S. (2001) Resort life cycle theory: Generating processes and estimation. *Annals of Tourism Research* 28 (4), 947–964.

Lundvall, B-A. (1993) *The Learning Economy: Challenges to Economic Theory and Policy.* Paper presented to the EAPE conference, Copenhagen, 27–28 October.

MacCannell, D. (1976) *The Tourist: A New Theory of the Leisure Class*. London: Macmillan.

MacKenzie, J.M. (1988) *The Empire of Nature. Hunting, Conservation and British Imperialism*. Manchester: Manchester University Press.

Madrigal, R. (1995) Residents' perceptions and the role of government. *Annals of Tourism Research* 22 (1), 86–102.

Mahon, G. (1980) *The Company that Bought the Boardwalk*. New York: Random House.

Mak, B. and Go, F. (1995) Matching global competition: Cooperation among Asia airlines. *Tourism Management* 16 (1), 61–65.

Mandelbrot, B. (1977) *The Fractal Geometry of Nature*. New York: W.H. Freeman.

Maneeorasert, M., Pokpong, K. and Prangsio, C. (1975) *Reconnaissance Survey of the Impact of Tourism in the Highlands*. Social and Economic Change Committee. Chiang Mai, Thailand: Tribal Research Institute.

Mann, K. and Lowe, B. (1956) *Teddy Bear.* RCA Records.

Mann, T. (1924) *The Magic Mountain*.

Manning, T. (1999) Indicators of tourism sustainability. *Tourism Management* 20 (2), 179–181.

Marchena Gomez, M. and Vera Rebollo, F. (1995) Coastal areas: Processes, typologies, prospects. In A. Montanari and A. Williams (eds) *European Tourism: Regions, Spaces and Restructuring* (pp. 111–126). Chichester, Wiley.

Markin, R.J. and Duncan, C.P. (1981) The transformation of retailing institutions: Beyond the wheel of retailing and life cycle theories. *Journal of Macromarketing* 1 (Spring), 58–66.

Markusen, A.R. (1985) *Profit Cycles, Oligopoly and Regional Development*. Cambridge, MA: MIT Press.

Markworth, A.J., Stringer, J. and Rollins, R.W. (1995) Deterministic chaos theory and its applications to materials science. *MRS Bulletin* 20 (7), 20–28.

Martin, B.S. (1999) The efficacy of growth machine theory in explaining resident perceptions of community tourism development. *Tourism Analysis* 4, 47–55.

Martin, B.S., McGuire, F.A. and Allen, L.A. (1998) Retirees' attitudes toward tourism: Implications for sustainable development. *Tourism Analysis* 3, 43–51.

Martin, B.S. and Uysal, M. (1990) An examination of the relationship between carrying capacity and the tourism lifecycle: Management and policy implications. *Journal of Environmental Management* 31, 327–333.

Martin, R. (1989) The new economic and politics of regional restructuring: The British experience. In L. Albrechts, F. Moulearts, P. Roberts and E. Swyngedouw (eds) *Regional Policy at the Crossroads* (pp. 27–51). London: Jessica Kingsley.

Mary Means & Associates, Inc. (2001) *Lancaster–York Heritage Region Management Action Plan*. Lancaster, PA.

Massey, D. (1978) Regionalism: Some current issues. *Capital and Class* 6, 106–125.

Massey, D. and Meegan, R. (1984) *Spatial Divisions of Labour: Social Structures and the Geography of Production*. London: MacMillan.

Massey, G. (1999) Product evolution: A Darwinian or Lamarckian phenomenon? *Journal of Product and Brand Management* 8 (4), 301–318.

Mathews, K.M., White, M.C. and Long, R.G. (1999) Why study the complexity sciences in the social sciences? *Human Relations* 52 (4), 439–462.

McCaskill, D. (1997) *From Tribal Peoples to Ethnic Minorities: The Transformation of Indigenous Peoples*. Chiang Mai, Thailand: Silkworm Books.

McCaskill, D. and Kampe, K. (1997) *Development or Domestication? Indigenous Peoples of Southeast Asia* (pp. 26–60). Thailand: Silkworm Books.

McElroy, J.L., deAlbuquerque, K. and Dioguardi, A. (1993) Applying the tourist destination life-cycle model to small Caribbean and Pacific Islands. *World Travel and Tourism Review* 236–244.

McKay, M.K. (1990) Tourism evolution in provincial parks: A guide to investment decisions. Unpublished B.A. thesis: Department of Geography, University of Western Ontario, London.

McKercher, B. (1999) A chaos approach to tourism. *Tourism Management* 20, 425–434.

McNair, M.P. (1958) Significant trends and developments in the postwar period. In A.B. Smith (ed.) *Competitive Distribution in a Free High Level Economy and its Implications for the University* (pp. 1–25). Pittsburgh, PA: University of Pittsburgh Press.

Meeks, H.A. (1986) *Time and Change in Vermont – A Human Geography*. Chester, CN.

Meethan, K. (2001) *Tourism in Global Society: Place, Culture and Consumption*. London: Palgrave.

Melly, G. (2002) You ain't nothing but an icon. *Observer Review* 28 July, 15.

Menzies, A. (1920) *Hawaii Nei 128 Years Ago. Journal of Archibald Menzies*. W.F. Wilson (ed.). Honolulu: The New Freedom.

Mercer, D. (1993) A two-decade test of product life cycle theory. *British Journal of Management* 4 (4), 269–274.

Messerli, H.R. (1993) Tourism area life cycle models and residents' perceptions: The case of Santa Fe, New Mexico (City Planning). Unpublished PhD Thesis, Cornell University.

Meyer, R. (1996) Waikiki faces major problems: Does new master plan hold solutions? *FIU Hospitality Review* 14 (1), 7–18.

Meyer-Arendt, K.L. (1985) The Grand Isle, Louisiana resort cycle. *Annals of Tourism Research* 12 (3), 449–465.

Meyer-Arendt, K. and Hartmann, R. (1998) *Casino Gambling in America: Origins, Trends, and Impacts*. Elmsford, NY: Cognizant Communications.

Meyer-Arendt, K.J., Sambrook, R.A. and Kermath, B.M. (1992) Resorts in the Dominican Republic: A typology. *Journal of Geography* 91, 219–225.

Middleton, V. and Hawkins, R. (1998) *Sustainable Tourism: A Marketing Perspective*. Oxford: Butterworth Heinemann.

Miles, R.E. and Snow, C.C. (1978) *Organisational Strategy, Structure and Process*. New York: McGraw Hill.

Mill, R.C. (1996) Societal marketing: Implications for tourism destinations. *Journal of Vacation Marketing* 2 (3), 215–221.

Miller, D. (1990) *The Icarus Paradox*. New York: Harper Business.

Miller, D. and Friessen, P.H. (1984) *Organisations: A Quantum View*. Englewood Cliffs, NJ: Prentice Hall.

Milne, S. (1998) Tourism and sustainable development: Exploring the global–local nexus. In C.M. Hall and A. Lew (eds) *Sustainable Tourism: A Geographical Perspective* (pp. 35–48). London: Longman.

Minniti, M. and Bygrave, W. (1999) The microfoundations of entrepreneurship. *Entrepreneurship Theory & Practice* 23 (4), 41–50.

Mintz, S. (1971) The Caribbean as a socio-cultural area. In M. Horowitz (ed.) *Peoples and Cultures of the Caribbean* (pp. 17–46). New York: Natural History Press.

Mintzberg, H. (2000) *The Rise and Fall of Strategic Planning*. London: Prentice Hall.

Mintzberg, H. and Waters, J.A. (1982). Tracking strategy in an entrepreneurial firm. *Academy of Management Journal* 25 (3), 465–499.

Miossec, J.M. (1976) *Elements pour une Theorie de l'Espace Touristique*. Centre des Hautes Études Touristique, Aix-en-Provence. Serie C, n. 36.

Miossec, J.M. (1977) Un modèle de l'espace touristique. *L'Espace Géographie* 1, 41–48.

Miskulin, D. (1994) A trip to the far past of Opatija tourism. In Proceedings, *150th Anniversary of Tourism in Opatija* (pp. 15–24). University of Rijeka, Faculty of Hotel Management, Opatija.

Mokyr, J. (2000) Evolutionary phenomena in technological change. In J. Zimon (ed.) *Technological Innovation as an Evolutionary Process* (pp. 52–65). Cambridge: Cambridge University Press.

Molotch, H. (1976) The city as a growth machine: Toward a political economy of place. *American Journal of Sociology* 82, 309–331.

Morecoft, J.D.W. and Dterman, J. (eds) (1994) *Modelling for Learning Organisations*. Portland, OR: Productivity Press.

Morgan, M. (1991) Dressing up to survive. *Tourism Management* 12 (1), 15–20.

Morgan, N.J. and Pritchard, A. (1999) *Power and Politics at the Seaside. The Development of Devon's Resorts in the Twentieth Century*. Exeter: University of Exeter Press.

Morrill, G.L. (1919) *Hawaiian Heathen and Others*. Chicago, IL: M.A. Donahue & Co.

Morrison, A.J. (1998) Small firm co-operative marketing in a peripheral tourism region. *International Journal of Contemporary Hospitality Management* 10 (5), 191–197.

Morrison, A., Rimmington, M. and Williams, C. (1999) *Entrepreneurship in the Hospitality, Tourism and Leisure Studies*. Oxford: Butterworth-Heinemann.

Moss, S.E., Ryan, C. and Wagoner, C.B. (2003) An empirical test of Butler's resort product life cycle: Forecasting casino winnings. *Journal of Travel Research* 41 (4), 393–399.

Mueller, S. and Thomas, A.S. (2000) Culture and entrepreneurial potential: A nine country study of locus of control and innovativeness. *Journal of Business Venturing* 16, 51–75.

Mueller, J.H., Schuessler, K.F. and Costner, H.L. (1970) *Statistical Reasoning in Sociology* (2nd edn). Boston, MA: Houghton Mifflin Co.

Murphy, P. (1985) *Tourism a Community Approach*. New York: Methuen.

Musick, J.R. (1898) *Hawaii. Our New Possessions*. New York: Funk & Wagnalls Company.

Nadeau, R. (1989) Le Tourisme Hivernale des Quebecois: De l'appel du sud au ski alpin. *TEOROS* 8 (3), 3–10. Montreal: UQAM.

Native Hawaiian Hospitality Association (2000) April 2000 Newsletter. On WWW at http://www.nahtha.org/april.htm. Accessed 22.3.2001.

Nelson, J.G. (1984) An external perspective on Parks Canada Future Strategies, 1986–2001. *Occasional paper #2*. Heritage Resources Centre Publication Series, University of Waterloo.

Nelson, J.G. (1987) National Parks and protected areas, national conservation strategies and sustainable development. *Geoforum* 18 (3), 291–319.

Nelson, R.R. and Winter, S.G. (1982) *An Evolutionary Theory of Economic Change*. Cambridge, MA: Harvard University Press.

Nice Matin (1971) Article Tourisme April 6. Nice: *Nice Matin*.

Nijkamp, P. and Reggiani, A. (1995) Non-linear evolution of dynamic spatial systems. The relevance of chaos and ecologically-based models. *Regional Science and Urban Economics* 25, 183–210.

Nilson, T.H. (1995) *Chaos Marketing: How to Win in a Turbulent World*. England: McGraw-Hill Book Company.

Nilsson, J-E. (1995) *Sweden in the Renewed Europe: Rise and Decline of an Industrial Nation*. Malmo: Liberhermods.

Nilsson, J-E. and Schamp, E. (1996) Restructuring of the European production system: Processes and consequences. *European Urban and Regional Studies* 3, 121–132.

Noble, I.R. and Slayter, R.O. (1981) Concepts and models of succession in vascular plant communities subject to recurrent fire. In A.M. Gill, R.H. Groves and I.R. Noble (eds) *Fire and the Australian Biota* (pp. 311–335). Canberra: Australian Academy of Sciences.

Normann, R. and Rairez, R. (1993) From value chain to value constellation: Designing interactive strategy. *Harvard Business Review* 71, 65–77.

Noronha, R. (1977) *Social and Cultural Dimensions of Tourism: A Review of the Literature in English*. Washington, DC: World Bank Working Paper.

Ober, F. (1908) *A Guide to the West Indies and Bermudas*. New York: Dodd, Mead & Co.

Oberhauser, A. (1987) Labour, production and the state: Decentralisation of the French automobile industry. *Regional Studies* 21, 445–458.

Ogilvie, F.W. (1933) *The Tourism Movement*. London: Staples Press.

Oglethope, M. (1984) Tourism in Malta – A crisis of dependence. *Leisure Studies* 12, 449–465.

O'Hare, G. and Barrett, H. (1997) The destination life cycle – international tourism in Peru. *Scottish Geographical Magazine* 113 (2), 66–73.

Olley, P. (1937) *Guide to Jamaica*. Kingston: The Tourist Trade Development Board.

Onkvisit, S. and Shaw, J.J. (1989) *Product Life Cycles and Product Management*. New York: Quorum Books.

Oppermann, M. (1995) Travel life cycle. *Annals of Tourism Research* 22 (3), 535–552.

Oppermann, M. (1998a) Destination threshold potential and the law of repeat visitation. *Journal of Travel Research* 37 (2), 131–137.

Oppermann, M. (1998b) What is new with the resort cycle? *Tourism Management* 19 (2), 179–180.

Oxford English Dictionary (1972) Oxford: The Clarendon Press.

Papatheodorou, A. (2001a) Why people travel to different places? *Annals of Tourism Research* 28 (1), 164–179.

Papatheodorou, A. (2001b) Tourism, transport geography and industrial economics: A synthesis in the context of Mediterranean Islands. *Anatolia* 12 (1), 23–34.

Papatheodorou, A. (2004) Exploring the evolution of Tourist Resorts. *Annals of Tourism Research* 31 (1), 219–237.

Paradise of the Pacific (1924) Survey of Hawaiian History Since Cook's Discovery 37 (7), 3–7.

Parks Canada (1994) *Guiding Principles and Operational Policies.* Minister of Supply and Services Canada.

Parks Canada (1997) *Banff National Park Management Plan.* Government of Canada.

Parks Canada (2002) Press Release: The Government of Canada announces action plan to protect Canada's natural heritage. October 3.

Paton, W. (1887) *Down the Islands: A Voyage to the Caribbees.* New York: Charles Scribners & Sons.

Patoskie J. (1992) Traditional tourist resorts: Problems and solutions Honolulu (Hawaii, USA). International Forum on Tourism to the Year 2000: Prospects and Challenges, Acapulco, Mexico.

Patoskie, J. and Ikeda, G. (1993) *Waikiki – The Evolution of an Urban Resort.* Honolulu: University of Hawaii. School of Travel Industry Management. Centre for Tourism Policy Studies.

Pattison, D.A. (1968) Tourism in the Firth of Clyde. Unpublished PhD thesis, Glasgow: University of Glasgow.

Pearce, D. (1989) *Tourist Development* (2nd edn). Harlow: Longman.

Pearce, D. (1993) Comparative studies in tourism research. In R.W.F. Butler and D.G. Pearce (eds) *Tourism Research: Critiques and Challenges* (pp. 21–35). London: Routledge.

Pearce, P. (1982) *The Social Psychology of Tourist Behaviour.* Oxford: Pergamon.

Peat, F.D. (1991) *The Philosopher's Stone: Chaos, Synchronicity and the Hidden Order of the World.* New York: Bantam.

Peet, R. (1998) *Modern Geographical Thought.* Oxford: Blackwell.

Pelgrave, F. (1994) *Whitecars.* Cairns: Pelgrave, F.

Peterson, D.W. and Moore, R.B. (1987) Geologic History and the Evolution of Geologic Concepts, Island of Hawaii. Washington D.C.: US G.P.O. (U.S.G.S. Professional Paper 1350.)

Phillippo, J. (1843) *Jamaica: Its Past and Present State.* London: John Snow.

Pimlott, J.A.R. (1947) *The Englishman's Holiday.* London: Faber.

Pine, B.J. and Gilmore, J.H. (1999) *The Experience Economy.* Boston, MA: Harvard Business School Press.

Pinfield, L.T. (1986) A field evaluation of perspectives on organisational decision making. *Administrative Science Quarterly* 31 (3), 414–450.

Piore, M. (1986) Perspectives on labour market flexibility. *Industrial Relations* 25, 146–166.

Piore, M. and Sabel, C. (1984) *The Second Industrial Divide: Possibilities for Prosperity.* New York: Basic Books.

Plog, S.C. (1972) Why destination areas rise and fall in popularity. Paper Presented at the Southern California Chapter of the Travel Research Bureau, October 10, 1972.

Plog, S.C. (1973) Why destinations areas rise and fall in popularity. *Cornell Hotel and Restaurant Association Quarterly* 13, 6–13.

Plog, S.C. (1991) Why destination areas rise and fall in popularity. In *Leisure Travel: Making It a Growth Market ... Again!* (pp. 75–84). New York: John Wiley & Sons, Inc.

Plog, S.C. (2001) Why destination areas rise and fall in popularity: An update of a Cornell Quarterly Classic. *Cornell Hotel and Restaurant Administration Quarterly* 42 (3), 13–24.

Pollard, J. and Rodriguez, R. (1993) Tourism and Torremolinos. Recession or reaction to environment. *Tourism Management* 12 (4), 247–258.

Polli, R. and Cook, V. (1969) Validity of the product life cycle. *The Journal of Business* 42 (4), 385–400.

Pollock, J. (1986) *Contemporary Theories of Knowledge*. Savage, MD: Rowman & Littlefield Publishers, Inc.

Porter, M. (1980) *Competitive Strategy*. New York: Free Press.

Potton Heritage Association (1993) Municipality of Potton, Mansonville; Pamphlet material: 1. Potton Hier et Aujourd'hui, 14 pages; 2. Les Bateaus du Lac, 3 pages; 3. The Mountain House, 4 pages; 4. Vale Perkins, 4 pages.

Power, T.M. (1995) Thinking about natural resource-dependent economies: Moving beyond the folk economics of the rear-view mirror. In R.L. Knight and S.F. Bates (eds) *A New Century for Natural Resource Management* (pp. 235–253). Washington DC: Island Press.

Pratt, A. (1991) Discourses of locality. *Environment and Planning A* 23 (2), 257–266.

Pred, A. (1966) *The Spatial Dynamics of U.S. Urban Industrial Growth*. Cambridge, MA: MIT Press.

Pred, A. (1984) Place as historically contingent process: Structuration and the time–geography of becoming places. *Annals of the Association of American Geographers* 74, 279–307.

Press Association (2002) Greek police arrest British tourists. *The Guardian* 29 June.

Prideaux, B. (2000) The resort development spectrum: A new approach to modelling resort development. *Tourism Management* 21, 225–240.

Priestley, G. and Mundet, L. (1998) The post-stagnation phase of the resort life-cycle. *Annals of Tourism Research* 25 (1), 85–111.

Prigogine, I. and Stengers, I. (1985) *Order Out of Chaos*. London: Flamingo.

Prosser, G. (1995) Tourism destination life cycles: Progress, problems and prospects. Paper to *National Tourism Research Conference*, Melbourne.

Prosser, G. (1997) The development of tourist destinations in Australia: A comparative analysis of the Gold Coast and Coffs Harbour. In R. Teare, B.F. Canziani and G. Brown (eds) *Global Directions: New Strategies for Hospitality and Tourism* (pp. 305–332). London: Cassell.

Prosser, G.M. and Cullen, P. (1987) Planning natural areas for sustainable tourism development. Proceedings 60th National Conference, Royal Australian Institute of Parks and Recreation, Canberra, October.

Pudney, J. (1953) *The Thomas Cook Story*. London: Michael Joseph Ltd.

Pukui, M.K., Elbert, S.H. and Mo'okini, E.T. (1974) *Place Names of Hawaii*. Honolulu: University of Hawaii Press.

Putnam, R. (1993) The prosperous community: Social capital and public life. *The American Prospect* 13, 35–42.

Queensland Government Tourist Bureau (1939) *Holiday Haunts*. Brisbane: Queensland Government Tourist Bureau.

Queensland Railways (1912) *Tours in the Cairns District*. Brisbane: Queensland Railways.

Rafool, M. and Loyacono, L. (1997) *Employment in the Travel and Tourism Industry*. Denver, CO: National Conference of State Legislatures.

Ray, D. (1988) The role of entrepreneurship in economic development. *Journal of Development Planning* 18, 3–18.

Regensberg, Fr. (without year, ~ 1911) Naturschutzparke in den Kolonien. Bearbeitet von Fr. Regensberg auf Grund der Rede des Herrn Prof. C.B. Schillings während der Tagung der Deutschen Kolonialgesellschaft in Stuttgart am 10. Juni 1911. In Verein Naturschutzpark (ed.) *Naturschutzparke in Deutschland und Österreich. Ein Mahnwort an das deutsche und österreichische Volk* (pp. 54–57). Stuttgart.

Republic of Kenya (1999) *Economic Survey 1999*. Nairobi: Republic of Kenya.

Reynolds, P.D. (1997) New and small firms in expanding markets. *Small Business Economics* 9, 79–84.

Richardson, S.L. (1986) A product life cycle approach to urban waterfronts: The revitalisation of Galveston. *Costal Zone Management Journal* 14 (1/2), 21–46.

Riegert, R. (1979) *Hidden Hawaii, the Adventurer's Guide*. Berkeley, CA: AND/OR Press.

Rink, D.R. and Swan, J.E. (1979) Product life cycle research: A literature review. *Journal of Business Research* 7, 219–242.

Ritchie, J.R.B. (1999) Crafting a value driven for a national tourism treasure. *Tourism Management* 20 (3), 273–282.

Ritchie, J.R.B. and Crouch, G.I. (2000) The competitive destination: A sustainability perspective. *Tourism Management* 21 (1), 1–7.

Roberts, W. (1948) *Lands of the Inner Sea: The West Indies and Bermuda*. New York: Coward McCann.

Rodney, W. (1972) *How Europe Underdeveloped Africa*. London: Bogle-Ouverture Publications.

Rodriguez-Pose, A. (1994) Socio-economic restructuring and regional change: Rethinking growth in the European Community. *Economic Geography* 70, 325–343.

Romanelli, E. and Tushman, M.L. (1994) Organisational transformation as punctuated equilibrium: An empirical test. *Academy of Management Journal* 37 (5), 1141–1166.

Romeril, M. (1989) Tourism – the environmental dimension. *Progress in Tourism, Recreation and Hospitality Management* (1), 103–113.

Rose, T.F. (1878) *Historical and Biographical Atlas of the New Jersey Coast* (p. 42). Philadelphia, PA: Woolman and Rose.

Rostow, W.W. (1960) *Stages of Economic Growth – A Non-communist Manifesto*. Cambridge, UK: Cambridge University Press.

Roth, V.J. and Klein, S. (1993) A theory of retail change. *International Review of Retail, Distribution and Consumer Research* 3 (2), 167–183.

Rubenstein, R.L. (1983) *The Age of Triage*. Boston, MA: Beacon Press.

Rubies, E.B. (2001) Improving public-private sectors cooperation in tourism: A new paradigm for destinations. *Tourism Review* 56 (3+4), 39–41.

Russell, D. (1987) Atlantic City's bet on gambling: Who won what? *Atlantic City Magazine* 11 (1).

Russell, R. (1995) Tourism development in Coolangatta: An historical perspective. Honors thesis, Griffith University, Gold Coast.

Russell, R. and Faulkner, B. (1998) Reliving the destination life cycle in Coolangatta. An historical perspective on the rise, decline and rejuvenation of an Australian seaside resort. In E. Laws, B. Faulkner and G. Moscardo (eds) *Embracing and Managing Change in Tourism: International Case Studies* (pp. 95–115). London: Routledge.

Russell, R. and Faulkner, B. (1999) Movers and shakers: Chaos makers in tourism development. *Tourism Management* 20, 411–423.

Russo, A.P. (2002) The vicious circle of tourism development in heritage cities. *Annals of Tourism Research* 29 (1), 165–182.

Russo, A.P. and van der Borg, J. (2002) Planning considerations for cultural tourism: A case study of four European cities. *Tourism Management* 23 (5).

Ruthen, R. (1993) Adapting to complexity. *Scientific American* 268, 130–140.

Rutter, J. (1998) They don't see eye to eye. *Lancaster Sunday News*. Lancaster, Pennsylvania, November 22.

Ryan, C. (1991) Tourism and marketing – a symbiotic relationship? *Tourism Management* 12 (2), 101–111.

Sabel, C. (1982) *Work and Politics*. Cambridge: Cambridge University Press.

Sabin, W. (1921) *Hawaii, U.S.A.: A Souvenir of 'The Crossroads of the Pacific'*. Honolulu: Paradise of the Pacific Publishing Company.

Sassen, S. (1995) Urban impacts of economic globalisation. In J. Bratchie *et al.* (eds) *Cities in Competition* (pp. 36–57). Melbourne: Longman.

Savary, J. (1995) Thomson consumer electronics: From national champion to global contender. In J-E. Nilsson, P. Dicken and J. Peck (eds) *The Internationalisaton Process: European Firms in Global Competition* (pp. 90–108). London: Chapman.

Schumpeter, J.A. (1934) *The Theory of Economic Development*. Cambridge, MA: Harvard University Press.

Schumpeter, J. (1939) *Business Cycles: A Theoretical, Historical and Statistical Analysis of the Capitalist Process*. New York: McGraw-Hill.

Schumpeter, J.A. (1996) *Capitalism, Socialism and Democracy*. London: Routledge.

Scott, R. (1957) Kailua-Kona shook up by tourist boom. Honolulu *Star Bulletin* 2 August, 12.

Shapiro, D. (1974) Nightmare not over for Kailua. Honolulu *Star Bulletin* 18 June, A12.

Shaw, G. and Williams, A.M. (1994, 2002) *Critical Issues in Tourism: A Geographical Perspective* (1st and 2nd edns). Oxford: Blackwell.

Shaw, G. and Williams, A.M. (1997) The private sector: Tourism entrepreneurship – a constraint or resource? In G. Shaw and A. Williams (eds) *The Rise and Fall of British Coastal Resorts* (pp. 117–136). London: Cassell.

Shaw, G. and Williams, A.M. (1998) Entrepreneurship, small business culture and tourism development. In D. Ioannides and K.D. Debbage (eds) *The Economic Geography of the Tourist Industry* (pp. 235–255). London: Routledge.

Shay, J.P. (1998) A multi-perspective, dynamic strategy model. Proceedings of the Third Annual Graduate Education and Graduate Students Research Conference in Hospitality and Tourism – Advances in Hospitality and Tourism Research, Houston.

Sheldon, P.J. and Abenoja, T. (2001) Resident attitudes in a mature destination: The case of Waikiki. *Tourism Management* 22 (4), 435–443.

Shields, M.J. (1987) Fantasy Island, *Southern* 2, 38.

Simon, H.A. (1991) Organisations and markets. *Journal of Economic Perspectives* 5 (2), 25–44.

Singh, S. (1998) Probing the product life cycle further. *Tourism Recreation Research* 23 (2), 61–63.

Skolnik, J. (1978) *House of Cards: The Legalization and Control of Casino Gambling.* Boston: Little Brown.

Slyworthy, A.J. (1996) *Value Migration.* Boston, MA: Harvard Business School Press.

Smart, G. (2002) Amish restaurants: Popular and illegal. *Lancaster Sunday News.* Lancaster, Pennsylvania, March 3.

Smilor, R.W. and Feeser, H.R. (1991) Chaos and the entrepreneurial process: Patterns and policy implications for technology entrepreneurship. *Journal of Business Venturing* 6, 165–172.

Smith, D. (1995) The inapplicability principle: What chaos means for social science. *Behavioral Science* 40, 22–40.

Smith, H. (2002) Ayia Napa puts the boot into rowdy tourists. *The Guardian* 17th June.

Smith, J. (1982) The Premium-Grind: The Atlantic City Casino Hybrid.

Smith, M. (1991) *The Future for British Seaside Resorts Insights D21–D26.* London: English Tourist Board.

Smith, M. (2002) Two parallel paths to a common goal? A critical analysis of sustainable tourism and cultural regeneration in the context of English seaside towns. Paper presented to 'Tourism Research 2002' conference, Cardiff, 4–7 September 2002.

Smith, R.A. (1992) Beach resort evolution: Implications for planning. *Annals of Tourism Research* 19, 304–322.

Smith, S.L.J. (1988) Defining tourism: A supply-side view. *Annals of Tourism Research* 15, 179–190.

Smith, S.L.J. (1994) The tourism product. *Annals of Tourism Research* 21 (3), 582–595.

Smith, V. (1978) *Hosts and Guests. The Anthropology of Tourism.* Oxford: Basil Blackwell.

Smith, V. and Eadington, W.R. (1994) *Tourism Alternatives, Potentials and Problems in the Development of Tourism.* Chichester: John Wiley and Sons.

Smyser, A.A. (1972) Changing Kona's uncertain future. Honolulu *Star Bulletin* 19 February, A11.

Snepenger, D.J. and Ditton, R.B. (1985) A longitudinal analysis of nationwide hunting and fishing indicators: 1955–1980. *Leisure Sciences* 7 (3), 297–319.

Snepenger, D.J. and Johnson, J.D. (1991) Political self-identification and the perception of economic, social and environmental impacts of tourism. *Annals of Tourism Research* 18 (3), 511–514.

Snepenger, D.J., Johnson, J.D. and Rasker, R. (1995) Travel-stimulated entrepreneurial migration. *Journal of Travel Research* 34 (1), 40–44.

Snepenger, D.J., O'Connell, R. and Snepenger, M. (2001) The embrace-withdrawal continuum scale: Operationalizing residents' responses toward tourism development. *Journal of Travel Research* 40 (2), 155–161.

Snow, R. and Wright, D. (1976) Coney Island: A case study in popular culture and technical change. *Journal of Popular Culture* 9, 960–975.

Societe des Musees Quebecois (1995) Repertoire des institutions museales du Quebec,-statistiques diverses.

Sodetani, N. (1985) Manago Hotel is a family tradition. Honolulu *Star Bulletin* 19 February, Section 1, 10.

Soja, E. (1989) *Postmodern Geographies: The Reassertion of Space in Critical Social Theory.* London: Verso.

Southward, W. (1966) Kailua-Kona mall plan site stirs debate. Sunday *Star Bulletin and Advertiser* 25 December, D6.

Southward, W. (1967) Kailua-Kona to resume talks on waterfront mall. Sunday *Star Bulletin and Advertiser* 17 September, D6.

Southward, W. (1968a) 8-step program is proposed for Kailua-Kona mall. Honolulu *Advertiser* 2 May, F9.

Southward, W. (1968b) 'Foundation only' as far as Kona condo can go. Honolulu *Advertiser* 23 August, A6.

Spirer, H. (1981) Life cycle. In A.C. Eurich (ed.) *Major Transitions in the Human Life Cycle* (pp. 1–61). Lexington, MA: Lexington Books.

Stabell, C.B. and Fjeldstad, O.D. (1998) Configuring value for competitive advantage: On chains, shops, and networks. *Strategic Management Journal* 19, 413–437.

Stankiewicz, R. (2000) The concept of 'design space'. In J. Zimon (ed.) *Technological Innovation as an Evolutionary Process* (pp. 234–247). Cambridge: Cambridge University Press.

Stansfield, C.A. (1972) The development of modern seaside resorts. *Parks and Recreation* 5 (10), 14–46.

Stansfield, C.A. (1978) Atlantic City and the resort cycle. Background to the legalization of gambling. *Annals of Tourism Research* 5 (2), 238–251.

Stansfield, C.A. and Rickert, J.E. (1970) The recreational business district. *Journal of Leisure Research* 2 (4), 213–225.

Stark, J. (1902) *Stark's Jamaican Guide.* Boston, MA: James H. Stark.

Steadman, P. (1979) *The Evolution of Designs. Biological Analogy in Architecture and the Applied Arts.* Cambridge: Cambridge University Press.

Steele, T., Lindley, R. and Blanden, B. (1998) *Lamarck's Signature. How Retrogenes are Changing Darwin's Natural Selection Paradigm.* Reading, MT: Perseus Books.

Stehle, P. (1994) *Order Chaos Order: The Transition From Classical to Quantum Physics.* New York: Oxford University Press.

Stermer, M. (1954) Flowers in the sky. Honolulu *Star Bulletin* 31 July, Magazine Section, 3.

Sternlieb, G. and Hughes, J. (1983) *The Atlantic City Gamble* (p. 3). MA: Harvard University Press.

Stevenson, R.L. (1973) *Travels in Hawaii.* Edited and with an Introduction by A. Grove Day. Honolulu: The University Press of Hawaii.

Stewart, C.S. (1831) *A Visit to the South Seas in 1829 and 1830.* New York: John P. Haven.

Stewart, I. (1990) *Does God Play Dice.* London: Penguin Books.

Stewart, I. (1993) A new order (complexity theory). *New Scientist* 137 (1859), 2–3.

Stoker, G. (1995) Governance as theory: Five propositions. *International Social Science Journal* 155.

Stoker, G. (ed.) (1999) *The New Management of British Local Governance* (pp. 1–21). Basingstoke: MacMillan Press Ltd.

Storper, M. and Walker, R. (1989) *The Capitalist Imperative: Territory, Technology and Industrial Growth.* Oxford: Blackwell.

Strapp, J.D. (1988) The resort cycle and second homes. *Annals of Tourism Research* 15 (4), 504–516.

Sturge, J. and Harvey, T. (1838) *The West Indies in 1837.* London: Hamilton, Adams & Co.

Sunday Star Bulletin and Advertiser (1984) First stages of a change. 22 July, G1.

Surin, K. (1998) Dependency theory's reanimation in the era of financial capital. *Cultural Logic* [electronic] 1 (2) 29 pp. On WWW at www.duke.edu/literature/dependency.htm. Accessed 12.9.2002.

Survey of TdA Participants (1995) executed by J. Lundgren in collaboration with the TdA, March.

Swarbrooke, J. (1995) *The Development and Management of Visitor Attractions*. Oxford: Butterworth-Heinemann.

Swarbrooke, J. (1999) *Sustainable Tourism Management*. Wallingford, Oxon: CAB International.

Tao, E. (1972) Dolphin amity found at last. Hawaii *Tribune Herald* 4 April, 1.

Tarrant, C. (1989) The UK hotel industry: Market restructuring and the need to respond to customer demands. *Tourism Management* 10, 187–191.

Taylor, F. (1973) The tourist industry in Jamaica, 1919 to 1939. *Social and Economic Studies* 22, 205–228.

Taylor, F. (1988) The ordeal of the infant hotel industry in Jamaica, 1890–1914. *Journal of Imperial and Commonwealth History* 16, 201–217.

Tellis, G.J. and Crawford, C.M. (1981) An evolutionary approach to product growth theory. *Journal of Marketing* 45, 125–132.

Teye, V., Sonmez, S.F. and Sirakaya, E. (2002) Residents' attitudes toward tourism development. *Annals of Tourism Research* 29 (3), 668–688.

The Atlantic City Convention and Visitors Authority (no date) On WWW at http://www.atlanticcitynj.com/. Accessed 6.3.2001.

The City and County of Honolulu-Office of the Mayor (no date) On WWW at http://www.co.honolulu.hi.us/mayor/goal-1.htm. Accessed 22.3.2001.

The Property Council of Australia, Gold Coast Chapter (2000) *Our Gold Coast: Refurbishing, Rejuvenating and Unifying the Gold Coast, The Edward de Bono Workshop: Strategic Statement and Future Directions*.

Theodoulou, M. (2000) Are party animals good news for Cyprus? *The Times* 27 May.

Theodoulou, M. (2001a) Clubbers' lesson: No E in Cyprus. *The Times* 19 June.

Theodoulou, M. (2001b) Cyprus drugs warning. *The Times* 4 August.

Thietart, R.A. and Forgues, B. (1995) Chaos theory and organisation. *Organization Science* 6 (1), 19–31.

Thomas, M. (1983) *Schooner from Windward: Two Centuries of Hawaiian Interisland Shipping*. Honolulu: University of Hawaii Press (A Kolowalu Book).

Thomas, M.J. (1991) Product development and management. In M. Baker (ed.) *The Marketing Book* (Vol. 2, pp. 284–296). Oxford: Butterworth-Heinemann.

Thomas, H. and Thomas, R. (1998) The implications for tourism of shifts in British local governance. *Progress in Tourism and Hospitality Research* 4 (4), 295–306.

Thompson, D.C. and Grimble, I. (1968) *The Future of the Highlands and Islands*. London: Routledge and Kegan Paul.

Thomson Holidays (1999) Statistics on UK Tour Operations. On WWW at www.thomson-holidays.com.

Thrum, T.G. Multiple years. *Thrum's Hawaiian Almanac and Annual*. Honolulu.

Tiebout, C.M. (1956) A pure theory of local expenditures. *Journal of Political Economy* 64 (3), 416–424.

Times, The (1860) *The Times* August 30.

Timmons, J. (1989) *The Entrepreneurial Mind*. Massachusetts: Brick House Publishing Company.

Timmons, J. (1994) *New Venture Creation*. Boston, MA: Irwin.

Timothy, D.J. and Boyd, S.W. (2003) *Heritage Tourism*. Harlow: Prentice Hall.

Timothy, D.J. and Butler, R.W. (1995) Cross-border shopping: A North-American perspective. *Annals of Tourism Research* 22 (1), 16–34.

Tinsley, R. and Lynch, P. (2001) Small tourism business networks and destination development. *International Journal of Hospitality Management* 20, 367–378.

Tirole, J. (1997) *The Theory of Industrial Organization*. Cambridge, MA: MIT Press.

Toh, R.S., Khan, H. and Koh, A-J. (2001) A travel balance approach for examining tourism area life cycles: The case of Singapore. *Journal of Travel Research* 39, 426–432.

Tomas P.S. (2000) Development and sustainability of aging tourist resorts. Future Strategies in the Balearic Islands (Spain) 29th International Geographic Congress, Cheju, Korea.

Toohey, B. (1994) *Tumbling Dice*. Melbourne: Heinemann.

Tooman, L.A. (1997) Applications of the life-cycle model in tourism. *Annals of Tourism Research* 24 (1), 214–234.

Tour des Art (2001) pamphlet.

Towner, J. (1985) The Grand Tour: A key phase in the history of tourism. *Annals of Tourism Research* 12, 297–333.

Towse, R. (1991) Venice as a superstar. Paper Presented at the Conference on 'The Economics of the Cities of Art', 13–15 May 1991, Venice, mimeo.

Travis, P. (1992) *The Seaside Fights Back, Insights C9-C18*. London: English Tourist Board.

Trellis, G.J. and Crawford, M.C. (1981) An evolutionary approach to product growth theory. *Journal of Marketing* 45 (Fall), 125–132.

Tremblay, P. (1998) The economic organization of tourism. *Annals of Tourism Research* 25 (4), 837–859.

Tribal Research Institute (1995) *The Hill Tribes of Thailand*. Chiang Mai, Thailand: Technical Service Club.

Tribe, J. (1997) The indiscipline of tourism. *Annals of Tourism Research* 24 (3), 638–653.

Trinidad and Tobago (1912) *Handbook of Trinidad and Tobago*. Port-of-Spain, Trinidad.

Truman, G., Jackson, J. and Longstreth, T. (1844) *Narrative of a Visit to the West Indies in 1840 and 1841*. Philadelphia, PA: Merrihew and Thompson.

Trusted, J. (1981) *An Introduction to the Philosophy of Knowledge*. London: The MacMillan Press, Ltd.

Tse, E.C. and Elwood, C.M. (1990) Synthesis of the life cycle concept with strategy and management. *International Journal of Hospitality Management* 9 (3), 223–236.

Tsonis, A. (1992) *Chaos From Theory to Applications*. New York: Plenum Press.

Tuchilsky, G. (1977) *The River Barons*.

Tune, J. (1980) The kings of real estate on Ali'i Drive. Sunday *Star Bulletin and Advertiser* 7 December, B1.

Turner, G. (1993) Tourism and the environment: The role of the seaside. In *Insights* (A125–131). London: British Tourist Authority/ English Tourist Board.

Turner, L. (1976) The international division of leisure: Tourism and the third world. *Annals of Tourism Research* 4 (1), 12–24.

Turner, L. and Ash, J. (1975) *The Golden Hordes: International Tourism and the Pleasure Periphery*. London: Constable.

Twain, M. (1966) *Mark Twain's Letters from Hawaii*. Edited with an Introduction by A. Grove Day. London: Chatto & Windus.

Twining-Ward, L. and Baum, T. (1998) Dilemmas facing mature island destinations: Cases from the Baltic. *Progress in Tourism, Recreation and Hospitality Management* 4 (3), 131–140.

Twining-Ward, L. and Twining-Ward, T. (1996) *Tourism Destination Development: The case of Bornholm and Gotland.* Nexo: Research Centre of Bornholm.

Twining-Ward, L. (1999) Towards sustainable tourism development: Observations from a distance. *Tourism Management* 20 (2), 187–188.

Urry, J. (1981) Localities, regions and social class. *International Journal of Urban and Regional Research* 5, 455–474.

Urry, J. (1988) Trading places. *New Society* 84 (1322), 7–9.

Urry, J. (1990) *The Tourist Gaze: Leisure and Travel in Contemporary Societies.* London: Sage Publications.

Urry, J. (1997) Cultural change and the seaside resort. In G. Shaw and A. Williams (eds) *The Rise and Fall of British Coastal Resorts* (pp. 102–113). London: Cassell.

UNESCO (2001) *Properties inscribed on the World Heritage List.* Paris: World Heritage Centre.

UNESCO (2002) *List of Biosphere Reserves.* Paris: MAB-Programme.

US Bureau of the Census (2000) On WWW at http://www.census.gov/dmd/www/products.html.

US Department of Housing and Urban Development (1995) Atlantic City: Consolidated Plan for 1995 Executive Summary. On WWW at http://www.hud.gov/cpes/nj/atlantnj.html. Accessed 22.2.2001.

van den Berg, L. and Braun, E. (1999) Urban competitiveness, marketing and the need for organising capacity. *Urban Studies* 36 (5–6), 987–999.

Van den Weg, H. (1982) Trends in design and development of facilities. *Tourism Management* 3, 303–307.

van der Borg, J. (1991) *Tourism and Urban Development.* Amsterdam: Thesis Publishers.

van der Borg, J. (2000) Tourism and the city: Some strategy guidelines for a sustainable tourism development. In H. Briassoulis, J. Stratten and J. van der Borg (eds) *Tourism and the Environment: Regional, Economic, Cultural and Policy Issues* (pp. 305–308). Rotterdam: Erasamus University.

van der Borg, J. and Gotti, G. (1995) Tourism and Cities of Art. UNESCO/ROSTE Technical Report n. 20, Venice.

van der Borg, J. *et al.* (2000) Study Programme on European Spatial Planning: Criteria For The Spatial Differentiation Of The EU Territory, Group 1.7 'Cultural Assets': Ed. by NORDREGIO, Stockholm.

van der Heijden, K. (1997) *Scenarios: The Art of Strategic Conversion.* Chichester: Wiley.

Var, T. and Kim, Y. (1989) Measurement and findings on the tourism impact. Unpublished Paper, Department of Recreation, Park and Tourism Sciences, Texas A&M University.

Veblen, T. (1970) *The Theory of the Leisure Class.* London: Unwin.

Vellas, F. and Becherel, L. (1995) *International Tourism: An Economic Perspective.* London: MacMillan Business Press Ltd.

Voase, R. (2002) The influence of political, economic and social change in a mature tourist destination: The case of the Isle of Thanet, South-East England. In R. Voase (ed.) *Tourism in Western Europe: A Collection of Case Histories* (pp. 61–84). Lincoln: The University of Lincoln.

Waikiki Improvement Association (1999) *Agenda Waikiki: Setting a Course for our Future.* On WWW at http://www.gurusoup.com/wia/programspage.html. Accessed 20.2.2001.

Walker, G. (1990) Geology. In W.L. Wagner, D.R. Herbst and S.H. Sohme (eds) *Manual of the Flowering Plants of Hawaii* (pp. 21–35). Honolulu: University of Hawaii Press.

Waldrop, M. (1992) *Complexity: The Emerging Science and the Edge of Order and Chaos*. London: Simon and Schuster/Penguin.

Wales Tourist Board (2000) Annual Report 1999–2000. On WWW at http://www.wales-tourist-board.gov.uk/attachments/1.pdf. Accessed 16.2.2001.

Wallerstein, I. (1974) *The Modern World-System I: Capitalist Agriculture and the Origins of the European World-Economy in the Sixteenth Century*. New York: Academic Press.

Wallerstein, I. (1980) *The Modern World-System II: Mercantilism and the Consolidation of the European World-Economy, 1600–1750*. New York: Academic Press.

Wallerstein, I. (1989) *The Modern World-System III: The Second Era of Great Expansion of the Capitalist World-Economy, 1730s–1840s*. New York: Academic Press.

Wall, G. (1982a) Cycles and capacity: Incipient growth or theory. *Annals of Tourism Research* 9 (2), 52–56.

Wall, G. (1982b) Cycles and capacity incipient theory or conceptual contradiction? *Tourism Management* 3 (3), 188–192.

Wang, P. and Godbey, G. (1994) A normative approach to tourism growth to the year 2000. *Journal of Travel Research* 33 (1), 33–37.

Ward, M. (1995) Butterflies and bifurcations: Can chaos theory contribute to our understanding of family systems. *Journal of Marriage and the Family* 57 (3), 629–638.

Weaver, D. (1993) Model of urban tourism for small Caribbean islands. *Geographical Review* 83, 134–140.

Weaver, D.B. (1986) The evolution of a heliotropic tourism landscape in the Caribbean. Paper Presented at the Association of American Geographers Annual Meeting, Minneapolis, MN, May 6, 1986.

Weaver, D.B. (1988) The evolution of a 'plantation' tourism landscape on the Caribbean Island of Antigua. *Tijdschrift Voor Econ. En Soc Geografie* 69, 319–331.

Weaver, D.B. (1990) Grand Cayman Island and the resort cycle concept. *The Journal of Travel Research* 29 (2), 9–15.

Weaver, D.B. (1992) Tourism and the functional transformation of the Antiguan landscape. In A.M. Conny (ed.) *Spatial Implications of Tourism* (pp. 161–175). Groningen: Geo Pers.

Weaver, D.B. (2000a) A broad context model of destination development scenarios. *Tourism Management* 21, 217–224.

Weaver, D.B. (2000b) The exploratory war-distorted destination life cycle. *International Journal of Tourism Research* 2 (3), 151–162.

Weaver, D. (2001) Mass tourism and alternative tourism in the Caribbean. In D. Harrison (ed.) *Tourism and the Less Developed World: Issues and Case Studies* (pp. 161–174). Wallingford, UK: CABI Publishing.

Weaver, D. (2003a) Managing ecotourism in the island microstate: The case of Dominica. In D. Diamantis and S. Geldenhuys (eds) *Ecotourism* (pp. 151–163). London: Continuum.

Weaver, D. (2003b) *The Encyclopaedia of Eco-tourism* (pp. 451–461). Wallingford: CAB International.

Weaver, D. and Oppermann, M. (2000) *Tourism Management*. Brisbane: John Wiley.

Weber, S. (1988) Life cycle of Croatian tourism product: What have we learned from the past. In *Europaische Tourismus und Freizeitforschung* (Band 6, pp. 37–51). Institute for Tourism and Leisure Studies, Vienna University of Economics and Business Administration.

Webster, A.G. (1914) The Evolution of Mt. Desert. *The Nation* 99 (256), 347–348.

Webster's New Twentieth Century Dictionary of the English Language (1983) Cleveland, OH: Simon and Schuster.

Weiss, R. (1994) *Learning from Strangers: The Art and Method of Qualitative Interview Studies*. New York: The Free Press.

Weizenegger, S. (2002) Ökotourismus und Großschutzgebietsmanagement: Von der Partizipation zum akteurszentrierten Ansatz im internationalen Naturschutz. In K.H. Erdmann and H.R. Bork (eds) *Naturschutz. Neue Ansätze, Konzepte und Strategien* (pp. 207–221). Bonn – Bad Godesberg: Bundesamt für Naturschutz, BfN-Skripten 67.

Welch, R.V. (1993) Capitalist restructuring and local economic development: Perspectives from an ultra-periphery city-economy. *Regional Studies* 27 (3), 237–249.

West, G. (1967) Elaborate Kona resort planned. Honolulu *Star Bulletin* 24 February, C1.

Wheeller, B. (1991) Tourism's troubled times. *Tourism Management* June.

Wheeller, B. (1993) Sustaining the ego. *Journal of Sustainable Tourism* 1 (2), 121–129.

Wheeller B. (1994) A carry-on up the jungle. *Tourism Management* 15 (3), 231–232.

Whitney, H.M. (1875/1890) *The Tourist's Guide Through the Hawaiian Islands, Descriptive of their Scenes and Scenery*. Honolulu: The Hawaiian Gazette Company.

Whittlesey, D. (1929) Sequent occupance. *Annals of the Association of American Geographers* 19, 162–165.

Wilkes, C. (1970) *Autobiography of Rear Admiral Charles Wilkes, U.S. Navy*. W.J. Morgan, D.B. Tyler, J.L. Leonhart and M.F. Loughlin (eds). Washington, D.C.: Department of the Navy. Naval History Division.

Wilkinson, P.F. (1987) Tourism in small island nations: A fragile dependence. *Leisure Studies* 26 (2), 127–146.

Wilkinson, P.F. (1996) Graphical images of the commonwealth Caribbean: The tourist area cycle of evolution. In L.C. Harrison and W. Husbands (eds) *Practicing Responsible Tourism International Case Studies in Tourism Planning, Policy and Development* (pp. 16–40). John Wiley and Sons.

Williams, A.M. (1995) Capital and transnationalisation of tourism. In A. Montanari and A. Williams (eds) *European Tourism: Regions, Spaces and Restructuring* (pp. 163–176). Chichester: Wiley.

Williams, A.M. and Shaw, G. (1998a) *Tourism and Economic Development: European Experiences*. Chichester: Wiley.

Williams, A.M. and Shaw, G. (1998b) Tourism and the environment: Sustainability and economic restructuring. In C.M Hall and A. Lew (eds) *Sustainable Tourism. A Geographical Perspective* (pp. 49–59). London: Longman.

Williams, A.M. and Shaw, G. (2002) Tourism, geography of. In *International Encyclopaedia of the Social and Behavioural Sciences*: 15800–15803.

Williams, A. and Zelinsky, W. (1970) On some patterns in international tourist flows. *Economic Geography* 46 (4), 549–567.

Williams, M.T. (1993) An expansion of the tourist site cycle model: The case of Minorca (Spain). *Journal of Tourism Studies* 4, 24–32.

Wilson, A. (1991) *The Culture of Nature: North American Landscape from Disney To Exxon*. Toronto, Ont.: Between the Lines.

Winchester, S. (1997) *The River at the Centre of the World*. London: Penguin.

Wolfe, R.I. (1948) The summer cottages of Ontario. Unpublished PhD thesis Toronto: University of Toronto.

Wolfe, R.I. (1952) Wasaga Beach – the divorce from the geographic environment. *The Canadian Geographer* 2, 57–66.

Wong, P.P. (1986) Tourism development and resorts on the east coast of Peninsular Malaysia. *Singapore Journal of Tropical Geography* 7, 152–162.

World Commission on Enviornment and Development (1987) *Our Common Future*. Oxford: Oxford University Press.

World Tourism Organisation (1980) *Manila Declaration*. Madrid: WTO.

World Tourism Organisation (1989) *The Hague Declaration*. Madrid: WTO.

Word Tourism Organisation (1993) Sustainable Tourism Development: Guide for Local Planners. Madrid: WTO.

World Tourism Organisation (1995) *Seminar on GATS Implications for Tourism*. Madrid: WTO.

World Tourism Organisation (1998) *Guide for local authorities on developing sustainable tourism*. Madrid: WTO.

World Tourism Organisation (2001) *International Cooperation Network for the Sustainable Management of Mass Tourism Coastal Destinations*. Madrid: WTO.

Wright, D.M. (1951) Schumpeter's political philosophy. In S.B. Harris (ed.) *Schumpeter, Social Scientist*. Cambridge: Harvard Press.

Wrigley, N. (1992) Sunk capital, the property crises and the restructuring of British food retailing. *Environment and Planning A* 24, 1521–1527.

Wrigley, N. (1998) Understanding store development programmes in post-property-crises UK food retailing. *Environment and Planning A* 30, 15–35.

Wrigley, N. and Lowe, M. (1996) *Retailing, Consumption and Capital*. Harlow: Longman.

Wrigley, N. and Lowe, M. (2002) *Reading Retail*. London: Arnold.

Xie, Y. (1995) Control and adjustment of the tourist area life cycle. *Tourism Tribune* 10 (2), 41–44.

Xu, H. (2001) Study on the potential tourists and life cycle of tourism product: A system dynamic approach. *System Engineering* 19 (3), 69–75.

Yale, P. (1995) *The Business of Tour Operations*. Harlow: Longman.

Yang, S. (1996) Doubts about the life cycle of a tourist product. *Tourism Tribune* 11 (1), 45–47.

Yi, Y. (2001) An analysis of the theory of life cycle in tourist areas. *Tourism Tribune* 16 (6), 31–33.

Yokeno, N. (1968) La Localisation de l'Industrie Touristique – Application de l'Analyse de Thunen-Weber. *Les Cahiers du Touirsme Serie C* No. 9, Aix en Provence.

Yoon, Charles & Associates, Inc. (1968) *Kealakehe Development Plan, North Kona, Hawai'i*. Honolulu: Prepared for the State Department of Land and Natural Resources.

Young, B. (1983) Touristisation of traditional Maltese fishing-farming villages. *Tourism Management* 12, 35–41.

Zago, M. (1997) L'Offerta Museale Veneziana. In G. Di Monte and I. Scaramuzzi (eds) *La Provincia Ospitale*. Bologna: Il Mulino.

Zh, L. (1997) On 'the theory of the life cycle of tourist destination'. A discussion with Yang Senlin. *Tourism Tribune* 12 (1), 38–40.

Zimon, J. (2000) Evolutionary models for technological change. In J. Zimon (ed.) *Technological Innovation as an Evolutionary Process* (pp. 3–12). Cambridge: Cambridge University Press.

Zurick, D.N. (1992) Adventure travel and sustainable tourism in the peripheral economy of Nepal. *Annals of the Association of American Geographers* 82, 608–628.